The German Epic in the Cold War

The German Epic in the Cold War

Peter Weiss, Uwe Johnson, and Alexander Kluge

Matthew D. Miller

NORTHWESTERN UNIVERSITY PRESS
EVANSTON, ILLINOIS

Northwestern University Press
www.nupress.northwestern.edu

Printed in the United States of America

10 9 8 7 6 5 4 3 2 1

Library of Congress Cataloging-in-Publication Data

Names: Miller, Matthew D., author.
Title: The German epic in the Cold War : Peter Weiss, Uwe Johnson, and Alexander Kluge / Matthew D. Miller.
Description: Evanston, Illinois : Northwestern University Press, 2018. | Includes bibliographical references and index.
Identifiers: LCCN 2017059457 | ISBN 9780810137325 (pbk. : alk. paper) | ISBN 9780810137332 (cloth : alk. paper) | ISBN 9780810137349 (ebook)
Subjects: LCSH: German fiction—20th century—History and criticism. | Weiss, Peter, 1916–1982. Ästhetik des Widerstands. | Johnson, Uwe, 1934–1984. Jahrestage. | Kluge, Alexander, 1932– Chronik der Gefühle. | Weiss, Peter, 1916–1982—Criticism and interpretation. | Johnson, Uwe, 1934–1984—Criticism and interpretation. | Kluge, Alexander, 1932– —Criticism and interpretation. | Cold War in literature.
Classification: LCC PT772 .M468 2018 | DDC 833.91409—dc23
LC record available at https://lccn.loc.gov/2017059457

For S.A.S.

CONTENTS

FIGURES

ACKNOWLEDGMENTS

The Low German expression "De Leng hett de Last" makes an appearance in a dialogue between Marie and her friend Francine in Uwe Johnson's *Jahrestage*. Associating the length of a task with its difficulty—"The more time you spend on a job, the harder it gets"—the phrase pertains both to Johnson's aspirations to see his epic tale through to its completion over some fourteen years as well as a study such as the one at hand, which sets *Jahrestage* in relation to Peter Weiss's *Die Ästhetik des Widerstands* and Alexander Kluge's *Chronik der Gefühle*. While this book has not been as long in the making as the epics it examines, it has incurred a number of personal debts along its way that I am keen to acknowledge here.

The project's conception dates back to the defense of a dissertation on the literary forms of dialectics in Kluge's prose writings and the dramatic works of Heiner Müller at Columbia University in 2007. In their review thereof, the members of my dissertation committee Andreas Huyssen, Harro Müller, Lydia Goehr, Stefan Andriopoulus, and Martin Puchner urged me to cast a wider net in my study of post-1945 German literature moving forward. I have been excited to follow this recommendation. Acquiring a broader purview of the field of German literary studies in the years since has enabled me to work out a new project and argument regarding literature written during the Cold War. The resulting shape thereof in this volume has benefited from the inspiration, advice, and guidance from mentors and colleagues in the field, beginning with the aforementioned Andreas and Harro, in whose seminars at Columbia I encountered the writers featured here. I thank Andreas especially for his ongoing support, also in more recent years.

Preliminary results of the research leading to *The German Epic in the Cold War* were presented at conferences of the German Studies Association and the Modern Language Association and at other symposium venues. These professional circuits constitute lifelines of the discipline and I am indebted to responses from numerous colleagues for their feedback on my project over the course of its development. While many of them will remain anonymous, I thank Leslie A. Adelson for her stellar directorship of the DAAD German Studies Summer Seminar "The Futures of Interdisciplinary Studies," held at Cornell University in 2012. It was there that I was granted opportunity to fine-tune my sensibility for literary futurity with Leslie and other colleagues as well as present aspects of my work on Peter Weiss. Second, the 2014 German Studies Association seminar on "Aesthetic Obstinacy" led by Richard

Langston and Claudia Benthien amounted to what has been perhaps the most productive experience I have had at the GSA to date, and I am especially indebted to Dick as well as seminar participant Sabine von Dirke for encouraging me in my work on Kluge in that context, which came to light as "*Eigensinn* in Transit: Reexamining a Concept for the Twenty-First Century," *Glass Shards: Alexander Kluge-Jahrbuch* 2 (2015): 83–102. I also thank Ela Gezen for the invitation to participate in the stimulating 2014 symposium at the University of Massachusetts Amherst on "Medium, Message and Method in Cultures of the Cold War." This opportunity facilitated a turning point of my theorization of the dimensions of epic in post-1945 literature, especially through conversations with fellow symposium participant Seth Howes. Other conference exchanges and collaborations at the GSA or NeMLA with Thomas Herold, Hunter Bivens, and Jennifer Hosek also helped me advance the argument elaborated in these pages. Across different stays in Germany, Thomas Ernst encouraged my contributions to German studies on site, Julia Tieke facilitated the advancement of my scholarly writing in German, and Falk Strehlow instilled in me a deeper appreciation for the concreteness of German literature's imaginative resources. Such connections are part of a larger web that has ensnared and channeled my passion for literary writing for some time. Chris Pavsek first introduced me to Kluge at Swarthmore College and intellectually formative years during graduate school at Columbia were fueled by conversations especially with Tomislav Zelic and also with Greg Williams, with whom I first read and presented on at least part of Weiss's *Ästhetik*.

With regard to my work on Uwe Johnson, I am deeply grateful to Holger Helbig and Antje Pautzke at the Uwe Johnson Research Center at the Universität Rostock for their outstanding hospitality and guidance during my two visits there in 2015 and 2016. Antje's expertise greatly facilitated my study of materials at the Uwe Johnson Archive on both occasions. Permissions to peruse archival holdings were kindly granted by Ulrich Fries and Raimund Fellinger in their respective capacities as representatives of the Johannes and Annitta Fries and the Peter Suhrkamp Foundations, as well as Gunilla Palmstierna-Weiss, who allowed me to read the epistolary exchange between Weiss and Johnson. Having enjoyed the opportunity to attend and participate in the stimulating 2016 Rostock conference *Uwe Johnson in seiner Zeit*, I revised the paper presented there with Antje and Holger's shrewd assistance and was able to publish it as "Uwe Johnson, Peter Weiss, und die Möglichkeiten des modernen Epos," *Johnson-Jahrbuch* (2016): 183–206. Participation in the conference also acquainted me with Gary Baker, whose pioneering work has informed my understanding of Johnson. And I am thankful to Willi Goetschel and Oliver Simons for providing feedback on my work on *Jahrestage*, particularly the article forthcoming in *Germanic Review*, "An Epic's Hydropoetics: On the Waters of Uwe Johnson's *Jahrestage*."

Closer to home, my work has benefited from participation in the Central New York Humanities Corridor Working Group "Perspectives on Europe from the Periphery." Funded from an award by the Andrew W. Mellon Foundation, our working group has provided a crucial venue for local scholarly exchange and I thank participating members Kathy Everly, Ken Friedman, Stefano Giannini, Libby Otto, and Karina von Tippelskirch for their constructive review of part of my manuscript and accompanying discussion. Colgate University has generously supported international faculty research through multiple grants enabling me to maintain a vibrant relationship with German studies in central Europe. The institution's faculty leave program afforded me the necessary time to complete much of the writing of the manuscript. And I have been privileged to enjoy the support of two colleagues in the Department of German, Claire Baldwin and Alan Swensen, in addition to that of other collegial interlocutors and friends in upstate New York.

The process of writing is far from solitary, and I am deeply grateful to those who have helped me see this publication through at Northwestern University Press, including Jane Bunker, for backing the project in her capacity as director there; two anonymous readers, who brought high levels of engagement and insight to my manuscript; Christi Stanforth for help with the copyediting; and Trevor Perri, Maggie Grossman, Marianne Jankowski, and Nathan MacBrien, whose oversight of the project and creative and editorial assistance made the process to book very smooth. Thanks also go to Steven Moore, for outfitting the index, to Colgate University, which provided a subvention grant to help the press offset a portion of the publishing costs, and to Suhrkamp Verlag, which granted permissions to reproduce images from Kluge's and Weiss's works.

In closing, I would like to acknowledge a kind of learning to which I am indebted that involves what might be called sharing in the art of living. On this score I express warm gratitude to my parents, Karen and Mel Miller, for all of their loving support over the years, as well as to April Sweeney, whose passion, enthusiasm, and artistic imagination generally and whose close-up support, patience, and encouragement during my work on this project specifically not only have ensured that the longitude of any project is, contrary to Johnson's fear, far from a burden, but have also made the shared art of living worth its while.

Hubbardsville, New York, 2017

ABBREVIATIONS

Throughout this study, citations from primary sources are indicated parenthetically in conformity with the following abbreviations key. Page numbers of existing English translations (where available) are followed by the pagination of the German originals (where relevant).

AN	Uwe Johnson, *Anniversaries: From the Life of Gesine Cresspahl*, trans. Leila Vennewitz (New York: Harcourt Brace Jovanovich, 1975).
AN II	*Anniversaries II: From the Life of Gesine Cresspahl*, trans. Leila Vennewitz and Walter Arndt (San Diego: Harcourt Brace Jovanovich, 1987).
AR	Alexander Kluge, *The Air Raid on Halberstadt on 8 April 1945*, trans. Martin Chalmers (New York: Seagull Books, 2014).
AoR	Peter Weiss, *The Aesthetics of Resistance: Volume 1*, trans. Joachim Neugroschel (Durham, N.C.: Duke University Press, 2005).
ÄdW	Peter Weiss, *Die Ästhetik des Widerstands*, vol. 3 of *Werke in sechs Bänden* (Frankfurt am Main: Suhrkamp Verlag, 1991).
AT	Theodor W. Adorno, *Aesthetic Theory*, trans. and ed. Robert Hullot-Kentor (Minneapolis: University of Minnesota Press, 1997); Theodor W. Adorno, *Ästhetische Theorie*, ed. Gretel Adorno and Rolf Tiedemann, vol. 7 of *Gesammelte Schriften in 20 Bänden*, ed. Rolf Tiedemann (Frankfurt am Main: Suhrkamp Verlag, 1997).
BU	Uwe Johnson, *Begleitumstände: Frankfurter Vorlesungen* (Frankfurt am Main: Suhrkamp Verlag, 1980).
BVG	*Berliner Verkehrsbetriebe* (the public transport company of Berlin)
CdG	Alexander Kluge, *Chronik der Gefühle*, 2 vols. (Frankfurt am Main: Suhrkamp Verlag, 2000).
ČSSR	Czechoslovak Socialist Republic
DMB	Alexander Kluge, "Die Macht der Bewußtseinsindustrie und das Schicksal unserer Öffentlichkeit," in *Industrialisierung des Bewußtseins: Eine kritische Auseinandersetzung mit den "neuen" Medien*, ed. Klaus von Bismarck et al. (Munich: Piper Verlag, 1985), 51–129.
DuM	Oskar Negt and Alexander Kluge, *Der unterschätzte Mensch: Gemeinsame Philosophie in zwei Bänden* (Frankfurt am Main: Zweitausendeins, 2001).
FRG	Federal Republic of Germany
GDR	German Democratic Republic

HO Alexander Kluge and Oskar Negt, *History and Obstinacy*, trans. Richard Langston et al. (New York: Zone Books, 2014).

JT Uwe Johnson, *Jahrestage: Aus dem Leben von Gesine Cresspahl*, 4 vols. (Frankfurt am Main: Suhrkamp Verlag, 1970–1983).

ME Franco Moretti, *Modern Epic: The World-System from Goethe to García Márquez*, trans. Quintin Hoare (New York: Verso, 1996).

NB Peter Weiss, *Notizbücher 1971–1980*, 2 vols. (Frankfurt am Main: Suhrkamp Verlag, 1981).

ND Theodor W. Adorno, *Negative Dialectics*, trans. E. B. Ashton (New York: Continuum, 1983); Theodor W. Adorno, *Negative Dialektik*, vol. 6 of *Gesammelte Schriften in 20 Bänden*, ed. Rolf Tiedemann (Frankfurt am Main: Suhrkamp Verlag, 1997).

TN György Lukács, *The Theory of the Novel: A Historico-Philosophical Essay on the Forms of Great Epic Literature*, trans. Anna Bostock (Cambridge, Mass.: MIT Press, 1971); Georg Lukács, *Die Theorie des Romans: Ein geschichtsphilosophischer Versuch über die Formen der großen Epik* (Munich: Deutscher Taschenbuch Verlag, 1994).

SED Sozialistische Einheitspartei Deutschlands, the Socialist Unity Party of East Germany.

SPD Sozialdemokratische Partei Deutschlands, the Social Democratic Party of (West) Germany.

UJA Uwe Johnson Archive Rostock (Depositum of the Johannes and Annitta Fries Foundation)

VPR Uwe Johnson, "Vorschläge zur Prüfung eines Romans," in *Romantheorie: Dokumentation ihrer Geschichte in Deutschland seit 1880*, ed. Eberhard Lämmert et al. (Cologne: Kiepenheuer & Witsch, 1975), 398–403.

The German Epic in the Cold War

Introduction

✦

A Genre for Cold Times

> An era of history . . . has lost its bearings, and . . . in the early years of the new millennium looks forward with more troubled perplexity than I recall in a long lifetime, guideless and mapless, to an unrecognizable future.
>
> —Eric Hobsbawm, *Fractured Times*

Cold Times?

This book is untimely in at least three senses. In everyday conversation, academic and otherwise, the topic of the modern epic tends to elicit consternation amid anyone familiar with the existence of the genre and its length. Who has time for that? No one, it would seem, is the implied answer, which immediately raises another question, as to when time was or where it might have gone. This leads to a second untimeliness, the period of the Cold War, in the context of which this study examines the modern epic's literary evolution. It is not so much that the Cold War may appear, despite claims of its reemergence amid tensions in Russian, U.S., and European relations in the second decade of the twenty-first century, as the present's ancient history. Rather, discernible in Cold War cultural documents, especially from the period's second half, are diagnostics attesting to time's standstill and even—in views confined to the large North Atlantic from Washington, D.C., to Moscow—to a standstill of history itself.[1] Did such a perceived stalemate afford people more time? Both of these resonances of the untimely relate to a third aspect of this book's focus on the genre of the modern epic, namely its appeal to literary imagination and writing in a present saturated by the plurality of media in a thoroughly technological lifeworld. If digital reality now constitutes human beings' second nature experienced as the first—so much so that for most members of the world's networked population, any space without a high-speed internet connection appears utterly anomalous—then the deflated status of the literary print medium must be regarded as a social fact. As the withering of literature's self-evidence draws large segments of the academic humanities into an accompanying devaluation, the disciplines thus affected will need to confront and develop responses to the displacement of their traditional object of inquiry in order to avoid suffering additional losses.

Addressing the phenomenon of an "industrialization of consciousness" driven by new media and their profit-oriented management in the 1980s, the German writer Alexander Kluge delivered a suggestive account of the relationship between our interaction with media and our experience of time. Underlying his argument is a strong valuation of two different organizations of human experience. Kluge pits one's own experience (*Eigenerfahrung*) against a kind of experience that has been expropriated (*enteignete Erfahrung*, DMB 99). The distinction relates to two temporal modalities. On the one hand, Kluge surmises, there is a tendency of media to expropriate time, such that interacting with any text, television show, film, and so on entails stark temporal forfeitures in the living of one's own life. Such a loss of time exemplifies what Kluge has characterized as *Zeitentzug* (time's withdrawal). On the other hand, there are works of art produced in such a way as to grant recipients more time than they cost, restoring, as it were, lost time and providing a surplus thereof for *Eigenerfahrung* (DMB 104).

Kluge's account of these two different qualities of time converts complex procedures of reception into critical categories. Any act of reading or other artistic reception involves an expenditure of one's own time as it is directed toward something other than the immediate self. In her related consideration of the experience of reading twentieth-century German literature's long narratives, Christa Karpenstein-Eßbach has addressed the basic features of the temporal transfer couched in Kluge's observations. There may be, she writes, a resistance to literature on the part of potential readers leery of losing themselves in a text or of passing into the experience of another, foreign world. But "for the time that novels demand, they return to us another time than that of our acute present."[2] In her ensuing account of a novel that broods paradigmatically over the character of time on the cusp of World War I—Thomas Mann's *Der Zauberberg* (*The Magic Mountain*), published in 1924—Karpenstein-Eßbach delineates the curious "life without time" that sets in at the alpine sanatorium.[3] If the protagonist Hans Castorp and his fellow sanatorium patients experience the eclipse of psychological as well as historical time, this may be due not only to the uniformity of the institutionally regulated lives they pass at some distance from modernity's bustle, but also to the absence of labor from their existence on the mountain. This in turn reveals the force of Kluge's use of "expropriation" to distinguish different experiences of time. In short, reading can amount to something like the enjoyment of one's own labor as a form of unalienated self-activity, which is what Kluge means by *Eigenerfahrung*.[4] And such an activity can yield unforeseen compensation for the losses incurred by investing one's time and energy in it. Of course, reading is never without contours and conditions: the former are set by the medium at hand, the latter by social factors determining access

Figure 1. Opening image from Alexander Kluge, *Die Lücke, die der Teufel läßt* (Frankfurt am Main: Suhrkamp, 2003), 6. Kluge's caption there reads: " 'Five mules, cut off by the flood waters of the Missouri, wait patiently to be rescued.' The fear of the animals in the picture above, their patience, the mass of water, what will happen in the next few days, all that is subjective-objective, i.e., it consists of facts and a living response" in Martin Chalmers and Michael Hulse's translation, *The Devil's Blind Spot: Tales from the New Century* (New York: New Directions, 2004), vi.

to the activity of reading itself. While Kluge challenges restrictions bearing on the latter, he also alludes to the need to discern whether and how any media allow for navigation and who can steer it (see *Eigensteuerung* vs. *Fremdsteuerung* in DMB 59, 104). For literature, this question turns largely on the medium's formal characteristics and the implications thereof for self-activity. As one can glean from these passages, Kluge sets high stakes on the production and reception of art. And, as we will see, he attributes great practical value to the kinds of exercises in navigation that literature offers. Kluge's demanding approach to art reflects the necessary conceptual anchorage that underlies much of his work's critical thrust and incisiveness. Such conceptual anchoring both opens the doors of an imagination in touch with human needs and provides orientation for survival strategies that we ignore only at

Figures 2–4. Cover images from the book jackets of *Chronik der Gefühle* and *Die Lücke, die der Teufel läßt*. Copyright © 2000, 2003 Suhrkamp Verlag Frankfurt am Main. All rights reserved.

our own possible peril. It also generates further guidelines for Kluge's broad inquiry into humanity's capacities for resisting the mysteriously dangerous realities that so often engulf us.

Whether the forces underlying such an engulfment have become more or less threatening in the new century—and for whom—is a question Kluge addresses from different historical, socio-theoretical, literary, and cinematic perspectives across his multimedial oeuvre. From the vantage point of this writing in 2015, the period of the Cold War—during which the writers discussed in this book developed their artistic agendas—might appear increasingly as a simpler and perhaps more peaceful age relative to our own.[5] The nomenclature itself is part of an identifiable ideological opposition rather than indicative of any bewildering obscurity (*Unübersichtlichkeit*) of the kind that has set in since. "Cold War" was a markedly Western term throughout the period's history that contrasted with the Soviet Union's appeal to "peaceful co-existence."[6] The latter phrase became current east of the continent's divide after Nikita Khrushchev's 1963 usage. In the global context of the time, however, processes of decolonization and proxy wars conducted outside the Northern Hemisphere were hardly free of bloodshed. Woefully inaccurate vis-à-vis such a context, the terms "Cold War" and "peaceful coexistence" applied at best to the bilateral relationship between the blocs. In the over twenty-five years since the thaw of the period in question, the scope and character of human violence, along with the perceptibility and interpretation thereof, have undergone tremendous metamorphoses. While the discourse of globalization has emerged to denote the organization of a world economy into a singularly dominant mode of production, such a process of increasing economic integration reveals a violent flip side, which continues to express itself in (ethno-)nationalist and/or (pseudo-)religious (i.e., cultural) terms that exacerbate hostilities the world over. It is not only that the violent disintegration of Yugoslavia rather than the peaceful unification of Germany appears as a dismal harbinger of the post-1989 world. Humanity's global track record since 1989 may also lend some retroactive credence to the Soviet Union's preferred term for the Cold War as a period of peaceful coexistence.

As culture has tended to supplant politics as a master term in the intractable discourse of a global society, the rise of cultural studies has had a great impact on the humanities. The ensuing predominance of culture as the humanities' common object of inquiry has displaced other guiding terms that once lent individual disciplines their sharper, if more self-confined contours. This cultural turn has brought advantages and disadvantages. For example, the expansion of the concept of text has facilitated the study of literary culture in the broader contexts of its social origins and functions. Such an approach can also fuel inquiry into the constitution of print- and text-based experiences amid the proliferation of other media and information and communication technologies. At the same time, working with an expanded concept of text also places demands on accounting for the specific qualities of a literary text as a work of art in contradistinction to other kinds of texts and media. As the cultural text we read has grown in scope, the specific aesthetic filtration through which any of its messages passes still bears heavily on questions of interpretation and critical analysis.

As an accompanying feature of globalization's uneven developments, culture's rise evinces more baneful dimensions. The tendency for frontlines of conflict to be drawn and enforced by divisive cultural concepts fantastically produced and grotesquely abused stands out in this regard. The widely debated value of humanities inquiry today is surely related to its ability to examine critically fault lines in the cultural expressions of conflict with an eye toward their historicization, interpretation, and transcendence.[7] In light of this task, this study's return to the Cold War as a legible period of coexistence as tenuous as it was challenging may prove of some service.[8] With divided Germany at the center of the bipolar world order, the fault line of which ran straight through Berlin, political discourse still held primacy over cultural discourse during the period: this granted international negotiations at least some purchase and provided a framework against which the claims of art could be measured and evaluated. Arguing for the cogence of the epic imagination that reemerged in remarkable if unlikely ways in works of German-language literature written after 1961, this study also appeals to the continuity of that imagination across the historical watershed of 1989–1991, those fast-paced years that witnessed the opening of the German-German border, the unification of Germany and the dissolution of the Soviet Union. Cold War variants of the modern epic in the German context not only reckoned with the preceding catastrophic phase of the continent's history and proceeded to map the complex repercussions thereof in Cold War (geo)politics. Out of its critical, resourceful work on twentieth-century pasts and presents, the modern epic imagination also wrested conditions under which possible futures could be envisioned, debated, and even made.[9] On both scores, the modern German epic's creative labor offers transferable lessons in political, social, and ethical orientation of no small importance in our current times beyond measure.

Cold War Epics

The argument substantiating such claims is the content of this book as a whole. This introduction outlines the study's scope and rationale by setting forth its selection of interconnected primary literary sources and offering a first cursory account of their historical and contemporary value. Chapter 1 lays out the study's groundwork from a literary-aesthetic vantage point. "Modern Epic Possibilities" presupposes the Cold War context of urban and ideological division most directly felt in Berlin in the wake of the Wall's construction in 1961 and the resulting spatiotemporal complexity of lived experience amid the geopolitical overdetermination of perception and movement, thought and action, and media and orientation. It approaches the question of the Cold War epic from a diachronic and theoretical angle to convey the stakes of the genre, explain the guiding questions and methodology of the study's literary analyses and present the larger arch of my argument regarding the course of the genre's development in the second half of the Cold War. In so doing, chapter 1 sets the stage for the analyses of the modern epic's literary evolution developed in the following three chapters, each of which focuses on one exemplary epic work. The epilogue recapitulates the main findings of the comparative assembly as a whole, with notes on the value of the epic imagination for the twenty-first century.

For starters, there is no single Cold War epic. Nor could there be. Moreover, the singularizing formulation in the book's title underscores the study's focus on the genre not for its own sake, but for what the modern epic can do as an enabling structure of meaning and insight, orientation and critique. The literary history of the genre traced in these pages concerns three works written in German (for the most part) between 1961 and 1989. These are Peter Weiss's *Die Ästhetik des Widerstands* (*The Aesthetics of Resistance*), the three volumes of which were published from 1975 to 1981; Uwe Johnson's *Jahrestage: Aus dem Leben von Gesine Cresspahl* (*Anniversaries: From the Life of Gesine Cresspahl*), the four volumes of which were published from 1970 to 1983; and Alexander Kluge's *Chronik der Gefühle* (*Chronicle of Feelings*), the two volumes of which were published not during the Cold War, but at the opening of the new millennium in 2000, along with all of Kluge's previous literary publications (with modifications) from 1962 to 1984 as well as scores of additional new stories.[10] As Kluge is the only of these authors to live through the Cold War's end, my account of his work not only treats *Chronik der Gefühle* as a monument to the period, but also addresses Kluge's active transfer of his project—which has continued, with ever-widening frames of reference, to issue imaginative cartographies of human life in the new millennium—to the post–Cold War age. While these literary works are by no means the only German-language representatives of the epic imagination during the period, they are, as I will argue, particularly indicative of the power and promise of socio-critical literature's ability to come to terms with social, political, and ethical challenges in the second half of the twentieth century in German-speaking Europe and beyond.[11]

As a second gloss on the book's title, it must be stressed that the Cold War epic in question here is not German in any straightforward national sense. Nor could it be—and not only due to the long-standing political instability of the signifier "Germany," which assumed some six different forms in the twentieth century alone. Contrary to the conventional association of the epic genre with a national horizon, the word "German" in the study's title designates the language of a genre that is transnationally oriented.[12] Such an orientation was doubtlessly conditioned by the authors' lived experiences of exile or other forms of displacement: from World War II through Cold

War geopolitics, the impact of history on the writers' biographies drove their emergent interests in delivering epic accounts and narrative maps of the world beyond the brittle national horizon. Each writer was nearly as nomadic as his wayfaring characters. Peter Weiss, the oldest of the three and never a citizen of any German state, was born in Nowawes near Potsdam in 1916. He was assigned the Czechoslovakian citizenship that his father, a Jewish Hungarian who had converted to Protestantism, adopted in the aftermath of Austria-Hungary's demise, whereas his mother was Swiss. Weiss spent his childhood in Bremen and Berlin. The forced migration of the family from Germany, which included stays near London and then in Varnsdorf, Czechoslovakia, before they settled in Sweden, began in 1935. Weiss joined them there in 1939, became a Swedish citizen in 1946, and resided in Stockholm until his death in 1982. Although he began writing in the language of his exile alongside artistic endeavors in painting and filmmaking, his literary breakthrough ensued when he returned to his native German, in which, beginning in 1960, he published a number of prose texts and plays of world renown prior to embarking on *Die Ästhetik des Widerstands* after 1968. Uwe Johnson was born in 1934 in Cammin, Pomerania, now in Poland, and was raised in nearby Anklam in western Pomerania. The advance of the Red Army at the end of the war compelled the westward migration of the family to the village of Recknitz and then the town of Güstrow in Mecklenburg. He began writing as a student in the coastal city of Rostock and then in Leipzig in the 1950s, but eventually moved to West Berlin in 1959. This "relocation" (*Umzug*), as Johnson preferred to describe his decision to leave East Germany, not only resulted from his growing frustration with the state's dictatorial practices and his own ordeals with party and police; it was also intimately caught up in Johnson's literary reckoning with the German Democratic Republic (GDR).[13] Keen to publish *Mutmassungen über Jakob* (*Speculations about Jakob*) after an earlier manuscript for another novel had been repeatedly rejected, Johnson came to the realization that his commitment to a critical, humanist socialism was incompatible with life in the state he would have preferred. *Mutmassungen* was published by the West German Suhrkamp Verlag the same year.[14] Thereafter, Johnson's migrations continued: to the United States, to Rome, back to the United States, and New York City, central to *Jahrestage*, then back to West Berlin, before settling in Sheerness-on-Sea in eastern England, where he died in 1984. Alexander Kluge was born in 1932 in Halberstadt in the state of Saxony-Anhalt to the east of what would later become the impassable border between the two German states. But he moved with his mother to West Berlin after his parents' divorce and the destruction of his hometown in 1945, and completed his secondary education there in 1949 before moving to West Germany, where he studied in Marburg and Frankfurt am Main.[15] In Frankfurt, where he also worked as a legal adviser for the Institute for Social Research, Kluge had the opportunity to make the acquaintance of Theodor W. Adorno. Skeptical of Kluge's literary ambitions and perhaps of the contemporary possibilities of the literary medium itself, Adorno sent him to Fritz Lang's film studio for an internship, where Kluge ended up spending much of his time in the cafeteria composing stories in notebooks, leading to his *Lebensläufe* in 1962. In conjunction with his first short film *Brutalität im Stein* (*Brutality in Stone*) in 1960, this publication marked the beginning of Kluge's long career of artistic production in various media.[16]

Such an overview of biographical dates and places reveals a common experience of migration shared by the three authors in different ways—none of them quite as direly as the more perilous migrations addressed in their narratives. This being said, migration goes hand in hand with the loss of home and identity for each. Yet none of their epics entertains any preoccupation with Germany as a *Kulturnation* that might have compensated for such loss. Nor could that notion provide any imaginary unity during the decades of political division from 1949 to 1990. The materialist orientation of Weiss, Johnson, and Kluge's epic tales, which ground ideational formations in economic and political history, abstains from and undercuts such cultural constructs. Their approach to Cold War division is not national, but (broadly) social, as well as, for Johnson especially, regional.[17] As intense as their literary examinations of German history are, each examines this history and its broader repercussions ex-centrically, from the margins, and with the "plurality of vision" that Edward Said has ascribed to the optics of exiles.[18] The Cold War epic could be written in neither Germany.[19]

A directly related curiosity of Cold War cultural politics is suggestive here. It concerns the literary historiography of the period. Generally speaking, the function of literary histories is at least twofold: for scholars and the reading public alike, such compendia present information on socio-historical and institutional contexts, aesthetic formations, and individual authors to provide orientation as well as possibilities for ascertaining larger connections and undertaking comparisons. In light of the structure of literary scholarship in Germanophone Europe, which remains oriented toward monographs on single authors that plumb depth at the expense of comparative breadth, such overviews can be quite useful. Second, literary histories, where they are nationally organized, as the humanities have been on both sides of the Atlantic for linguistic and philological reasons for decades, are also involved in the curious art of narrating the nation, which often includes the assimilation of literary culture to the spirit of a people even where literary production challenges actually existing national political formations. Thus, in the vexed competition for cultural legacies (*Kulturerbe*) and legitimation in the Cold War context of German division, the following finding is perhaps not entirely surprising: the condition of postwar division appeared so solid, even final, that virtually all of the German literary histories published in East or West Germany during the period treated literary texts written in either political state as completely separate phenomena (i.e., in separate volumes).[20]

This raises the question—especially given the aforementioned signposts of Weiss, Johnson, and Kluge's cross-border migrations—of each author's categorization in the nationalizing narratives of cultural history. No official (i.e., publishable) East German literary history would integrate any of them, despite Weiss's emphatic declaration of solidarity with socialism in 1965, the proximity of his artistic production thereafter to the socialist project, and his repeated trips to East Germany and discussions with politicians and artists (theater-makers) there.[21] While Johnson was featured prominently in Wolfgang Emmerich's (West German) history of GDR literature, which grasped East Germany as the very lifeblood of Johnson's creative work, all three authors were identified (and appropriated) as West German authors in literary histories written in and about West Germany.[22] To be sure, each participated extensively in the West German public sphere, especially Kluge, whose involvement in West German film politics and television production (from his coauthorship of the 1962 Oberhausen Manifesto, which launched New German Cinema, onward), theoretical collaborations with Oskar Negt (which addressed German politics at crucial historical junctures), and even a great deal of the thematic orientation of his storytelling up to 1984 suggest how intimately his work was related to the FRG, also as a space of national culture.[23] Nonetheless, the literary-historical integration of Weiss, Johnson, and Kluge into West Germany was tenuous given that none of the three was born in that state, and only one of them ever lived there in any continuity. In retrospect, as with so much of the Cold War, it is easier to recognize how much Weiss, Johnson, and Kluge's *Lebensläufe* (which renders "curriculum vitae" and in German contains the literal connotation of "walks through life") outstripped the national categories current in the cultural historiography of the time. Seen from within the Cold War period, the geopolitical present on which such categories rested appeared permanent rather than anomalous.[24]

The process leading to division's seeming permanence was tumultuous in the making. The foregoing biographical sketch reveals a second commonality on this front: although Weiss nearly belonged to an older generation than Johnson and Kluge, each writer began publishing around 1960, at what was to be a critical juncture of the German question in the Cold War. The erection of the Berlin Wall in 1961 provided a kind of temporary clarification as to what the relationship between the Germanies—and the blocs—would look like.[25] As the closest observer of German-German division, Johnson was quick to grasp Berlin as a "model for encounters between the two world orders."[26] He elevated the border to a literary category that demanded "the transformation of epic techniques and language until they proved adequate to the unprecedented situation."[27] Johnson's story "Eine Kneipe geht verloren" (A Bar Goes Lost), which narrated a young West Berlin woman's selfless efforts to help East Berliners cross the German-German border, provided a telling example thereof.[28] Its plotline related to Johnson's 1965 novel

Zwei Ansichten (*Two Views*), where the Wall's central role helped confirm his reputation (at his annoyance) as the "poet of the two Germanies" (*Dichter der beiden Deutschland*).[29] The Wall's construction also compelled the transgressive assistance Gesine Cresspahl's friend Anita Gantlik lends to East Germans' westward relocations, as recounted in *Jahrestage* (*JT* 1623).[30] And yet, these signposts in Johnson's work notwithstanding, Berlin's militarized border did not become a great point of focus in the Cold War epics considered here, *Jahrestage* included.[31] As a clear manifestation of the political domination of space, however, the Wall very much served as the best-known signifier for the country, the continent, and the world's division during the period, and in this way also pointed to the curious conditions for artistic work during the Cold War's second half, not to mention life in the divided city. The far-reaching repercussions of the Wall's construction thus proved to be in play even where the Wall itself was not.

Concrete division impacted the arts in material and ideational ways. Any art produced within each Germany was subject to ideological celebration or ideologically driven neglect, if not condemnation, often in relation to the competing state and its ideology. Such "culture wars" were always and fairly transparently political. Material division in Berlin also confronted art with special challenges due to the spatial scission driven into the middle of the German metropolis as well as the dominant role of leading media, such as radio and television, which, transcending the imposed divide, tended to monopolize reality's representation to the detriment of the kind of cognitive mapping that the arts could deliver.[32] Any artistic responses to such Cold War pressures were thus bound to relate as much to informational media in their politicized function as to other artistic media.[33] As will be seen in the chapters that follow, the modern epic's rejuvenation in the Cold War was fueled in part by its interaction with other artistic and nonartistic media. This interaction reveals a connotation of the term "epic" that is important to this study. In addition to its designation of an identifiable literary genre, "epic" here concerns the general artistic practice of what Bertolt Brecht, in his work on epic theater, called "the separation of [a work's] elements."[34] In contrast to the obfuscating politicization of perception often effected by leading media in their alignment with ideology, the kind of separation Brecht called for can be implemented to afford recipients' senses freer opportunities for apprehending and responding to reality. Weiss, Johnson, and Kluge's works certainly square with this call. Amid the spatiotemporal complexities of post-1961 Berlin realities, they undertake epic mediations of the Cold War askew of geopolitical predeterminations, enabling readers to orient themselves in emancipatory ways.

Wielding a monopoly on political power in the GDR, East Germany's Socialist Unity Party (SED) orchestrated and ordered the sealing of the state's borders in response to the increasing migration of East Germans westward in search of better lives. But the SED could not stem the migration of the literary-cartographic imagination, which assumes epic proportions in Weiss, Johnson, and Kluge's aspirations to map the material, geopolitical and social complexities of the Cold War.[35] Whereas their very biographies resisted subsumption into the categories of national politics current until 1990, a reappraisal of their written works today can reveal the ways in which they surpass the time-spaces of their inception, execution, and first reception. The authors' migration backgrounds do not simply drive the forms and trajectories of literary oeuvres (*Lebenswerke*) that stand in for and reconstitute fictional homes and identities parallel to those denied by the course of history. The dialectics of each writer's immersion in and disengagement from the time-spaces of history he aspires to narrate builds on intricate combinations of documentation and fiction, mimesis and construction, and anchorage and projection: these constitute shared features of Weiss, Johnson, and Kluge's epic pursuits of reality. As discussed in chapter 1, their literary projects remain beholden to a narrative realism as critical as it is self-reflexive: dialectically materialist in their immersions into presents and pasts, Weiss, Johnson, and Kluge's chronicles approximate the genre of historical fiction, but also generate questions and answers about how to survive and/or change the societies of which they are part. In so doing, each realist project also intervenes in the history it depicts in view of its possibilities and alternatives: having worked through past travails of the antifascist resistance against Nazism, the nameless chronicler of Weiss's *Die Ästhetik des Widerstands* concludes his epic in the subjunctive to confer the book's conception of aesthetic resistance to the future; with *Jahrestage*, Johnson and his fictional protagonist-narrator Gesine Cresspahl set a "world against the world" (VPR 403) by undertaking the (co)narration of history for "when we are dead" (cf. *AN* 108, 254/*JT* 151, 385); and Kluge, whose literary and theoretical endeavors (with Oskar Negt) can alike be described as bottled messages for posterity,[36] embraces a critical practice for which his repeated narrations of the Battle of Stalingrad in *Schlachtbeschreibung* (*Description of a Battle*) can be taken as paradigmatic: at the beginning the text's re-editions in 1978[37] and 2000, Kluge instructed readers to proceed with an interest turned away (*abgewendet*) from the given political state of German history (*CdG* 1:511). Each of these turns suggests that amid all of modernity's continuing time-space compression,[38] Weiss, Johnson, and Kluge's modern literary works unfold in and address themselves to vaster, longer, slower—that is, epic—swaths of time.

In anticipation of the analyses that follow in chapters 2–4, the basic features of each epic's relation to the times and spaces of its narration can be spelled out in further detail. For starters, Weiss's *Die Ästhetik des Widerstands* does not deliver any straightforward literary cartography of the Cold War. Rather, it begins in medias res in a past Berlin to narrate the international antifascist resistance movement in the years 1937–1945 and speaks to time-spaces outside this framework via historical reconstruction, allusion and/or implication, as when the narrator traces capitalist exploitation back to ancient social formations or grounds subsequently emerging Cold War divisions in political conflicts at the end of World War II. Throughout the tale, Weiss's narrator, whose fictional profile resembles the author's in some respects,[39] remains embedded in the story as an unusual unity of the epic's narrative and narrated times into which readers are likewise drawn.[40] Weiss himself did not take large part in the antifascist movement, but his fiction assiduously reconstructs the historical context and its challenges, which the narrator relates from his autodiegetic perspective. As the growing power of the Nazi dictatorship compels the migration of its designated enemies, we accompany the narrator, and intermittently his family members, comrades, and connections, on a journey leading from Berlin to Warnsdorf (Varnsdorf), Czechoslovakia, to Spain, where he participates in the republican cause during the Spanish Civil War, through Paris on his way to Stockholm in officially neutral Sweden, where he learns of the traumatic experiences of his mother during the war as well as recounts the harrowing demise of his friends in Berlin. Across this journey, as the narrator and fellow opponents of fascism confront and/or seek to subvert the Nazi dictatorship, their own efforts to achieve emancipation are juxtaposed to the "global net" (*weltweites Netz*) that repeatedly threatens to engulf them from without (*AoR* 117/*ÄdW* 1:137). As restrictions on underground life in Nazi Germany and occupied or collaborating Europe compound foregoing social restrictions placed on the protagonists' proletarian existence, their emancipatory aspirations revert to more rudimentary tasks of orientation and survival. Steered by the autodidactic education on which the characters have embarked, these tasks evince broad contours on Weiss's watch. Across their fight against fascism and their quest for survival, the characters' attempts to map changing situations are enhanced by their appropriation of artistic culture, their study of history, and their numerous protracted cognition-oriented dialogues. Their work is *Die Ästhetik des Widerstands*' own: throughout, the epic persists in dichotomously demarcating the fault lines of the struggles faced by its many characters, narrator included: unity and difference, perspectives from above and below (both within the Left's political organizations and beyond), friend and foe, inclusion and exclusion, sight and blindness are binaries that run like red threads through the book's pages and do not diminish at its end. As the narrator chronicles the period, his efforts ultimately culminate, by implication in the artful construction of the book's final chapter, in Weiss's present and thereby invite the transfer of the work's lessons in political and aesthetic orientation to a new phase. Transposing his narrator's epic labor into the Cold War present, Weiss both apprehends national, continental and global divisiveness in the "new, smoldering war" that emerges out of World War II's end and will "overshadow life for decades" (*ÄdW* 3:262) and exposes the temporal construction underlying his narrator's ability to deliver the epic tale as a whole. This consists in the curiously sustained tension between the narrator as protagonist and writer. The former repeatedly questions the viability of the latter, and can only anticipate what the latter achieves in fact and deed: the articulate, even resonant narration of the indescribable experiences in the book's narrated time.[41] Reflecting on the defeats and deaths of the dark years, the ambitious project of the progressive fusion of politics and art in a revolutionary culture is less jettisoned as futile than reasserted in a new key. On my reading in chapter 2, "Epic's Impossible Return," Weiss's work bequeaths legacies of aesthetic resistance to its Cold War present as well as posterity.

In some contrast to Weiss's project with which it has been compared, Johnson's *Jahrestage* inverts the relation between the narrative present and narrated time. The epic proceeds from its frame narrative in the present, Gesine Cresspahl's New York City in 1967, backward into the past. The former remains in the foreground throughout the daily chapters of Johnson's genially selected and politically tumultuous year from August 20, 1967, to August 20, 1968, each date of which is marked on the literary calendar except for the first, which begins on the New Jersey coast. The epic's spatial coordinates are delivered as exactingly: the narration of urban life in New York City is continually interspersed with references to the narrative present's antipodally construed vanishing points—the war in Vietnam and the Prague Spring in Czechoslovakia. Indeed, the global reach of this Cold War epic ensures not only that it is polyperspectival, but also multilingual, such that English, Czech, Russian, Italian, Danish, and Low German (*Niederdeutsch*, i.e., *Platt*) find their way onto Johnson's pages as part of translator Gesine's environs. That last idiom points to the temporal migration of Cresspahl's consciousness into the past with which her spatial orientation in the political present must be supplemented. The prolonged embedded narrative that Gesine recounts for herself and to her daughter Marie revolves around her family's history in the fictional (East) German town of Jerichow (based loosely on Klütz in northwestern Mecklenburg), which Cresspahl left via West Berlin for the West German city of Düsseldorf in 1953, only to continue on to the United States in 1961. As part of the GDR she fled, Cresspahl's Mecklenburg home remains inaccessible to her in the epic's present, but it is the site at which Johnson—through Gesine's narration—brings the same calamitous years (and more) as Weiss's *Ästhetik* into focus. In August 1968, as Cresspahl's reconstruction of the past reaches the narrative present in a culmination resembling Weiss's construction, mother and daughter are depicted one last time during a stopover in Denmark en route to Prague in the Czechoslovak Socialist Republic (ČSSR). The hopefulness and anticipation accompanying the journey are overshadowed by (readers' historical knowledge of) the Soviet suppression of the Prague Spring, which began on the night of, and thus right after, the epic calendar's final entry. As the projected space of the narrative's future—and perhaps Johnson's own hope for a human socialism—suffers eclipse, *Jahrestage* ends inconclusively at the Danish coast. Whereas Weiss's *Die Ästhetik des Widerstands* achieved epic integration by artfully circumscribing the future, Johnson's epic probe of the Cold War in *Jahrestage* teeters on the brink of temporal integration's limits in a narrative that appears to succumb to the politico-economic domination of space, but not without delivering an unparalleled investigation of life's presents, pasts, and futures in the Cold War. Culling transferable lessons of orientation from Johnson's "anatomy of a century in a permanent state of crisis,"[42] chapter 3, "Time-Spaces of Epic Narration," also argues for the transhistorical validity of *Jahrestage*'s clairvoyance beyond its narrated times.

Finally, in significant contrast to Weiss and Johnson, Kluge's *Chronik der Gefühle* is set far beyond any single narrative thread in time, save the dispersed narration of human feelings themselves. As these assume resonant articulation in the many truncated short stories that populate Kluge's two large volumes, their migrations are unconstrained by any centripetal force of narration or overarching story line. Yet Kluge's *Chronik* is organized in terms of a general structure akin to the work of memory operative in Johnson's epic especially. As Kluge highlights in the collection's foreword, the cumulative presentation of his storytelling proceeds, "like memory," for the most part from his most recently written stories backward in time, only to return in the final chapter, "Der lange Marsch des Urvertrauens" (The Long March of Primordial Trust), to the broadest sweeps of time and space (*CdG* 1:7; 2:923). My approach to Kluge's literary work as a highly unusual instantiation of the modern epic genre nonetheless ties it to the Cold War in two basic ways. First, whereas Kluge adopted an epic format for the comprehensive publication of his storytelling only in 2000 (and has maintained this format for the subsequent continuation of his writing), I argue in chapter 4, "Epic Storytelling and Human Survival," that the determinate dates of *Chronik der Gefühle*'s formidable sprawl remain 1945 and 1989 as watersheds of the collection's temporal framework.[43] Second, the very architecture of Kluge's approach to epic storytelling is itself anchored in the conditions of narration in the Cold War: his literary cartography radicalizes the relative independence of the epic's parts in constructive mimesis of catastrophic history, the explosions of which have consequence for narrative form.[44] As a result, the trajectories of Kluge's manifold space- and time-travelers need not (indeed, cannot) congeal into an integrated narrative epic featuring a single story line of the kind still privileged by Weiss and, more loosely, Johnson, however vast and differentiated the narratives of *Die Ästhetik des Widerstands* and *Jahrestage* may be. The structure of temporal integration—time's "wholeness," however long—that underlay Weiss and Johnson's undertakings implodes on Kluge's watch, which enables him to preside over the epic's transformation into a network of storytelling. In Kluge's narrative network, neither space nor time is subordinate to the other, and time is no longer constrained by chronological conceptions of linearity in the story. The shift in question is also palpable in Kluge's repeated calls for "maps of human experience" that he delivers in his notorious practice of cross-mapping, whereby disparate discourses are interrelated on the model of hiking through the Harz (a mountain range in the middle of Germany) with a map of London.[45] Epic reasserts itself according to a constellated model of narration appropriate to the spatiotemporal compression and expansion, including time's "uncanniness" (*CdG* 2:11; *Unheimlichkeit*), that Kluge diagnoses as constitutive features of modern and Cold War realities. In these two senses, then, Kluge's wayfarers remain as grounded in the Cold War context as the others: while characters are held back by the unredeemed and unredeemable pasts of (not only German) history, as vehicles of longer range feelings and human capacities, their stories also stretch across "time-spaces that last longer than a life-history: the stars, eons, generations" intimated in Kluge's introductory note to *Chronik*'s concluding chapter (*CdG* 2:923). As the foregoing overview has aimed to suggest, violent pasts, Cold War presents, and anticipated, yet unforeseeable futures constituted serious challenges to representation in epic literature in view of which Weiss, Johnson, and Kluge's works would develop unconventional, diverse, and powerful responses.

Storytelling's Revival after Catastrophe

Abounding in time and space travel, the German epics of the Cold War still gravitated toward the catastrophic history of the twentieth century's darkest years in Europe. The epic was not simply up against the challenge of rendering the geopolitical and material complexities of Cold War space legible and navigable. The modern German epic also had to return to the very causes of the like in the catastrophes Nazi Germany brought about. The shadows cast thereby rendered the modern epic's reemergence in postwar Europe unlikely, if not dubious.

The unlikelihood of literature's strong return in the postwar period stemmed from a number of factors. The greatest concerned the hitherto unimaginable atrocities committed by Nazi Germany in the World War it began and the genocide of millions in the Shoah it organized. The perception of the German language's irretrievable demolition by the Nazi dictatorship only added to the notion that such horrors could not be represented at all, and most certainly not (yet) in the language of the perpetrators.[46] In the immediate aftermath of the war, West German literature first reduced itself to existential fundamentals in rubble literature (*Trümmerliteratur*) amid delays in coming to terms with what had transpired during the previous twelve years of dictatorship. Undeterred by any confusion regarding the emergence of Nazism out of the Weimar Republic's (read: capitalism's) crises, East German literature announced and celebrated the construction of a system that would guard against future lapses into barbarism. Given the SED's strict oversight of literary publication, the analysis thereof would make for a different kind of case study. Suffice it to say here that the GDR's founding myth as the antifascist and therefore better Germany did not necessarily guarantee concrete confrontation with the past. Yet the past's repression and/or transfiguration (*Verklärung*) could not possibly hold in either state indefinitely. Juridical and political developments such as the trial of Adolf Eichmann in Jerusalem in 1961–1962, the prosecution of additional perpetrators in the Auschwitz trials conducted in Frankfurt in 1963–1965, questions about the German past and the complicity of the older generation raised in the (West German) student movement (also driven by opposition to U.S. military involvement in Vietnam), and the contributions of intellectuals in the German public spheres on Germans' inability to mourn, the repression of its past, and lingering democratic deficits (in both German states) also paved the way for literary contributions, however delayed, to the serious reexamination of the past and the work of remembrance and mourning.[47] Thus, prior to the "incredulity toward metanarratives" that Jean-François Lyotard would soon diagnose in his analysis of postmodernism, against Karl Markus Michel's 1968 declaration of literature's death in the leading (West) German leftist journal *Kursbuch*, against the competition from other media reflected in the literary scholar Peter Demetz's "sobering thought" that the 1979 American telecast *Holocaust* "shocked millions of viewers into thinking more about Germany than any books or plays had been able to do" and against the plethora of cultural production revolving around the Holocaust and World War II that has emerged since then (which demonstrates less that the subject matter is inexpressible than that the unsayable can also be exploited through its conversion into kitsch), a key task still fell to epic literature in the German context, which could hardly be ignored nor further neglected: the difficult revival of a storytelling that would fathom, account for and work through catastrophe.[48] In other words, World War II and the Shoah demanded adequate and appropriate means of representation, which were neither easy to establish nor constant.[49] Not only life, history, and thinking, but also literary production faced a caesura.[50] In a probing article on Weiss's *Ästhetik*, the German literary scholar Burkhardt Lindner warned of the dangers of neutralization (*Verharmlosung*) in any literature's approach to this past: "After Auschwitz, Gulag, and Hiroshima . . . we must ask whether we can still lay serious claim to the power of epic memory as the 19th-cenutry novel did."[51] As the undertaking to remember and tell could by no means be discarded save with even worse consequences, the call went out for the generation of new forms of representation and communication with which one could even embark on the attempt. The German epic in the Cold War was not to be the epic of old.[52]

The work of the German philosopher, social critic, and aesthetic theorist Theodor W. Adorno remains a stringent context for thinking through such a task. From the 1947 *Dialektik der Aufklärung* (*Dialectic of Enlightenment*) that he cowrote with Max Horkheimer during the war through *Negative*

Dialektik (1966), in which he elaborated a new form of the categorical imperative mandating that Auschwitz not be repeated, Adorno's thought was deeply invested in questions of representation and mediation with a focus on the baneful entwinement of rationality and social reality under the aegis of domination. Returning to Frankfurt am Main along with Horkheimer after the war, Adorno did not tire of seeking to advance awareness and self-reflection in the German public sphere on the country's past and the shadows it cast over all aspects of life. A pressing issue for Adorno was the seamless restoration of German "culture," in particular the continuation of artistic traditions, which he diagnosed as ideological perversion. In his meditations on metaphysics with which *Negative Dialectics* concluded, Adorno underscored that culture had failed utterly in the face of Nazism. Culture's death and the resulting "stench" thereof consigned it to "garbage" (*ND* 366/359). This was no facile subjective judgment of taste, but an ethical concern that cut to culture's core: "In restoring itself after the things that happened without resistance in its own countryside, culture has turned entirely into the ideology it had been potentially—had been ever since it presumed, in opposition to material existence, to inspire that existence with the light denied it by the separation of the mind from manual labor" (*ND* 367/359–360). While Adorno included the expressions of the cultural critic he himself was in such judgments, his claim that all post-Auschwitz culture was garbage did not so much issue an absolute verdict as speak to the stringency of the challenge to refuse culture's ideological restoration. Adorno turned the question of the feasibility of any culture in Germany to the caesura: "Nothing can be saved unchanged, nothing that has not passed through the portal of its death" (*ND* 391–392/384). The negation of culture—out of which it might self-critically reemerge transformed[53]—applied to artistic production as a whole, including the entire reservoir of literature preexisting Auschwitz, and it is in this context that Adorno's 1955 claim that to "write poetry after Auschwitz is barbaric, and this corrodes even the knowledge of why it has become impossible to write poetry today" must be situated.[54]

Here too, the widely circulated passage issued neither a final verdict nor a prohibition. Misunderstanding might have been mitigated by reference to Adorno's account of art's service to the "subject's urge to express itself" and the "need to lend a voice to suffering" (*ND* 17/29). He meant this in no merely compensatory sense: reactivating a conception of art as the "consciousness of plight" (*Bewußtsein von Nöten*) that Adorno saw in Hegel, the former's posthumously published *Ästhetische Theorie* (*Aesthetic Theory*) ascribed to the whole world an objective need for art (*AT* 18 and 37/35 and 50). Needs continued in any case, as Adorno wrote there, "mute in themselves, [awaiting] the expression that artworks fulfill by proxy" (*AT* 345/512). Art's substitutive articulations of need stood in for a transcendence that art itself could neither deliver nor prefigure in any direct manner. Hence Adorno's own predilection for all those works of art—music and literature being the media on which he focused most—that absorbed the negative state of the world, registered the impossibility of representation, and reflected their always already commodified status under reigning relations of production. Adorno thus codified the continuation of a dark modernism for which the experience of death and meaninglessness were constitutive. He did not thereby envision a transgression of limits so much as impress them upon us. No artistic canon emerged from this, about which in any case there could be no positive prescriptions, only an awareness of what was no longer tenable, convincing, or even palatable. Adorno's contributions to debates about prose-based narration similarly reflected his insistence on the negation of continuity in artistic traditions. More determinate than abstract, such negations were relevant to concrete situations and tasks ascertainable therein: against the backdrop of his sweeping claim that "it is no longer possible to tell a story [*erzählen*]," Adorno emphasized that if "*the novel wants to remain true to its realistic heritage and tell how things really are, it must abandon a realism that only aids the façade in its work of camouflage by reproducing it.*"[55] While the novel, after such abandonment, was to land on territory not charted by Adorno himself, he nonetheless suggested the possibility for critical resets of realist narration in passages such as this.

Adorno's tremendously resourceful *Aesthetic Theory* abounded in paradoxes revolving around "the communication of the uncommunicable" to outline the paths by which artistic production might be able to resonate in modern society postcatastrophe (*AT* 196/292). His notion of art as a unique form of social labor and force of production in its own right suggested how the circle of manual and mental labor severed by cultural ideology might be dialectically squared (*aufgehoben*—at least theoretically) and is particularly germane to this study's approach to what epic mediations of society can accomplish.[56] An appreciation of the positive legacies of Adorno's contributions also allows for a more balanced understanding of even his grimmest assessments. After witnessing the circulation of his association of poetry with barbarism, Adorno reformulated his point to express the following:

> Perennial suffering has as much right to expression as a tortured man has to scream; hence it may have been wrong to say that after Auschwitz you could no longer write poems. But it is not wrong to raise the less cultural question whether after Auschwitz you can go on living—especially whether one who escaped by accident, one who by rights [*rechtens*] should have been killed, may go on living. (*ND* 362–363/355)

While the air doubtlessly thins in such lines, what resonates in the passage is not only a syndrome of survivor guilt. The weight of its "whether" can still be read as a "how." Adorno's writing, reckoning, from *Minima Moralia: Reflexionen aus dem beschädigten Leben* (*Minima Moralia: Reflections from Damaged Life*) onward, with life's very livability in a wrong society, did not yield resignation so much as it urged thoroughgoing philosophical, ethical, and aesthetic examination of the character of life's continuation after catastrophe and under conditions not chosen. Such inquiry continues to have cultural dimensions also. If the conditions for Auschwitz, which Adorno thought to be neither subjectively nor objectively overcome postwar,[57] or to put the matter more generally, if catastrophic potentials still prevail in modern society's objective constitution and its ubiquitous pathologies, then human survival itself turns into a question that must be approached from as many angles as possible. While the urgency of the question of survival may have appeared to subside after World War II, amid the precarious stabilizations of life in Cold War Europe it hardly ceased, but had to be reformulated under changed conditions.[58]

From Postwar Epic to Epic Futures

Adorno's approach to the question of cultural production after Auschwitz suggests at least two touchstones relevant to postwar epics. With regard to the portal of death, Adorno clearly only deemed culture to be beyond its inner contradictions and irreparable failures where it demonstrated itself capable of coming to terms with human suffering. This is ground zero in Weiss, Johnson, and Kluge's diverse approaches to historical catastrophe and the traumas it induced. As the German literary scholar Günter Holtz has written, Weiss and Johnson's books are to be read as "Totenbücher" (literally, "books of the dead"; also a colloquial term for obituaries). "They are certainly no works of literature in any conventional sense of entertainment," Holtz continued, "nor can they be subsumed into the tradition of an informative-enlightening literature. They pass history on to later generations as ongoing suffering and action, such that the silent appeals of the murdered and departed may be given voice."[59] In both Weiss and Johnson's works as well as Kluge's, the dead are quite literally speaking to the later-born, to whom the postwar German epic ascribes a tremendous responsibility stemming from its unavoidable subject matter. The new categorical imperative demands as much vigilance in artistic production as in any other part of culture.

Second, in their various literary passages through death's portals, Weiss, Johnson, and Kluge's works undertake extensive dialogue with the deceased. Their attempts to actualize such dialogues result in ethical and practical reformulations of the question of survival to which literary art can contribute in ways that Adorno may not have imagined.[60] While art's autonomy was de rigueur for Adorno, Weiss, Johnson, and Kluge extend it to include art's practical use-values—including the kind of counsel (*Rat*) that Walter Benjamin associated with storytelling—for the living.[61] Aesthetics is not confined in their modern epics to conventional categories of art's merely contemplative valorization, but rather denotes an undertaking in practical orientation with high stakes. As Jost Hermand underscored in an article on Weiss's *Ästhetik*, the task was "to reclaim newly humanized territory from threatening chaos through the strenuous labor of the word."[62] Far from culminating in any morbidity or melancholia of the kind that "Totenbücher" might imply, the necromantic art of the postwar epic serves the living, as the descendants of the deceased, embracing an optimism of the will in the forms of hopefulness and even, at times, levity (*Heiterkeit*). In other words, the possibility of surviving and the aims of storytelling go hand in hand in the modern epic as an aspirational genre.[63] Modern epic *Totenbücher* become "handbooks" (*Gebrauchsbücher*) for the living.[64]

A further dimension of the postwar epic's temporality must be underscored in this context. As discussed above, the imperative to reckon with the crimes and repercussions of Germany's Nazi past constituted a key premise of any tenable reset of artistic, here literary culture. As the energies of social and political critique came to a head in West Berlin, West Germany and elsewhere during the decade 1963–1973—a ten-year period for which the premiere of Rolf Hochhuth's play *Der Stellvertreter* (*The Deputy*) in 1963 and the economic-historical watershed of the 1973 oil crisis can serve as cornerstones in this context—the confrontation with the past also reignited the question of the organization of society as such. The decisive framing of the human future as something that could be shaped and of history as a process that could be steered to the end of emancipation made itself felt on numerous levels of society and at multifold sites of political action—from student protests in Western capitalist countries to the Prague Spring in Czechoslovakia, from writers' (such as Günter Grass's) involvement in SPD election campaigns to the notion that literature itself could be an agent in the process of social and political transformation. The debates raging through German feuilletons about Peter Weiss's play *Die Ermittlung* (*The Investigation*)—which was based on the aforementioned Auschwitz trials in Frankfurt, was written subsequent to Weiss's express commitment to socialism, and opened simultaneously on some twenty-five West and East German stages in October 1965—not only attested to the attention coordinated efforts in the arts could command in the public sphere at the time.[65] They also indicated how much society's future course hung in the balance west as well as east of the wall. But for how long? The rise of the SPD, which would continue to govern the FRG as the leading partner in the social-liberal coalition until 1982, was celebrated, but then also bemoaned as the exigencies of governance ensured that political transformation would assume the form of long and slow marches through the institutional structures of the country. Conversely, in the GDR, the 1973 designation by the SED Central Committee's new General Secretary Erich Honecker of the socialism that actually existed (*real existierender Sozialismus*) as a relatively independent phase appeared, to East German citizens and intellectuals alike, as a forfeiture of the socialist project's purchase and promise.[66] In conjunction with the oil crisis that has in retrospect been grasped as the harbinger of capitalism's reorganization into a newly global phase—one in which neoliberalism has appeared to go hand in hand with a reshaping of the *zoon politikon* into a mostly consuming animal—the furor of critique yielded to a climate of resignation, with the leading questions and revolutionary pushes of the decade—and of 1968 as its cardinal pivotal year—sliding into an obscurer distance amid the period's postprocessing. Against these proclivities of the age, the German epic in the Cold War constituted a reset and reexamination of social emancipation on a larger scale. The genre is marked not only by its postcatastrophic position, but also its post-1968 inquiry into what became of the socially and politically critical energies of the period after their perceived exhaustion, miscarriage, or obsolescence. Such an approach—a great backtracking and reassessment—has most convincingly been attributed to Weiss,[67] is explicitly worked out, in an offbeat, apprehensive, and mysteriously abstentious way, in Johnson's *Jahrestage*, and clearly informs Kluge's elaboration of his radar through *Chronik*'s engagement with the scenes and discourse of 1968, as in the "Tage der politischen Universität" (Days of the Political University) sections and the aforementioned "Long March" chapter. Where *Die Ästhetik des Widerstands* fiercely reasserts the link between literature and social emancipation, *Jahrestage* examines the connection vis-à-vis (diminishing?) sites of political actionability, whereas the post-1989 *Chronik*, along with Kluge's subsequent works, persists in framing the question of emancipation as an open-ended task of investigative orientation across vast land- and timescapes.

Totenbücher of the postwar era and living epics for the future, Weiss, Johnson, and Kluge's epics constitute three different *Lebenswerke* in the multiple senses of what this compound word "life-work" can imply: culminating oeuvres of each author's narrative endeavors in the literary medium, exponents of the epic imagination's vitality, and handbooks dedicated to survival. Shy of returning to the teaching of the good life—the "Lehre vom richtigen Leben" that Adorno had evoked as something obsolete at the opening of *Minima Moralia*[68]—all three stake claims to human emancipation through self-activity. The commonalities of their projects notwithstanding, existing scholarship has yet to account fully for the force of the modern epic's surprising postwar return represented by their works. To be sure, the German scholarship on each writer has become so formidable that it virtually defies overview. While the canonization of Weiss's *Ästhetik*, influentially dubbed a "book of the century" (*Jahrhundertbuch*),[69] has turned its assessment almost into a rite of passage for literary critics and scholars, studies on Johnson, if less broadly pursued, are as voluminous, and the scholarship on Kluge, whose work newly enjoys, like the other two, regular examination in a yearbook, continues unabated.[70] Each body of scholarship displays a rich history of reception and provides in-depth understandings of each writer. Yet the organization of such academic work into monographs, replete with their requisite specializations, has consigned comparisons of the three mostly to literary histories, in which each author appears briefly as part of broad formations, as in Ralf Schnell's suggestive rubric "Counter-Stories" (*Gegengeschichten*, a term mobilized by Kluge's poetics) that constituted the "smallest common denominator of a diverse [West German] literature" at the beginning of the 1980s and subsumed along with Kluge, Johnson, and Weiss, writers such as Heinrich Böll, Günter Grass, Peter Handke, Wolfgang Hildesheimer, and Martin Walser.[71]

To fill the gap between a specialist literature oriented to individual authors and the overviews offered by literary history, this study's synoptic approach to Weiss, Johnson, and Kluge's works as participants in the history of the postcatastrophic chapter of the modern epic genre proceeds at a "medium level."[72] Scholarship on Weiss, Johnson, and Kluge has occasionally sounded the treatment of their works through the lens of epic as a desideratum.[73] Focusing on the literary structure of the genre and its network-character facilitates the comparison of their epic works beyond approaches centered on individual authors. And yet—to return to my opening remarks on literature's social standing today—the self-evidence of this generic structure can be as little taken for granted as literature itself.[74] *The German Epic in the Cold War* accordingly foregrounds Weiss, Johnson, and Kluge's interrogations of narrative's feasibility in the aftermath of catastrophe and emphasizes the epic's reconstitution in a plural media landscape with which the literary medium can and must interact. Thus, in addition to drawing on the expertise of the German and international literary scholarship and its existing comparisons (e.g., of Johnson and Weiss, of Weiss and Kluge) to trace this reconstitutive piece of cultural labor, I also integrate media-theoretical considerations, where relevant, from the broader field of cultural studies to highlight the modern epic's contemporary value in its specificity. Addressing some of the most ambitious literary works of the twentieth century, this book's essays cannot possibly be definitive or exhaustive given the scope of the material. Rather, as exercises in comparative reading, they endeavor to convey what it is like to engage with epic literature today. Following Kluge, who has championed storytelling as a means of survival and a network that can console,[75] this book's chapters ask whether and how the genre was able to provide orientation and warmth amid cold times, and whether it can offer a human warmth obscured, if not obliterated, by the hot outbreaks of violence prevailing across the globe today. Presenting methodological considerations informing my comparative analysis of what Weiss, Johnson, and Kluge's works aspired to accomplish in the Cold War, the following chapter zeroes in on the genre in which the modern epic imagination takes shape.

Chapter 1

✦

Modern Epic Possibilities

Tasks and Techniques of a Genre

From *Blitzkriegen* and flights no epic can emerge . . . What genre could capture the collapse of our experience of time?

—Karl Schlögel, *Die Mitte liegt ostwärts*

Thinking today is *also*, whatever else it is, an attempt to think the world system as such.

—Fredric Jameson, *The Geopolitical Aesthetic*

See Gesine Lisbeth? In telling a story one has to think of everything.

—Uwe Johnson, *Jahrestage*

Conceptualizing an Unlikely Genre

Novel, chronicle, encyclopedia, constellation, monument, counterstories, network: of the generic categories that might capture the innovations in narrative form advanced in Peter Weiss, Uwe Johnson, and Alexander Kluge's prose works, this study adopts "modern epic" as the organizing principle of its comparative investigation. The name of the genre itself has been regarded as something of a self-contradiction. Whether in Schlögel's remark cited above regarding epic's inability to capture the collapse of our experience of time in the twentieth century or in Lindner's warning, cited in the introduction, regarding postcatastrophic returns to "the power of epic memory" operative in the nineteenth-century novel, our association of epic with ancient or otherwise past and no longer viable modes of narration remains firm. Yet "modern epic" is not meant to beg any questions here. While literary criticism and scholarship have periodically been beset by works outstripping conventional taxonomies and the expectations ingrained by them, generic categories must be derived from actual artistic products. A long-standing central tenet of German aesthetic theory holds that the form and content (including, as "material," previously developed aesthetic forms, *AT* 35/59) of any artistic production unfold in dialectical interrelation.[1] In lockstep with this precept, Weiss's *Ästhetik*, Johnson's *Jahrestage*, and Kluge's *Chronik* remobilize characteristic features of the epic and advance formal innovations of the genre to generate creative and realistic forms of narration appropriate to historically specific contexts and suggestive of the epic imagination's future purchase. Modern epic constitutes a common denominator for the comparative evaluation of their accomplishments not simply due to the general resonance which "epic" (usually as the adjective *episch*) still holds in German as an attribute of all literary prose (in contrast to dramatic or lyrical genres). That would do little to limit the field. Rather, the reconstruction of the literary-aesthetic and theoretical discourse on the concept of modern epic and what such a genre can entail enables us to distinguish it from other narrative modes. The following pages thus lay the theoretical groundwork for the analyses elaborated in the study's main chapters by reviewing and intervening in this discourse, highlighting interconnected features of Weiss, Johnson, and Kluge's projects as instantiations of the modern epic, and outlining an arch of the genre's possibilities that the synoptic treatment of their works suggests.

Modern epic is a literary-historical category developed by the comparatist Franco Moretti. In his 1996 study named after the genre, originally published in Italian as *Opere Mondo*, Moretti focuses on challenges pertaining to the literary narration of increasingly complex modern social conditions from Goethe's *Faust* through modernism to Gabriel García Márquez's *One Hundred Years of Solitude*. Tracing the evolution of the modern epic while accounting for the emergence and different uses of specific literary techniques, Moretti delivers a testament to the undiminished power of prose's formally innovative possibilities against claims regarding the medium's obsolescence. His study operates against the backdrop of foregoing theorizations of literary forms vis-à-vis their historical moments and themes. While Moretti's reliance on a Darwinian model of evolution only loosely parallels the emphasis in German aesthetics on form and content's dialectical relationship, his advocacy of the modern epic returns us to a conceptual point of departure in Hegel's *Aesthetics*, parts of which Moretti cites at the outset of his study:

> The epic [Hegel lectured] . . . acquires as its object the occurrence of an action which in the whole breadth of its circumstances and relations must gain access to our contemplation as a rich event connected with the total world of a nation and epoch [*in sich totalen Welt einer Nation und Zeit*]. . . . This whole [*Totalität*] comprises both the religious consciousness, springing from all the depths of the human

> spirit, and also concrete existence, political and domestic life right down to the details of external existence, human needs and means for their satisfaction; and epic animates this whole by developing it in close contact with individuals, because what is universal and substantive enters poetry only as the living presence of the spirit.[2]

Against the background of Hegel's criteria, which were oriented to the epic of antiquity, Moretti unravels modern epic responses to the genre's putatively impossible task: the narration of totality under the conditions of modernity. Because what Hegel called the "living presence of the spirit" no longer encompassed universality, substance, and individuals' lives in any straightforward relation, the prospects for encapsulating modernity in some totalizing poetic form seemed bleak (*ME* 12ff.). On Hegel's account, the epic of yore had benefited from the allegedly poetic content of a bygone age (*poetischer Weltzustand*) in which individual heroic actions—most curiously in the context of war—could be holistically and concretely narrated in connection with the spiritual unity of a people (*Volksgeist*).[3] The genre of the novel, by contrast, which Hegel treated derivatively as the "modern *bourgeois* epic" (*moderne* bürgerliche *Epopöe*), takes shape against the background of a whole world (*totalen Welt*) that is "already prosaically ordered" in a way "diametrically opposed to the requirements which we found irremissible for genuine epic."[4] Although Hegel would not have put it this way, such "prosaic ordering" would include the abstraction and reification in modern social relations deemed resistant to mediation in and by artistic semblance, at least as Hegel imagined it: "Art," he had famously pronounced in the introduction to his lectures, "considered in its highest vocation, is and remains for us a thing of the past."[5] The encyclopedic comprehension of art Hegel delivered in his *Aesthetics* situated its object of study within a larger system in which the task of modernity's fullest self-comprehension fell to philosophy. Whereas the relegations of absolute wisdom suggested that "modern epic" was an oxymoron in terms, the claim that such a genre was constitutively flawed was driven by a philosophy of history that could be challenged.

The young György Lukács set himself to precisely such a task. His *Theory of the Novel: A Historico-Philosophical Essay on the Forms of Great Epic Literature*, written at the beginning of World War I and published in German in 1920, revisited Hegel's discussion to prolong, in part, its differentiation of epic and novel as well as challenge the larger implications thereof. Confirming the obsolescence of epic time diagnosed in Hegel's *Aesthetics*, Lukács focused on the modern novel as the "expression of transcendental homelessness" (*TN* 41/32). In contrast to the symmetry of sense and the senses, the world and the self, art's models and copies (*Vorbild* and *Abbild*) in an epic age in which the "starry sky" supplied orientation to individuals as "the map of all possible paths," the modern novel and its individual characters are fundamentally disoriented—and searching (*TN* 29, 37, 60/21, 29, 51). "The novel is the epic of an age in which the extensive totality of life is no longer directly given, in which the immanence of meaning in life has become a problem, yet which still thinks in terms of totality" (*TN* 56/47; *und das dennoch die Gesinnung zur Totalität hat*). Where such a *Gesinnung* to totality remains, it must somehow create (*erschaffen*) a totality that is no longer apprehensible concretely (*TN* 37/29). Extensive totality, in short, gives way to a totality that is expressive or genetic.[6] Lukács's investigation thus turns to a consideration of novelistic form: "All the fissures and rents (*Risse und Abgründe*) which are inherent in the historical situation must be drawn into the form-giving process and cannot nor should be disguised by compositional means" (*TN* 60/51).[7] The modern novel's (philosophical) history can be read as a search for forms for narrating life in the contingent world in which modernity's problematical individuals find themselves (*TN* 78/67). In contrast to the spatial orientation evinced by the ancient epic's topographical tendencies, time serves as the plane of development for the transcendentally homeless in the modern novel, hope and remembrance the only dimensions of meaning's constitution (*TN* 124/110). Thus, in his evaluation of Gustave Flaubert's novel of disillusionment *L'Éducation sentimentale*, Lukács claimed that the desolation in the estrangement between self and world depicted there is overcome by time: "The unrestricted, uninterrupted flow [*Strömen*] of time is the unifying principle of the homogeneity that rubs the sharp edges off each heterogeneous fragment and establishes a relationship . . . between them. Time brings order into the chaos of men's lives and gives it the semblance of a spontaneously flowering, organic entity" (*TN* 125/111). While Lukács also attributed to Flaubert the attainment of "truly epic objectivity," *L'Éducation sentimentale* stands out as an exemplary illustration of a specifically novelistic achievement of totality via the temporal integration of the story (*TN* 128–129/114–115). Having grasped time as the very plane on which the novel grapples with modernity, Lukács identified a principle of great consequence for the modern epic[8] as well as for the subsequent development of his own thought, which proceeded to theorize both the historical emergence (in revolutionary praxis) of "a new complete totality [that] could be built out of all [modernity's] substances and relationships" (*TN* 152/137) and the narration thereof in realist literature.[9]

Retrospective of Hegel and Lukács's approaches, the contemporary literary scholar Massimo Fusillo has described both accounts of the novel's derivation from the epic genre of a bygone age as a "critical myth."[10] Fusillo observes the historical trajectory of the generic distinction in question to be thornier than they presented it: he grasps epic and novel as "bundles of transcultural constants" that intermix and appear in different variations at different times.[11] While the distinctions *The Theory of the Novel* generates between epic and novel are thus bound to demarcate tendencies, rather than absolute differences, the following initial extraction from Lukács's study remains of heuristic value for ascertaining modern epic emphases and possibilities:

Epic	Novel
Extensive totality	Creative totality
Narrating in space	Narrating through time
Collective	Individual
Social reality	Psychological reality[12]

As we will see, modern epic works oscillate between these poles and in some cases surpass them, a development Lukács anticipated in his outgoing sketch of Russian literature, in which he ascertained a reconstitution of the epic out of the modern novel.[13]

This final step of *The Theory of the Novel* relates to a larger contribution to be gleaned from Lukács's book, namely its implicit contestation of the restrictions Hegel had placed on modern literature's relation to social totality. At the end of *Aesthetics*'s discussion of art's romantic form (understood there in its systematic place as Hegel's umbrella term for modern art), Hegel had granted art a freedom to be enjoyed once the relationship between form and content no longer stood under the sign of dialectical necessitation.[14] Hegel was claiming, in other words, that in the wake of any pressing need to find specific artistic expression for social content, the artist's experiments in form were set free, yet at the price of their larger social significance.[15] This stands at considerable odds with *The Theory of the Novel*, which demonstrated how much the development of literary forms was motivated by the inner dynamics of modern social life, the trappings of which literature could powerfully reveal. The pronouncements of a social philosophy—the triumphant streaks of Hegel's larger theory of modernity being conspicuously absent from *The Theory of the Novel*'s pages—must have proven of little consolation to Lukács, for whom philosophical discourse could not reach into and touch human life at the concrete levels at which it was lived. As Fredric Jameson underscored in his essay on Lukács in *Marxism and Form*, "Pure thought never has absolute value as a privileged means of access to reality. On the contrary, it is narration which is for [Lukács] the absolute" and which qualifies literature not simply as a competitor of social theory, but also as a means for contesting the very ground of the latter's diagnoses.[16] In short, Lukács's focus on literary aesthetics was wresting the self-comprehension of modernity away from of its confinement to philosophical discourse.[17]

This is not to say that Lukács was under any illusions regarding art's social power. His musings on Russian epic novels emphasized that art would never by itself be able to bring about lost substance (*TN* 152/137). And his later work on realism would pin the tenability of narrative to "those moments of history in which human life can be apprehended in terms of concrete, individual confrontations and dramas, in which some basic general truth of life can be told through the vehicle of the individual story, the individual plot."[18] Yet as the author of *The Theory of the Novel* was clearly still grappling with literature's relation to the social totality, the question remained as to whether Lukács's "will to reestablish epic narration" granted literature any anticipatory social role.[19] This relates to a further distinction between epic and novelistic form that has shifted back and forth over the course of the genres' histories, namely the question of open versus closed narrative structure, which is also a question of integration and endings. Fusillo observes the oscillating application of the open/closed distinction to the two genres from Homer's (epically open) *Iliad* and (novelistically closed) *Odyssey* onward, whereas Moretti touts the reversion of "centripetal epic and centrifugal novel . . . *pace* Bakhtin" into its opposite, whereby the epic appears as "the polyphonic form" specializing "in the heterogeneous space of the world-system."[20] Lukács's handling of the question in *The Theory of the Novel* derived from his tendency to treat totality generally as a closed structure there. On his approach, the question of beginnings and endings only became problematic under modern conditions. This is because the ancient epic putatively enjoyed an unbroken relationship to the social totality as an organic whole of which it was part (*TN* 66/57): epic tales could begin in medias res and end at will as the narrative receded into a known and shared world of myth. While "we [moderns] cannot breathe in a closed world" (*TN* 33/25), Lukács modeled even the modern novel's temporal totality on the integrated enclosure of the unified story, not its fragmentation, not, in other words, any open deferral to social developments that literature could by itself not bring about. Yet in concluding his essay with an eye toward future epics of the "new world," Lukács himself opted for a form open to history (*TN* 152/137). History's force pierces the totality of yore and is the reason for which no modern totality could possibly be grasped in terms of organic closure. What remains in and for the modern epic is thus a *Gesinnung zur Totalität* and the value of "thinking in terms of totality" that I elaborate below. For a book emphasizing the shattering punctuation of totality in modernity, Lukács's ending is a consistent one.[21]

Literary Evolution

Against such sweeping historico-philosophical exercises, Franco Moretti's study frames the "basic components of the modern epic" not "as *desirable innovations*, but as *problems to be solved*" (*ME* 94, emphasis there). The author of *Modern Epic* thereby supplants the dialectical necessitation inherent to any motivated artistic approach to modern reality with an evolutionary model for understanding literary morphology. On Moretti's model, experimentation in literary devices offers up virtually random variations of form that are then socially selected in the process of literature's evolutionary history (*ME* 6, 181). Moretti demonstrates the explanatory purchase of such an approach by focusing mostly on chapters of the genre's evolution prior to World War II.[22] As a result of his methodology, the course he charts for the genre differs from the modern epic's subsequent development in the Cold War context. *Modern Epic* nonetheless proves valuable to an assessment of Weiss, Johnson, and Kluge's postcatastrophic works in multiple ways: whereas Moretti's conception of the genre establishes the modern epic as a viable category of world literature, his survey of its devices suggests what Weiss, Johnson, and Kluge could inherit and reshape in their own experiments with the genre. Moreover, Moretti's construal of literary evolution in terms of problems and their solutions can be utilized within the dialectical elaboration of the modern epic's postwar trajectory.

Laying some of the groundwork for his later theory of distant reading that would occasion animated discussion in literary studies, Moretti's *Modern Epic* familiarizes us with a searching genre and a dynamic taxonomy of "flawed masterpieces" that labor resourcefully on Hegel's oxymoron (*ME* 5). As action yields to imagination, the would-be epic hero (e.g., Goethe's Faust) is transformed into a passive spectator, whose actions are diabolically facilitated by another, Mephistopheles (*ME* 16–17), that devil who embodies and hides the violence (of the West's aspirations to universal dominion) that the genre denies and disavows (*ME* 34, 25). Nonsynchronicity (Ernst Bloch's *Ungleichzeitigkeit*) emerges amid the "smashing of linear time" (*ME* 51) in a genre that delights in digressions characteristic of its encyclopedic ambitions (*ME* 38, 49). The very perspective of the modern epic, in contrast to the novel, which Moretti associates with the "compact and homogeneous spaces" of locale or nation, appears off-center, takes shape at the margins and is oriented toward "the world-system as a whole" (*ME* 47, 50). The second half of the book features a "stream of consciousness" (which Moretti sets in quotes to grasp more accurately the role of the preconscious in James Joyce's *Ulysses*) that is championed for its embrace of meaninglessness, a comportment that enables Leopold Bloom to survive in the urban metropolis (*ME* 167, 156). In the problem-and-solution structure that Moretti has adopted, this even leads to the elaboration of "an enriching passivity" in the form of the consumer and an "immediately visible totality . . . [in the] world of consumption" (*ME* 143). A polyphony of voices and styles newly unmotivated by any anthropocentrism takes over as "institutional language" (*ME* 192, 196) in a development that Kluge's practice of cross-mapping will confirm, but not with any of the finality with which Moretti appears to end his book, namely with a thesis on the epic novel as an enchanting technology (*ME* 249). The larger ramifications of such developments—with which

Moretti doubtlessly also wishes to provoke his readers—are ambiguous. Yet in such passages, if not before, his appeal to the social selection operative in his evolutionary model of literary morphology, on the one hand, and his insistence on the autonomy of the cultural sphere (*ME* 90), on the other, appear, if not contradictory, then at least to have been driving to questionable ends. Noticeably voided on this front, as literary "solutions" appear to mesh seamlessly with capitalism and technology alike, is the spirited, motivated questioning and searching character of Lukács's approach, in the absence of which Moretti's discussion appears to allow little room for the interventionist appeals we encounter in the modern epic's subsequent history.[23]

Totality and Realism in the Modern Epic

The modern epic's postcatastrophic course appears to refute Moretti's skepticism regarding the roles of artistic motivation and any historically inflected dialectics of literary form. Both are present in Weiss, Johnson, and Kluge's retentions of epic links to society's totality and their embrace of the experimentally realist practices that would render it. While their respective commitments to totality may make their projects appear abstruse from postmodern perspectives, their works do not stand and fall with this category.[24] Under modern conditions in which history has become a dynamically constitutive force, any aspiration to totality—either as a theoretical orientation to society as a whole or an aesthetic orientation to the encapsulating circumscription thereof in some tale—will remain asymptotic.[25] More interesting, therefore, is how "thinking in terms of totality" (Lukács's *Gesinnung zur Totalität*) can drive circumspective pursuits of reality in literature. In Weiss, Johnson, and Kluge, the postwar modern epic critically approximates society's totality in general conformity with the standing of the concept in Hegelian Marxism, where "thinking in totality" pertains to the precept that all social and historical phenomena, including that of literature itself, must be addressed and grasped in their mediation by the social totality.[26] While literature infrequently "thinks in totality" in the discursive language of theory, the modern epic's orientation to totality points to the participation of literature and narrative—which must command the ability to transcend the reification of what appears immediate—in mediating activity.[27] Designating this activity as mediation, rather than in the traditional terminology of reality's literary representation, will prove of further consequence.

The literary mediation of reality relates to the second, creative dimension of totality in the modern epic, namely as a literary-aesthetic category for the stories it aspires to narrate. This speaks directly to the role aesthetic decisions and techniques play in marking the contours and boundaries of narrative, not least since "infinite forms," as Moretti playfully taunts the genre with the early Lukács, "do not exist" (*ME* 97). Modern epic narration must generate its own spatiotemporal boundaries or, in lieu thereof, some other tenable response to the problem of totality's resistance to poetic encapsulation. The whole tale—of the international antifascist resistance and its legacies (Weiss), of the labor of memory and the project of a democratic socialism (Johnson), of catastrophic modernity and its avoidance (Kluge)—cannot, and yet must, be told. As we will see, to do so each epic makes stark decisions with regard to its story, narration, and address. The ostensible story of Weiss's "book of the century"[28] is restricted to about eight of its years; Johnson controls the narrative present of *Jahrestage* by the artifice of calendar and narrative contract; and Kluge's *Chronik* avoids the problem of one story's framework altogether by developing a complexly constellated approach to the narration of society's essential characteristics. Formally innovative initiatives abound on the level of narration in all three works: in each case thereof, we witness suggestive orchestrations of incompletion by which epic boundlessness is given different kinds of open form. In this, the modern epic's "problem-solving vocation" parts ways with Moretti, who characterizes this vocation as the reduction of modern history's tensions by way of the epic's ability to "make existence more comprehensible, and more acceptable" (*ME* 6). Against such symbolic affirmation, Weiss, Johnson, and Kluge reopen the whole question of human emancipation, expanding its scope and reasserting its stakes in principled opposition to history's unacceptable preclusion of emancipatory possibilities.

Realist Practices and Open Forms

As much as Lukács's discussion paved the way for the modern epic's trajectory in German as well as other contexts, in undertaking attempts to reconstitute realist narration postcatastrophe, Weiss, Johnson, and Kluge are procedurally more indebted to Lukács's erstwhile antagonist in political-aesthetic matters Bertolt Brecht. Brecht's influential diagnosis of realism's challenges in the twentieth century proved seminal for the literary methods Weiss, Johnson, and Kluge would deploy to probe the Cold War and its recent pasts:

> The situation thereby becomes so complicated that a simple "representation of reality" ["*Wiedergabe der Realität*"] says something about reality less than ever before. A photograph of the Krupp Works or of A.E.G. yields nearly nothing about these institutions. Actual reality has slipped into the functional. The reification of human relationships, such as the factory, no longer produces the latter. So there is in fact "something to build up," something "artificial," "contrived." . . . [Thus] art is necessary.[29]

Few other passages capture the task-oriented development of artistic forms as succinctly. Brecht's understanding of the dynamic interrelation of form and content in artistic approaches to modern reality can be regarded as a generally operative principle governing realism's formal experimentation and Weiss, Johnson, and Kluge write in this tradition.[30] What is more, Brecht's formulation grasped realism's challenge on the very level of artistic semblance that Hegel and Lukács deemed so imperiled by the relationship between concretion and abstraction in modernity. For realism to reveal "the causal complexes of society/unmask the prevailing view of things as the view of those who are in power/write from the standpoint of the class which offers the broadest solutions for the pressing difficulties in which human society is caught up/emphasize the element of development/make possible the concrete, and make possible abstraction from it" meant that art "in the scientific age" would clearly need to draw widely on extra-aesthetic models of understanding also.[31] In a short text prompted by questions about the representability of the contemporary world on the stage, Brecht envisaged art and science as partners in revealing the world's changeability, especially if the latter concept could be applied to the social world as much as it had been to nature.[32] Art's relation to abstraction and concretion alike stood to be enhanced by theatrical work that unfolded in conjunction with scientific and socio-theoretical knowledge. Working up such synergies, the revolution of aesthetic forms set on rendering society's core mechanisms more transparent.

The challenges Brecht outlined in 1931 became perceptibly more difficult postcatastrophe, pressing—as a concrete problem for works of prose—on the feasibility of narration itself. One could not proceed from any omniscience. Weiss, Johnson, and Kluge register a first repercussion of historical content at this very level: by repeatedly thematizing narration as fundamentally uncertain, Weiss, Johnson, and Kluge absorb its non-self-evidence into the "form-giving process" (*TN* 60/51). If a recurring leitmotif of Weiss's epic is the question "How could all this be depicted?" (*AoR* 112/*ÄdW* 1:130), to which—in the long run (and it is a marathon)—the narrator will have delivered an answer in the form of the tale itself as well as a "transcendental" account of the conditions of its possibility,[33] Johnson begins by sensitively wresting epic language out of the Atlantic Ocean's ebb and flow: "Long waves sweep slanting against the beach, hump muscled backs, raise trembling combs that tip over at the greenest summit. The taut roll, already streaked with white, enfolds a hollow space of air that is crushed by the clear mass as if a secret had been created and destroyed there. . . . The word for the short waves of the Baltic was choppity [*ist kabbelig gewesen*]" (*AN* 3/*JT* 7). The opening of Johnson's *Jahrestage* enticingly zeroes in on the story to be told as a secretive space caught in the waves' taut roll. Still more telling is a detail not captured in the translation: the absence of the simple past in the final sentence of the German. The English verb "was" renders not *war*, but rather—and perhaps unexpectedly—the present perfect *ist gewesen*. Johnson thereby eschews the very *episches Präteritum* that Thomas Mann had famously elevated to epic prose's quintessential vehicle in his description of the narrator as "that conjurer who murmurs in past tenses" (*den raunenden Beschwörer des Imperfekts*) in his foreword to *Der Zauberberg*.[34] Abstaining from the imperfect, the past participle of Johnson's present perfect tense indelibly emphasizes the pastness not only of that which is to be retrieved, but also of the very language that would do so.

In some contrast to the intricate subtleties to be gleaned from Johnson's prose, Kluge often foregrounds narration's challenges more explicitly, at least at the level of his programmatic statements, which often involve a degree of theoretical abstraction. At the beginning of his *"Unheimlichkeit der Zeit"* collection with which the second volume of *Chronik der Gefühle* opens, Kluge, after referring to the bombing he witnessed of his hometown, intones that there will be no classical, harmonious forms. "We human beings are bound [*bestimmt*] by the war that form and content wage on one another" (*CdG* 2:11). But this strife is concealed, in a second repercussion of history on narration that Kluge explains in another context, by the false novel society composes in its attempts to tailor us (*zuschneiden*) to *its* requirements.[35] To society's "novel of reality," Kluge opposes a different kind of artistic object or assembly thereof ("'Kunstgegenstand,' ein Aggregat von Kunstgegenständen") in a realism that combines exactitude and protest.[36] Note the strategy: Kluge describes what passes for reality in terms of the falsity of its realistic appeals and putative transparency, which are shams, so as to oppose them with an equally constructed, yet exacting art of protest that repeatedly draws attention to its constructed character. That contesting conceptions of reality rage at each other at the level of form calls for distinguishing between them. Kluge therefore elaborates, with Oskar Negt, the task of antagonistic realism in a poetologically significant passage of *Geschichte und Eigensinn*:

> One can imagine the problem of antagonistic realism as the analysis of a site of an explosion. The explosion has strewn about objects [*Gegenstände*] into a circumference. The violence of the explosion, i.e., its cause, is no longer present at the site; it must be reconstructed from out of the results. . . . The dispersal of things corresponds to the dispersal of the subjective capacities throughout the social totality, i.e., across historical relations, the industrial landscape and in the inner commonwealth [of the body]. . . . The analysis of what has happened [is to be supplemented by] the collection of what the explosion has scattered. (*DuM* 2:348)

The explosive force presents a problem both because it eludes any direct representation, which thus places considerable demands on its mediation, and because of the sheer destruction it has caused, from which no reconstruction of the objects and capacities scattered about can readily ensue.[37] Kluge's epic prose operates on the terrain of this twofold challenge. In so doing, his stories strive to fathom the conditions of history's explosive forces so that these might be demystified as well as reconnect elements torn asunder to circumscribe humanity's emancipatory potentials. Such ambitious work demands an expansion of the optics of Brecht's function-oriented conception of realism. Negt and Kluge deliver no less. They start with the "known coordinates of the horizontal and vertical," which speak to the five senses and to mediated experience respectively (*HO* 236/*DuM* 2:511). The former are *Nähesinne*, direct senses for what is near and concrete, whereas the vertical dimension speaks to the role of the *Fernsinne*, indirect senses for what is far, including a historical sense.[38] The indirect senses must also be able to deal in abstraction (*DuM* 2:597). To these as well as Brecht's functional dimension (which they cite and describe as the coordinate of heteronomy), Negt and Kluge add reality's irrational, imaginary, and revolutionary dimensions (*HO* 236–240/*DuM* 2:511–515). These last three present different ways of conceiving human responses to modern reality's pressures. The now sixfold set constitutes a matrix of subjective-objective reality that Kluge explores across his epic prose, as addressed in chapter 4 below.

In addition to his influential conception of realism, Brecht's work evinces a specific resonance of epic crucial to Weiss, Johnson, and Kluge's works. It stems from Brecht's whole notion and practice of epic theater. Adapting and developing epic, prose-bound practices of distanciation and defamiliarization (or estrangement) for the stage, Brecht sought to enhance theater's socio-critical and emancipatory capacities. Adhering to Brecht's call for a "separation of [the artwork's] elements" (*Trennung der Elemente*),[39] via which the activity of readers, like Brecht's spectators, could be fostered, the modern epic employs Brecht's theatrical advances in the medium of prose. Contributing to the dissolution of the work's self-sufficient status as a putative organic whole, artistic practices of separation assume various forms in the modern epic and can include such techniques as the interruption of narrative sequences as well as related montage-like assemblies of the kind Walter Benjamin championed in his reading of Alfred Döblin's *Berlin Alexanderplatz*,[40] emphases on artifice in the use of documentary materials, the cultivation of tension between empathetic and distancing modes (i.e., the collapse and reconstruction of aesthetic distance), as well as historicizing imperatives (often underscored by the use of gestural indicators).[41] While the exact character of each epic's differentiated integration of such elements is a matter of literary analysis to be addressed in relevant contexts, its effects can be summarized as training in what Kluge calls the capacity for drawing distinctions (*Unterscheidungsvermögen*).[42] The epic that occasioned a raging debate about the actual character of its practices of separation (or rather its alleged obfuscation thereof) is the one that engages with Brecht's theory and practice most explicitly: a sustained and seminal portion of the second volume of Weiss's *Ästhetik* is devoted to the narrator's work on the project of a dramatic epic (*ÄdW* 2:177; *dramatische Epik*) that Brecht himself no longer saw through. As I discuss in chapter 2, Brecht's Engelbrekt drama—which was to focus on a fifteenth-century Swedish peasant uprising in the middle of World War II—represents a crucial turning point in *Die Ästhetik* to questions of artistic production. Weiss's narrator's very phrase "dramatische Epik" reads as a clear chiastic inversion of Brecht's epic theater. It signals less a return to any kind of Aristotelian aesthetics than a transmedial appropriation of Brecht's theatrical innovations (as well as theater's more traditional elements such as dialogue and, via narrative simulation, embodied polyperspectivism) back into the epic mode.[43] In this, the modern epic evinces the value of medial cross-fertilization for critical artistic production as well as reception.

The dissolution of the work's self-sufficient status, the training of the capacity for drawing distinctions through practices of artistic separation, and the fundamentally asymptotic relation to totality constitute aspects of the modern epic's removal of its own fourth wall. While the genre's transnational orientation can be gleaned from Moretti's remarks about the relationship between the modern epic and the world-system as well as Michael Denning's chapter "The Novelists' International," referenced in the introduction, on Weiss, Johnson, and Kluge's watches especially, epic narration turns emphatically to recipients and readers as participants in the modern world each epic is seeking to re-create. As Weiss's narrator anticipates, his writings would "address people who might be found anywhere, whatever their background, internationalism would be the criterion for my affiliation [. . . and I would] seek connections beyond the borders of states and tongues" (*AoR* 117/*ÄdW* 1:136). Becoming more pronounced during the modern epic's Cold War phase, such appeals to recipients point to a dimension of the genre underexplored in Moretti's study.[44] Open, even fragmentary narrative need not arouse suspicion as an impossibly infinite form demanding reintegration in the work lest it be taken as indicative of the faultiness of the writer's conception or execution of the tale. Weiss, Johnson, and Kluge all deal in different ways with fragments not only as the inevitable results of catastrophic history, but also as elements of a formal structure via which works defer to their dispersed appropriations by readers, whose activities can further test, enlarge, and concretize epic aspirations. As noted in the introduction, such a practical turn is by no means foreign to Weiss, Johnson, and Kluge's conception of aesthetic autonomy. In his foreword to *Chronik*, Kluge underscores that readers must "verify, what applies to them" (*CdG* 1:7). What is more, each epic work both models the interpretation of reality and the practical applications thereof within its diegesis[45] and invites the nondiegetic extension of such activity. The modern epic thereby invests less in its self-sufficiency as a work (*Werk*) than in the coproduction of its work (*Arbeit*), including the relation of such work to the totality of which it is part. Johnson grasps the writer's construal of relations not as part of any truth or purity, but as the process of truth's ascertainment (*Wahrheitsfindung*),[46] over which the author wields no authority: "Defend your independence until the last page of the book," he advises the reader of novels. "You have earned the right to a story. The delivery of a quintessence or moral is a breach of the contract. With the novel, the story is promised [*versprochen*]. What is to be said to that is for you to say."[47] Totality is rendered by open form not simply because extensive totality is neither final nor concretely given to apprehension, but because it is not in the purview of any individual, absolute philosopher, epic poet, or political party. Such appeals to readers—like the polyphony of the epics themselves—follow less any logic of recognition and desire for validation on the part of author or work than a necessary deferral to the social processes and movements in and through which the author's labor might live.[48] Over the historical course of a work's reception, moreover, its address can vary as widely as the orientations of any of those who might appropriate it, especially in the passage of the modern epic to an age no longer conceivable via Cold War coordinates. By anticipating, thematizing, and inviting its critical reception, each work becomes part of a larger network of dynamic relations, in which literary knowledge and its practical implications have a place.

An essay by Thomas Metscher, "On the Necessary Plurality of Artistic Forms: Notes on the Problem of a Theory of Modern Epic Poetics," remains instructive for its relevant elucidation of the connection between procedurally experimental and open realist forms on the one hand and social practice on the other.[49] Informed by the great experiments of Weiss's *Die Ästhetik des Widerstands*, Metscher's essay surveyed and then left behind long-standing twentieth-century aesthetic debates between realist, expressionist, and modernist positions that remained politically charged in German contexts from World War I through the end of the GDR. Metscher advocated the procedural pluralism of realist practices, also for the socialist contexts in which formal experimentation was being repressed. The 1986 essay, published by a West German philosopher in a leading East German scholarly journal, is a great document of Cold War aesthetics and the weight cultural programs still carried in what would retrospectively become known as the waning period's last years. The very style and diction in which Metscher defined realism as the "most complex, most stringent (*dichteste*), deepest and most comprehensive level of the artistic penetration of reality and appropriation of the world (*Wirklichkeitsdurchdringung und Weltaneignung*) that is possible at a given historical moment" suggests the then-lingering urgency of literary aesthetics (1640). While Metscher pinned realism to a broadly conceived function of representation (his use of *Abbildfunktion* presupposes extra-aesthetic reality as literature's main point of reference), realism itself was bound to no specific aesthetic forms whatsoever. Even modernist tendencies toward abstraction and fragmentation of the kind that Lukács decried could not be excluded, lest realism prove unable to operate on the "world-historical front of time (to speak with a concept of Ernst Bloch)" (1641). In thus ordaining a "realistic avant-garde," Metscher enthusiastically appealed to realism's experimentation in form as a timely continuation of the dialectics of form and content in narrative prose. Moreover, the feasibility of realist narration—in its recognition of the primacy of praxis, according to Metscher—was linked to the possibility and meaningfulness of social action, at least in principle (1646). Thus, in the 1980s, at a time when many in the GDR, and Kluge himself in the FRG, found themselves at a loss for having anything to tell amid the future's putative eclipse on both sides of ossified ideological opposition,[50] Metscher's account of modern epic poetics, which was not confined to German coordinates but oriented to world literary production, confirmed and celebrated the fact that "realism lives"—also as a vehicle of hope (1640). That it continued at all, Metscher surmised, was due not to some randomness of variation or the selection of its forms by extra-aesthetic social forces, but rather, in a context of "complex class confrontation as well as new media of mass communication along with their ideological formation and manipulation," to "[authors'] conscious ideological and ethically political decisions" (1645). That Metscher did not specify the subject of such decisions exactingly—hence my reinsertion of "authors" into the citation—may have rendered his position amenable to East German cultural politics, but what remains valid about Metscher's essay today is its justification of motivated realism as an aesthetic program for socially troubled times. As the open forms of Weiss, Johnson, and Kluge's experimental realisms make clear, the quality of the authors' decisions will turn largely on the relations each work establishes to questions of practical and social emancipation.

Media, Mediation, and Mapping

The foregoing section's account of the motivations underlying experimentation in realist practices relates to a third repercussion of historical content impacting the postwar modern epic. More than any of the works featured in Moretti's study, Weiss, Johnson, and Kluge's epics interact extensively with artistic, journalistic, and entertainment media.[51] The uncertainty of narration and the struggle for realism against society's falsely realistic narratives often comes to a head in the different forms this interaction assumes. Exploiting the cross-fertilization of the arts for literary production, Weiss's *Ästhetik* abounds in ekphrases and diegetic interpretations of the visual arts that his protagonists study to enhance their orientation. *Jahrestage*'s points of reference more frequently concern nonartistic media such as the *New York Times* that Gesine Cresspahl avidly peruses; vast sections of this and other newspapers are woven into Johnson's chronicle of a year. Kluge's stories, on the other hand, often unfold as visual prose (*Bildprosa*), an intermedial practice suggestive of the larger contours of his vast multimedial network of production, which encompasses films, television shows, and DVD projects. By outfitting itself with such features, the modern epic can appeal to and even appear to absorb other media as productive extensions of its own realist aspirations to totality (as is not seldom the case in Weiss and part of Johnson's use of the

New York Times). Alternatively, it can draw critical attention to and even contest the mediation of content by other media (as in Johnson's more scrutinizing use of newspapers and *Jahrestage*'s staging of competition between radio and television or the differential relations Kluge establishes between text and image and between different communication media).[52]

In light of such practices, the value of grasping the modern epic's activity in terms of mediation (rather than other competing terms for this activity, not only representation, but also *Darstellung*, *Erscheinen*, and constellation) becomes clear.[53] In a methodologically suggestive contribution to the conceptual history and study of media, John Guillory recommends drawing on the different connotations of mediation in a related way: the English word speaks both to the socio-theoretical conception of mediation (i.e., *Vermittlung*, in Hegel through Jürgen Habermas) as well as practices of different media (*Medialisierung*), which are not exactly the same thing.[54] Addressing the work of media within a Hegelian-Marxist framework of mediation raises our awareness of the stakes of what media (fail to) do. Moreover, contrasting representation and mediation, Guillory appeals to the ways in which the "more inclusive" latter concept underscores the complex processes by which media make objects in the world appear.[55] He also follows the logic of *Vermittlung*'s insistence on the referral of any one phenomenon, artistic or otherwise, to the social totality of which it is a part. On this two-sided approach, there will always be "more reality" to mediation than to representation.[56] That the modern epic's mediation of reality unfolds at levels of *Vermittlung* and *Medialisierung* alike indicates its self-reflexivity in a multimedial landscape in which literature is no longer, if ever it was, a leading medium (*Leitmedium*) of society. Amid the competition of literature with radio, television, film, and other media and entertainment arts that took shape during the Cold War, the attractiveness of a medium that self-reflexively combines *Vermittlung* and *Medialisierung* should have been apparent. In the wake of digital revolution and ensuing miniaturization that hypersaturate the lifeworld in various communication technologies, the self-reflexivity cultivated by the modern epic has become an even timelier anomaly.

A side-glance at a contribution to media studies can help ascertain the challenge faced by the modern epic on this front. In their widely referenced study *Remediation: Understanding New Media*, Jay David Bolter and Richard Grusin identified in remediation a general principle in the history of media, whereby each new medium—oscillating between the satisfaction of human desires for transparent immediacy and our delight in opaque hypermediacy—builds on and refashions previous media in a struggle for legitimacy and influence.[57] While Bolter and Grusin focus on digital media and their technological ability to remediate any other medium, they also note the "ways in which older media refashion themselves to answer the challenges of new media."[58] That "no medium, it seems, can now function independently and establish its own separate and purified space of cultural meaning" convincingly describes a situation of ever-intensifying mediations of the lifeworld that blend into one another in a web of internet-facilitated interrelations now experienced as second nature, if not terribly natural.[59] If literature is to have any space in this, it must clearly be "built up," to keep with Brecht's phrasing. It cannot proceed on any model of its own self-evidence in ignorance of its environs.

In a 1966 essay that reads prescient in this regard, Theodor W. Adorno addressed the erosion of the boundaries that once distinguished the arts from one another. In lieu of expressing any nostalgia for past purities—which would be susceptible to his own critique of artistic culture's ideology—Adorno noted how artistic transgressions placed new demands on ascertaining how and where meaning is aesthetically constituted in any artistic phenomenon. With an eye toward substantive evaluation, Adorno argued that "the clash between the work of art and the world of objects [which, in the context of his argument, also includes other media and artistic genres] becomes productive, and the work authentic, only where this clash is allowed to happen [*allein dort, wo es diesen Gegensatz immanent austrägt*] and to objectify itself by its friction with the thing it devours."[60] A work of art can neither ignore the heterogeneous material through which it might become art at all, nor can it fail to process and thereby establish a relation to such material on its own terms. The translator's addition of the word "friction" to render the passage into English insightfully underscores the antagonism Adorno is suggesting, for such friction marks the border at which an aesthetic relation (e.g., between two heterogeneous media) is being established at the site of a separation (in Brecht's sense). The claim speaks to Weiss, Johnson, and Kluge's epics insofar as each of these, while abounding in medial transpositions of heterogeneous materials (e.g., the Engelbrekt drama, Kluge's retelling of other novel or film endings) and other kinds of intermedial references (e.g., ekphrasis, the narrativization of Gesine or her daughter Marie's reading of the *New York Times*, but also the evocation of film techniques such as montage), processes reality autonomously through the medium of literature, even as each stretches this medium to its limits, not just in terms of length, but also through the concretization of socio-theoretical mediation in narrative. By and large, *Die Ästhetik des Widerstands*, *Jahrestage*, and *Chronik der Gefühle* do not constitute intermedial experiments by combining different media—although Kluge's incorporation of visual materials into his prose stories demand to be addressed in this way. Rather, the modern epic mediates reality as well as remediates other media-specific renditions of that reality in and through its own literary medium. In outlining such features of modern epic texts in these ways, I rely on the conceptual precision that Romanist Irina Rajewsky has brought to the study of intertextuality and intermediality.[61] By facilitating the differentiation of the kinds of remediation addressed by Bolter and Grusin, Rajewsky enables us not only to grasp how specific kinds of intermedial references and practices of remediation constitute meaning in a work of literature such as the modern epic. Her approach also helps us to identify the friction between different media as an aesthetically constituted phenomenon in Adorno's sense. In this way, focusing critically on procedures of mediation and remediation between and within different media, as can be seen in the—for Kluge *more trustworthy*[62]—relationality established in the modern epic, also suggests the value of transferring Brecht's separation of elements—each of which may play a role in reality's *Vermittlung*—to our navigations through digital and technological landscapes.[63]

In contrast to Bolter and Grusin's description of new media, over the course of which "reality" appears to recede amid the impossibility of immediacy and the opacity of hypermediacy, the modern epic's exercises in mediation and remediation serve realist orientation from the perspective of human interests.[64] Weiss, Johnson, and Kluge's alternative media practices make up for precisely what the media, in their collusion with market imperatives, fail to do: facilitate our own orientation to reality. In this, their works participate in the task of an aesthetic of cognitive mapping to which Fredric Jameson has ascribed such a critical function. In *Postmodernism, or, The Cultural Logic of Late Capitalism*, Jameson advocates aesthetic mapping practices integral to "a pedagogical political culture which seeks to endow the individual subject with some new heightened sense of its place in the global system" and thereby contribute to critical orientation in the "bewildering new world space of late or multinational capital," the beginnings of which Jameson, writing at the Cold War's end, dates to the early 1970s.[65] While Jameson does not ground his elaboration of cognitive mapping in the epic genre specifically, the following overview highlights the suggestive overlap of his discussion with the aesthetics of the modern epic in Weiss, Johnson, and Kluge.

The value of Jameson's conception of an aesthetic of cognitive mapping consists first in his combination of the empirical and phenomenological tasks of orienting oneself in space with the larger and more complex tasks of orienting oneself to social structures, which, in the age of multinational capitalism, have become global in scale. Jameson develops the former dimension from the work of Kevin Lynch on the ways in which people generate mental maps of cities to navigate urban spaces. With regard to the latter, Jameson frames our relationship to the social totality via recourse to Louis Althusser's conception of ideology as "'the representation of the subject's *Imaginary* relationship to his or her *Real* [i.e., social and material] conditions of existence.'"[66] In Althusser, Jameson relates, the function of ideology served to bridge the "gap . . . between existential experience and scientific knowledge" of the social structure as a whole. This includes "the ways in which we all necessarily *also* cognitively map our individual social relationship to local, national, and international class realities."[67] Part of the postmodern challenge—and the continued urgency of an aesthetic of cognitive mapping today—stems from the concern that under scrutiny such relations appear utterly enigmatic to us: neither ideology in its classical function nor any other readily available alternative story lines appear to deliver compelling representations of individual subjects' relationships to "that vaster and properly unrepresentable totality" of an entire world system, the machinations of which inscrutably condition the fabric of our lives.[68]

Second, Jameson's diachronic approach to the problem of orientation—which is perennial but manifests itself differently at different times—presents us with an opportunity to appreciate its challenges and their potential redress. While Jameson's strokes are broad, by grasping the difficulties of phenomenological and social orientation according to a three-phase model of capitalist history he brings some historicizing precision to the problems of totality's representation witnessed in Hegel and Lukács above.[69] In the age of imperialism, Jameson explains, "the truth of [individual] experience [already] no longer coincides with the place in which it takes place," which is to say that its mediation becomes a problem for any representational account of an individual or social group's relationship to the real, including that delivered by the modernist prose of the period, which in many cases obliquely filtered the "global colonial system" through the syntax of poetic language and the monadism of individual consciousnesses.[70] Amid the complexities of life subsequently emerging in the postmodern spaces of multinational capitalism Jameson analyzes, disorientation only accrues as we are inserted "as individual subjects into a multidimensional set of radically discontinuous realities, whose frames range from the still surviving spaces of bourgeois private life all the way to the unimaginable decentering of global capital itself."[71] While Jameson emphasizes the challenges that fall on any viable aesthetic of cognitive mapping, including the notion that "there may be historical situations"—such as our own—in which the "production of functioning and living ideologies . . . is not possible at all," artistic production's aspirations to map the unrepresentable social totality are not imaginary in any pejorative sense. Jameson confirms such approaches as crucial interventions in the Symbolic order that are of great critical value even where they must fail.[72] Such failures are not so much related to the inability to produce mimetic maps in any literal sense. On the contrary, Jameson reformulates the logic of art's constructive mimesis of reality to underscore that there can and will be "no true maps" and that cognitive mapping engages necessarily in artistic experiments and projective figurations.[73]

Jameson's account of cognitive mapping warrants additions relevant to the modern epic. Notably, Jameson frames his culminating discussion of cognitive mapping's task in *Postmodernism* vis-à-vis media. As a counterhegemonic strategy that constitutes "an integral part of any socialist political project," art's cognitive maps present alternatives to the media's ideological functions.[74] In its implicit competition with the media, critical artistic mapping makes its "media term" explicitly present "as an *analogon* or material interpretant for this or that more directly representational social model" in what Jameson identifies as a triangular structure unique to postmodernism.[75]

Weiss, Johnson, and Kluge's use of autodiegetic narrators and their foregrounding of narrative uncertainty are ways in which the modern epic's media term reveals the whole task of mediation in its proper light, that is, as bridgework between experience and truth. Furthermore, the importance of such a competition between revealed and concealed practices of mediation becomes even more pointed in the current situation, in which the postmodern disorientation that so concerned Jameson has passed into a digital age in which such disorientation is glossed over and filled in by newly orienting media devices: global positioning systems obviate the need for Lynch's mental maps as much as the information and communication technologies known as "social media" simulate our relation to some larger social reality, however virtual. Henceforth, our Imaginary relationship to the Real proceeds as digitally mediated masquerade, not only obscuring what Jameson, with Althusser, calls the "real conditions of existence," but also debasing—through both deprivation and flood—human sensory experience itself. That such digital mediators are feeble bridges with no small effect on the human psyche and the human being's own ability to navigate an inhabited world is perhaps palpable in the desperation that sets in when an internet connection is interrupted or a smartphone lost. Given this situation, redoubled efforts in realism—including the kind found in Negt and Kluge's expansion of the senses addressed above—speak to actual needs in the reconstitution of human agency unexpropriated by the commodity devices of miniaturization.

Second, Jameson's reformulation of the older concept of class consciousness into his account of cognitive mapping[76] relates to Weiss, Johnson, and Kluge's demarcations of the direction and perspective of such an aesthetic in the epic. All three attempts to map the social totality of the Cold War confront obstacles that compel recourse to vertical metaphors of power. There is great consensus in the scholarly literature in ascribing importance to the perspective operative in Weiss, Johnson, and Kluge's epics as a "view from below":[77] whether it be Weiss's characterization of the proletarian conquest of culture in view of a scientific age "from deep down" (*AoR* 163/*ÄdW* 1:188), Johnson's interest in and solidarity with "simple people"[78] as well as his rendering of the retrievable past in the image of a "great gray cat behind the windowpane, seen from very far below as with a child's eyes" (*AN* 47/*JT* 64), or the plight of Kluge's characters under the falling bombs, who stand in need of orientation denied them in the immediate moment of crisis (as in the "strategy from below" section of Kluge's narration of the bombing of Halberstadt, *AR* 27ff./*CdG* 2:43ff.), there can be little question as to which side of power such modern epics place themselves and what kind of service their exercises in mapping is meant to provide. It unfolds as little as Jameson's according to a logic of class in any narrow sense. Nor does the vertical schematization—which is perhaps best understood as shorthand—imply that society's antagonisms are theoretically fixed. More broadly, against cartographic reason's practices of domination—from its abuses in the colonial world system through capital's production and manipulation of space as well as the design of military campaigns that Kluge's charts mimic (e.g., *AR* 40–41, 48/*CdG* 2:52–53, 58–59) to its digital outgrowth into the surveillance of individuals and entire peoples, which map, to remain with the vertical metaphor, from above—the aesthetic practices of cognitive mapping in Weiss, Johnson, and Kluge venture the more arduous task of mapping human emancipation from below. In service to human survival and self-empowerment, such mapping treats given scenarios of false, misleading, and/or dangerous mediation with healthy doses of skepticism. Intervening across the Imaginary (a position sometimes occupied by the consciousness of their characters), the responses of Weiss, Johnson, and Kluge's works to Real conditions of existence reexamine, wear down, and overturn ossified (mis)representations of modern social realities in the Symbolic order. Constructively mediating a totality that refuses direct representation, their collective commitment to realist practices confirms the modern epic's place in the kind of pedagogic political culture that Jameson's work has continued to champion.

Epic, Emancipation, and Education

Plumbing the prospects of human being's orientation via literary experiment, the modern epic qualifies as a likely practitioner of an aesthetic of cognitive mapping to which Jameson ascribes such high stakes. While the task-work he outlines can feasibly be taken up by any art, the epic's relation to narration in space—as highlighted in the discussion of Lukács above—and its circumspective approach to the social totality, including collective life therein, constitute features that compel the epic's further distinction from the genre of the novel. Moretti, who emphasized differences between epic and novelistic approaches to space, is not the only scholar to value the delimitation of the two prose genres. In her study of *How Novels Think: The Limits of Individualism from 1719–1900*, Anglicist Nancy Armstrong has narrowed down the novel's definition and scope, pinning it to the history of liberal individualism. On her account, the novel engenders, disciplines, and defends the individual as a reality and as a category: so powerful is the genre's "ideological core"—the (re)production and universalization of the modern individual subject—that Armstrong "cannot quite believe that any novel can reach in and modify the ideological core of the genre and still remain a novel."[79] Thus, the novel's epic turn away from the self-enclosed individual and the integrated narrative that would confirm him,[80] which became palpable in modern epic works such as Joyce's *Ulysses* and Döblin's *Berlin Alexanderplatz*, already marks a vanishing point of Armstrong's conception. Absent from Armstrong's focused study, the epic's twentieth-century return, as theorized in the literary-aesthetic discourse addressed in this chapter, signals a passage beyond or at least askew of individualism's horizon. Whereas Armstrong ties the novelistic genre to the discursive categories and practices of a bourgeois world,[81] the underpinnings of which carry over into the global exportation and adoption of its mode of production today, the Cold War epic was situated between the first and second worlds, even reaching into the third. While the genre could hardly strip down such global divisions, its multifold traverse thereof placed the Cold War epic in a position to read and narrate the fissures of social contradictions and possible orientations thereunto on a broad scale. What is more, that the dialectics of such reading and narration were more palpable during that period than our own by no means consigns the modern epic project to any historical dustbin. Rather, peering critically through the Cold War to time's epic dimensions, the genre impresses upon us the value of stories that, as Walter Benjamin put it, "do not expend themselves." Preserving and concentrating "its strength and capable of releasing it after a long time . . . the story . . . resembles the seeds of grain which have lain for centuries in the chambers of the pyramids shut up air-tight and have retained their germinative power to this day."[82] Duration, Benjamin wrote in a related piece, "is a criterion of epic writing far more than of other types of literature. Duration not in time, but in the reader. The true reader reads epic in order to 'retain' it."[83] The modern epic offers reservoirs of such time.

An untimely genre? The signposts of the modern epic canvassed here suggest otherwise. Its motivated commitment to totality, its enlargement of human optics and senses via realist experimentations and constructions, its reassertion of self-critical narration in the face of narrative's uncertainty, its appropriation of epic theater's advances in and for prose, its thematization of existing social movements and those on the cusp of emergence, its labor on media and its own labor of mediation, its practices of cognitive mapping that would serve emancipatory spatial and social orientation and, finally, its modulations of intensive and extensive time are all indicative of its force as a literary genre. The course of the Cold War epic in the German context is determined by its assembly of these variegated elements: from Weiss's controversial unification thereof in *Die Ästhetik des Widerstands*, which is perhaps already the last epic to evoke novelistic integration, through the wondrous artifice of Johnson's *Jahrestage*, which exemplarily situates the epic in the clutches of geopolitical history, to Kluge, whose short narratives populate the hollows of epic's imploded form to remediate humanity's potentials, the postwar evolution of the modern epic is a rich trajectory, full of advances and retreats. The axis of its narration, when viewed comparatively through Moretti's diachronic structure of representational problems and their solutions via the innovation of literary techniques, already suggests something of the genre's arch: from the centripetal force of Weiss's narrator as a single medium through which all that transpires in the three-volume story is filtered,[84] through the controlled multiplication of acts of narration in Johnson, who first contracts with his main character Gesine Cresspahl to recount twentieth-century history and then duplicates this twofold structure to incorporate voices of contiguous generations by way of Gesine's deceased Jerichow relatives, on the one hand, and her daughter Marie, on the other, to feature a quartet of narrative voices in his four-volume opus, to Kluge's *Chronik*, the two volumes of which are filled by spatiotemporally disperse narratives oscillating between the different ways Kluge self-reflexively marks his own activity as a narrator and the seeming disappearance of narration into the materials assembled, the epic undergoes an entropic democratization in form.[85] As Weiss's integrative balancing act between unity and difference yields to Johnson's polyphonic contract, and as the complex, yet ultimately singular story lines of each yield to Kluge's radicalization of the principle of the independence of epic's parts in an ever-expanding network of constellated narration, epic's modern content does not elude literary form, nor do the stories' endemic antagonisms slacken amid the disintegration of their overarching story line, nor again are epic's spaces of hope eclipsed so much as multiplied and searchingly reasserted in new keys. The innovations of prose narration constitute an unfurling of the epic imagination that will continue as long as the need for epic and what it can offer resonate unfulfilled.

A rich trajectory, the epic's postwar course, and while it is not without difficulty, its many pages repay invested time. The emphases on the multidimensional and conceptual intricacies of the modern epic's labor outlined in this chapter may appear to suggest the opposition of the genre to the emotions, including that of pleasure. This could not be further from the case. First, by opening itself to uncharted zones between reason, its barbaric destruction, and its marginalized others, each epic seeks to redress the opposition of emotion and intellect: Weiss through the correction of reason's terrors by way of fantasy, dreams, and hopes as well as by working through trauma, Johnson by way of creating a fictional world in which the traumas of invented persons reverberate as truly as their hopes,[86] and Kluge by way of foregrounding, narrating and analyzing feelings in a continuation of Robert Musil's call for precision in the soul.[87] In response to the question, which Kluge is regularly compelled to field, as to why he does not make things a little easier for recipients, Kluge counters with a reference to a commercial he once saw on television. It depicted a family sanctuary under a rainbow in a scene narrated by a child. The advertisement, on Kluge's account infantilizing in tone and content, was for a Reagan-era SDI missile defense system, and one problem it suggests is the vast discrepancy between undeveloped emotional life, which the infantilizing commercial perpetuated by exploiting a politics of fear, and the hyperadvancement of physics.[88] Chronicling human feelings, Kluge's work aspires to remedy such gaps.

The veritable difficulties of modern epic content stem from its stubborn assertion of emancipation in a catastrophic history that appears to deny it utterly. Most reproached for its cultivation of difficulty is the epic that stands at the beginning of the process of form's entropic democratization charted in the following chapters. But its centripetal formal structure is no correlate to an authoritarianism that it contests throughout: as the narrator and fellow travelers amass a vast education from below that unfolds in analogy to labor's other dimensions,[89] Weiss's *Ästhetik* is most explicit and most generous in tirelessly narrating the processes via which critical appropriation and reconstitution of culture are attainable. In aspiring to teach what human emancipation might look like and entail, it cannot dictate. A relevant discussion of art embedded in the epic intimates the book's reception by contrast. Weiss's character Heilmann claims that the socialist realism in question there "cannot suffice for the worker. No matter how squarely it places him in the middle of events, it nevertheless underestimates him by granting him only one aspect of reality. He must feel that tailored themes prevent him from making up his own mind" (*AoR* 57/*ÄdW* 1:68).

Building the difficulty of the content into its forms, the modern epic's uncompromising treatment of reality ensues not out of a desire to overwhelm, but rather out of the respect each writer holds for potential readers. "It is possible," Johnson insisted in response to a question in an interview with the German broadcaster NDR as to who would read a thousand pages of anything anymore, "for people to take stock of a larger epic magnitude."[90] Prompting the emancipatory activation of recipients, epic difficulty unfolds as the promise and pleasure of self-purpose.[91] Called on to navigate and coproduce the epic's networks, readers are not subjected to a heteronymous relation controlled by authors, who in any case place the literary text in its autonomy on a higher plane than their individual agencies as creative laborers.[92] Aspiring to produce frameworks in which freedom might prevail,[93] Weiss, Johnson, and Kluge's works supply contours for readers' experiences as processes leading to outcomes that ultimately fall outside their purview.

Critical theory has advanced the claim that human beings cannot remain "indifferent to the restriction of their rational capacities" and their self-actualization.[94] If this is so, it is hard to see how the modern epic's cultivation of self-activity could be divorced from pleasure. Not only does such pleasure not equal complicity, to oppose a line from the *Dialectic of Enlightenment*'s treatment of the culture industry.[95] The modern epic facilitates the unfolding of pleasure in and as self-empowerment. Amid the heteronymous distribution of human feelings into antithetical domains of labor and entertainment, Bertolt Brecht's insistence on the relationship between pleasure and learning,[96] so basic as to appear trite, reminds us of the pleasures labor can yield in its passage from an alienated activity imposed to a self-activity unexpropriated. For Weiss scholar Robert Cohen, writing against the negative connotations the terms "labor," "achievement," and "effort" assume in capitalist society, "there is a kind of labor that does not lead to fatigue and accommodation but brings about a lively stubbornness. There is a kind of achievement that is not to the detriment of others but for the benefit of all. There is a kind of effort that does not cost one's leisure but serves everyone's liberation. Beyond all the difficulties, the involvement with *The Aesthetics of Resistance* is of this kind."[97] Cohen thus zeroes in on a link between the pleasures of unalienated self-activity that take shape in the epic and the larger political value thereof. This brings us back to the social practice of reading. As a site of self-activity and self-purpose, as a space for building up and developing thought and the emotions in the full play of human faculties, as a training ground of spatial and social orientation broadly conceived, epic space possesses tremendous social value, as crucial as it is difficult to access. Overall, its difficulty has less to do with its literary form than the general social and temporal inaccessibility of unalienated activity today. Precisely because of the larger social value of the modern epic's ability to foster self-activity, it is a site that demands expansion, which is what has prompted Kluge's multimedial outreach, as discussed in chapter 4 below.[98] If the expansion of this kind of space is also a political project, it comes along with pedagogic directives. If the whole task of education can be still be conceived in terms of the facilitation of human self-emancipation, then the Cold War epic can be considered as one of its textbooks, written from another age.

Chapter 2

Epic's Impossible Return

Peter Weiss's *Die Ästhetik des Widerstands*

> That a human being could give another freedom was a preposterous notion. Freedom, that she could only attain herself.
>
> —Charlotte Bischoff via interior monologue in *Die Ästhetik des Widerstands*

Epic Resets

Peter Weiss's *Die Ästhetik des Widerstands* famously begins in medias res: ensconcing readers in a scene of great strife depicted by the Pergamon Altar and its friezes in the Berlin museum named after it, it is a dramatic opening. Only gradually do the temporal and spatial coordinates of the narrative attain focus. The subject of the friezes, "The Battle between the Gods and the Giants," initially foregrounded in the text's simulation of a process of direct perception, shifts into a background against which three young protagonists—the unnamed narrator and his friends Coppi and Heilmann—assume shape. Their discussion of the visit to the altar in the narrated time of Weiss's book on September 22, 1937, continues over the course of the next several chapters in an exchange that lays the groundwork for a most unusual novel's development of a politico-philosophical aesthetics for the twentieth century and beyond (*AoR* 7/*ÄdW* 1:12).

The first chapter mounts a literary remediation of the Pergamon Altar, cuing themes crucial to *Die Ästhetik des Widerstands* as a whole. Each is as significant for the work's poetics as for its content. The issues are compactly demonstrated and enacted in the protagonists' confrontation with ancient myth. The first concerns their ascertainment of the whole from out of the altar's fragmented parts. The very appearance of the altar presents a twofold challenge in this regard: since its scope and complexity as a large monumental public work of art outstrips what the eye can grasp in a single moment, it necessarily temporalizes perception in the act of reception to a great degree. Second, because the altar—the ruins of which German archaeologists excavated in Turkey in the 1870s and 1880s and then, in an arrangement with the Ottoman Empire, appropriated and transported to Berlin for reconstruction—could not be restored in its entirety, the missing components of its imagery have to be filled in by the imagination and/or research.[1] The protagonists' ensuing hermeneutic activity builds on their perceptions in conjunction with a book Heilmann has brought along (*AoR* 4/*ÄdW* 1:8). As their interpretation of the Gigantomachy also attends to its palimpsests, the ostensible depiction of the Greek gods' victory over Gaea—demoness of the earth and mother of Giants and Titans, Cyclopes and Furies—is translated into the terms of ancient social class history. In this way, the "mythical disguise" in which "historic events" were cloaked and immortalized is stripped of its timeless character (*AoR* 5/*ÄdW* 1:9). Revealing the function of such art to consist in the legitimation of worldly political power—here that of the Attalid dynasty—the protagonists also register the restriction of art's enjoyment to the privileged (*AoR* 5/*ÄdW* 1:9). Yet in their discussion they are also able to establish the footholds of a different approach to the work. This is made possible by the neutralization of the altar's function couched in Coppi's question as to whether the monument possesses a "value in its own right, belonging to anyone who steps in front of it" (*AoR* 8/*ÄdW* 1:12). In fact, its effects can neither be controlled by the intentions of the power holders who commissioned it, nor does the artwork prescribe restrictions on its reception. Heilmann confirms the interpretative reversal under way by attending further to its "dichotomy" (*AoR* 8/*ÄdW* 1:13; *Zwiespalt*). The very presence of the besieged and their torment in the struggle allows for an identification with what the protagonists call "our race" (*AoR* 6/*ÄdW* 1:10; *unser Geschlecht* is construed there in terms of class) and for an appreciation of the aesthetic accomplishments made possible by the laboring classes, both of which suggest class struggle's vast continuity.[2] In these ways, *Die Ästhetik*'s interaction with the altar evinces the project of a broadly conceived emancipation on which the proletarian narrator and his friends, comrades, and members of their class are embarking. Their collective program is driven by a utopian vision of humanity, of which Heilmann is the initial spokesperson in the following chapter (*AoR* 13/*ÄdW* 1:18).

As much as the vision of an emancipated humanity inspires members of the antifascist movement, it is not one that can be readily fulfilled. The circumstances for the protagonists' emancipatory aspirations could not be much worse. Those who step in front of the altar appear not as themselves, but in camouflage, as suggested by the brown shirt Heilmann has donned (*AoR* 7/*ÄdW* 1:11–12). Living underground—Coppi is engaged in illegal political activity, the narrator is preparing for his departure to join the International Brigades in the Spanish Civil War—they are as invisible in Nazi Germany's public sphere as Hercules is absent from the frieze. Only a "sign bearing [the latter's] name, and the paw of a lion's skin that had cloaked him" have remained (*AoR* 7/*ÄdW* 1:11). Although the myth places Hercules on the side of the gods, the protagonists deem him one of their own. Coppi, who along with the narrator tends to represent the claims of a positive representational aesthetics in the discussions that follow in the former's kitchen,[3] regards Hercules's absence as an omen of their own predicament. But it is not necessarily ominous: Heilmann, the staunchest proponent of the avant-garde and aesthetic experimentation among the comrades, exploits the frieze's gap in representation. Responding to Coppi's call that they create their own image of the Hercules they miss on the frieze, Heilmann advances a refunctionalization of the hero by solidifying Hercules's alignment with the enslaved by the end of the next chapter (*AoR* 20/*ÄdW* 1:25). Thus does Hercules become a leading motif (*Leitbild*) of *Die Ästhetik*, the novel's first entirely absent, yet resonant image produced via literary imagination and narration.[4] In this work's extensive interaction with the visual arts (its "Gang zu den Bildern")[5] and literary works—from which Weiss's narrator and fellow travelers repeatedly derive inspiration, accumulate energies of resistance and establish orientation, effectively activating an extensively networked living archive[6] for themselves as well as posterity—such a beginning is well worth remembering. One may find in it both an assertion of liberation's long march as well as a highly crystallized form of Weiss's own intent in writing *Die Ästhetik des Widerstands* to "sketch what I earlier never saw" (*NB* 50).

As the fury of its first chapter—barely intimated in these introductory remarks—draws to a close, *Die Ästhetik* artfully presses upon readers the direness of the protagonists' struggle. The chapter's framing is characteristic of the book's epic coups. On leaving the museum, Heilmann points out an inversion in the altar's spatial function. The friezes, once featured on the altar's erstwhile base displaying outward, were, for the purposes of the museum exhibition, mounted on the north, west, and south walls to enclose onlookers facing the altar on the east side of the room. "Something the viewer was to grasp by slowly circling it was now surrounding him instead" (*AoR* 10/*ÄdW* 1:15). Bereft of its relation to "the Aegean sky," the enclosure of the altar and its onlookers in Berlin echoes the very first words of the book: "All around us" (*AoR* 3/*ÄdW* 1:7; *Rings um uns*) not only to convey the politically induced claustrophobia the characters are made to endure, but also to underscore the administered isolation of art in the museum experience, from which the protagonists must extrapolate and refunctionalize its meaning and significance in order for art's practical and existential (noncultic and noncommodified) value to be actualized in their present. What is more, as the altar's inverted appearance becomes part of a series of "dizzying" contrasts—from Ancient Greece, to the Babylonia of the next exhibit room, to the noise of "the rhythmic smashing of hobnailed boots" in the urban space just outside the museum—Weiss's narration underscores the general need for orientational readjustment (*AoR* 11/*ÄdW* 1:15). The text thereby effectively cuts through the chaos of the war-torn agony of the bodies on the Pergamon friezes, the time-space compression inhering in the museum's practices of acquiring and displaying world history, and the present political reality, metonymically captured in the reference to Nazi boots. Weiss will have his narrator repeatedly deliver such cross-cutting mediation—of art, history, and the present situation—to enact a broadly conceived aesthetic mapping of narrated spaces in what makes for part of this novel's epic turn.[7]

Aesthetic Culture and Modern Epic

> Back then, when we found ourselves in the middle of events, we recognized only that [culture] was full of antagonisms, an overview was not to be had. In order to win a picture of our history we first had to draw lines between paltry points of reference and create connections across chasms.
>
> —*Die Ästhetik*'s narrator in volume 3

A work of great literary, aesthetic, political and existential intensity, the content of *Die Ästhetik des Widerstands*'s epic drive has often been characterized first in terms of its examination of the historical challenges faced by the antifascist Popular Front movement and the impact a disunited Left would have on Europe after World War II amid the continent's ensuing geopolitical division.[8] This is the story Weiss's epic renders dramatically in its narrated time, where resistance primarily concerns the struggle against the Nazi dictatorship and European fascisms. Curiously, with just a few modifications, the endeavor just described would almost qualify as an epic in the old style of Hegel's imagination discussed in the foregoing chapter: an emphasis on action in an age of (unsung antifascist) heroes, a living presence of the spirit (amid politically committed comrades), a spiritual unity (of the Left), a totalizing poetic form replete with a beginning in medias res and an ending by which a well-nigh omniscient narrator sinks the tale organically into the lives of its audience. Closer examination debunks such semblance. As action yields to discussion and reflection, as any presence of spirit has to be mustered from out of despair, as unity proves elusive, the totalizing poetic form circumscribes more than integrates individual and collective experiences. And the foundation of a would-be omniscience is destabilized by the question of whether the story can be told at all: this genuine concern in face of a catastrophic modernity's mid-twentieth-century horrors generates a degree of self-reflexivity that Hegel would have found absent from antiquity's epic poetry. As *Die Ästhetik*'s narrator follows the claims of two of the book's many teachers—Charlotte Bischoff and Max Hodann—on the impossibility of restoring any culture without fully coming to terms with what had transpired (cf. *ÄdW* 3:236, 242, 246, 259), epic resets would and could not come about automatically.

Coupling reflection on the historical process with self-reflection on the literary mediation thereof, *Die Ästhetik des Widerstands* does not so much restore culture—not to mention pretend that its availability is self-evident—as advance its transformative re-creation. It does so by embracing a conception and practice of aesthetics as a site and force of humanization through cultural labor. This is what makes the work as difficult and arduous as it is valuable and pleasurable, in the sense identified by Robert Cohen cited at the end of the previous chapter. This characterization follows a degree of consensus in recent Weiss scholarship that has emphasized the significance of this unusual work of literary art's own aesthetic and intermedial practices.[9] At the same time, it is more broadly formulated to grasp the key elements of Weiss's undertaking in their relation to one another. The specific inflection *Die Ästhetik* gives each of these large terms—aesthetics, humanization, labor, and culture—makes for the sharp and still timely contours of Weiss's contribution. For that reason, this section provides an overview of their configuration in Weiss's modern epic.

Save for its standing in the title, the first term is less explicitly mobilized than the others on the pages of *Die Ästhetik* itself. But the foregoing consideration of *Die Ästhetik*'s first chapter already points to Weiss's dynamic emphasis on the story's aesthetic dimension. The titular term is not exactly synonymous with art; rather, it encompasses both the ancient meaning of aesthetics as sensory perception as well as the faculties of fantasy and imagination that we associate with art. The most basic embodied human functions—the general activity of the senses, orientation in time and space, sensitivity to the modalities thereof, along with remembrance, fantasy, and the imagination—are all aesthetic procedures for Weiss. Such activity is underscored both in the aesthetic focus of the protagonists' quest to emancipate themselves through education as well as in the following seminal passage attributed to Max Hodann:

> Art, said Hodann, intervenes at precisely that point at which all philosophies and ideologies stop, it emerges from entelechy, that enigmatic force inherent to all living beings, in order to steer life and, should it suffer damage, restore it, it belongs to the mnestic functions, which in the brain, in the centers of the visual and the acoustic, of spatial and temporal orientation, preserve everything that has been perceived and make it, down into our nervous stimuli, available to us, without the traces of this mental capacity for remembrance ever having been able to be pinned down via dissection. (*ÄdW* 3:134)

Hodann's claims permit a distinction between art and the mental capacity in question: art is an outgrowth and objectification of the latter, the aesthetic capacity, which makes aesthetics the broader and more fundamental term. It appears as resistance in the context of a structurally antagonistic society that prescribes passivity and estranged labor to whole classes. On this front, the autodidactic project undertaken by Weiss's proletarian protagonists amounts to a politically rebellious self-overcoming (*AoR* 45/*ÄdW* 1:53; *Selbstüberwindung*, translated as "strength of mind") of those whose activity society's division of mental and manual labor otherwise relegates to the latter category. Rattling at the constitution of class division in society's predetermination of the self, the protagonists' discussions of art and daily life and work experiences alike explicitly thematize sensory activity to train the self's human capacities beyond those contingently prescribed.[10] In Weiss's book, aesthetics ranges from the reappropriation of one's senses and the activity of making-sense through the reception and production of works of art to ways of dealing with, surviving, and moving beyond existential threats.[11] In conjunction with artworks as exemplary vehicles of resistance, fantasy, and imagination objectified, aesthetics' schools—aesthetic experiences diversely conceived—provide essential tools to survival as well as self-development. In this way, the book's first anchor rests in the aesthetic imagination it mobilizes on the fronts of perception and interpretation, orientation and decision-making, action and memorialization. On the basis of its priority, aesthetics also serves as the testing ground for any political course of action and partisanship, facilitating the critical reappraisal of revolutionary struggle that *Die Ästhetik* delivers.

A basic capacity of human beings, aesthetics points to the second term in the series. Humanization indicates first the repossession and development of aesthetic faculties against their expropriation and debilitation amid unfavorable political and economic conditions. Pinned to the prospects of individual and social emancipation, humanization speaks to a liberation larger than the defeat of Nazi Germany. In initial descriptions of the process, the narrator underscores its broad anthropological underpinnings. In the face of socially induced speechlessness or muteness, "attempts to escape [such conditions] belonged to the functions of our existence [*Dasein*]" (*AoR* 45, translation modified/*ÄdW* 1:54). The aspiration to *Mündigkeit* (maturity, self-representation, even: linguistic fluency) in the full philosophical sense the Enlightenment bestowed on this concept will have clear implications for the book's conception of political practice.[12] The achievement of voice and articulateness not only foreshadows the narrator's own aesthetic journey to becoming a writer and *Die Ästhetik*'s critique of authoritarian political practice. It is also frames emergence out of suppression in ontogenetic and—with the first-person plural characteristically predominant here—phylogenetic terms.[13] Echoing this broader vision near the end of the war, a disillusioned Hodann appeals to humanization and humanity amid his frustration with the political struggle (cf., e.g., *ÄdW* 3:248). But "the words truth and humanity, like the concepts of ethics and morality, had virtually become infamous by their political misuse" (*ÄdW* 3:134). While *Die Ästhetik*'s investment in aesthetic experiences as sites of humanization is unmistakable, there is little tenable recourse to the humanist discourse that failed to prevent humanity's unprecedented destruction. While the anthropological concept of humanization constitutes a linchpin of *Die Ästhetik*'s reinitiation of the larger struggle for emancipation, its content and purchase demand political and materialist reformulation vis-à-vis the specific contexts in which its realization is threatened or undermined entirely.

Concern for the myriad tensions between the power of historically specific social, economic, and political forces on the one hand and the impetus toward a broadly conceived humanization on the other drives *Die Ästhetik*'s sustained interrogation of the possibilities and travesties of art and politics. As the narrative advances its comprehensive examination of the antifascist movement in the historical period in question, the core of Weiss's response to the Left's defeats becomes ascertainable in aesthetic education's relation to social and political emancipation. As can be anticipated from the foregoing, the crux of the connection lies in the self-activity of human beings. Fantasy and resistance are therefore fused in one of the book's frequently cited lines—from its reception of Picasso's *Guernica* at the end of the Spanish Civil War—on imagination (*Phantasie*) that "lived so long as human beings who resisted lived" (*AoR* 298/*ÄdW* 1:339). So too does the narrator willfully draw an analogy between joining the Communist Party and visiting the Louvre in an interrelated embrace of "struggle without compromise" and "the absolute freedom of fantasy" (*ÄdW* 2:19). While this association is echoed in Willi Münzenberg's recollection of the vision of a total material and intellectual revolution anticipated in the intercourse of the political and cultural avant-gardes in Zurich's Spiegelgasse during World War I (*ÄdW* 2:55–59), the claims attributed to Hodann on art's equivalence to humanity highlight art's ability to make up for what politics cannot fulfill (*ÄdW* 3:135).[14]

As the arch of this small assembly of emblematic passages suggests, Weiss unfolds the necessity and scope of aesthetic resistance by attending to deep disturbances in politics. The emphasis on the autodidactic nature of *Die Ästhetik*'s emancipatory project relates directly to a critical point sounded in the book's analyses of the difficulties encountered in the international Left's attempts to procure tenable political unity across linguistic, ideological, and organizational barriers. Strategically imperative to success, the enforcement of political unity too often goes hand in hand with the suppression of dissenters, incurring all manner of democratic deficits. While the many instances of the clashes staged in *Die Ästhetik* between the necessity of establishing political unity and the repression of differences in viewpoints refuse summary, the book's dialogical labor on oppositions shows its strength by lending each standpoint its force and validity.[15] Thus, while the leading role of the Soviet Union and its influence on antifascist strategy through the Communist International (Comintern) are grasped as historical necessity, the repressive hardships and harsh reprisals for deviance induced by unity's enforcement not only frame unity as a recurring aporia, but also submit its enforcement to ethical review and critique.

A relevant thread from Weiss's treatment of the Spanish Civil War in the second half of the first volume illustrates this point. It begins to take shape with the character Münzer, who voices criticism of the Left's authoritarian practices with regard to the suppression of anarchists and the orchestration of solidarity at the price of individual agency. Admonishing that it "would be deadly for us, who are fighting for a future goal, to take a stance that the people coming after us would have to renounce" (*AoR* 219/*ÄdW* 1:249), Münzer's approach to means-ends relations insists on the consistency and temporal unity of emancipation in every action: "If we fail [to liberate] ourselves, then it will have no consequences for us" (*AoR* 199/*ÄdW* 1:226), he argues in a variation of Marx's third thesis on Feuerbach, thereby refusing the subordination of passive individuals to party directives and of the present to a future.[16] Where Hodann subsequently seeks to grasp the complex relationship between theory and praxis more probingly in a review of Soviet history, even he ends up attesting—perhaps unintentionally in the following sentence's preposition—to the lingering estrangement of revolutionary activity: "We are inconspicuous *next to* the locomotive of history, even if we ourselves are the ones who, with our unique and singular actions, made it start moving" (*AoR* 222, my emphasis/*ÄdW* 1:253).[17] The introduction of Marcauer's perspective into debates about the political purges in the Soviet Union in March 1938 only intensifies the respective forces of argument and counterargument. In a chapter marked by Weiss's deft threefold weave of communism's Stalinization, the *Anschluss* of Austria to Nazi Germany, and the increasingly imperiled plight of republican Spain, Marcauer directs fierce skepticism at her comrades' rationalizations of the trials. Echoing and sharpening Hodann's own earlier remarks on the relation of the organization of private and sexual life to the struggle for liberation (*AoR* 228–230/*ÄdW* 1:260–262), she tells them their explanations are distorted "because you remain trapped in your male world" (*AoR* 257/*ÄdW* 1:293). To her the reported events in the Soviet Union suggested no tragedy—and certainly no catharsis—but only the madness of a male world "letting off steam" in a house upheld by belief alone (*AoR* 258–259/*ÄdW* 1:294). As her criticism of past and present policy takes on increasingly acerbic tones, Marcauer is taken prisoner in the following chapter and disappears from the novel (cf. *ÄdW* 3:43), but not without leaving a powerful and—as we will see—influential trace.[18]

The example of such a thread underscores Weiss's committed attention to the multiple voices of *Die Ästhetik*'s many debates. The spiraling advancement (cf. *AoR* 63/*ÄdW* 1:74) of dialogical opposition in its narrated time doubtlessly expands the work's optics in its narrative present. Wherever one side appears to gain the upper hand in the historical reality of practice, as seen in the impact of Soviet policy during the time, Weiss reinforces the perspectives of skeptics and visionaries,[19] reaching, where necessary, to seemingly marginal characters such as the narrator's father and mother, Münzer,

Marcauer, and Rogeby, as well as imaginatively strengthening the voices of better-known historical persons, including the aforementioned Heilmann, Coppi, Hodann, and Münzenberg, as well as Karin Boye, Bischoff, and many others.[20] "The characters in this book," wrote Weiss in his *Notizbücher*, "are historical, just as all the sites and events are authentic, but everything is treated freely in accordance with the novel form" (*NB* 926). While those still living "may not recognize themselves in the novel's characters," its author attempted "not to impute anything to [any of them] that they themselves could not have done or said" (*NB* 927), lines that are taken up into the work's final self-reflection on the time and space it traverses to tell its story (*ÄdW* 3:265–266).

Weiss's free treatment of the historical content is neither facile nor easygoing. Part of a larger motivated agenda, the work's dialogical plurality enables him not only to represent "every moment of the irresolvable conflicts" in collectivity "as a movement of absolutes."[21] *Die Ästhetik* also makes good in form—where dialogue holds out against party directives—and content—self-emancipation—on precisely those shortcomings identified in the object of its critique, to challenge the claims and deformations of official communism without jettisoning communism in principle. The anonymous narrator especially refrains from doing so, as in the debates with his father and SPD member (*AoR* 108–109/*ÄdW* 1:126), where the former's anticipation of joining the Communist Party may come across as naive in light of the whole power of *Die Ästhetik*'s retrospective review and critique of totalitarianism's germs. To the extent that *Die Ästhetik*'s dialogical approach was read as a critique of communism from a standpoint of idealistic solidarity, it may have contributed to Heiner Müller's ambivalent caricature of its author as a monk of utopia,[22] but it must be acknowledged that Weiss's laborious efforts to separate communism's alleged bankruptcy in the wake of Stalinism (and today in the wake of actually existing socialism's collapse) from its alternative future potentials were part and parcel of his insistence on long term political emancipation from below. Settling accounts with totalitarian abuses, *Die Ästhetik* wagers no less than a democratic affirmation and reassertion of those aspirations for which communism was the vehicle. In this respect, assessing the work on its own terms in the twenty-first century may pose certain difficulties.[23] Although *Die Ästhetik*'s predication on reviving and renewing resistance after the historical defeats suffered by the Left in the twentieth century's darkest moments qualify it directly to a present in which capitalism has triumphed globally, today, where the verdict on communism appears completely sealed, the transhistorical validity of *Die Ästhetik*'s vision may not enjoy much purchase on these political terms.[24] And yet the truth-content of works of art does not wither in such a way.[25] From its author's consideration of class struggle as eternal[26] to its defiance of external criteria masquerading as measures of truth, *Die Ästhetik* not only opposes in spirit and practice the very marginalization to which it is subjected. Unfavorable as the current conditions of its reception may be, it remains possible to frame the importance of Weiss's broad-minded conception of aesthetic resistance to questions of emancipation in global capitalism.

Hence my approach to Weiss's contribution in terms of this fourfold general vocabulary to which we can return. The activity emphasized in the descriptions of aesthetics and humanization above points to the metapolitical conception of labor through which Weiss's *Ästhetik* gains transhistorical traction. As with the others, labor appears in sweeping anthropological terms, especially in the formulations attributed to the narrator's father: "His motto was the Marxist proposition that labor constitutes the creative principle, the essence of the human species" (*AoR* 308/*ÄdW* 1:351). Affirming his activity and himself, the narrator's father even embraces labor under conditions of estrangement, which gives rise to the curious image of the "paid laborer" behaving as if he "were in a socialized factory" (ibid.). Yet if the trajectory of time reveals a revolutionary or at least progressive dimension—to which the narrator's not infrequent appeals to emancipation's advances, however long and slow, attest (e.g., *AoR* 61/*ÄdW* 1:72, 2:238)—then his father, a lodestar not only in his embrace of labor but also in his advocacy of political praxis's democratic baseline,[27] is just ahead of its curve, planting seeds of the future in the present. Labor thus complements and concretizes aesthetic activity's humanizing dimension. By insisting on the analogy between intellectual and physical forms of labor, as drawn by the Swedish communist Rogeby in his conarration of the history of social democracy in Sweden (*ÄdW* 2:281), in the narrator's father's equalization of art and literature and tools and machines as means of production (*AoR* 308/*ÄdW* 1:350), or later on in the narrator's refusal to allow any gap to emerge between his own manual and intellectual activities (*ÄdW* 3:45), *Die Ästhetik* approaches culture from the perspective of labor. In so doing, it displaces and overrides the former's ideology with a conception that stands culture on its feet, paving the way for its transformative reconstitution postcatastrophe.[28]

The strength of *Die Ästhetik*'s development of a labor theory of culture consists first in its defiance of manual and mental labor as fundamentally different kinds of human activity. Without reducing either to the other, Weiss interrelates forms of physical and intellectual work in suggestive ways, expanding the range of each while opposing the socially antagonistic form of their separation from one another (e.g., *AoR* 310/*ÄdW* 1:353, *ÄdW* 3:45). Weiss's book can thus be read in conjunction with Adorno's critique of the restoration of cultural ideology in Germany after Auschwitz, discussed in the introduction.[29] At stake is not merely the facilitation of greater access to culture (e.g., via some enhancement of its circulation), but a transformative reconceptualization of culture itself. Something other than the division of mental and manual labor is meant when "we talk about our culture, it is precisely this activeness that is the basis of everything surrounding us in the country and the cities" (*AoR* 310/*ÄdW* 1:352–353). In the positions articulated at the end of *Die Ästhetik*'s first volume, the narrator's father delivers something of a theoretical summation of what has preceded in the aesthetic exercises of the book hitherto. For while the young protagonists are concerned with the accessibility of art and the expansion thereof to greater numbers of people, their self-education foregrounds the enactment of cultural reception as a process of (self-)transformative appropriation they themselves must undertake. The strong emphasis on the laborious nature of the activity of an appropriation for which (1) the protagonists are ill prepared and (2) culture in its bourgeois association was not intended[30] retracts the distinction between the reception (enjoyment or consumption) and production (creation) of cultural works. This model of "productive reception"[31] yields unprecedented results in Heilmann, Coppi, and the narrator's sessions, where the protagonists not only follow with great interest nineteenth-century and socialist realist depictions of workers' lives, but also read Dante to grapple with Nazism and Kafka's *Das Schloß* (*The Castle*) as a proletarian novel (*AoR* 50–61, 67–74/*ÄdW* 1:60–72, 79–88; *AoR* 149–156/*ÄdW* 1:171–180). The most sustained and intense episode of productive reception may be found in the chapters surrounding the transition from the first to the second volumes. The exploration there of Picasso's *Guernica*, Delacroix's *Liberty Leading the People*, Géricault's *The Raft of the Medusa*, Goya's *The Third of May 1808*, Menzel's *Iron Rolling Mill*, Koehler's *The Strike*, and Munch's *Workers Returning Home* (*AoR* 292–317/*ÄdW* 1:332–360) demonstrates *Die Ästhetik*'s literary remediation of other artistic media in full force: the text proceeds from a deliberative exposition of these artworks to inspired departures of epic language from its sources (e.g., *AoR* 317/*ÄdW* 1:360–361), returning again via additional research on Géricault to yield the surprising elimination of the difference between the recipient and the work of art altogether as the narrator himself appears alongside the marooned castaways on the *Medusa*'s raft (*ÄdW* 2:13).

The productive and transformative reception of artworks fuels *Die Ästhetik*'s expansion of culture as well as the self-conception of those delving into it. In addition to unsettling and overturning canonized interpretations of works in fresh proletarian contact, the liberating appropriation of culture transforms the recipients themselves. Aesthetic humanization is self-transformation, outstripping society's predetermination of the self. Predicated on overcoming the identity socially prescribed to them, the protagonists raise self-transformation to a principle to be vigilantly upheld throughout. Their appropriation of culture from a proletarian standpoint is neither redundant nor reductive, but spurred on by the ability of avant-garde works to explode a recipient's preestablished conceptions of self and reality (*AoR* 54/*ÄdW* 1:64).[32] The transformation in question assumes still larger dimensions in those scenarios of collective reception more common to *Die Ästhetik*, where self-transformation enjoys its greatest enhancement.[33] The principle of ongoing collective self-transformation sets artistic engagement outside any facile self-affirmation and guards against perpetuating any single condition in which the proletariat may find itself, whether this be an exclusion prescribed to it by capitalist relations of production or a specific stage reached in a revolutionary process.

This leads to a third salient point of *Die Ästhetik*'s labor theory of culture, which concerns the character of culture's refunctionalization under way in its proletarian appropriation. Removed from the bourgeois relations of production in which they exist for a certain class and are qualified as a certain kind of leisurely consumption and/or intellectual enjoyment, artworks are inserted into an alternative circuit of production, circulation, and reception.[34] This process of appropriation

> could never mean simply taking over cultural values from the hands of people who with their privileges had formerly served the rulers, for that would have involved adopting the depoliticization of culture, the rejection of the class struggle. Instead, there had to be a reciprocity between the things that had been shaped and the quest for an expression of their own. While we acquired culture, that overall mechanism, of which culture had been a component, had to be destroyed. . . . Once they were put on the ground of the proletariat and interpreted there, the works of literature, art, philosophy would gain a new meaning. (*AoR* 163/*ÄdW* 1:188)

Derived from Antonio Gramsci's writings on cultural hegemony, the guidelines articulated here drive *Die Ästhetik*'s project of cultural conquest undertaken by Heilmann, Coppi, and the narrator and are seen through on the level of the narrator's indirect rendering of the whole tale.[35] By inserting artworks into a network of its own crafting, *Die Ästhetik* produces cultural production's own relations[36] and "guards against the reduction of culture to commodification."[37] The "new meaning" of "the works of literature, art, and philosophy" is devoid of the capitalist valorization of culture in the commodity form. *Die Ästhetik*'s "counter-archive"[38] primarily concerns not the canonization of a different selection of artworks—most of its references feature established pre-avant-garde works from the European tradition[39]—but their revaluation and refunctionalization: in the relations *Die Ästhetik* entertains for the reception and production of art, questions of exchange-value and external valorization evaporate into questions of use-value and the creative labor process. In so doing, the project does not so much reject the doctrine of aesthetic autonomy as reformulate it. Where such a doctrine—including that of art's value for its own sake—has gone hand in hand with art's commodification under capitalist relations of cultural production (a social fact that the doctrine perhaps still thinly disguises), reenvisioning the use-value of art amounts less to the feared reduction of its hallowed scope to the status of mere instrument or political weapon than to an expansion of art's autonomy unconstrained by the bracketing of its practical, political, and existential dimensions. Devoid of false emphases that accrue to art under pressures of commodification and regimes of bourgeois distinction, the broad-minded and self-critical scrupulousness characteristic of Weiss's treatment of artworks in the narrative render them more proximate to life—including extreme life—than art's institutional administration promotes. In this way, the labor theory of culture advanced by *Die Ästhetik* investigates what art can be like when it is permitted to generate social value on its own terms.[40]

As far-reaching and ambitious as *Die Ästhetik*'s approach to culture is, founding it on labor inevitably raises the issue as to whether and how all human experiences could possibly be addressed in terms of the latter. This question is the narrator's own and the issue turns on the category of totality operative for him in Weiss's book. The subject-centered, genetic, and expressive conception of totality—emphasized at the outset (*AoR* 46/*ÄdW* 1:54–55) and corresponding to the book's (self-)critique of the Left as well as the living labor of narration itself—faces two other poles. The first can be characterized as that wider field of culture's universality found in artworks (e.g., *ÄdW* 2:33) as repositories of all the dead cultural labor that can be reactivated in productive reception.[41] The narrator demonstrates a budding sense for such universal connectivity over the course of the work (e.g., *AoR* 148–149/*ÄdW* 1:171, *ÄdW* 2:68, 256). As formidable a task as the realignment of culture to labor appears, it is undoubtedly the second pole that marks the potential limit to *Die Ästhetik*'s espousal of its narrative labor's expressive totality. This pole concerns the dark zones, contradictions, and zero-points of the historical story confronted, from the Soviet purges through the horrors of the Shoah. That the narrator might at all rise to the task of fathoming and rendering such breaking points stems from his labor's other-directedness, its exposure to objective materials, its self-transformative processual intercourse with the world and the experiences of others. The crux of Weiss's dialectical conception of totality thus rests in the necessary balancing act between labor's subjective-objective motivation and its principled openness to challenges and contradictions on which its "thinking in terms of totality" might feed or falter.[42]

Aesthetic culture's "universal connections" (*ÄdW* 2:256) are voided by precisely those events that bring the epic narrator's drive to a halt. Stumbling blocks derive not only from the complexity of events that compel the narrator to repeatedly wonder "how all this [could ever] be depicted . . . how could what we were experiencing . . . be delineated in such a way that we could recognize ourselves in it" (*AoR* 112/*ÄdW* 1:130). They also pertain to the model itself: if, with Hodann, art is a continuous struggle against self-abandonment (*ÄdW* 3:134), the self-fortification the narrator achieves through a rationalizing approach to art (as well as politics) is challenged on a personal level by Rosalinde Ossietzky, for example, who considers his belief in the necessity of the "sober judgment" of events on the eve of war and his appeals to a "politics of rationality" banefully wishful thinking (*ÄdW*

2:171–173). Additionally, Swedish writer Karin Boye's work is read as overwhelming "the entire theoretically constructed existence of the young worker who wanted to become a writer" (*ÄdW* 3:38). Similarly, her claims and convictions—articulated during the peripatetic conversations of the two in Alingsås—nearly send the narrator's "rational system" into a tailspin (ibid.). The strongest single injunction to narration's feasibility is seen in the slow demise of the narrator's mother after the traumas she experienced while in flight across sites of genocide in Eastern Europe on her way to Sweden with his father, whose rationalizing attempts to clarify and explain what happened drove her experiences "into a greater darkness" (*ÄdW* 3:125). Reunited with his parents in 1940, the narrator conveys that "until then there was no contradiction between life and art, rather it was in art that reality could achieve its highest articulation. But now that my mother's life grew more distant from me, so too did art" (*ÄdW* 3:130–131). Amid the inconceivability of finding any form for the reality of his mother's experience and her demise, the narrator can only process his own failure. And yet:

> Our inability to follow my mother was not determined by anything metaphysical or mystical, we just did not yet have any register for that which exceeded the apparent, our helplessness was provisional, had not our entire development demonstrated that concrete judgments could be built up out of first intuitions and approximating investigations. If something was present dreamlike in the form of a germ, it was also already part of our reality. (*ÄdW* 3:135)

Recoiling from his inability to respond to or aid his mother to any avail in the time narrated, the son refrains from relegating her—or anyone else's—experience to a completely other or irretrievable realm, but rather insists on its adjacency to a shared world. In this way, Weiss has his narrator retain expressive totality's processual character: as a give-and-take between self and other, reception and production, pen and paper and source media, such an approach corresponds to the necessarily asymptotic character of totality in the modern epic, as discussed in the previous chapter. But what is more telling in this context is the narrator's reference to the realm of dreams. The recourse to the oneiric intensifies in *Die Ästhetik*'s third volume to address precisely those experiences that defy totality's rationalizing management.[43] In lieu of pretending to have successfully integrated his mother's experiences into his tale, the narrator is pressed to deliver a delineation of languages, which blazes a trail for surmounting narration's limits. After the language of politics, the wartime media language with its mathematical and geographic, economic and military points of reference, and the gray language of personal masquerades, it is the interplay between the language of writing and the almost entirely visual and acoustic language of dreams that provides an outline for further elaborations on a totality (*Gesamtheit*) that cannot be grasped (*ÄdW* 3:148–149). The tenability of such elaborations—and that of aesthetic culture as a whole—would derive from its attentiveness to the deep debasement of humanity that has taken place (*ÄdW* 3:241–242).[44] Hodann, resigning from the Free German League of Culture that he cofounded in Sweden, would no longer follow through on this vision for culture's critical reconstitution after catastrophe. This leaves it to the narrator, whose accomplishments in *Die Ästhetik* must be measured by this benchmark—that is, the book's proximity to human suffering and the ways it comes to terms with it.

The reconstitution of aesthetic culture thus envisioned requires the time and space that Weiss's *Ästhetik* allots it. As the irreducibly edgy literary work that it is, replete with historical reconstruction, political and philosophical essayism, second- and thirdhand reports of what the embedded narrator does not himself experience, descriptive and narrative ekphrases of visual and other artistic media, not to mention its numerous intricate plays of literary artifice, *Die Ästhetik des Widerstands* refuses any straightforward argument regarding its political content or position: so many are the arguments it unfolds that any attempt to pinpoint its contribution along discursive lines would end up having to recapitulate at least something of the aesthetic journey—a proletarian odyssey—through which all of its content is filtered. Hence the most suggestive approaches have inquired into *Die Ästhetik*'s unusual status as a literary work. In doing so, many have highlighted the epic character of Weiss's self-described novel. Providing "ten working theses" on *Die Ästhetik*, Klaus Scherpe drew attention to the work's relation to other literary genres, including the "left *Heimatroman*," autobiography, the bildungsroman and the historical novel. Because *Die Ästhetik*'s "collective fiction" leaves each of these behind, Scherpe chooses to refer provisionally to the work as a "novel/epic."[45] In another account, Andreas Huyssen, in view of the "monumental, solemn, and highly rhythmic ductus of its language, the extended curves of seemingly interminable syntactic blocks, the presentation of history as a machinery of death, and the strange oscillation of the narrator's identity between fragmented subjectivity and anonymity," described the book as "an attempt to recreate the epic out of the failure of the avant-garde."[46] Fredric Jameson, on the other hand, discussing *Die Ästhetik*'s defiance of the separation of art and politics common to the postwar period, wrote of Weiss's attempt "virtually by fiat and by an effort of the will, to put the two [political and aesthetic] vanguards back together" (*AoR* xviii), and Peter Bürger, in view of *Die Ästhetik*'s reactualization of the avant-garde's call to suffuse art with life, grasped the work's epic character as a response to theoretical debates on the functions of instrumental and autonomous literature.[47] Taken together, these claims underscore the scope of Weiss's renewal efforts. *Die Ästhetik*'s redefinition and reconstitution of culture after catastrophe occurs through the reassertion of epic itself. In development of the genre's touchstones outlined in the previous chapter, the following sections focus on Weiss's book as a modern epic by examining the peculiar narration of its tale as a mode of resistance, its literary mobilization of other media to craft its own narrative maps and networks, and, finally, the space it carves out for (the genre's) polyphonic futures. By addressing these elements of Weiss's renewal of the epic genre, the chapter outlines *Die Ästhetik*'s lingering resonance for a century beyond the author's imagination.

Narration as Resistance

> He equated the struggle for truth in art with rebellion against demagoguery, for him artistic labor was inseparable from social and political reality. The destructiveness descending on Spain was meant to wipe out not only people and cities, but also the ability to express things.
>
> —the narrator on Picasso in volume 1

While the visit to the Pergamon Altar serves as *Die Ästhetik*'s immediate point of departure, the initiation of the long arch of the autodiegetic narrator's journey to becoming the book's author begins with the exposition of the protagonists' project of an emancipatory education in the first volume's fifth chapter. Ultimately, *the* action of the book is the fictional tale of its own writing. Weiss's complex handling of the story's narration evinces his direct confrontation with and proposed solution to the challenges of the modern epic genre. As discussed in the previous chapter, these stem from the perceived contradiction between modernity's prosaically ordered totality and the poetic encapsulation thereof in epic form. The challenge is exacerbated in the modern epic postcatastrophe due to its express orientation to historically specific content. To renew the epic in the face thereof, Weiss turns the very question of his project's feasibility into *Die Ästhetik*'s structuring principle. The questions put to the representability of historical events and experiences—posed repeatedly by the narrator himself (*AoR* 112/*ÄdW* 1:130; *AoR* 117/*ÄdW* 1:135; *ÄdW* 3:25, 42) and faced by other reporting and writing characters, such as (Lise) Lindbaek reporting on the Spanish Civil War (*AoR* 243/*ÄdW* 1:277) and (Jakob) Rosner working as the "Hieronymus"[48] of the Comintern (*ÄdW* 2:206–209)—not only sound a recurring leitmotiv of the book's query. They are also integral to the epic's sustained self-reflexivity. The question of the modern epic's possibility also structures the book's times, including the curious temporality of the narration itself.

Die Ästhetik des Widerstands's narration of events from the context of the antifascist resistance from 1937 to 1945 is overlaid with the narrator's path to becoming a writer. While the turning points of this process, along with the narrator himself, are all embedded in the epic's narrated time, what is especially curious about this thread's arch is that the autodiegetic narrator—in accordance with Weiss's process-oriented conception of expressive totality discussed above—never once treats the tale as written. Anticipating a zero-point in his prospective account of the execution of his friends Heilmann and Coppi, along with other members of the Red Orchestra (*Rote Kapelle*), in Berlin-Plötzensee in December 1942, he predicts that his "hand would become lame on the paper" (*ÄdW* 3:267), thereby holding out until the very end on the feasibility of the tale that has unfolded before readers' eyes on Weiss's thousand pages. This curiosity has led to the necessity of distinguishing between the narrator as a figure in the novel (the *Roman-Ich*) from that (same) narrator who is for all practical purposes the story's source (its *Ich-Autor*), anchored outside the novel's diegetic time in a future the former only ever anticipates and which can be considered identical to Weiss's own time and perspective.[49] Weiss scholar Burkhardt Lindner, who introduced this useful distinction between the autodiegetic and heterodiegetic roles played by the narrator, has subjected the two-tiered temporality of Weiss's construction and the irritations it can engender to sustained analysis.[50] These include points of contiguity and difference between the narrator's auto- and heterodiegetic roles, a relationship Weiss orchestrates in a cunning approach to modern epic form.

To grasp it, one must take a step back to reconsider *Die Ästhetik*'s narrator in view of the scholarship's assessments. In the spirit and practice of *Die Ästhetik* itself, the strongest approaches can be taken up to mark possibilities in the spectrum of interpretation. For starters, the book's two-dimensional temporal structure is not terribly novel. Focusing on the fictional tale of the embedded narrator's rise to authorship, one arrives readily at the not unfamiliar genre of the bildungsroman of the artist, as highlighted by Weiss scholars Jochen Vogt and Michael Hofmann. The former not only stresses *Die Ästhetik*'s literary-historical provenance in this way, he also stakes claims for Weiss's developmentally achieved "epic integration" of disparate and contradictory elements.[51] Indeed, *Die Ästhetik*'s structure evokes the most notorious bildungsroman of all: G. W. F. Hegel's *Phänomenologie des Geistes* (*Phenomenology of Spirit*), the two-tiered temporality of which featured its embedded protagonist—in changing guises of consciousness, self-consciousness, reason, and spirit—undertaking a perilous journey of doubt, "or more precisely one of despair," the outcome of which could not be known to it in the process.[52] In some analogy to Hegel's spirit—which Adorno proposed to read as social labor (*gesellschaftliche Arbeit*)[53]—*Die Ästhetik*'s narrator makes all manner of developmental advances that readers can interpret in light of the whole, even if the narrator is never presented as fully recuperating them for himself. On Hegelian terms, the autodiegetic narrator's advances hold *an sich* (i.e., *für uns*) and are thus apprehensible by readers, but not yet real for the embedded narrator (*an und für sich*).[54] In other words, self-consciousness is projected as a goal, but its would-be wisdom is not absolute: it remains an open cleft. In fact, as suggested above with regard to the narrator's confrontation with his mother's demise, any pretense to such recuperation would only feign totality's unachievable closure. *Die Ästhetik* decisively refrains from this. As a result, in contrast to the retrospection to which Hegelian dialectics—in its embrace of totality recuperated—confines wisdom, the cognitive and practical orientation of Weiss's highly motivated narrator is directed toward the future as well as the past. His anticipatory comportment—reflected in the recurring question as to the modern epic's feasibility, which often works like a Brechtian alienation effect to interrupt the narrative's flow and our absorption into it—contributes to *Die Ästhetik*'s self-reflexivity, pausing and resetting its rhythms for readers to see, appreciate, or question, even challenge, its inner workings.[55] In his benchmark study *Ästhetische Erfahrung in der historischen Krise*, Michael Hofmann has contextualized the novel's self-reflexivity in the tradition of transcendental literature to explain how Weiss, who has his narrator foreground and meet the representational challenges of his activity, delivers a thoroughgoing account of the conditions of *Die Ästhetik*'s possibility.[56] Indeed, Hofmann reconstructs the developmental stages thereof in affirmation of Weiss's fiction.[57] In so doing, his influential study lays out what can also be considered *Die Ästhetik*'s generosity: an engaging blueprint for emancipation, Weiss's fiction offers no less for Hofmann than parameters for the practice of freedom beyond domination.[58]

By focusing on the fiction of the narrator's becoming a writer within Weiss's larger historical tale, Hofmann's interpretation—like Vogt's—navigates the terrain of the book as the literary-aesthetic accomplishment that it is. At the same time, the narrator's story—and these two interpretations thereof—speak less directly to how *Weiss* came to write it. This transpires in fact at a different level, which *Die Ästhetik*, as Lindner puts it, "performs."[59] Such an approach, which Lindner has also provocatively addressed in terms of Weiss's "falsification" of his own biography, adopts a more skeptical view of the accomplishments of the fiction.[60] Mindful of the overlaps and differences between Weiss and the autodiegetic narrator, Lindner's work distinguishes between the book's real and fictional construction, zeroing in on the ways in which Weiss's own work clearly differs from that of *Die Ästhetik*'s narrator.[61] Lindner thus exposes and interrogates what I described in the preceding paragraph as the book's generosity as a ruse.[62] As revealing as Lindner's approach is and as much as it adds to our understanding of Weiss's work, it is less clear that the ruse is as dangerous as Lindner implies. Nor need Weiss's own work be pitted against that of the narrator. Even where the former is different from and larger than the latter, the narrator's labor is also Weiss's own.

Further textual analysis substantiates the claim that the power and generosity of Weiss's fiction prevails over and against its alleged masquerade. The status of book's core question invites a relevant clarification. "How could all this be depicted, I wondered. . . . The form would be monstrous, would cause dizziness. It would let people sense how inadequate the description of the shortest stretch of road would be by opening the multivalence of every direction taken" (*AoR* 112/*ÄdW* 1:130). What could be irritating here is that the heterodiegetic role of the narrator is already delivering an answer to the question he poses autodiegetically. In fact, this answer squares so well with Weiss's own that it has been taken as a positive moment of the epic's self-reflexivity.[63] The narrator's expression of such a project's anticipated execution in the subjunctive is characteristic. A feigned question? It seems one could argue this, namely that the path of despair is as fabricated here as in Hegel, in light of each tale's eventual completion. Yet I take this in neither case to be true. For starters, one can speculate—against any opposition of the imaginative to the real—that the despair dramatized in the respective narratives of the *Phenomenology* and *Die Ästhetik* is doubtlessly each author's own. Such speculation aside, it is far from a banal consideration to note Weiss's publication of *Die Ästhetik* as a work-in-progress in separate volumes over the course of six years. Weiss thus earnestly embarked on a process the end of which was not in sight, which is to suggest that the guiding question of *Die Ästhetik*'s feasibility was open to its author as well.[64] The publishing choice, in other words, came at a great risk, since Weiss's own anticipations—along with those of the narrator across all three volumes—aspired to, but could not pronounce, let alone control the narrative's orchestration prior to its actual completion.[65]

Other interminglings of author and narrator—implausible within the logic of the book's narrated time—can be read as suggestive self-reflections of the epic work as a whole. Thus, when the narrator relates his family's nomadic biography in the first volume prior to more express articulations of his becoming a writer later in the book, his considerations indicate Weiss's own confrontation with his material:

> Neither my mother nor any chronicler had ever set about depicting the old-fashioned fairy-tale quality of this milieu [in her native Strasbourg], there had been no trace of homeyness [*Heimischsein*], of security [*Geborgenheit*], my mother and her sisters had begun earning their livelihood as young girls, they drifted apart, never got together again, the changing places, the travels, the arrivals in strange cities *were linked not to epic impressions* but to the question of whether a job could be found here. (*AoR* 115, my emphasis/*ÄdW* 1:134)

Characteristic of the narrator's curious ability to put himself in other places and even others' minds—the perspectival shift is especially palpable in the adverb "here"—the passage suggests a tension between the practical exigencies of nomadic life and any epic sensitivity. The narrator associates the latter with that tradition of prose writing "from *Wilhelm Meister* to *Buddenbrooks*" (ibid.) modeled on property ownership, and later describe such works as exponents of the "individualized novel" (*AoR* 160/*ÄdW* 1:185). This indicates that no generic differentiation of the epic and novel is being advanced in the passage itself. Yet while the narrator denies his mother the epic sensitivity in question, the very next page of his own prose confirms that "books, people, pictures" were "the solidities in a life that otherwise knew only unsteadiness" (*AoR* 116/*ÄdW* 1:135) to confirm the problem-oriented work-in-progress that is seeking epic form for its content. This will demand innovations of the kind already operative in the first volume, including the collectivizing reading of Kafka's *The Castle* as a proletarian novel and the individualizing reading of Neukrantz's *Barricades in Wedding*—"the first work that made me wish to set down something myself, make something visible" (*AoR* 159/*ÄdW* 1:183)—by which the narrator subverts conventional canonical categories.

Third, the convergence of Weiss's own work with that of his heterodiegetic narrator and the partial overlap between the biographical stations of the autodiegetic narrator and Weiss himself warrant greater scrutiny of the kind that can explain Weiss's alterations. On this score, the term "wishful biography" (*Wunschbiographie*) would not be so bad—the aspirations of Weiss's fiction are inconceivable without the category of the wish—if it had not been turned against Weiss as an individual. But it also misses the point of Weiss's use of the narrator as a vehicle for collective fiction. Two key aspects of Weiss's estrangement of his own biography in the figure of the narrator point in this direction. Both are symbolically charged. The first is the often-cited birth date of the narrator, November 8, 1917 (*AoR* 25, 221/*ÄdW* 1:31–32, 252), one year before Weiss's own and the night of the October Revolution on the Julian calendar. The symbolism elevates the narrator to a representative of the aspirations of an entire class.[66] Second, in confirmation of the fictional narrator's separation from Weiss, including the Jewish background of the latter's father, the non-Jewish narrator's mother is told by her landlady to remove herself from a bench in Varnsdorf, which was not meant for Jews (*AoR* 164/*ÄdW* 1:189). She forestalls her son's protest, however, explaining to him that "after being called a Jew several times because of her dark hair, she had declared herself a Jew, which, however, made it difficult for her and Father to find another apartment" in the town (*AoR* 164/*ÄdW* 1:189).[67] This self-identification—as a play with fiction in the fiction—not only is driven by the empathy with victims ascribed to Weiss's entire oeuvre.[68] It also sets up the narrator's reckoning with his mother's witnessing the Shoah in the third volume referenced above.[69]

Weiss's additions to historical fact in the literary remediation thereof lend *Die Ästhetik* great force. The book's ruse is not so much a problem as a strength that allows for both the epic's dramatic effects—including readers' absorption into them—and possibilities for discerning the details of Weiss's own artifice. As the work collapses and reconstitutes aesthetic distance, it is seldom if ever impossible to establish one's whereabouts as a reader. Indeed, *Die Ästhetik*'s epic orientation in and toward space, immediately highlighted in the chapter following the narrator's reconstruction of aspects of his mother's biography (*AoR* 117–123/*ÄdW* 1:135–143), serves as the basis for its further distinction from the novelistic genre.[70] Martin Rector's previously cited "Örtlichkeit und Phantasie" addresses space as the central dimension of human perception of Weiss's book.[71] Setting the work's spatial imagination against its orchestrated temporalities, Rector takes issue with the implications of Vogt and others' references to the genre of the bildungsroman and its concomitant emphasis on temporal development. Underscoring *Die Ästhetik*'s topical and topographic tendencies, Rector paves the way for its assessment as a modern epic in the sense defined by this study. Suggestively arguing that the book's spaces are linked on the model of a network (*Vernetzung*),[72] Rector, in his criticism of Vogt, nonetheless overstates the opposition between spatial and temporal organization to the detriment of grasping their interrelation in Weiss's work. Contrasting the constitution of *Die Ästhetik* in principle with that of the integrative bildungsroman, Rector contends that its basic movement is not successive but iterative. It unfolds, he writes, not via "the epic 'and then' but rather an always newly restarting [*immer wieder neu ansetzendes*] 'and yet' [*und doch*]. That is the formula for the resistance in question."[73] What Rector has described is indeed neither associable with the epic of yore nor especially with most bildungsromans, but is certainly part and parcel of the modern epic's motivated dialectics—and *Die Ästhetik*'s unwieldy traverse of space as well as time. Nuances aside, there are fewer contradictions between these scholarly approaches than there are ways of accommodating them in view of *Die Ästhetik*'s expansive optics. Taken together, the insights Vogt, Hofmann, Lindner, and Rector offer permit further elaboration of the epic narrator's role in two interrelated directions. The narrator's function as a vehicle for a larger collectivity and the book's advancement of writing as a force of production present crucial modifications of the novelistic genre of the educated bourgeoisie. In so doing, they prove integral to Weiss's assertion of modern epic narration as resistance and reveal the potentials of *Die Ästhetik*'s democraticization of epic form.

The perplexities engendered by Weiss's narrator turn largely on his oscillation between the autodiegetic and heterodiegetic roles described above. In neither is he particularly individualized or granted much personal psychological depth.[74] In the former role, Weiss has him rather recede into the background of the events he depicts, while in the latter he almost looms over them. As *Die Ästhetik*'s author maintained, the character, though neither fixed nor unified, serves as the "unifying center of the whole book,"[75] its focal point (not its perspective),[76] in some contrast to the more memorable agents therein. Commentators were accordingly quick to emphasize the narrator's role as a "point of coordination" (*Koordinationspunkt*),[77] a witness, chronicler and mediator (*Vermittler*),[78] a chorus,[79] and even a medium (*Medium*) for the whole,[80] in which, as Weiss himself noted, all of the contrasts and differences of opinion were refracted (*NB* 810). Every passage cited hitherto in this chapter comes to readers via this narrator, whose heterodiegetic role unfolds from the first pages as a seemingly omniscient (*auktorialer*) narrator, even as his own ground-level perspective as an embedded character is prone to blindness: "It was normal to get your bearings blindly, to wangle every bit of information on the sly" (*AoR* 130/*ÄdW* 1:151), a predicament that compels the time of action to yield to the time of reflection in the narrator's mediating activity (cf. *ÄdW* 3:261).

The facilitation of the narrator's mediating function goes hand in hand with his recession behind what he relates.[81] Weiss's technique strongly echoes a trajectory of the modern epic genre analyzed by Franco Moretti. For Moretti, it is the removal of the would-be hero from the epic's sphere of action that enabled Goethe in *Faust* and Joyce in *Ulysses* to rediscover totality in and for modernity.[82] But neither Faust nor Leopold Bloom is linked to either tale's narration in the emphatic way that Weiss's centripetal character is. This may make him—and his seemingly surreal abilities to fly over Berlin (*AoR* 79–81/*ÄdW* 1:93–95), enjoy focalized access to other characters' interior monologues, and deliver sweeping accounts of historical time—appear more ethereally unreal than they. While the unusual expansiveness of the character's consciousness[83] has generated considerable discussion in the scholarship, the narrator himself characterizes his function in telling ways, from the pointed anticipation of his future role as a "blank page" to be written by collective experiences (*AoR* 268/*ÄdW* 1:305) through his self-description as a register and bearer of his own cultural network (*ÄdW* 2:68) and his role a "messenger, medium, assistant" (*ÄdW* 2:204) to others in a reference to his activity in the Swedish underground, to his inheritance of Bertolt Brecht's project for the Engelbrekt drama (*ÄdW* 2:176). Facilitating his turn to production, his collaboration with the playwright leads to a crystallization of his self-conception as a "chronicler conveying collective thought" (*ÄdW* 2:306). Such points of contiguity between the character and his narrating role stress the collective dimension of his writerly activity: "As if dictated to him through a chorus [. . . his] consciousness was filled with the process of writing" (ibid.). The position achieved not only establishes the point of departure for the third volume in which, according to Weiss, aesthetics is no longer defined through speaking about artworks or offering analysis, but rather—after the means of expression have been conquered—"expresses itself directly" (*NB* 817, 781; *schlägt sich direkt nieder*). It also warrants Jochen Vogt's characterization of the narrator as the emergent consciousness of a class, a quality that sets *Die Ästhetik*'s mediator outside the framework of the bourgeois novel of education.[84]

An additionally suggestive account of Weiss's narrator grasps him as an angel of history. Perceiving him to "grow wings," Ursula Heukenkamp has claimed that this "persistent companion, comrade and messenger resembles an angel."[85] While this leads Heukenkamp to Walter Benjamin's famous commentary on Paul Klee's *Angelus Novus* in the former's "Theses on the Philosophy of History," her aperçu can be substantiated via Weiss's own remediating activity in the epic. During his stay in Paris in the fall of 1938 between the end of the Spanish Civil War and his arrival in Sweden, the narrator makes a return visit to the Louvre. The last impression he retains from "an infinite series of pictures" being packed away on the eve of imminent war was that of a flying St. Ranier (*ÄdW* 2:40–41). The intermedial reference is to *The Blessed Ranieri Frees the Poor from a Florentine Jail* by Stefano di Giovanni, also known as Sassetta, as the Renaissance painter is called in Weiss's text. The narrator's ekphrasis of the painting, depicted in figure 5, is characteristically meticulous. Rendering perception in real time in the manner of the Pergamon Altar's remediation, the narrator's description is interrupted by the evacuation of the museum under way. Yet Weiss's juxtaposition creates an interesting visual interplay between the painting's subject matter captured in its title and the museum visitors being ushered out by Louvre attendants. As the latter's calls and bells sound through the exhibition halls, the narrator notes that this little painting, measuring about seventeen by twenty-five inches and modest in aspiration compared to Géricault's furious work, "suddenly took up more space within me" (*ÄdW* 2:41). Without yet being about to pinpoint the image's significance, the narrator, hastened along by an attendant, depicts his retreat from the scene in the following way: "Turned backwards, my gaze fixed on [Sassetta's] horizontal flyer, I distanced myself [from this picture], sensing relief, levity [*Leichtigkeit*], already ladders were being set up, the disassembly began, we were thrown out into the mobilization, into the expectation of war. Hang him, hang him, the loudspeakers roared on Monday, in a familiar way, as the gang leader [*Bandenführer*] stirred up animosity against [Czechoslovakian president Edvard] Beneš [*Benesch*]" (*ÄdW* 2:41–42). In a complete inversion of the deliverance facilitated by Ranier's angelic powers, Weiss's narrating angel is no guardian, but rather himself expelled from the temple (*ÄdW* 2:40), his only temporary source of protection (*Schutz*) and stability (*Halt*) into a greater exposure, in a movement echoing that of Benjamin's *Angelus Novus*. The fast turns of Weiss's prose in the sequence create a sharp contrast between the reassuring effect St. Ranier has on the narrator and Europe's rapidly deteriorating political situation. In light thereof, it seems odd that the narrator—whose despairing uncertainty abounds in the next chapter—claims any sense of relief. Whereas art can have no immediately implementable effect on life outside the museum, Weiss's unlikely inscription of the narrator into this chorus of angels alongside Sassetta, Klee, and Benjamin's is significant vis-à-vis an imperiled Europe on the eve of war. If he figures at all as an angel of history, this derives not simply from the victims-oriented morality that Heukenkamp associates with his angelic characteristics.[86] Ranier's flight serves as no ethereal illusion, but as a subjective anchor of hope wrested from the despair of the existing situation. In a reversal of the directionality Benjamin ascribed to Klee's *Angelus Novus*, whose gaze affixes to the past while being hurled forward by the storm of putative progress,[87] the narrator gazes via Sassetta's angelic Ranieri into a future from which the present repels him. Yet by anchoring this view within himself, his struggle for survival enjoys an ideational foothold: if Hercules is the protagonists' lodestar of action, Ranier indicates the direction thereof, its

Figure 5. Stefano di Giovanni (Sassetta), *The Blessed Ranieri Frees the Poor from a Florentine Jail* (1437–1444)

social content as well as its future-oriented aspirations. In conjunction with the narrator's function as the book's medium, the remediation of Sassetta's painting contributes to the transformation of the epic into a field of concretized hope at work.

In such ways, the deflation of the narrator as a person and the remediation of artworks that occur through him as a medium work in tandem to open the epic field to further experiment and invite narrative pluralization. A second component of Weiss's democraticization of epic form is facilitated by the narrator's figuration of writing as a force of production, integral to *Die Ästhetik*'s labor-oriented approach to culture. The narrator repeatedly focuses on writing as a craft or instrument (*Handwerk* at *ÄdW* 1:183, 3:30, 134; *Instrument* at *ÄdW* 2:306). This tool proves as crucial to culture's appropriation as it is to the book's conception of narration as resistance. As indicated in the epigraph to this section, *Die Ästhetik* also grasps the struggle against fascism as a struggle for expression. As explained in the previous section, Weiss's *Ästhetik* lays out the relations of cultural production into which expression's linguistic tool is being inserted in order for it to wield fully its endemic force: "When artists from a middle-class background [*aus dem Bürgertum*] expressed their disgust [with society], their non-belonging, they remained stuck in their background by digging in individual pain; but by writing they got closer to the people who viewed their activity as an unnecessary, luxurious extravagance" (*AoR* 162/*ÄdW* 1:186). On the one hand, the passage frames writing as a technology with a teleology of its own, independent of a writer's background. On the other, it immediately inscribes the tool's neutrality into an alternative teleology that clearly gravitates to the cause of the narrator's "people." A politically determined codification? In the same chapter, the narrator claims that the protagonists' "efforts to conquer art and literature could have no other purpose [*Wahrheit*] than to strengthen the togetherness of people who had so far sensed only their isolation. If we wanted to flee to the intrinsic value of an artwork, we risked winding up in a vacuum" (*AoR* 159–160/*ÄdW* 1:184).

The question as to whether Weiss is overdetermining the force's teleology turns on a larger claim about the directionality of society's productive forces. As with *Die Ästhetik*'s labor-oriented approach to culture, the issue of writing's inherent directionality corresponds to an important thread of Adorno's *Aesthetic Theory*, which underscores the entwinement of aesthetic and social forces of production: "The aesthetic force of production is the same as that of productive labor [*der nützlichen Arbeit*] and has the same teleology; and what may be called aesthetic relations of production—all that in which the productive force is embedded and in which it is active—are sedimentations or imprintings of social relations of production" (*AT* 5/16).[88] As Peter Uwe Hohendahl has most recently argued, it is precisely Adorno's conception of "all artworks . . . as the result of human labor under changing historical and cultural conditions" that makes *Aesthetic Theory*, in its materialist aspect, such an important and relevant work for twenty-first-century aesthetics.[89] At the same time, an ambivalence hovers about the passage cited, which turns on the notion of productive or useful labor. While one may envision "use-value" rather than exchange-value in Adorno's reference to *nützliche Arbeit*, the teleology the two forces share—reading the passage within the context of *Aesthetic Theory*'s larger argumentative framework—culminates in the commodification they suffer amid capital's valorization of their use. Weiss knows that the independent teleology his narrator ascribes to writing cannot unfold automatically. It is no neutral question to be waited out. Hence *Die Ästhetik*'s subjective strain: concertedly inserting the productive force in question into alternative relations of cultural production, the narrator advances the value writing can enjoy this side of commodity production. Resonating in motivation, hope, the quest for survival, and all those aspects of intentionality that Adorno believed were either irrelevant to or interfered with the successful execution of any artistic work and that Weiss captures in the overarching titular motif of resistance itself, the subjective factor is something *Die Ästhetik* emphatically affirms.[90]

The narrator's conception of writing as a force of production provides the respective focal points of this chapter's final two sections. First, writing's insertion into alternative relations of production renders service to the book's multidimensional practices of orientation. In *Die Ästhetik*'s development of an aesthetic of cognitive mapping, writing's use-value can be measured according to needs: the need for spatial, temporal, and political orientation as well as the epic expression thereof. To such ends, Weiss's assertion of the modern epic genre gains traction through the book's reliance on and remediation of art itself. In pursuit of this thread, "Media, Maps, and Networks" addresses the function of *Die Ästhetik*'s intermedial characteristics as an additional component of Weiss's solution to the challenges of modern epic form.

Second, in emphasizing the subjective motivation of artistic production without gluing it to the personhood of any single individual, writing—including that of *Die Ästhetik* itself—is not subject to any authorial monopoly.[91] The broad metapolitical claim on art and literature's roles in "strengthening togetherness" rather mandates precisely the kind of openness that the book's critical analysis of political unity's enforcement found lacking. In conjunction with the narrator's depersonalized role as a medium rather than an authority, *Die Ästhetik* makes it clear that the force of production in question—writing, voice, self-expression—is a tool to be shared for its humanizing potential to be real. The narrator's conception of writing as such a force of collectivized production thus serves as the theoretical nexus of the epic's polyphonic turn. Through the narrator and emergent conarrator Bischoff, the voices of the vanquished resonate posthumously after and against their historical elimination by fascism and subsequent erasure in what is called cultural memory. Telling their story not only constitutes an unlikely pyrrhic victory against their erstwhile victors and the finality of the latter's crimes. The polyphonic means by which it is accomplished confer the resistant potentials of narration to posterity for subsequent appropriation, elaboration, and expansion. In so doing, *Die Ästhetik* speaks to futures beyond its purview.

Media, Maps, and Networks

> Our relationship to art, to fine art, music, literature, is nothing other than some inventory we have within ourselves, some reservoir of things that constantly enables us to actualize our experiences, isn't it?
>
> —Peter Weiss in conversation with Burkhardt Lindner

In epic expansion of the literary medium's optics, *Die Ästhetik*'s extensive interaction with and production of media, maps, and networks build a new Hemeroskopeion for dwarfs. The characterization derives from the ancient name of the Spanish city of Denia, on the western perimeter of the Mediterranean (*AoR* 286/*ÄdW* 1:325). As the International Brigades are being disbanded, the narrator visits a hilltop overlooking the Spanish city with Lindbaek in search of ruins of the Greek temple alleged to have once stood there. They attribute the foundation of the city to seafaring Phocaeans, whose trade and barter must have benefited for a time from the fortuitous position of their settlement. The narrator swiftly appropriates the Greek name for "watchtower" in his ensuing remediation of Géricault, Delacroix, and Goya's paintings: "In measuring their strength against transience, [these artists] outlined small standpoints, observation posts, setting up and fortifying a Hemeroskopeion" (*AoR* 307/*ÄdW* 1:349). While the motif of the dwarf recurs in different ways across *Die Ästhetik*'s pages, its use here marks the perspective not of seafaring adventurers intent on economic exploitation, but that of those below for whom the metaphorical watchtower is being erected as part of *Die Ästhetik*'s countercartography: "What dwarfs we were," the narrator muses en route to the Louvre in the "overwhelming" city of Paris, the next station of his temporary exile (*ÄdW* 2:39).[92] Although the scope and movements of *Die Ästhetik*'s optics are as multifaceted as Oskar Negt and Alexander Kluge's extension of Brecht's function-oriented conception of realism discussed in the preceding chapter[93] and thus do not admit of being captured by any single metaphor, Hemeroskopeion provides a key example of the breadth with which Weiss resets epic through the remediation of its source materials.

Media, maps, and networks constitute integral components of *Die Ästhetik*'s remediating work. Weiss's book outfits each of these terms with its own expanse. As discussed in the previous chapter, Fredric Jameson has championed critical artistic attempts to advance orientation in and vis-à-vis the unrepresentable totality of society in reference to an aesthetic of cognitive mapping. In conformity with Jameson's conception thereof, the function of Weiss's media term is made explicit in the narrator's self-description of his role as medium and mediator. The term "media" is also privileged in *Die Ästhetik*'s comparative references to the arts. Leaving the future task of his artistic work as yet undetermined in his Spanish summer of 1938, the narrator remarks that the "only thing that had set in was a timbre which made it appear that I would be able to express all thoughts and experiences. Words or images, whatever was needed, would be their media" (*AoR* 268/*ÄdW* 1:305). A similarly ecumenical conception of the value of artistic media in their plurality is sounded in Münzenberg's recollection of the relationship between politics and art in the avant-garde movement: "We did not need to demand that art, which had taken on the task of overthrowing mental reality, also had to have a political mission. [Art] delivered that to which its media were best suited" (*ÄdW* 2:62). Where *Die Ästhetik* presents a principled openness vis-à-vis artistic media as the primary sources of its research into aesthetic resistance, the telos of its remediation remains, in the final product, the printed word of the literary medium.

For this reason, none of *Die Ästhetik*'s maps are literal, but concern literary practices of spatial and temporal location. Its narrative maps can be identified on the level of its macrostructure, as Martin Rector has pointed out regarding the division of the book's chapters and subvolumes by locality:[94] Berlin and then Varnsdorf feature in the first half of the first volume, while

Spain is the site of its second half. Paris and then Stockholm feature in the second volume, whereas the third's first half continues mostly in Alingsås as well as Stockholm and then in its second half returns, via the narrator's reliance on Bischoff, to Berlin. Narrative maps also emerge out of the aesthetic activities of characters' self-localizations. Few chapters fail to foreground their milieus, whether these be interiors, as in the focus on the kitchen, or the cities mapped via the identification of street names, house numbers, bridges, and even public elevators. Interesting counterpoints to the descriptions of rooms highlighted in Rector and Jameson's accounts of *Die Ästhetik*'s spatial practices are given in Stockholm.[95] For example, on his walks the character Stahlmann absorbs the city into the "epic he carried within himself" (*ÄdW* 3:97). Like Coppi's father in Berlin,[96] Stahlmann suffocates amid his confinement to interiors in the underground resistance and longs for expanses of the kind he enjoys on Stockholm's Väster bridge (*ÄdW* 3:94). In a related contrast of opposed poles, Bischoff, arrested as an illegal shortly after her arrival in Stockholm, takes her first stroll around the Swedish capital accompanied by a policewoman on the eve of her (ultimately aborted) deportation to Nazi Germany (*ÄdW* 2:77–84). The chapter not only plays through perspectival contrasts of the policewoman and the communist, oversight and blindness, publicity and clandestinity, and freedom and incarceration in remarkable ways. It also features an elevator ride at the Stockholm locks between Lake Mälaren and the Baltic Sea (*ÄdW* 2:83–84). *Die Ästhetik* regularly localizes with such detail and the importance of such sites to Weiss's epic realism is confirmed by the *Notizbücher*'s inclusion of photographs (see figures 6 and 7). Veridical touchstones of modern epic objectivity, they are not included for their own sake and, like the interiors, are never described on the static model of ownership; rather, they function as points of orientation amid the migrations of members of the resistance living "from moment to moment" (*AoR* 28/*ÄdW* 1:35; *auf Abbruch*). Moreover, bridges and locks, like the canals featured in the photographs Weiss collected in his *Notizbücher*, concretely disclose the multifold significance of the epic's networks.[97]

Die Ästhetik mobilizes networks in at least three ways. On the story's most basic level, network connotes that system of underground relations connecting members of the international antifascist resistance to one another against the global net threatening to engulf them from without (*AoR* 117/*ÄdW* 1:137). Thus Funk (Herbert Wehner), who also goes by the pseudonym Svensson, toils away in his Stockholm interior mapping out the connections of the resistance—"from out of encrypted names and dates he began to put a blueprint together . . . drawing bundles of radial lines from himself to those below"—to see what could be accomplished (*ÄdW* 3:54). On a second level, network designates the web (*ÄdW* 2:255; *Gewebe*) of aesthetic culture's reach, both in the broad sense of the human aesthetic faculty's perspectival points of contrast and poles of orientation in sensory fields as well as the emotional and symbolic poles rendered through the narrator's extensive

Blick über Stockholm. Im Hintergrund die Altstadt, in der Mitte die Väster-Brücke, vorn rechts Lilla Essingen

Figure 6. Väster Bridge, Stockholm (*NB* 811)

Der »Maria«-Fahrstuhl an der Schleuse

Figure 7. The Maria Lift in Stockholm's Slussen District (*NB* 474–475). Bischoff's elevator? The likelier site of Bischoff's lookout is Stockholm's Katarina Lift, which was operational in 1939. Excerpts from Peter Weiss, *Notizbücher 1971–1980*, 2 vols., 811, 474–475.

engagement with artworks. The political resistance's orchestration of its actions and the narrator's refunctionalization of art are indicative of the relations *Die Ästhetik* establishes for human labor and reveal "network" to be the appropriate term for what the protagonists tend to describe in terms of a genetic totality. Their claim that totality—here a comprehensive set of guidelines for their thought, orientation, and action—"had to be newly created" (*AoR* 46, syntax corrected/*ÄdW* 1:55) concerns the realignment of culture in a network of their own making.[98] Generating the relations of practical political orientation and artistic reception and production, the construction of such a network is akin to establishing an "apparatus of reproduction" the populace did not otherwise possess (*AoR* 308/*ÄdW* 1:351). With the emergence of a cultural network in this sense, *Die Ästhetik*'s counterarchive is transformed via its internalization by individuals into a living archive and operative register within: Bischoff and the narrator represent the political and artistic wings of such activity respectively (cf. *ÄdW* 2:112; *ÄdW* 2:315, 68). Whereas *Die Ästhetik* narrates the appropriation of networks by individuals in a linear fashion, it also invites the actualization of epic networks according to a variety of spatiotemporal logics, as Martin Rector's appeal to *Die Ästhetik*'s nonlinear model of networking (*Vernetzung*) suggests and as the much differently constituted network-character of Alexander Kluge's epic prose would confirm in the modern epic's subsequent course.[99]

Against this backdrop of *Die Ästhetik*'s robust work with media, maps, and networks, two specific dimensions of the narrator's function of medium and mediator further demonstrate Weiss's response to the challenges of modern epic form. As noted above, *Die Ästhetik*'s remediating practices assimilate all of its source materials—regardless of their own medial character—into the monomedial literary epic. Intertextual references to other literary works are often related to the narrator's self-referential tale of becoming an author. Intermedial references to nonliterary works of art such as paintings and architecture tend to relate to the historical tale he is seeking to shape. Such transformations of material from one media source to another constitute medial transpositions in the sense described by Irina Rajewsky.[100] Largely narrativizing its source works, *Die Ästhetik* incorporates nonliterary materials into its pages, drawing on them for the sake of literary expression. Medial transpositions can then either take on a life of their own in the literary medium, as in the flight of the narrator's epic language at the end of the first volume, which spiritedly departs from the series of paintings discussed there (*AoR* 317/*ÄdW* 1:361), or can sustain prolonged interaction between the literary remediation under way and the source medium, as in the returns of the narrator's ekphrases to paintings' details, which condition their literary interpretation and use. Where remediations evoke techniques of nonliterary media, as in the narrator's use of abrupt juxtapositions and contrast, they resemble Rajewsky's narrower definition of intermedial references that establish an interplay between two media, even where only one is present.[101] The two aspects of the epic's remediating work that I have in mind are both integral to *Die Ästhetik*'s larger project of cognitive mapping but deliver orientation through different means with distinct effects. The first concerns the status of literary montage mobilized in the narrator's relation of his work with Brecht on the Engelbrekt drama to the narration of World War II, whereas the second pertains to the narrator's reliance on artworks to describe otherwise unrepresentable events in the narrated time of the story.

At the center of Weiss's epic lies the long Engelbrekt sequence featuring the narrator's collaboration with Bertolt Brecht at the outset of World War II. Engelbrekt was a leader of a peasant revolt in fifteenth-century Sweden that attracted Brecht's attention during his Stockholm exile. In describing the fictional collaboration, the narrator remediates a scant fragment of a plan for a play into an extensive piece of prose. As addressed by the scholarship, the multifold importance of the sequence stems from its facilitation of the narrator's explicit turn from the reception to the production of art,[102] his increasing familiarization with his Swedish milieu,[103] its implications for understanding Weiss's relationship to Brecht and Brechtian aesthetics,[104] the delivery—in the narrator's transposition of Brecht's dramatic fragment—of what one commentator has described as a novel within the novel,[105] and, finally, through this last, the self-reflection of *Die Ästhetik* as a dramatic epic in its own right.[106] As the narrator relates his work with Brecht on their project for the theater, *Die Ästhetik*'s intertextual references merge with both medial transpositions and intermedial references to create a formidable epic prose: "Never before," he notes, "had the treatment of an artistic problem presented itself to me under such unrelenting antagonism as in this winter [of 1939–1940], never before was it clearer how the artistic action [*Handlung*] played itself out right there where societal forces confronted one another most intensely" (*ÄdW* 2:213). As this passage suggests, the work on a drama for Engelbrekt is closely associated with the autodiegetic narrator's present. As indicated by the narrator's commentary on Picasso, the attempt to avail oneself of aesthetic orientation and expression had to be undertaken precisely in the moment of its greatest unlikelihood: "During war one can only speak about war when the task is to fathom its causes" (*ÄdW* 2:193), *Die Ästhetik*'s Brecht proclaims. The Engelbrekt drama was precisely one such attempt to investigate aspiration and defeat and thereby "contribute to knowledge of the irregularities, ups-and-downs, gaps, and leaps in the process of world revolution" (Brecht in *ÄdW* 2:234). While the task of Engelbrekt as an epic drama was to "do justice to the bifurcations and separations, contradictions and ambivalences of events" (*ÄdW* 2:177), Brecht himself, in his sweeping search for events' patterns, also despaired of finding explanations for "the catastrophe by which we were afflicted" in view of the incommensurability between his models, historical case studies, and the present crisis (*ÄdW* 2:257). This raises the stakes for his assistant's narration of the play, which continues the project Brecht jettisoned.

Whereas the narrator comes to regard Brecht's treatment of the Engelbrekt project as an occasion for the latter's exercises in style and experimentation with dramatic forms (*ÄdW* 2:213–214), his own report continues Brecht's cognitive interest in the material not simply by relating Engelbrekt's downfall near the end of *Die Ästhetik*'s second volume (*ÄdW* 2:306–310).[107] Cohen's and Tobias Mandel's commentaries have emphasized the fact that the Engelbrekt drama is not to be found—*pace* Gudrun Klatt's reference to *Die Ästhetik*'s inner novel—within its pages as a self-contained work of prose, but is rather interwoven with other material in an array of assemblies characteristic of *Die Ästhetik*'s intricate weaves.[108] A suggestive chapter from Weiss's quirky remediation of the dramatic fragment reveals the form of *Die Ästhetik*'s text to be more telling than the Engelbrekt thread in its isolation. "We found ourselves in a war on two fronts, followed Engelbrekt through the blowing snow, entrenched ourselves in our besieged city" (*ÄdW* 2:248), it begins, the snow of which appears to blur the very distinction between *Die Ästhetik*'s present and its fifteenth-century source story. In fact, what follows is a cross-cutting interplay between the narrated present of March 1940 and the narrated past of Engelbrekt's January 1436, in which the narrator's quick shifts between time-spaces at first make for disorienting reading, then reveal the entire chapter as an attempt to exploit parallels between Engelbrekt's plight and the resistance's own. The narrator's reference to the two fronts of the war—not its military, but its economic and the political aspects—are analogous to those Engelbrekt faced. Stockholm—owing to Sweden's at least partial compliance with Nazi demands—is besieged in both accounts. The consolidation of elites against Engelbrekt is mirrored in the increasing pressure on Swedish communists leading to the arson attack against the offices of the communist paper *Norrskensflamman* in Luleå (*ÄdW* 2:250). Characteristic of the narrator's weave of the two layers are passages constituting a kind of literary montage, for example: "Union leaders terrorized union representatives who were communist, with one communiqué after another they tried to force their exclusion. . . . While reactionary powers appeared to gain the upper hand, the representatives of democratic traditions mustered a counter-offensive. Engelbrekt, for the fourth time, set out for Stockholm, with peasant armies" (*ÄdW* 2:248). Or, still more sharply: "The workers of the city greeted the peasant soldiers. The ignition charges in the party building in Luleå were detonated" (*ÄdW* 2:252). The narrator's own mediating activity comes to the fore in such passages. While some commentators have attested to an opposition between montage and mediation,[109] others have associated *Die Ästhetik*'s use of such montage and related techniques with film.[110] In this light, the passages just cited constitute what Lugder Claßen and Jochen Vogt describe as parallel and contrastive montage techniques respectively.[111] While the narrator cites Brecht's appeal to the activity of writing as montage,[112] he also criticizes the playwright's tendency to conceal the difference between the product assembled and its source materials (*ÄdW* 2:272). Although Lindner levels this same critique against *Die Ästhetik*,[113] the narrator's description of the work on Engelbrekt allows both for the discernment of source materials—he lists the historians' accounts he has been studying on this same page—and maintains the separation of elements on the level of effect. The very character of the cuts between Engelbrekt and the narrated present both foreground their separation and entertain continuities, including parallels in antagonists' conspiracies and Engelbrekt's paradoxical relation to the people he led (*ÄdW* 2:255).[114] Differentiating and splicing together different times, the narrator's presentation compresses the epic's temporal dimension, analogous to the compression of space in Brecht's appeal to the use of the telescope to grasp disparate and distant connections.[115] In short, the techniques of a chapter that endures the Winter War in Europe's north between night and day, snow and fire, and the Soviet Union and Finland enhance the epic's direct sense for what is near and concrete (*Nähesinn*) and thereby the sense it can make of its narrated present.[116]

If the twenty-ninth chapter of volume 2 can be said to compress time via montage, a second technique of literary remediation in Weiss's epic constitutes its flip side: "Brecht could not let go of an image that we had come across, a medieval view of the city with an astronomical depiction of solar relations. . . . Brecht did not want to dispense with the cosmic phenomena, which, pointing to large spaces of time, contrasted with the revolutionary moment and at the same time anchored it within a continuity" (*ÄdW* 2:251). The inclusion of such a cosmic dimension points to *Die Ästhetik*'s epic expansion of time. The book's extension of its optics into what is far—its indirect senses (*Fernsinne*)—is facilitated by the literary remediation featured in the many detours the narrator takes around the direct depiction of events. The modern epic's key question as to "how all this [could] be depicted"—remediation's recurring segue—is frequently answered via recourse to other art. Obverses of montage's retrieval of the past to map the present, such detours reenlarge the present, situating it in the greater course of epic time.

The narrator spends less than a full year in Spain, yet its beginning already boded a "cosmic length of time" (*AoR* 185/*ÄdW* 1:211). His first visit to Brecht—on the island of Lidingö in the Stockholm archipelago, where Brecht is staying in volume 2—is prompted by the latter's interest in reports from the Spanish Civil War and the causes of the republican defeat. Where Lindner describes the character Branting's report as "traumatized language" and ascribes this to aspects of the narrator's own reconstruction,[117] the latter's response to Brecht's questions are couched—in what he relates heterodiegetically, not in what his character says to Brecht—in Pieter Brueghel the Elder's paintings *Dulle Griet* and *The Triumph of Death*, reproduced in the book Brecht is passing around the room (*ÄdW* 2:147–148). "Often I asked myself," the narrator relates to *Die Ästhetik*'s readers as he takes the book into his hands, "in what way the impressions of the war could be reproduced, they always lost, even by more exacting description, something of their essence" (*ÄdW* 2:149). In the face of such a challenge, the narrator's ekphrasis of the two paintings serves as the detour required to describe what happened in Spain: "Lured forth by the figure of the Megaira, all of that which was underlying erupted" onto the surface of Brueghel's images (ibid.). The ekphrasis—characteristically intense on two scant pages of the epic—speaks to two main aspects of the embedded narrator's report, which, stumbling about and self-interrupting like Branting's, notes both the insufficiency of idealistic brigadiers to imagine their defeat[118] as well as their repression of all those "uncanny" aspects of the Left's in-fights (*ÄdW* 2:150–151). In the narrator's commentary, Brueghel draws viewers into the paintings' multifold scenes, even allowing them to adopt the view of the patients the narrator treated during his work as a paramedic in Spain:

> Whoever found himself feverish from wounds was most likely to recognize the outbreak of a hellish domination, often we heard requests from those whose eyes had been shot out, whose arms or legs had been torn off to remove this animal, this goat, this owl, this nagging carp from his bedside. . . . Once the threshold into the unreal was overcome, the appearances reproduced by Brueghel assumed an immediate concreteness. (*ÄdW* 2:150)

While the aesthetic perception and imagination fueled by such surreal optics compensate for political idealism's insufficient fantasy, the full breadth of the "phantasmagorias of deceitfulness, betrayal, shamelessness, and outrages" as well as the "business of making rumors, deception, and intrigue" in Brueghel's scenes allude to practices on both sides of the war in Spain. The narrator exposes the effects thereof on the Left as a partial cause for its defeat, even as he suggests that the repression of anything upsetting trust in the leadership was unavoidable (*ÄdW* 2:150–151). With Brueghel's faces "scratched into the retina [*Netzhaut*] of his eye" (*ÄdW* 2:151), the narrator's mobilization of the paintings to think through what happened in Spain puts his inner network on exemplary display, while simultaneously demonstrating art's encapsulation of the continuities of larger patterns across historical time's expanses.

Die Ästhetik undertakes another important representational detour amid the narrator's struggle to process his mother's experiences and death. Even as he chastises himself for his inability to come to the aid of his mother or doubts ever being able to access what occurred to her, as discussed above, her very appearance—at the narrator's reunion with his parents at the beginning of volume 3—is already being committed to myth. At the end of the opening chapter there, her face, "large, gray, worn out by the images that had imposed themselves on it, a stone mask, the eyes blind on the fractured surface," is identified as the face of Gaea, the demoness of the earth from the Pergamon frieze with which the epic began (*ÄdW* 3:20). Swiftly converting his own experience into art, the narrator tenuously draws on Ancient Greek myth in order to confront effects of the Shoah. The context is scene for another curious mobilization of a piece of the European cultural tradition. Few taboos, we must realize by now, befall its multifold redeployment. With Hodann, the narrator turns to Albrecht Dürer's *Melencholia I* as a summa of one of *Die Ästhetik*'s most probing chapters. Torn between the "blindness" into which his thoughts of his deceased mother had driven him (*ÄdW* 3:123) and his father's rationalizing insistence on identifying catastrophe's causes by naming the large industries responsible for genocide and blaming also himself and all of the workers who upheld them (*ÄdW* 3:125–129), the narrator "asked [himself] yet again how all of this would ever lend itself to expression" (*ÄdW* 3:125). Images of indistinct origin and "movements of a corporeal kind" populate the chapter as the ground zero of a literary art yet to be achieved (*ÄdW* 3:131). In the meantime, Dürer's engraving stands in for the representation of his mother's experiences that elude his father's Marxist diagnosis as well as any other register of which the writer-to-be could avail himself in that moment. "It was almost as if art captivated us more by sinking us into the unnamable than any boost. Thus did my mother persist," according to Hodann, whose lines are reproduced by the narrator's use of indirect speech, like Dürer's Melencholia (*ÄdW* 3:132). But while mother and Melencholia merge in the otherworldly attributes of the engraving, the ekphrasis that unfolds over the next three pages otherwise turns away from her. Leading back into the world of work, it reads, on the whole, as an affirmative rather than critical self-reflection and reassertion of the narrator's literary task, replete with the instruments of labor that place the remediation in closer proximity to his father's discourse than his mother's experiences. It delivers no encapsulation of the latter, but remains consistent with the provisional character of the narrator's efforts, which he foregrounds and second-guesses. In this way, the reliance on the engraving does not, in contrast to the nonrational and surrealist function to which Brueghel's paintings are put, provide for a representation found wanting in the story. Dürer's *Melencholia* speaks not to temporal continuity of the object of reference—the Shoah itself, as witnessed by the narrator's mother—but to the subjective continuity of the efforts of his labor. The self-referential remediation is shakier, undertaken out of an interest in probing art's ability to serve history's victims, the only possible reset of aesthetic culture that Hodann could imagine as legitimate (*ÄdW* 3:241–242). Where the discussion of *Melencholia* ends with Hodann's triumphant claims about art as part of life's mysterious entelechy, the remediation of Dürer does not fulfill the narrator's wish to bring his mother's experiences closer. Rather, it frames aesthetic culture's reach with an open verdict.

A final example attests less to the remediation of source materials seen in the narrator's ekphrases of Brueghel and Dürer's works than to a mediation of historical time on the model of the chronicle, albeit unusually deployed. At the end of the Spanish Civil War and from the epic lookout of Hemeroskopeion, the narrator scales class struggle's well-nigh cosmic duration. Tracing the arch of some twenty-five hundred years of Spanish history from antiquity at a blazing speed on the final few pages of the chapter relating the excursion to the Denia hilltop, the narrator's chronicle invites comparison to "one of the most beautiful stories we have by the incomparable Johann Peter Hebel."[119] Where Walter Benjamin lauded Hebel's "Unexpected Reunion" (*Unverhofftes Wiedersehen*) for grafting the global and fatal dimensions of natural history into the span of his character's lifetime, Weiss has his narrator proceed from speculations on Denia's foundation, through the economically driven upheavals of ancient colonial exploits in Mediterranean space (which includes an early dating of industrialization to the metal works of the sixth and seventh centuries BCE), the rises and falls of a host of rulers amid the razing and rebuilding of cities, a review of the Roman empire's incursions throughout the region and many other details, all conveyed via a Marxist analytical apparatus projected, as this briefest of descriptions suggests, far backward into history long before capitalism's official emergence (*AoR* 284–290/*ÄdW* 1:322–330). The passage thus makes for a considerable condensation (*Raffung*) of narrated time.[120] In taking leave of antiquity—vis-à-vis which the narrator notes a despairing proximity (*AoR* 287/*ÄdW* 1:326)—the presentation accelerates still more:

> The peasants rebelled against the Romans, in the vast migrations Vandals, Suebi, and Alani inundated the country, the Visigoths founded a kingdom here, the Berber Moors thronged in from the South, Arabian caliphs instituted their rule and were superseded by Christian kings in Castille, Asturia, Léon, the rural populace fought for its rights, achieved self-administration, independence for a while, was again subjugated in Aragón, constant insurrections, constant battles, knives, sickles, pickaxes tore into flesh, blood soaked the earth. (*AoR* 289–290/*ÄdW* 1:329)

Characteristic of the flights of *Die Ästhetik*'s epic language is the compression of historical details first into general motifs ("constant insurrections, constant battles") and then into series of nouns ("knives, sickles, pickaxes"), confirming, as it were, "the history of humanity [as] the history of butchery," to cite Hodann's later designation (*ÄdW* 3:47). As a whole, the passage, which continues up to Spain's fate at the end of its Civil War in the epic's narrated present, delivers precisely that kind of "model of the world's course" that Benjamin saw as the chronicler's jurisdiction, in contrast to the task of the historian.[121] Following Benjamin's secularization of the medieval chronicle, the "great inscrutable course" envisioned by *Die Ästhetik* runs the gamut of class struggle through the violent cycles of resistance and suppression without relinquishing its persistent investment in the "efforts, . . . incalculable sacrifices and victims" (*AoR* 290/*ÄdW* 1:330) that stand out at the end of the narrator's rendition of emancipation's long arch in Spain. In this, resistance appears bound more to a cosmology of class than a politics. *Die Ästhetik* extends its radar beyond its intensive focus on European history's darkest hours from 1937 through 1945. Even as the narrator emphasizes the necessity of asserting resistance at the unlikeliest points of its success, *Die Ästhetik* ultimately recuperates emancipation's long-term prospects from out of the great range of its defeats, that is, over and against its verifiability at any one point of historical time. The epic's mediation of historical time thus lays groundwork for the futures of resistance and emancipation beyond the time of its narration, including that of the heterodiegetic narrator, whose time and perspective, in the final chapter's address of the fault lines of the Cold War, merge with Weiss's own.

Epic's Polyphonic Futures

> There were three calculations of time. One from abiogenesis to the end of the world. One from her birth to her death. One for the duration of the task. This was the calculation now valid.
>
> —Bischoff via interior monologue in volume 3

Expanding its epic optics out of the critique of the historical forms of resistance it examines in its story, *Die Ästhetik*'s extensive reassessment of revolutionary struggle relates as much to the antifascist resistance movement as it does to its author's more recent past and the protest energies associated with the year 1968. Driven by the perceived exhaustion, miscarriage, suppression or obsolescence of revolutionary energy, *Die Ästhetik*'s epic self-expansion rescues and rechannels emancipatory aspirations in long time. Transforming the shape of emancipation itself, *Die Ästhetik* opens its framework of resistance to futures beyond its purview. While the experience of the Left's defeat mandated a critical retrospection of measures taken in the historical process, *Die Ästhetik* adheres to the labor-oriented model of resistance and reflection adopted by the narrator as a character and executed by him as the work's implicit writer. Whereas the antagonisms of Weiss's book appear theoretically fixed in terms of class struggle, its model warrants further review in light of both the narrator's self-reflexive inventories of its limits and the express interest he articulates in a newly emergent "revolutionary, universal culture" at the end of the war (*ÄdW* 3:258). This last phrase confirms the connection between culture and humanization discussed above and also raises its stakes via the use of such adjectives. In this context, those stakes can be reformulated: When is epic? and For whom is epic? are implicit questions Weiss develops by unfolding *Die Ästhetik*'s class cosmology in relation to forms of gender, racial, and cultural difference. Looking back at *Die Ästhetik*, Weiss conveyed his own awareness of resistance's multiple forms in reference to "the ecological movement . . . the women's movement."[122] In lieu of pitting the focal points of social movements against one another, Weiss remained in search of their common denominators in the context of a Marxist humanism. This commitment is palpable in the ways his epic interweaves threads of feminist resistance, racial and cultural alterity, and the imagination of the future. Probing such intersections, *Die Ästhetik* modifies its narrator's drive toward a totality that he cannot seal into an epic field on which relations between unity and difference might be newly reformulated. In conjunction with *Die Ästhetik*'s decisively polyphonic fivefold conclusion, each thread plays a powerful role in the book's deferral to the social movements of the future.

As noted above, the thread of resistance's feminist aesthetic begins with Marcauer's critique of the men's party and runs through *Die Ästhetik*'s whole assembly of strong female characters. Their latent strength is palpable even where—and for Weiss because—it is marginalized: during the first visit to Brecht, for example, the remediation of Brueghel addressed above is framed by the narrator's reference to Brecht's coworker Margarete Steffin, who lays the Brueghel book aside for the narrator to pick up, and Helene Weigel, on whom the narrator's gaze falls while delivering his report (*ÄdW* 2:149, 152). The reference to each provides the segue for the narrator's criticism of Brecht's patriarchal behavior there. In the next chapter at Lidingö, these women, along with others, form a counterchorus that directs sharp criticism at the Molotov-Ribbentrop Pact the men are at pains to defend (*ÄdW* 2:167) in a continuation of Marcauer's challenges to party-loyal rationalizations of political deformations.[123]

While the narrator can attend critically to the role gender plays in relations between those around him, Rosalinde Ossietzky and Karin Boye expose and challenge his own fetishization of (a questionable) rationality, offsetting thereby his centripetal function. This decentering of the narrator explains the third volume's polyphonic turn, especially in its second half. *Die Ästhetik*'s polyphonic procedure was already evident in its abundant dialogues and the narrator's function as a medium for other voices. In the third volume, this structural feature is intensified. This pertains not only to a narrative requirement of the story, whereby the narrator, who remains in Stockholm throughout the war, necessarily relies on reports from others in order to relate scenes from the German capital.[124] It can also be read as the epic's incipient integration of the feminist resistance articulated hitherto. At the very least, the autodiegetic, if not the heterodiegetic narrator relinquishes his voice to cede to that of *Die Ästhetik*'s emergent conarrator Charlotte Bischoff. This protagonist's importance to the epic stems first from the fact that much of what is found in the third volume is either unfathomable without her implied delivery of materials and reports to the narrator or (implicitly) narrated by herself. In volume 2, one could already sense a liberation of Bischoff's interior monologue from the narrator's interference: the remarkable chapter introducing Stockholm is focused entirely on her perspective (*ÄdW* 2:77–85). While she shares with the narrator the function of a medium in conjunction with her subordinate role in the party (*ÄdW* 3:228) and figures as a messenger and scout (ÄdW 3:64; *Bote*) sent by Funk/Svensson/Wehner on a clandestine journey via freight ship from Gothenburg via the Kattegat and then the Kiel Canal on to Bremen and into Nazi Germany, her voice and activity also stand on their own, marking centrifugal forces in the balancing act *Die Ästhetik* is coming to perform.[125]

Extending and accentuating the feminist critique of the party (e.g., *ÄdW* 3:80–82), Bischoff also serves as a key political agent thereof, defying the abjecting logic of women's exclusion.[126] While she bears bruises of her political labor (cf. e.g., *ÄdW* 2:144, 165), her survival of the scouting mission to Germany—in contrast to the numerous deaths suffered by fellow resistance fighters there—renders her voice integral to the narration of the whole. Preserving the "memory of the faces, voices, and paths shared with the dead," Bischoff, notebook at hand in 1944 in *Die Ästhetik*'s third-to-last chapter, initiates the narration of the resistance against its obliteration, recording every name and story possible, each of which would warrant a whole biography (*ÄdW* 3:223; *Lebensbuch*).[127] In so doing, she, like the narrator, passes over into a function for a larger collective: her consciousness "filled with the dead, her own death had to appear as a collective death" (*ÄdW* 3:232). At the same time, individualized as a future teacher, Bischoff's activity follows through on the model of history's evaluation articulated by Heilmann in the letter he writes to the narrator, which Bischoff, we are given to understand, later delivers. Whereas Bischoff notes that her murdered comrades were in no search of immortality, but rather fulfilled by the actions they undertook in life (*ÄdW* 3:226), Heilmann, lamenting that more robust legacies could not be bequeathed by those meeting untimely deaths, calls for the evaluation of their accomplishments via other criteria: "A new scale would have to be found via which the weight of their lives could be proven" (*ÄdW* 3:202). Separated from her friends' execution at Plötzensee by the largest temporal gap in *Die Ästhetik*'s narrated time, Bischoff's project to narrate and memorialize the antifascist resistance movement provides for such a scale by anticipating the future's address of the past,[128] including its hopes, intentions, and aspirations, thereby laying the groundwork for a future Germany seems unlikely to have, "bereft of almost all of those who could have given it a new face" (*ÄdW* 3:239).

These aspects of Bischoff's activity both place her in close proximity to another female narrator of the modern epic, Uwe Johnson's Gesine Cresspahl, addressed in the following chapter, as well as speak to the trajectory of trust relations so integral to Alexander Kluge's epic narration of feelings in *Chronik der Gefühle*, examined in chapter 4. An uncharacteristically gentle scene from exilic life in Stockholm puts the "trust in an expanded sense" that Bischoff attributes to the relations between resistance members (*ÄdW* 3:223) on exemplary display. Running into Bischoff and (the character Gerda) Lindner at an immigration office in the Swedish capital, the narrator relates the subjective and objective atmosphere of their togetherness. The "open bright view of the water" across the Riddarfjärden grants them a "feeling of security" (*ÄdW* 2:118; *Geborgenheit*). The whole scene, in which women constitute a majority, stands out among *Die Ästhetik*'s many group discussions for being less tense and antagonistic. Bischoff also advances the book's self-reflection on its own frame of reference in this chapter. With a far-reaching perspective, she puts the disadvantages and plight faced by the three comrades in March 1939 into a larger context: "What is this pompous Europe, she said, over and against the gigantic, still unexpended areas of the earth, from which a power will once rise that will commit our shoddy present to oblivion" (*ÄdW* 2:115). Bischoff's activation of indirect sense (*Fernsinn*) does not so much render their own small deeds meaningless as set them in relation to that larger "universal order" of butchery and resistance that *Die Ästhetik* proposes as the world's course.[129] In so doing, Bischoff appears as something of a mouthpiece for Weiss's own turn to the third world internationalism of the kind marked by *Die Ästhetik*'s emphasis on Géricault's African whom the narrator highlights on the raft of the *Medusa* (*AoR* 303/*ÄdW* 1:345) as well as the excursion into alterity undertaken by Stahlmann on his visit to Angkor Wat in Cambodia, later related to the narrator during a stroll through Stockholm (*ÄdW* 3:93–108). In conjunction with Bischoff's provincialization of Europe, such cases represent *Die Ästhetik*'s most far-reaching global references in space. And yet the approach to cultural alterity signaled in these examples appears to run analogous to what would have to be undertaken on the diverse European continent also. In Sweden as in Spain, settling in and acting effectively are pinned to the learning-process of becoming familiar with the foreign via narrative appropriation. "This field of activity," the narrator notes in Cueva during the Civil War, "this tactical image, this map of Spain had not yet been transformed into a living structure containing encounters with people, specific ways of seeing and expressing things" (*AoR* 235/*ÄdW* 1:267). As the narrator substantiates this challenge in the following chapter's juxtaposition of emigration to political exile, the former mode of experience appears as a site of all the specific questions of cultural mediation that the latter overrides in its focus on the continuity of one's activism across different venues (*AoR* 240/*ÄdW* 1:272).[130] While Hodann holds himself up in reference to that continuity, the text implicitly indicates that the power of resistance—not to mention the attainment of political unity—presupposes the labor of transcultural and translational mediation.

The alienating experience of emigration returns in Rosalinde Ossietzky's story in an especially telling weave. Not only does she highlight the intersection of "being a woman and being an emigrant" (*ÄdW* 2:138) as particularly debilitating. With "black hair and brownish skin" inherited from her mother's Indian descent (*ÄdW* 2:131), Ossietzky is marked as racially other across the European spaces of her exile and subjected to racist aggression. "You know," she says in the summation she delivers with a sardonic laugh to the narrator from his bed at the chapter's end, "I have now finally sunk from the highest caste down to the untouchables" (*ÄdW* 2:138). While Ossietzky's depiction of social differentiation in such terms can still be amalgamated to the narrator's model of class struggle, *Die Ästhetik* tends to set the signposts of non-European antagonisms into view at the outer limits of its radius, on the horizons of its work. Whereas the novel decisively frames its totalizing imagination as a drive unfulfilled, the narrative has clearly established an impetus for relating, if not incorporating, all of the social challenges it finds and scouts to its cosmology of class. Nothing less would warrant its repeated appeals to the universal in culture. Yet a friction may persist between the universality of class struggle and the representation of differences less directly related to labor. While the former is raised to cosmic dimensions on the level of content, the task of the labor-oriented mediation of social difference prevails as the book's method and is set into motion on the level of its form. If and where resistance's many sites refuse unifying or overarching solidification, the figure of unity—still featured, if more faintly, in the story as an open call by its end (cf. *ÄdW* 3:239)—must cede to questions of the relationality of manifold social differences to one another as fault lines in the folds of epic time. Labor will clearly have a role to play in the task of this mediation on the level of method. It is likewise an indispensable anchor on the level of content, and yet may no longer serve as the sole common denominator of social difference's many forms. Such a modification, where necessary, would enhance the investigative scope and quality of any inquiry into resistance as well as its ecumenical reach.

The balancing act *Die Ästhetik* performs between labor and the world relates to a final oscillation, if not ambivalence, in the work's conception of time. As noted above, Weiss's epic stages at least five endings. The last of these does not so much close the epic as reinstate resistance's futures. The first ending is the aforementioned letter Heilmann sends "To Unknown" (*ÄdW* 3:199). It is a bottled message, infused with an orientation to the future, not only in its search of a scale on which the defeated resistance could be weighed, but also in the trepidation Heilmann expresses regarding its delivery, knowing "that much time may pass until that which I write may reach you, if at all" (*ÄdW* 3:200). Heilmann would have liked to have written everything differently, but his "time is short. And the paper used up" (*ÄdW* 3:210). The following chapter documents the elimination of that time's anchor on earth by recounting the execution of Heilmann, Coppi, and other members of the Red Orchestra in reports that came to Bischoff via the attending clergyman Poelchau, who told them to his friend Reichwein (*ÄdW* 3:231). The third ending is Bischoff's chapter from 1944, addressed above, which reasserts the perspective into the future, whereas the fourth is dedicated to Hodann's work on the Free German League of Culture and supplemented, in Weiss's

Notizbücher, with the epitaph on Hodann (*NB* 898–925), which does not refrain from depicting *Die Ästhetik*'s own teacher in his helplessness (*NB* 916). This leaves the narrator's own concluding chapter, which connects with Heilmann and Bischoff's to anticipate the continuation of the resistance into the postwar period, in the epic's famous return to the Pergamon frieze, highlighting again the absence of Hercules and the presence of the paw of a lion's skin as a position anyone rising up through self-empowerment could assume.

The epic's multifold ending invites a final redress of the book's conception of time due not only to the lingering oscillation between resistance and defeat, as suggested in this overview, but also to its pendulum's sway between past and future in Weiss's model of the world's course. Martin Rector has focused on this pendulum in terms of existential threat and resistance to attest to *Die Ästhetik*'s mythic modulation of the variability of the perpetually same (*Varianz des Immergleichen*), which also allows its reflections on defeat to be reactualized at different historical junctures.[131] While Rector's formulation captures the work's long rhythms and its epic expansion of time, Thomas Metscher has reinstated the progressive dimension into epic time by describing *Die Ästhetik*'s structure in terms of concentrically expanding circles, from its 1937–1945 story to the time of the heterodiegetic narrator and Weiss himself from the war's end to 1980 and to the time—incorporated through *Die Ästhetik*'s remediation of artworks—of the history of humanity itself, which Metscher schematizes in terms of Marxist historiography.[132] In making the case for this, Metscher also confirms the work's organic structure of development (which includes the more-than-iterative, accumulative development of the narrator himself) that he has described as a linchpin of epic form.[133] Ultimately, the value of *Die Ästhetik* can be ascertained by weighing its cultural labor on its own scale to demonstrate how it grants orientation, meaning, and hope. Against Cold War dialectics and the accompanying widespread impression of the helplessness of individuals, *Die Ästhetik*'s unlikely reassertion of the epic—as genre and as imagination—in the atomic age ushered in by the U.S.'s "new big bang" (*ÄdW* 3:264; *Urknall*) stakes out fields for the continued analysis and pursuit of emancipation against the barriers that encumber it.

Chapter 3

Time-Spaces of Epic Narration

Uwe Johnson's *Jahrestage*

> From the point of view of epic, existence is an ocean. Nothing is more epic than the sea.
>
> —Walter Benjamin, "The Crisis of the Novel"

An Epic's Hydropoetics

At the beginning of the essay "On Epic Naiveté," Theodor W. Adorno invoked the beating of the sea on the rocky coast and the roaring of heavy water in Homer's *Odyssey* as the sounds of "epic discourse."[1] He proceeded to mark epic as an anachronistic undertaking. In an age dominated by interchangeability, the epic aspiration to "report on something worth reporting on, something that is not the same as everything else, not exchangeable" appeared as inherently fraught as the original attempt to distill particularity from the eternal sameness of the mythic world.[2] This did not confirm the epic's futility for Adorno. On the contrary, even the short essay, not to mention the more elaborate reading of Homer that Max Horkheimer and Adorno put forth in the *Dialectic of Enlightenment*, unfolded the critical potentials of epic narration from its naive investment in the unique. While Adorno associated this naïveté with a "stubborn clinging" to the "blind contemplation of the particular," he ultimately validated epic language's ability, however imperiled, to intimate "what once was" in its singularity.[3] This ability stemmed from epic's equivocal relation to its mythic material. Teasing out moments of epic narration's tendencies toward generalization and particularization, autonomization and mimesis, Adorno cautiously, yet assuredly confirmed narrative's capacity to deliver the uniqueness of real events, craft images thereof in language, and insinuate the pitfalls of a rationalizing discourse that would order and classify them.[4]

The equivocality of epic language was part and parcel of enlightenment's primordial departure from myth. While Horkheimer and Adorno's now classical text, especially in its first chapter and first excursus, attended to the regressions incurred wherever enlightenment aspired to master myth, it also elevated art and aesthetic experiences, wherever possible to paradigmatic sites of nondomination and reconciliation.[5] In its utopian rather than calamitous form, the entwinement of myth and enlightenment points less to any state of return than to processes of nonidentical experiences. While initial reviews characterized both Peter Weiss's *Die Ästhetik des Widerstands* and Uwe Johnson's *Jahrestage: Aus dem Leben von Gesine Cresspahl* as anachronistic in their returns to realist narration and archaic in their appeals to myth—both allegedly fell behind the modernist experimentation for the advancement of which their previously published works had been championed[6]—closer examination reveals the nonidentical status of myth in these modern epics as a template for transformative appropriation and variation.

Whereas Weiss's reworking of myths from the world of classical antiquity in *Die Ästhetik des Widerstands* proceeded explicitly through his narrative ekphrasis of the Pergamon altar and a politicizing refunctionalization of figures such as Hercules, the mythical substrate of Johnson's epic has proven a matter of greater debate. Situating *Jahrestage* within the trajectory of the urban epic (*Großstadt-Epos*), Johnson scholar Bernd Neumann has written that "what the myth of the *Odyssey* is for Joyce and the legend of Job for Döblin [in *Berlin Alexanderplatz*] is for Johnson the repressed Holocaust."[7] While the Shoah, despite what the structural parallelism of Neumann's sentence appears to suggest, could hardly serve as an equivalent in this series of references, in view of its force "above all in the Mecklenburg thread of its narrative," Neumann identified *Jahrestage*'s "archaic dimension, its, if you will, participation in myth" in this very substrate.[8] While many scholars have concurred with Neumann in claiming the Shoah's centrality to *Jahrestage*, they have more appropriately stressed the historical character of the epic's content. For Jochen Hörisch, *Jahrestage*, in contrast to Joyce's novel, "does not mythologize its material; rather it shapes it into rhythmic patterns" of daily and yearly repetition and deviation.[9] Ingeborg Gerlach's characterization of *Jahrestage*'s Jerichow narrative as myth is no sweeping claim, but rather carefully couched in Gesine Cresspahl's perspective, in which her own past has *become* mythic prehistory.[10] Norbert Mecklenburg has described *Jahrestage*'s focus on the historical fact of German responsibility for the genocide as an "ethical-political and at the same time epic 'a priori.'"[11] An "irreducible condition of the literary presentation of German history in the twentieth century,"[12] the gravity of the Shoah in *Jahrestage* may have appeared akin to the weight of myth, yet was historical through and through and treated as such in Johnson's postcatastrophic epic.

The quasi-mythic substrate of *Jahrestage* is elemental: from its Lake District to the Baltic coast, Mecklenburg is full of water. Parallel to the mythic opening of Weiss's *Die Ästhetik des Widerstands* at the Pergamon Altar is Johnson's retrieval of the narrative from coastal waters in the epic's first paragraph highlighted in chapter 1 above (*AN* 3/*JT* 7). The natural element is repeatedly evoked, as has been widely recognized, at key junctures of the epic, including the openings of volumes 2 and 3, and the closing of its fourth and final volume.[13] The sole undated chapter, *Jahrestage*'s first may evince a deeper epic time, but like the Mecklenburg backstory in which its waters resonantly pool, *Jahrestage*'s historicizing imperative ensures that Johnson's immersion of his narrative and characters in such an element is as differentiated and particularized as the rest of the epic's contents.

In some contrast, then, to Adorno's juxtaposition of the "solid ground" of narrative differentiation to the "amorphous flood of myth" as the "eternally invariant,"[14] Johnson's hydropoetics draw seas and lakes, waves and rain, swimming lessons and excursions, Hades-crossings to isles of the deceased and the undertows of psychic time all into *Jahrestage*'s historicizing pool. Against the perception of water's eternal sameness, Johnson's attention to detail in the thoroughgoing specification of the epic's contents[15] contains many nuances, not only by regularly incorporating reports on the weather, as in a note on a humid atmosphere's effects on New York City's pollution (e.g., *AN* 48/*JT* 65), but also by distinguishing among the unique characteristics H_2O assumes: "chlorine-green, tepid, and tight" in the swimming pool at the Upper West Side Hotel Marseille (*AN* 318/*JT* 487), poisoned from the discharges of industries into the Hudson River (*AN* 360–364/*JT* 559–563), soft and calcium carbonate-free, but dirtied in Heinrich Cresspahl's rain barrel (*AN* 405/*JT* 616), clearer than ever from Gesine's uncle Paepcke's well on Fischland at the Baltic coast (*AN II*, 68/*JT* 881), heavy and black in Patton Lake in a landscape "chemically treated . . . for people who pay" somewhere in upstate New York (*AN II*, 151–154/*JT* 1017–1020), and brackish in the Baltic that rattles pebbles about Gesine and Marie's ankles (*AN II*, 644/*JT* 1891). No mere leitmotiv accompanying the story of its protagonist—"a native of Mecklenburg and avid swimmer"[16]—*Jahrestage*'s elemental waters are not exactly integrated into the epic on the model of what Neumann celebrated in the title of his chapter "The Completion of *Jahrestage* or the Unification of all Water."[17] While Neumann alluded to water as the substance of continual transformation,[18] Ralf Schnell has emphasized that in *Jahrestage*'s return to the sea—here the Danish coast—at its end, Johnson's image of aquatic nature—which resists any "organological embedment" (*organologische Einbettung*)—did not come around full circle.[19] It did not even reach Mecklenburg, which remains inaccessible to Gesine in the epic's frame narrative. With the waters of seas, lakes, and pools outweighing those of rivers, *Jahrestage*'s hydropoetics stand under the sign of not confluence, but divergence.[20] The unification of its narrative streams is not so much geared toward closure as poignantly orchestrated through artifice. To read *Jahrestage* is to bathe in all kinds of different waters.

Far from resting in any stylistic archaisms, the mythic character of *Jahrestage*'s aquatic element serves as a facilitator of different kinds of stories, akin in its function to Johnson's conception of the Berlin Wall as an instigator of literary innovation cited in the introduction. Beyond its status as a resonant epic image of nature that doubtlessly channels Gesine and Johnson's own orientations to their Mecklenburg homes, water figures importantly in *Jahrestage*'s hydropoetics as a marker of biographical history, a liminal existential space, a site of memory's enactment, and a conduit of migration.[21] These come together in the remarkable inventory Gesine offers at the beginning of *Jahrestage*'s third volume, where she lists the heterogeneous waters of her life as portals of spatiotemporal travel as well as recreational pleasure. "And you came swimming all the way from Mecklenburg!" Marie exclaims in an attempt to commemorate her mother's successful transit near the chapter's end (*AN II*, 154/*JT* 1019). Yet the waters of Gesine's memory remain heavy and dark. And her migration often resembles a derelict flight: "Derelict: wouldn't that word apply to the English of Mrs. Cresspahl, who is trying to sell her labors in a country that uses this kind of language as to a drifting ship without pilot or crew?" (*AN II*, 1/*JT* 776). One the book's sharpest maritime metaphors, the passage anticipates the prominence metaphors of flow and fluidity would attain in an age of global capitalism.

Hydropoetics is not merely topical for Gesine's story. In its focus on the organization of a literary work's narrative currents, the conceptual metaphor can be wielded to interrelate and distinguish *Jahrestage*'s novelistic and epic features. Johnson himself was not averse to characterizing the reporting of the "Diary of the World" (*AN II*, 399/*JT* 1509) in terms of an epic spate (*AN* 55/*JT* 74; *epischen Fluß*). But in contrast to the *New York Times*, whose epic characteristics are not accompanied by the same degree of self-reflexivity as Johnson's literary experiment, the narrative spates of *Jahrestage* operate in complex registers of time and space. To be sure, at the most basic level, readers can follow Gesine Cresspahl's life in linear, chronological time. Yet the difficulties of her quest to reconstruct and come to terms with the past go hand in hand with the disjointed, seemingly disconnected, montage-like character of *Jahrestage*'s chapters that suggest the discontinuity of Gesine's memory-work. The challenge is marked early on: in her first explicit characterization of memory's function, the past palpably eludes the mind's controlling grasp: "To be inside [the past] again, to enter into that again. There is no such thing" (*AN* 47/*JT* 63). The question of ontological and temporal difference suggests the difficulty of the telling: "If only memory could contain the past in the receptacles we use to sort the elements of present reality!" (*AN* 47/*JT* 63; see also *AN* 320/*JT* 490). Recalcitrant to being captured at will and according to plan, the past would appear to refuse any straightforward linear narration. Johnson dramatizes all this in the process of Cresspahl's remembrance so much that the reconstruction of the Jerichow story, which ultimately *is* retrieved and more or less told from start to finish, may come at great surprise. What is more, that Gesine's reconstruction of the past (mindful of the inability of any return) is devoted to her orientation in the present with an eye to the future underscores the link between Johnson's protagonist and linear time's forward march. Finally, Johnson's contractual structure for the day-to-day narration of Gesine's New York life from around August 20, 1967, to August 20, 1968, appears to reinforce *Jahrestage*'s foundation on linear temporality.

At the next level of consideration, however, the recapitulation of the Jerichow story, replete with forward and backward movements and ellipses along the temporal axis of Gesine's narration, suggests another ordering in time. Gesine's storytelling abounds in temporal discordances, many of which revolve around the traumatic knots of her experiences.[22] The past frequently reveals itself as coterminous with Gesine's narrative present. Combining chronological and calendrical time,[23] *Jahrestage* develops the connection couched in the double entendre of the title between anniversaries and the more literal meaning of *Jahrestage* as days of the year.[24] Within the decisive artifice of the quotidian marking of time the more cyclical, more expansive, and more epic time of the calendar makes itself felt. As the calendar and its time provide the deeper principle for *Jahrestage*'s temporal construction, the work folds the chronos of Gesine's life into a fuller swath of history of which she becomes a medium.[25] In this way, the positions of the frame and embedded narratives become inverted vis-à-vis one another. Whereas Gesine sets on delivering an account of her past to herself and Marie in the former, her narrative present rather appears, over the course of *Jahrestage*'s execution, as an outgrowth of the latter. The mise-en-abyme-like relationship between the two narrative frameworks has contributed to the overall breadth of *Jahrestage*'s interpretations, oscillating, as they have, between focuses on pasts and futures, closure and openness, fatalism and hopefulness (or apocalypse and utopia), morality and politics, singularity and exemplarity, and other binary oppositions.

A reformulation of these observations in hydropoetical terms can help make sense of the work's dual temporalities as well as its epic relation to space. For starters, linear time, that of the novel and its subject (and the horizons of each), would be akin to stream and river. This dimension of *Jahrestage* coincides with the work's focus on Gesine and her project to retrieve the past in order to understand "where she came from, what made her into what she is"[26] and thereby to find and verify her place in a world in which she has never really settled. As D. G. Bond has pointed out, such a description of *Jahrestage* evokes György Lukács's account of the modern novel as a searching genre of and for transcendentally homeless individuals.[27] The paths Gesine treads through the past toward self-understanding already make for a compassionate and gripping tale. At the same time, *Jahrestage*'s intricate weaves of past and present, of embedded and frame narratives reveal not only that Gesine's problems are as historical as they are transcendental, but also suggests that Cresspahl—contrary to Johnson's emphases on the centripetal function of Gesine's consciousness for the whole[28]—cannot herself be considered some final arbiter of the history of the twentieth century her author reveals through the narration of her life, reading, and stories.[29] In short, the novelistic spates of *Jahrestage*'s streams and rivers are directed into the epic's sea.

While Gesine's stories are organized through Johnson's use of the calendar that provides a larger temporal framework for the mediation of her life, the image of their ebb and flow naturally evoke the space of the sea with which Walter Benjamin so closely associated the epic genre. As part of a decidedly postcatastrophic instantiation of the genre, *Jahrestage* is flooded with the violence of history. But the streams of its narrative do not culminate therein: there is no return to identity in *Jahrestage*'s waves, save the identity of a nonidentical story. This is granted Gesine, "child that she/I was" (*AN* 4; *AN II*, 644/*JT* 8, 1891): proceeding according to chronos's forward flow, her life story is wrought from the waters of putative mythic sameness as a contingent singularity. In other words, in their reentry into the ocean from which they were exemplarily concretized, *Jahrestage*'s narrative spates take shape according to a logic of tidal fluctuation. Their nonidentical variation most definitely includes the category of possibility that Gesine explicitly admits of her own stories about the past (*AN* 103/*JT* 144). As in *Jahrestage*'s chapter on repetition (*JT* 913–915), *Wiederholung* (which also connotes review) provides for the discernment of deviation and difference (*JT* 914; *Abweichungen*): in its contingent singularity, the story of Gesine's life presents one possibility among others. The stories and days from her life are full of concrete possibilities for difference and variation. What is more, by providing a model for the coexistence of different times in space, the epic ocean reveals the partially permeable boundaries of Gesine's stories with regard to geography as well as history. To be sure, *abstract* possibility has as little purchase in space as it does in time. Ontological differences in the latter are to Gesine's memory work what demarcation lines are to her free movement (cf. *AN II*, 153/*JT* 1018). Nonetheless, *Jahrestage*'s transoceanic space-travel pertains not only to Gesine's real and imagined migrations across the geopolitical landscapes of the Cold War, but also to the more general aesthetic of cognitive mapping that *Jahrestage* delivers. Gesine's list of the waters in which she has swum—an epic technique through and through[30]—not only attests to differences in the waters themselves, but also frames her passageways through the unexchangeable spaces of the larger world. It thereby connects to a spatiotemporal orientation that is not only of value to Cresspahl herself. Gesine's catalogue of lakes provides a key example of what Norbert Mecklenburg has called Johnson's "topical narration . . . an explicitly object-related, problem-oriented, and argumentative storytelling"[31] with which one can associate *Jahrestage*'s investigative and mapping tendencies alike. These go hand in hand with other epic (Brechtian) techniques of interruption and estrangement that Mecklenburg and others have analyzed as key components of *Jahrestage*'s supra-individual mediation of society.[32] Advancing learning about trajectories of societal as well as personal development in fulfillment of its author's conception of an enlightening literature,[33] *Jahrestage*'s spatiotemporally vast mediation of society supersedes the strictures, worldviews, and practices of the novelistic genre highlighted in chapter 1, allowing readers great scopes of play in their reception of the work.

To account for this last epic feature of *Jahrestage*, I draw on Severin Strasky's compelling characterization of *Jahrestage*'s paradoxical unity in terms of the undulating movement of waves.[34] While Strasky emphasizes the principle of *Jahrestage*'s segmented and fragmented narration to account for the diversity of its waters, the image of the sea's waves captures metaphorically the internally differentiated unity of the book as a whole. Each chapter constitutes a wave, similar and different to the others, wrought from yearlong residence at the coasts of modern epic. As with the duality of *Jahrestage*'s Jerichow and New York City narratives, the complexity of the work's hydropoetically conceived unity permits a broad range of respective emphases on its centripetal and centrifugal pulls. Building on Mecklenburg's account of the relative independence of *Jahrestage*'s components,[35] D. G. Bond has made a case for the desubjectification and detemporalization of the book's reception,[36] noting that *Jahrestage* "need not be the object of a contemplative armchair read but a book with a distinct use-value—not unlike a reference work—to be read in parts, as a series of episodes each of which may be returned to at will."[37] While the appearance of segmentation and relative independence of *Jahrestage*'s various waters neither sublates chronology nor forecloses future time, it may displace the categories of individual consciousness and "the time of the subject"[38] from their sovereignty over *Jahrestage*'s interpretation. What this invites is not a mistaking of any single lake (*den See*) for the sea (*die See*), but the productiveness of perennial returns to *Jahrestage*'s various waters and currents in which readers may swim at their discretion.[39] In this conceptual metaphoric usage, water and the activity of swimming therein appropriately convey what reading such a work is like. As physical submersion into an element, swimming is a strenuous pleasure, more intense than the refreshment of bathing in daily life. Such a pleasure is not a given: the issue of water's accessibility is raised in *Jahrestage* in numerous ways, not just vis-à-vis pollution or Cold War geopolitics, but also in Gesine's recollection of her student days in Halle, where swimming lessons compensated for her infrequent access to a shower in her apartment building (*AN II*, 596/*JT* 1831). Nor is there guarantee of any solid ground in light of the ever-present danger of drowning, even for Mecklenburg's human amphibians (*AN II*, 597/*JT* 1831). In this, *Jahrestage*'s waters suggest society's perilous mediation of individual lives, first and foremost that of Gesine herself, swimming in and through the currents and pools of sociohistorical time. Mustering a poetic redress of such mediation, *Jahrestage* reaches us across the divide between the Cold War and its future presents, granting us swimming lessons in reading for our own times.

This chapter sets its further course on a fuller exposition of Johnson's approach to modern epic form first by investigating his curious contract with *Jahrestage*'s narrative "point of coordination,"[40] its "mediating character" (*vermittelnde Figur*),[41] its "synapse" (*Umschaltestelle*):[42] the autodiegetic narrator Gesine Cresspahl, who is herself more comprehensively embedded in the narrative than the unnamed narrator of Weiss's *Die Ästhetik des Widerstands*. Ascertaining her work as the book's memory and medium,[43] my account trains its gaze on lessons to be culled from Cresspahl's orientation to the possibilities of life and action in the Cold War landscapes she reads, traverses, and narrates. In so doing, the chapter also explores the epic techniques via which *Jahrestage* establishes its Cold War cartography with an emphasis, in the concluding section, on *Jahrestage*'s mediation of Gesine's relationship to Prague as a prescient critical genealogy of the global present.

Person and Contract

> *Who's telling this story, Gesine?*
> *We both are. Surely that's obvious, Johnson.*
> —Cresspahl and Johnson on November 3, 1967 (italics there)

> For Cresspahl the Führer was someone with whom he had no contract.
> —Heinrich Cresspahl on January 31, 1968

A migrating mediator, *Jahrestage*'s embedded narrator is something of a derelict, without party or pilot. In both *Jahrestage* and Johnson's own extensive commentaries, Gesine Cresspahl is framed less as a main character than as her own person.[44] The fifth definition of *Person* in Jakob and Wilhelm Grimm's dictionary highlights a relevant connotation of its German usage: "the independent, self-conscious and rational individual in his [or her] singularity."[45] *Jahrestage* exploits this semantic register to deploy "person" emphatically across its pages. The first reference to Gesine's relationship to the *New York Times* relates that she engages with the paper as if it were "a person" (*AN* 10/*JT* 15). The personification allows this interaction to assume the quality of a conversation with a resourceful, if fallible authority. On first viewing the Riverside Drive apartment in which she will reside with her mother, Gesine's then four-year-old daughter Marie is greeted by its departing inhabitants—a young Danish and a young Swiss woman—"solemnly and politely, as a person" (*AN* 20/*JT* 28). A residue of European tactfulness in the American city? Mrs. Cresspahl, "the German" (*AN* 45, 104; *AN II*, 164, 536/*JT* 61, 145, 161, 1035, 1259, 1734) who emigrated to the United States six years prior to *Jahrestage*'s narrative present, is known for her formality and respectfulness. Her adjustments to the new milieu and the prospects of raising her daughter in it make for alluring scenes of cross-cultural navigation. Gesine's reorientation also raises the question of the transferability of her political convictions to the New York environment.[46] The process is replete with stumbling blocks of the kind highlighted in Gesine's hostile reaction to the racism of a Jewish real estate agent in Queens: "The child [Marie] wanted to know what [her mother] had meant, 'You bastard of a Jew,' and realized that miracles [*Wunder*] can happen, saw the suitcase with her toys from the hotel being driven up, felt she was already on a plane, tomorrow she would be home. Gesine was ready to give up. You can't live among such people" (*AN* 14–15/*JT* 21). While Gesine's anti-anti-Semitism has already been established in the text, it fails at this intersection to prevail with any consistency as the antiracism into which she would seek to convert it. For the reader, the surprise (*Wunder*) is Gesine's own regression into countering racism with an anti-Semitic remark. Her subsequent appeals to a morally pure, if thinly populated, universe[47] present standards she struggles to uphold on the level of her own behavior. Where such an episode points to Cresspahl's fallibility, her decision to send Marie to a private Catholic school exemplifies further dissonances in her multinational life across cultures. While the school promises that Marie would "be treated as a separate and independent person" and "her abilities . . . recognized and developed as early as possible" (*AN* 73/*JT* 100), Gesine's choice contradicts her idealistic commitment to socialism. The practical decisions she makes in New York City elicit consternation and critique from unidentified interlocutors in a follow-up chapter on September 19. In such ways, *Jahrestage* frames challenges faced by Gesine as questions and problems to be solved.[48]

Such signposts are surface indications of the iceberg thawing in *Jahrestage*'s mediation of Gesine's American life. While the work's calendrical form may evince, in its seriality, the appearance of an abstract procedure in Johnson's quotidian marking of time, the author both imbues this structure with a novelistic arch and diversifies its form and content from within to grant the time-spaces of his undertaking their epic scope, while retaining Gesine's role as *Jahrestage*'s central person and narrator in conformity with the work's subtitle. The gradual buildup over the course of the first two hundred pages or so introduces protagonists Gesine and Marie in their milieu and establishes the epic's internal rationale. Highlights of the former concern Gesine's employment at the international New York bank served by her training in translation and finance; the initiation of the Jerichow narrative and an introduction to the town from her father Heinrich's perspective; Marie's (self-) introduction via her own catalogue; Riverside Drive and the Upper West Side as an imaginary home (*AN* 118/*JT* 173; *unsere Heimat . . . ist eingebildet*); Gesine's habitual review of the *New York Times*; and readers' piecemeal introduction to *Jahrestage*'s large host of characters, including Mrs. Ferwalter, D. E., Francine, and many more. As for the long tale's rationale: the September 10 chapter, which features Marie's insertion of a question into Gesine's reconstruction of her parents' 1931 Jerichow engagement, is the first to reveal explicitly that Gesine's retrieval and narration of the past are taking place within the narrated present (*AN* 53/*JT* 72). After having grappled earlier with memory's reliability, Gesine comments on the function of her storytelling for Marie in her first recorded message (*AN* 102/*JT* 143; *Phonopost*) to her friend D. E. on October 5: "Marie insists on my continuing my account of how it was when Grandmother married Grandfather. Her questions sharpen my imagination [*meine Vorstellungen*], and her listening looks attentive. . . . But what she wants to know is not the past, not even her own. For her these are [*es ist*] a presentation of possibilities [*Möglichkeiten*] from which she believes herself immune, and in another sense stories [*Geschichten*]" (*AN* 103/*JT* 143–144). In its construction of the narrative world that follows, *Jahrestage* expounds Marie's connection to her mother, that of her mother to her family history, and the weight of political history bearing down on every individual amid the recession of such immunity.[49] Gesine's phrasing of the "presentation of possibilities" nonetheless harmonizes with the epic's hydropoetics described above: taking *Möglichkeiten* together with *Geschichten*, her postulation of "how things might have been" (*AN* 361/*JT* 560) relates both to the self-reflexive narration of history in the subjunctive and the possibilities of individuals' actions within it.[50] The commitment to grasping the societal mediation of such possibilities by no means entails a presentation of history as predetermined. Rather, *Jahrestage* holds to its own line on history as "a concept or draft" (*AN II*, 644/*JT* 1891; *Geschichte ist ein Entwurf*).[51] It offers but a version of reality, against which readers, along with Marie, can measure and ascertain their own (VPR 402–403). It is in this differential relationship that Gesine's stories, couched in the modality of possibility in the dual sense of what is told and how such content is told, assume the character not of an authoritative model to be followed, but of a template for living in and working through historical time.

The category of possibility at work in *Jahrestage* includes the labor of the imagination, but as in Robert Musil's earlier modern epic *Der Mann ohne Eigenschaften* (*The Man without Qualities*),[52] it remains wedded to plausibility and precision. *Jahrestage*'s possibilities unfold within the logic of Johnson's realism. Part and parcel of Johnson's literary search for truth in a book that refuses to jettison the substance of reality as its anchor,[53] the review of possibilities is staged repeatedly, most often in the dialogic exchanges between Gesine and Marie.[54] Occasionally punctuating the flow of Gesine's stories, Marie's interjectory reactions and questions contribute to Gesine's self-reflexive delivery of the Jerichow tale. Subjected to this privileged listener's review, the beguiling assertions of Gesine's narration of the past within *Jahrestage*'s frame narrative yield to stops, checks, and restarts. But Marie does not figure as the prevailing instance of control. Numerous signs indicate that Gesine's stories to Marie both exceed and take a different form from what we read on *Jahrestage*'s pages[55] and that what *Jahrestage* has Gesine relate is not all directed to her daughter.[56] Readers come to realize the redaction of Gesine's narration by another. As Johnson noted in an interview, although (the fictional) Cresspahl was "present during [the text's] transcription" over which she could exercise her "right of veto"[57] and although she herself delivers the manuscript of *Jahrestage* itself to her former teacher Kliefoth near the end of the New York adventure (*AN II*, 644/*JT* 1891), the author possessed the right to follow up on and where necessary correct Gesine's memory to ensure that what was transcribed resembled "how things really were" (*wie es tatsächlich gewesen ist*).[58] Coupled with the mediation of Gesine as a character within the *Jahrestage* story, Johnson's "editorial" mediation of her narrative efforts and memory both enhances the author's literary quest for truth and reveals the fundamentally fictional means thereof. In this, the dereliction of Gesine's hydropoetical plight is orchestrated and constrained by Johnson as its pilot.

Johnson's cunning response to the challenges of modern epic form consists in the division of labor's narration by contract between two people for the course of one year. Johnson's staging of his contractual arrangement with Cresspahl is *Jahrestage*'s basic fiction and its sustaining lie. Uwe Johnson and Gesine Cresspahl's "teamwork"[59] lends cohesiveness to the work's epic forays as well as provides for the management of its closure. Based on a contract (*Vertrag*) rather than trust (*Vertrauen*),[60] the transaction does not cynically concede the relations of literary production in capitalist society. *Vertrag* is a positive term for Johnson.[61] As the epigraph from Heinrich Cresspahl's perspective above suggests, contracts provide for real interpersonal relations and obligations. Nowhere does the Führer's hold on power appear as any legitimate piece of a social contract, but rather its absolute controversion.[62] Indeed, the idea of the social contract provides a source for the sense of fairness and justice with which Johnson holds fascist, socialist, or capitalist practices to the fire without preinvesting in a completely different social order.[63]

"*One year I have given you. Thus our contract*" (*JT* 1426): the arrangement for Cresspahl and Johnson's conarration of a year splits the narrative voice in two in Gesine's and Comrade Writer's shared New York City present.[64] It is the poetological foundation of the epic's polyphony, swiftly multiplied via the incorporation of numerous other voices and perspectives, including Gesine's father Heinrich and other relatives and acquaintances from Jerichow with whom Gesine is also in dialogue, Marie's deceased father Jakob, Marie herself, interlocutors in the metropolis, as well as that of the newspaper personified into the figure of the aunt who serves as a local surrogate on foreign U.S. territory for the family Gesine does not have there. The plurality of voices and perspectives makes for an abundant interplay amid the plethora of positions, so much so that both the respective authorities of Gesine's narrative voice as well as that of he who commits it to literature sometimes appear to dissolve across the year's advance.

Of course, behind the contract and the elaborate orchestration of the epic's polyphony alike stands the actual Uwe Johnson (not to be confused with the Comrade Writer who makes infrequent appearances in the text), just as much as the actual Peter Weiss stood behind the curious autodiegetic narrator he sends on a journey to becoming *Die Ästhetik*'s author. The comparison to Weiss's scheme for reconstituting epic narration in an age of its unlikelihood yields other findings. As discussed in chapter 2 above, Weiss developed a response to the narrative challenges of modern epic form by dividing his single narrator into autodiegetic and heterodiegetic roles; in the process of becoming the implied author of the whole, Weiss's narrator also serves as a medium for all of the other voices of *Die Ästhetik*'s dramatis personae. On the whole, *Die Ästhetik* adheres to and reinforces time—emphatically projected from antiquity through its conclusion into readers' futures in Weiss's full-fledged model of the world's course—as the plane of dynamic subjective and social development. This contrasts with Johnson's division of narrative labor onto different individuals in space. In *Jahrestage*, the singular and sweepingly unifying force of Weiss's narrator yields to the contestation of viewpoint in an arrangement in which Gesine occupies the position of *Die Ästhetik*'s autodiegetic and Comrade Writer that of its heterodiegetic narrator. What is more, by decisively restricting the contract to a year—one in which he would be "richly presented by [the events of] reality [*reich beschenkt von der Wirklichkeit*]"[65]—Johnson not only provides a stopgap to epic time's potentially infinite ebb and flow, he also crafts a genial solution to the problem of epic closure. Within the temporally fixed calendrical framework—an artificial totality that contains the past, but not the future, save as a modality of hope and projection—*Jahrestage* can unfold its urban and provincial topographies. Finally, Johnson's fictional contract serves as the structural vehicle for the epic's self-reflexivity, both on the level of Gesine's attempts to recapture the past, as noted above, and on the level of Johnson's own efforts to mediate the history of the twentieth century hitherto. A piece of artifice more resembling an ocean liner than the perilous raft on which Weiss's narrator occasionally finds himself, the contract surely feigns the conditions of *Jahrestage*'s own possibility as a literary text,[66] and yet, as with Weiss, can absolutely be taken seriously as a piece of *Jahrestage*'s real poetology and Johnson's own self-obligation to uphold his part of the agreement and complete the project.[67]

This last observation points to the status of *Jahrestage* as a *Wunschbiographie*, again not in the facile sense in which the term was turned against Weiss, but rather as a denomination for the literary aspiration to find a coherent form for the narration of one's times. A finding from the Uwe Johnson Archive in Rostock is suggestive on this score. In his own copy of the second volume of Weiss's *Notizbücher 1971–1980*, Johnson marked all of Weiss's references to death there as well as the following passage: "I am a schizophrenic, holding myself up for more than 8 years with this novelistic life [*Roman-Leben*]. It is as if that which has been artistically created has become part of my own life, everything that takes place here is true for me."[68] Weiss's description of his work on *Die Ästhetik* could not have hit Johnson closer to home; at least it is hard to imagine that the latter did not find it relevant to his own work on

Jahrestage. Accordingly, charges leveled at *Jahrestage*, whose author was seen to "be playing a little hide-and-seek and calling himself Gesine Cresspahl" were perhaps unsurprising.[69] While literary critics were swift to scrutinize Cresspahl as a kind of "*wunschbiographische*" alter ego of the writer who created her and remained wary of *Jahrestage*'s "contract" as a questionable deceit, Johnson's confidence in the procedure established was evident from his own account of the differences between his biography and Gesine's: his delineation in *Begleitumstände* both countered the aperçu of the singular identity of person (character) and author (*Verfasser*) and prolonged the enchantment of the parallels (*BU* 440–444). As with Weiss's narrator, Gesine's biography is altered in suggestive and symbolic ways that reveal the power of fictional transformation. Whereas Weiss's postdated his own birth to have his narrator's coincide with the beginning of the October revolution, Gesine's is dated to March 3, 1933—predating Johnson's own by less than a year and half—to dovetail with the imprisonment of German communist Ernst Thälmann and the effective beginning of the Nazi terror (*AN* 136/*JT* 202).[70] Where Weiss's symbolic chronology dovetails with his work's focus on the travails of the antifascist resistance, Gesine's preoccupation with the deaths of others—most sharply with Jewish victims of the Nazi dictatorship—inform her keen awareness, as if carried within her as a permanent part of her posttraumatic consciousness, of "belonging to a people that butchered another in too large a number" (*JT* 232). This sensitivity propels *Jahrestage*'s sustained inquiry into how to live (and how to write of the attempt to live) after Auschwitz.[71] On a lighter note, while the careers of Cresspahl and Johnson clearly differ, there are a number of geographic overlaps in their migrations, culminating in Johnson's providing Gesine and Marie with his own family's address and telephone number in the apartment on Riverside Drive in Manhattan (*AN* 104/*JT* 145), which sets Gesine's projected departure from New York City in the direction of Prague into sharp relief. Striking in Johnson's comparison of himself to Cresspahl is also his attention to gender, which he identifies as a factor in determining his relocation to West Berlin (because he would be free there of the military service compulsory for West German men), whereas Gesine faced no such consideration, but surely others (*BU* 442–443).[72] One sees quickly: Johnson insists both on the differences between himself and his artistic creation as well as on the independent reality of the latter. As Ralf Schnell has written in a clarification of the relationship between Cresspahl and Johnson, the I of the text—whether Gesine's or the Writer's—is not Uwe Johnson, at least not in any immediate sense, but mediated through narrative technique: "Gesine is not a projection, but rather part of his life, an integral part as well as a medium of its communication."[73] Where Johnson can feign an alibi for his work by appealing to Gesine's cofacilitation thereof, their contract binds her to him as much as him to her, fueling the literary play of identity and difference in the presentation of life possibilities and their critical review, thereby outfitting the epic with a spectrum of situationally bound investigations into Cold War living.[74] Wishful biography is thus transformed into a graphic of so many wishes, perhaps nowhere more compactly presented than in the explicit anniversary correspondence between the New York and Jerichow narratives on St. Nicholas Day: featuring Heinrich Cresspahl itemizing his hopes for the coming year in a Christmas spirit thirty-three years prior to December 6, 1967, the chapter closes jarringly with a note on his picking up an application for a membership in the Nazi Party that he would not pursue (*AN* 270–274/*JT* 414–418).[75] No mere personal fantasy or play of hide-and-seek, Johnson's ulterior novelistic life—to continue the parallel with Weiss's note—graphs wishes in historical time. The tenability of its account stands and falls with the work's ability to capture and speak to the texture of the world's historical course within the parallel fictional world it sets against it.

As can be gleaned from the above, the stakes for *Jahrestage* are as high as for *Die Ästhetik*, but also of a different kind. The shared starting point rests in reconstituting the postcatastrophic narration of what once was via the genre's self-reflexive deployment of its autodiegetic narrators. In lieu of presupposing the self-evidence of literary narrative in an age of its uncertainty, both works foreground the tasks and struggles of mediation—in some contrast to the nonliterary media on which the genre's narrators set to work—as the bridge-building between experience, truth, and justice that it is. This activity, which includes the remediation of media populating the epics' environments, constitutes an additional common denominator between *Die Ästhetik* and *Jahrestage*, and yet the epics' respective interactions with media—as sites where epic senses can be cultivated, built up, and developed—differ sharply in their actual procedures. To ascertain differences in the techniques of literary remediation employed in the modern epic as well as the specifics of *Jahrestage*'s contribution in this regard, the next section delves into Johnson's work on media and his book's assembly of a living archive from out of its twentieth-century investigations.

Media and Archives

> That is not to be believed; could it be true?
>
> —January 26, 1968

> For Cresspahl these were things he had never heard before. . . . And yet these were all familiar things, seen merely from a different viewpoint, seen fresh.
>
> —December 28, 1968

Jerichow residents Heinrich Cresspahl and Jakob Abs both possess the curious ability to train their gazes into the distance (*AN* 120, 347, *AN II*,

264, 391/*JT* 176, 532, 1234, 1478; *die Augen auf Fernsicht stellen*). Such a predisposition likely stems from their sojourns by ship, train, and horse carriage across sea and land. Of the faculties of the human sensorium explored in *Jahrestage*, sight stands out as a sense to be trained. The thematization of various characters' abilities to see through and across space and time recurs throughout its chapters.[76] In both the Jerichow and New York City narratives, the faculty is endowed primarily with political significance and concerns interpretations of events that bear on individuals' judgments and decisions for or against specific courses of action: Gesine interrogates her father's ability—not without repartee—to read Germany's future history out of the events of 1933 (*AN* 117, 233–234, 257, 312/*JT* 169, 348, 391, 470), processes the memory of her own perceptions of war as a child (*AN* 324; *AN II*, 71, 114/*JT* 494–495, 885, 955), and reflects on Marie's conception of the war in Vietnam that she cannot see (*AN* 322/*JT* 492). A necessary if by itself insufficient component of the kind of informed behavior to which Gesine aspires (*AN* 142/*JT* 209–210), seeing is itself conditioned by wishes and feelings, habits and socialization. *Jahrestage* subjects the faculty of sight to investigation in order to ascertain the kinds of insight human beings can achieve vis-à-vis the processes determining the fabric of their lives.

Seeing is not the only faculty in question in the epic's examination of the human sensorium. The essay Marie composes for a homework assignment "I Look Out the Window" relates images of a fire on Ninety-Sixth Street to her mother's recollection of the war only at the latter's protest: "No . . . I said it smelled like war," Gesine clarifies with a nod to the power of the olfactory sense (*AN* 122/*JT* 179). Yet contrary to the madeleines of another age, the senses of smell and taste are, like "Gustafsson's famous fish salad" (cf. *AN* 47/*JT* 64), unreliable mnemonics in *Jahrestage* and not prominently featured in the narrative.[77] More significant is the role of the auditory, where radio, the Nazi usurpation of public spaces, and then the air-raid alert sirens and bombs of war—not to mention the many reverberations of noise in the American metropolis (*AN* 157–159/*JT* 240–243)—constitute the sounds with which modern epic discourse must contend.[78] Whether Heinrich Cresspahl's "Volksempfänger, 'people's receiver' " or Alexander Paepcke's "Blaupunkt magic-eye radio" with access to the BBC (*AN II*, 44/*JT* 835), references to radio point to the important role media play in both strands of the narrative.[79] Communication technologies populating the epic include such radios as well as letters, tape recordings, telegrams, teletypewriters, polygraphs, and photographs. These material media constitute prosthetic extensions of the human sensorium into spaces and times beyond immediate experience, as crucial to the epic's expansion of optics as they are dangerous. Cresspahl's perusal of the newspapers from his 1933 purview while still in England indicates part of the challenge: "For eight months Cresspahl could watch from the outside how the Nazis were setting up their state. . . . Since he had been living in towns he had read the newspapers . . . slowly, as recreation almost, and with a deep-rooted suspicion that reserved for his own eyes proof of the truth of the news" (*AN* 233–234/*JT* 348). While the ubiquity of medial misrepresentation warrants Cresspahl's skepticism, the passage simultaneously questions the trust placed in one's own ability to see: the already apparent baneful political trajectory of Germany does not countervail against Cresspahl's decision to return. Gesine's characterization of her father's stubborn comportment alludes to the fraught interplay between the use of one's own sense(s) and the necessary reliance on their medial enhancement.

Basic rudiments of epic orientation in time and space, the faculties of seeing and listening are for sensing and distinguishing what is near and what is far.[80] *Jahrestage*'s examination of the reliability of prosthetic extensions of the senses is particularly evident in the book's interaction with the nonliterary print medium of the newspaper, most prominently the *New York Times*. The scholarship has accordingly devoted considerable attention to Johnson's use thereof to reveal its changing function in the epic and advance different lines of interpretation regarding *Jahrestage*'s intermedial practices. Documenting the present for Gesine, the *New York Times* she avidly peruses can appear as a substitute for her own more direct experience.[81] At the same time, the paper facilitates an appropriate self-contextualization of the foreigner's frame of reference in the metropolis (*AN* 55/*JT* 74) as well as a compression and expansion of time and space for the senses (*AN* 90/*JT* 127). By and large, Johnson's use of the paper constitutes a medial transposition of highly filtered source material, ranging from brief intermedial references to stories reported in the *Times* through lengthier paraphrases of reports to direct translations, for which Johnson includes the *Times* copyright. As commentators have noted and as a perusal of Johnson's own archival scrapbooks of the paper confirm, there is a particularly heavy thematic emphasis on violence in relation to the Vietnam War, political strife and crime in U.S. urban centers, and the long postwar shadows cast by recent catastrophes.[82] The subjective imprint of these focal points is clear enough. But even as Gesine and Marie's processes of selective reception are marked in the narrative and even as Johnson was keen to insist on the absorption of all the documentary material into Gesine's consciousness,[83] the epic extensiveness of *Jahrestage*'s remediation of journalistic content places an unusual burden on readers' suspension of disbelief regarding the assiduousness of Gesine's daily activity.

Deborah L. Horzen has sounded this last point in her insightful study of *Jahrestage*'s use of the *New York Times*.[84] Demonstrating *Jahrestage*'s narrative adaptation of newspaper materials to its own structure and themes, Horzen's grasps the book's newspaper both as an "authentic channel of information about current events" and a "virtually infinite narrative background for Gesine's reflections and reconstructions."[85] In drawing attention to *Jahrestage*'s multifold orchestration of documentary material, however, Horzen's "Fitting the News to the Novel" also ascertains an overall reduction in the truth-content of *Jahrestage*'s objectivity, since she regards the mediation of the material by Gesine as still "more prejudiced" than the paper.[86] In regularly questioning the paper's news reporting and editorial practices, however, the attention Gesine pays to reality's mediation by the *Times* signals an important concern of her own storytelling.[87] Readers are de facto confronted with alternative, competing mediators: the tenability of Gesine's reporting and that of her Auntie Times will turn both on the veracity of their contents as well as the character of the relationships they maintain with their points of reference and intended audiences.

Over the course of *Jahrestage*, Gesine's reliance on the *New York Times* yields to an increasingly skeptical comportment vis-à-vis the medium, more reminiscent of her father's "deep-rooted suspicion" of news outlets. If Cresspahl's disbelief of British reports of the Nazis' rise to power proved less than credible, Gesine's occasional withholding of creditability from the *Times* yields benefits. To be sure, the skepticism on display possesses a dual character indicative of Cresspahl and Johnson's narrative teamwork. The effect is such that Gesine's repartees to *Times* articles may first reflect her own pre-established positions or convictions, as demonstrated by the sharp entry into the September 4 chapter on Labor Day:

> Are we to believe this? That more than three hundred Czechoslovak intellectuals have launched an appeal to the West to join in a protest campaign against their own censorship authorities, and of all people to the author John Steinbeck? We don't think we will believe this. Steinbeck has visited the war in Vietnam and what he saw there did not displease him. Nevertheless, the New York *Times* seems to believe the report and publishes it on the front page. (*AN* 37/*JT* 51)

In contrast to the many news items that populate *Jahrestage* without any explicit response on Gesine's part, this entry couches the intermedial reference to the report within her expression of incredulity. The vigor of the chapter's opening paragraph surely derives from the entwinement of the three key issues at hand: U.S. military pursuits in Southeast Asia that spur Gesine's refusal to settle too comfortably into her new home, political turmoil in the Czechoslovakia that she will elevate into the space of her epic hope, and—here perhaps Johnson's more so than Cresspahl's—interest in the question of the public role of writers in contemporary politics. As the *Kommentar* on *Jahrestage* has documented, Gesine's politically sagacious suspicion in this case was correct: the appeal referred to there was forged.[88] While the skepticism directed at the *Times* also applies to its editorial decision to credit its source and feature the report on its first page, the pronominal "we" in the passage points to a more general incredulity directed at the *Times*' reporting. The crux of the intermedial practice on display derives from Johnson's use of Gesine as a checking mechanism for reality's mediation, the reliability of which cannot be taken for granted simply because it appears in such a trusted paper. *Jahrestage*'s source material—devoid of its "inherent objectivity"[89] in this case—proves an untrustworthy mediation. Note the fierce competition of reality's respective mediations: it cannot derive from any claim regarding the ultimate unattainability of truth, but rather its reinstatement as a criterion for the tenability of journalism and storytelling alike. Nowhere does *Jahrestage* disavow the process of truth's ascertainment that ingrains the book's moral fiber.[90]

Gesine's relation to the *New York Times* nonetheless abounds more in esteem than in any abstract ideological opposition (cf. *AN* 120–121/*JT* 176–177). All criticism and parody of the medium aside, the *Times* remains a key "dispenser of [the] reality" (*AN* 399/*JT* 609; *Lieferantin von Wirklichkeit*) that *Jahrestage* refuses to jettison. In this formulation, the paper—like Johnson's own installments of *Jahrestage* (*BU* 428; *Lieferungen*)—is granted the status of a good to be used, like a tool. This pinpoints the function of media in their proper role, not as reality itself, but the potential means of its unraveling. For this reason, all media—including Moscow and Prague papers on which Gesine also draws in mapping the Cold War—demand the kind of problem-oriented scrutiny modeled in *Jahrestage*'s interaction with the *Times*, lest Gesine's concession of her own "defenselessness" vis-à-vis her aunt come true (*AN* 338/*JT* 518).

A particularly telling example of *Jahrestage*'s examination of the character of reality's mediation appears in its January 27 chapter. Following up on a report on the communications industry's false image of U.S. minorities and their absence from positions in the media, the *Times* wants to provide readers with glimpses into its editorial offices, in what seems an effort to reveal the conditions of its work behind the scenes with greater transparency. In describing how it crafts its reporting of the news, the *Times* presumes to have demonstrated how every reader's question will have been answered, a notion at which *Jahrestage* directs particular scorn (*JT* 648).[91] The *Times*' self-commentary is clearly a piece of self-marketing. It may even be humorously intended, though Cresspahl and Johnson turn such intent on its head here.[92] The problem remains that the paper's own exercise in self-reflexivity takes shape as an attack on readers' agency: the whole process of questioning and answering, as exercises of readers' own faculties, is being usurped by the editors. Johnson's chapter exposes the paper's hubris by formulating—against the pettier concerns staged in the *Times* article—questions the paper has in fact not answered. Here the collective pronoun stands not only for Cresspahl and Johnson's teamwork, but also for the whole reading public: why, for example, does the *Times* downplay reports from the Fulbright Commission on the travesties of the U.S.'s Vietnam War policy? Why has it newly limited reports on the Vietnam War dead to U.S. soldiers from the New York region (*JT* 648–649)? In both cases, Johnson ventriloquizes the paper's suppression of such ulterior questions—"The question is incorrectly posed. . . . One cannot look at the matter in that way"—revealing thereby the narrower discursive confines through which the "fitness" of the news for print is being established. "Any questions? Fit to print?" The German chapter ends with the English phrases, exposing such fitness as a sham and the mediation of the *Times* as a dangerous affront. In their treatment of the *Times*' fitness clause as untranslatable (*AN* 120/*JT* 176), Johnson and Cresspahl ultimately reject it as a criterion for truth's ascertainment. Fitness may govern the *Times*' management of editorial decisions, it may even provide for enticing stories and novels, yet in conformity with the claim that Johnson is using the fictional status of Gesine and her own reading for the purposes of a general aesthetic of cognitive mapping, the news that Horzen fits to Johnson's novel simultaneously provides an occasion for that genre's epic turn and the expansion of its cartographic efforts. The modern epic will not be governed by fitness.

Thus, in contrast to the extensive reliance of Weiss's *Die Ästhetik des Widerstands* on works of art for generating its model of the world's course as a long trajectory of emancipation, *Jahrestage* implicitly and explicitly champions a principled scrutiny vis-à-vis its nonartistic source materials. Yet a second function of Gesine's remediation of the *New York Times* relates much more closely to the "living archives" mobilized in Weiss's epic. Cresspahl's vast inventory of world events—replete with its disjointed, non-self-contained maps of past, present, and future—constitutes nothing short of a sourcebook for informed living. A relevant "archivological" interpretation thereof has been advanced by Eva Schauerte.[93] Zeroing in on the intermediality between the newspaper and the literary work's calendar format, Schauerte highlights the importance of Johnson's own practice of archiving the news in the scrapbooks underlying *Jahrestage*'s literary remediations. Detailing this practice from the predigital age as a "materialized labor of memory" by which Johnson rendered the fleeting medium of the paper more durable, Schauerte accounts for the establishment of an "anchor between external, past reality and time and the narratological operations of the author and his persons" in Johnson's workshop.[94] She accordingly works up its significance in relation to *Jahrestage*'s own thematization of two archives operative in its pages. The first is that of Gesine's partner D. E., who has converted "his memory into knowledge . . . [but] no longer lives with these things" from the past save as components "summoned on demand" (*AN* 227/*JT* 339). This relates to his ability, in the role of "planner, protector, initiator" (*AN II*, 226/*JT* 1150), to navigate the world with seemingly little effort, as on his trip to Richmond, England, with Gesine and Marie, recollected in the November 22 chapter, where D. E.'s eagerness to please does not exactly render his worldly-wise ways more endearing. Gesine, on the contrary, and in the words of D. E.'s handwritten letter to the recipient of his modern romantic appeals, perseveres differently. For D. E.'s Gesine, "rain, death, and the ocean" are still real; all about her there is a "past filled with characters, a present that includes the dead" (*AN II*, 30/*JT* 817). Whereas Schauerte proceeds to substantiate the distinction between Gesine and D. E.'s respective living and dead archives in relation to the memory experiment of the October 27–28 chapters,[95] D. E.'s depiction of his friend already points to the connection between her living archive and the storytelling it serves. In contrast to D. E.'s inventories that ossify information and objectify knowledge to render it instrumental, Gesine's repository quickens through the narration of the past, transforming it into aesthetic experience in and for the present. While D. E. can organize the 1966 tour of Richmond that Marie found less than exciting (*AN* 225/*JT* 335), Gesine can narrate it as the tale that draws her daughter—and readers—into the past's possibilities.[96] As Schauerte notes, *Jahrestage*'s adaptation of past and present reality through the paper and other extraliterary historical sources is predicated on a retraction of the opposition Walter Benjamin had maintained between the information of new media and epic narration.[97] And as Holger Helbig has shown in an essay on *Jahrestage*'s citational and narrative practices, Johnson maintains a strategy of "higher transcription" to transform its source materials into art.[98] Analyzing the June 18 chapter, Helbig demonstrates how *Jahrestage*'s remediation of its source materials satisfies the dual criteria of historical veracity and aesthetic success in a non-conflicting way.[99] Such an achievement does not take place for its own sake in *Jahrestage*, but informs the larger vision of Gesine's and the epic's own aesthetic imagination.

With this account of *Jahrestage*'s intermediality, one has arrived at the crux of the work's own tenability. "Living archive" most pertinently concerns the production of stories in, with, and through which one can live. Marie's New Year's gift to her mother is key in this regard: she not only constructs a model of Gesine's Jerichow home based on her mother's stories but also, in reviewing her progress with Gesine, notes that she will equip the attic for subsequent chapters (*JT* 540; *Für das, was nun kommt*). Such rooms are narrative chambers; *Jahrestage*'s chapters are stations of an at least temporary residence, passageways for dwelling.[100] Whereas Marie, perhaps because she perceives her own identity as New Yorker and American as stable, visualizes Gesine's stories in terms of the physical home, the living archive cannot be a house for Gesine, but must be and remain mobile. A more appropriate image might have been any number of seafaring vessels with which to sail the epic's hydropoetic waves, such as the Station Island Ferry, which Marie appreciates as "a house that drives . . . a street between the islands that takes itself across" (*AN* 67/*JT* 91; *die sich selbst übersetzt*). Surmising that "where I am from is no longer" (*AN* 255; translation modified/*JT* 386), Gesine elevates stories to the status of a home that is not otherwise to be had save through the telling: her tales achieve their tenability as products of one's narrative labor in and on the world, scrutinized as to the conditions of their own possibility, tested according to intermingled criteria of truth and plausibility, and wielded as tentative, yet powerful constructs in the knowledge of their ultimate difference from the realities they are set against.[101] At issue is not merely the appropriation of the past or one's background (*AN II*, 30/*JT* 817;

Herkunft) for the sake of its memorialization. Homesickness has only ever meant "train station" to Gesine.[102] For Cresspahl and the project of her life, the living archive's value manifests itself in the affirmation of a portable and future-oriented identity. When, how and where Gesine's stories are headed, where they are taking her, that is, what their larger implications are—such questions are entrained over the course of *Jahrestage*'s epic probe of space and time in the progression of its year.

Nowhere is the principle of home-making through storytelling demonstrated more triumphantly than in the lead-up to the epic's ominous conclusion. Accelerating in leaps and bounds over the spaces and times on which *Jahrestage* has lingered, Gesine's stories approximate the narrative present to become coterminous with the reach of Marie's conscious memory by the final chapters of the fourth volume. It is here that Marie introduces a refrain to herald the value of (storytelling's) hospitality. It emerges with her welcoming Gesine to the San Francisco they visit briefly on August 15 during her mother's attempt to shield her daughter from the news of D. E.'s death (*AN II*, 609/*JT* 1845). The next day, after Gesine has recounted her relocation from Mecklenburg to West Berlin in 1953 on the return trip to New York, Marie modifies her English refrain: "Welcome home, Gesine!" (*AN II*, 617/*JT* 1855). Last, at the end of the next chapter, as Gesine's narration of the past has reached the American metropolis, Marie celebrates the homecoming of the tale: "In New York I turned four. Finally we have arrived where my memory knows its way around. Welcome home!" (*AN II*, 631/*JT* 1875; *wo meine Erinnerung Bescheid weiß*). Marie's announcement occurs on the very page to which Johnson ascribes the completion of the manuscript within the fiction (*AN II*, 644/*JT* 1891). The provisional August 17 conclusion of the *Jahrestage* story presents a tentative, complex, and paradoxical homecoming. As Marie gains at least partial control of the narrative, Gesine's ripostes to her daughter are either absent from these sections of the text or take place via detours, as in the delayed response to Marie's interjectory appeals to homesickness (*AN II*, 620/*JT* 1860–1861). Above and beyond Marie and Gesine's own reflections on their present and future transit, the fraying texture of the larger literary mediation under way in these chapters is particularly suggestive. Marie's exclamatory homecoming cheer not only stands in sharp contrast to their impending departure for Prague. It must also be read against the entwinement of A. M.'s letter to Cresspahl that Gesine reads as clearing her psychologically for work[103] and the August 17 chapter on the discourse of the past's mastery (*AN II*, 617ff./*JT* 1856ff.). In short, Marie's diction and formulations perform and yet undermine the closure at hand: "Knowledge is power [*Gelernt ist gelernt*], Gesine. Go ahead and tell it" (*AN II*, 625, 626/*JT* 1867, 1868), she repeats in another refrain, as if coaxing Gesine to the finish line, resting assuredly atop the past participle (*gelernt*) that skepticism of the past's mastery (*Bewältigung*)—"To accomplish. To master" (*AN II*, 622/*JT* 1864; rendered in English in the German text)—would prohibit. Marie's formulation of the narrative's arrival modifies her mother's own articulation of her life project. Where Gesine wanted to "*find out about things. At least to live with my eyes open*" (*AN* 142/*JT* 209–210; *Bescheid zu lernen. Wenigstens mit Kenntnis zu leben*), Marie replaces the active verb "to learn" (*lernen*) with a seemingly possessive "knowing" (*Bescheid wissen*). Her comment, which contrasts with Gesine's projected activation of her learning on the eve of the Prague journey, can be read as a slippage that tacitly reminds readers of the fallacy of claiming too firm a hold on memory and knowledge. The point of arrival ebbs. Begging anew the question of memory's ability to ascertain the past, Marie is already conferring the narrative to the larger sea from which it would reemerge and be relived in some newly admixed nonidentical variation. In this way, *Jahrestage* confirms its narrative undertaking as a medium for perennial returns and differential repetitions, retaining the living character of an archive to be reactualized at need and whim.

Emphatic at its closing, *Jahrestage*'s orientation to its heterodiegetic future is marked in numerous ways throughout the text. One of the most intriguing aspects of the work's futurity concerns a missive Gesine files in her living archive midway through *Jahrestage*'s year. On February 7, she composes a letter to her daughter regarding "something I want to keep from you for another eight years" (*AN* 446/*JT* 687). The letter is more forthright and didactic than many of the stories Gesine tells for "when she is dead" (*AN* 108, 254/*JT* 151, 385, cf. 1048). What it contains is a mother's explanation and justification of her newfound enthusiasm for the socialist reform course she sees taking shape in Czechoslovakia. Detecting signs of the possibility of a "new beginning" there, Gesine regards this horizon of her life as a great personal and societal opportunity to which she would commit herself fully (*AN* 447–448/*JT* 688–690). Placing the logic of her interpretation of events, her reasoning and accompanying conclusions on full display in the letter, Gesine directs her bottled message to the appropriate time of its comprehensibility, when Marie will be of age, so that her daughter might understand Gesine's reasoning on its own terms and in its own time.[104] The subjective transfer of a mother's message through the portals of time will remain fraught, the letter a future-oriented projectile of a possibly derelict project Gesine will not be able to control, not only because the objective trajectory of political history in Czechoslovakia will take its own course, but also because Gesine can steer others' understanding of her chosen course of action only up to a point. With Gesine's decision to ride this larger wave, the texture of her relationship to the Prague Spring comes to constitute the most beguiling trajectory of the entire narrative. Against a Cold War that makes life opportunities as difficult to see as they are to judge, *Jahrestage* amasses a cartography of its times, from Gesine, who keeps tracking it, clinging to life as a project, in search of self-actualization, outward. To ascertain how Gesine's Prague becomes visible to her in this way, the next section provides a brief overview of *Jahrestage*'s mapping techniques, before, in the concluding section, turning to its mediation of Gesine's space of epic hope as a contribution to a critical understanding of society's development.

Mapping the Cold War

Tell her, Gesine. . . . Improve on what we did.

—April 22, 1968

You say you come from the German Baltic? But the land comes to an end up there!

—Kreslil to Cresspahl on March 28, 1968

Gesine's storytelling in *Jahrestage* extends from the engagement of Marie's grandparents Heinrich Cresspahl and Lisbeth Papenbrock in 1931 to the epic's narrative present. As much as the Nazi dictatorship, world war and the Shoah constitute gravitational pulls thereof, by the end of the second volume, Gesine has arrived at the beginning of Jerichow's "New Era" (*AN II*, 159/*JT* 1029), as she designates the caesura of 1945. Though she claims the period would prove "good training" (*AN II*, 146/*JT* 1001), from the beginning of her account of the Soviet occupation of the town, Gesine finds herself beset by new difficulties in the telling. The concern recurs across *Jahrestage*'s third volume. Beseeched by her deceased relatives to improve on their own example—of parenting, educating, living?—Gesine, mindful of the power of Cold War opposition to overwrite mentalities, hesitates for a moment, fearing that Marie will draw the wrong conclusions—for example, conflate Soviet domination with socialism as a political project *tout court*—from a full reckoning with postwar history in Europe's East. As Gesine's recapitulation of her family history morphs into that of her own life, the Jerichow and New York City narratives become increasingly intertwined under the sign of geopolitics. As an overwhelming codeterminant bearing down on individual political decisions, the context places strains on Gesine and Marie's efforts to orient themselves across Johnson's tumultuous year, revealing *Jahrestage* to be an epic of the Cold War more than of any other.

Adhering to its frame narrative in conformity with its contractual arrangement, *Jahrestage* does not depict the present as some repetition of the past. Gesine reads the news with politico-historical vigilance to pinpoint how and where catastrophic history can be overcome, whence the vigor of her scrutiny. As her direct and indirect gaze befalls past, present, and future across Jerichow, New York, and Prague, *Jahrestage* abounds in myriad juxtapositions of its different contents. The epic's curious practice of montage has accordingly attracted attention. Despite Johnson's own reservations regarding the term,[105] montage can be used to delineate the various cross-cutting techniques by which Cresspahl and Johnson navigate swiftly between spatially and temporally disparate sites. The procedure occurs in at least two different ways within individual chapters. Montage effects can derive, for example, from those chapters modeled on chronicle narration. On December 18 (*AN* 312–315/*JT* 471–475), February 12 (*AN* 461–463/*JT* 710–723), March 12 (*AN II*, 58–61/*JT* 856–862), and elsewhere, Johnson deploys the techniques of a chronicler's swift sequencing of events and leaps from one character's perspective to another to compress space and time and advance the past's narration.[106] The October 3 chapter, by contrast, evinces a more modernist version of montage at work. Like others composed as vignettes, the chapter's beginning and end supply a frame for its heterogeneous contents. Its outer edges are marked by Gesine's financial maintenance of gravesites, first via the bill from one Emmy Creutz in Jerichow, last by (Jakob's mother) Marie Abs, who lies buried in the West German city of Hanover (*AN* 98–100/*JT* 137–140). The text oscillates back and forth between these signposts, paragraph by paragraph, interspersing paraphrases of *New York Times* articles and excerpts from Creutz's communiqué. References to U.S. bombing strikes in Vietnam, the capture of Nazi war criminal Erich Rajakowitsch in Istria, repercussions of Stalinist purges in the USSR, a Darmstadt trial against members of the SS, and declining support for the war in Vietnam by the U.S. public comprise the former. In the latter, Gesine receives the documentation of Creutz's work at the Jerichow church cemetery and a detailed request for the compensation thereof in the form of purchases from capitalist markets.

One of *Jahrestage*'s most intense chapters, the rapid delivery on October 3 highlights the epic's range of themes before their rhythmic recurrences may have impressed themselves on readers. Gesine also recounts the suicide of Amalie Creutz, who preceded Emmy as the cemetery caretaker Erich Creutz's wife. Like the diminished friendliness in Emmy's tone to Gesine, the episode is contextualized only hundreds of pages later (*AN II*, 107, 264–265/*JT* 944, 1235). Standing by itself as it does, the reference to Amalie is turned, along with the other items, into an assembly that coheres around the theme of death in an arrangement where no one item is granted more importance than another. But the chapter's components are also not equivalent. The montage draws no balance: the disparity between the barter-like exchange between Gesine and Emmy and the automatic payment set up as a bank transfer for Abs's grave is mirrored in the differences between Nazi, Stalinist, and U.S. violence. The amplification of difference runs counter to Marie's interest in establishing correlations between past and present, as when she alleges a connection between Jerichow residents' initial ostracization of the daughter (Gesine) of the appointed mayor (Heinrich) cooperating with the Russians and the treatment of Francine as an African American girl at Marie's otherwise all-white school. Gesine warns her daughter not to compare elements across times and contexts (*JT* 1048; *Vergleich es nicht*), whereby Marie remains no less free to draw the conclusions she works out in her own thoughts. Where a too-facile drawing of analogies risks misrecognizing the present, *Jahrestage*'s montage assemblies fuel training in the differentiating power of epic optics.[107]

The October 3 chapter's somber focus on a scene of nonconvergent deaths is offset only by the sun that shines onto Emmy's gravesite plantings—"pansies" renders *Stiefmütterchen* there, the "little stepmothers" growing over Heinrich and Jakob's Jerichow graves, but not Lisbeth's (*AN* 99/*JT* 138). Its montage stands out for the intense abruptness of its shifts and resulting juxtapositions. *Jahrestage*'s chapters usually contain fewer, such that montage effects will more often make themselves felt between the days of its year. Stemming from Johnson's strategic arrangements of the material, key indications of this more general technique include the chapters on and around October 21, with the resulting juxtaposition of the narration of Gesine's birth to Heinrich Cresspahl's clandestine cooperation with the SPD in Lübeck and the mass demonstration in Washington, D.C., against the war in Vietnam that Gesine failed to attend but prefers to read about (*AN* 136–139/*JT* 206–210). Featuring Gesine's first tape-recorded message to her daughter, the November 29 chapter ends with her faltering attempt to speak to Marie about the latter's father Jakob and an apology. It is preceded by Gesine's receiving an admonishing letter in response to her earlier inquiry to GDR authorities regarding the number of Jewish summer guests at the nearby town Rande prior to 1933 and followed by her account of her father's rebuke of Mannig Susemihl, who had visited him in Richmond in 1933 to enlist his help in anti-Nazi activities. The chapters beginning mid-February, on the other hand, interweave—amid Gesine's illness—the narration of the pogrom on November 9, 1938, during which Lisbeth witnesses the murder of eight-year-old Marie Tannebaum; slaps the perpetrator, Nazi mayor and chief of police Friedrich Jansen, in the face; and commits suicide thereafter, and that of Marie's difficulties with Francine, whom she and Gesine "lose" to the welfare authorities, who demand that Francine be reunited with her mother (*AN* 499–501/*JT* 769–774). In such clusters, the epic's political nerve centers are being worked out, if inconclusively. In the first case, Gesine's abstention from politics is contrasted with that of her father's participation, even as both comportments read as instinctual in context there. In the second, Heinrich's considered refusal to help Susemihl contrasts with Gesine's pointed inquiry to Rande, the conspiracy-theoretical response to which both suspects her of intent to defame the GDR and is undersigned by one Susemihl (*AN* 253/*JT* 384–385). In the third, Lisbeth's fictional fate is inscribed into the history of persecution in Nazi Germany and placed in contrasting proximity to race relations in New York City. Reading *Jahrestage* with an eye for such juxtapositions reveals the orchestration of numerous parallels. They create no identities across times, but supply the present with a backdrop against which the grain of individuals' conditionings, comportments, and decisions can be examined and evaluated.

When undertaken within the narrative present, *Jahrestage*'s assemblies splice different spaces together to yield a geopolitically inflected aesthetic of cognitive mapping. Whereas Gesine's well-nigh ascetic abstention from politics in the U.S. can resemble a strategy of hibernation,[108] the rationales she offers for her choices reveal suggestive clues about her orientation. In response to her relatives' rebuke, Gesine defends her absence from the October 21 demonstration in Washington by attempting to walk them through the coordinates of the interpretation of her actions according to the bipolar Cold War matrix of the blocs: "A rejection of North American expansion in Asia would be twisted into approval of Soviet expansion" (*AN* 141/*JT* 208), she maintains, which her relatives regard as a piece of intellectually rationalizing nonsense. Although she attends peace rallies with and for Marie (*AN II*, 185–189/*JT* 1069–1075), the larger interpretative context—hypermediated, often conspiracy-theoretical, and in any case heavily impacted by the dominant geopolitical ideologies on ample display in the papers—remains ever-present to Gesine, who scoffs at others' overvaluations of individuals' influence (see, e.g., *JT* 894). Whereas such signs have contributed to readers' impressions of Cresspahl's deep-seated pessimism, she also demonstrates the ability to see through her own and others' equations wrought via the geopolitical matrix (*AN* 442/*JT* 682; *Gleichungen*). Her notes critical of student protests—such as those at Columbia University recounted in the May 1 chapter—are not entirely unfounded; they betray at least some analytical precision (*JT* 1091–1096). Setting forth itemizations of events and their threads as summer approaches, she phones Anita Gantlik to discuss student protests in West Berlin, where the assassination of Martin Luther King Jr. in Memphis on April 4 is perceived as a not-quite-comprehensible precedent for the assassination attempt on the West German student leader Rudi Dutschke on April 11 (*JT* 988–989); interlaces reports on student protests in New York City and Warsaw (*JT* 863), Paris and Prague (*JT* 1106–1107); juxtaposes French, Polish, East German, and Czechoslovakian Communists' actions to one another (*AN II*, 246/*JT* 1199–1200); and tracks and translates news from Prague for professional (e.g., *JT* 1037) and personal reasons (*JT* 1446). Across 1968's transnational scope, Gesine is clearly plotting spaces of her possible engagement. Notably, whereas Western protest energies are directed against the U.S.'s war in Vietnam (*JT* 201) and where "1968" as a protest year may still loom in the minds of Westerners as a Western phenomenon, Gesine's radar traverses the geopolitical divide, identifying socialist Czechoslovakia's perceived spring as the time-space most worthy of her attention. Her focus stems not simply from the work for which she is commissioned by her employer and vice president of the New York bank Mr. de Rosny, who has spotted an opportunity for establishing financial relations with the ČSSR, but rather from Gesine's reflections on the preconditions of her political engagement: the prospects of a democratic socialism alone compel Cresspahl to convert her apprehensive cognition-oriented lifestyle into committed participation.

That such an option emerges at all as a space on *Jahrestage*'s realistically overdetermined cartography of the Cold War may seem a small wonder. As Gesine interprets this political window of 1968 as the concrete possibility[109] of a better future she can help build, Prague becomes the space of her epic hope on which Johnson's literary mediation of life in the Cold War turns.

Spaces of Epic Hope

> How much more often will hope construct a foundation for itself out of nothing other than rational building-blocks and maintain with irrational walls a room in which disappointment will later find comfortable residence?
>
> —March 25, 1968

> Four political systems attempted to change her person.
>
> —Johnson on Gesine

As historical difference accrues between *Jahrestage*'s literary cartography of the twentieth century and the ulterior shores of a post–Cold War age, the transhistorical validity of Johnson's accomplishment has come into question. Whereas Johnson's reckoning with totalitarian aspects of the Soviet occupation and the GDR received renewed interest in the wake of German unification, in a review of Johnson scholarship in 2001 Greg Bond provocatively claimed that *Jahrestage*'s key concerns—coming to terms with German guilt and grappling with individual human beings' orientation vis-à-vis Cold War division—rendered the work obsolete in the new century.[110] While the changed constellation did not imply the work's irrelevance for Bond, who still found *Jahrestage*'s adherence to these two questions exemplary,[111] Horst Turk has delivered a poignant response to the charge in "Europäische Konstellationen: Zur Aktualität Uwe Johnsons." Turk's reappraisal lays out paths for *Jahrestage*'s transfer into the new century by attending to the lingering urgency of its concerns, including not only the sagacity of its "Kapitalismus-Kritik"[112] but also the work's modulations of solidarity and integrity as well as its sustained analysis of the conditions of personal engagement and commitment, which Turk relates to contemporary politico-philosophical discussions.[113] In fact, *Jahrestage*'s examination of the prospects and meaning of individual action in the Cold War provides a prescient genealogy of the global present that has emerged in its wake.[114] Elliptically fused with the critical historical watershed of the Prague Spring, *Jahrestage*'s diagnosis of its own time is perched at the brink of its end. Johnson's evocative culmination of the epic renders the transition from one age to another newly legible and transfers potentials for renewed orientation through *Jahrestage*'s own terminal horizon.

This thesis befits both the many details of *Jahrestage*'s treatment of social history in the narrative's pasts and presents as well as its mediation of Gesine's relationship to Prague as the space of her—and the epic's own—hope. The thematic and formal dimensions of this trajectory hardly constitute uncharted territory in *Jahrestage* scholarship. Yet rereading *Jahrestage*'s rendering of Cold War history from a distance can confirm the value of the epic's adventurous radial tour through space and time for the futures beyond its purview. The economic and political points of focus in *Jahrestage*'s Prague plotline, the orchestrated features of the epic's closing, and the repercussions thereof for the further evolution of the modern epic genre point to the power of Johnson's work in its historical transfer. Treating these issues in conjunction with one another, the concluding section of this chapter also situates *Jahrestage* within the larger arch of the modern epic's course charted in this study.

Jahrestage renders the multifaceted economic and political dimensions of Gesine's emerging relationship to Prague equally palpable. As with the strong tows of the epic's many narrative currents and tensions, economic and political perspectives on this site take shape from above and below with unyielding fierceness. Their entwinement is inscribed into Gesine's orientation to Prague from the beginning. Her embedded individual perspective from below is dually conditioned by her unwavering commitment to a human socialism, on the one hand, and her employment at the bank under the direction of Mr. de Rosny, on the other. In the emerging liberalization of the Czechoslovak Socialist Republic, de Rosny has spotted an opportunity for the expansion of his institution's affairs and with that of finance capital itself. The apparent contradiction in which Gesine is thus embroiled is lost on no one, least of all Marie, who discerns dishonesty in her mother's claiming "to favor the socialist cause" while working in "a capitalist country, in a bank!" (*AN II*, 157/*JT* 1025). Where some mystery lingered about her father's commitment to espionage for Great Britain during the war (*AN II*, 24–28/*JT* 809–814), there is no real secret to Gesine's position, not least because she clearly regards her employment as a contingent and temporary way to provide for herself and her daughter. Gesine is never herself at work, which she does not regard as part of a fulfilled life (*AN II*, 163/*JT* 619, 1035, 1334, 1472). Johnson's two-sided description of Gesine's activity—objectively tasked with laying the groundwork for de Rosny's loan of hard currency to the Czechoslovak republic (see *AN II*, 88/*JT* 915), subjectively driven by the chance to "help repair a socialist economy" and the prospects of life there (*BU* 422)—sought to confirm the tenability of her approach to Prague.[115] While the implication of subjective control over the task at hand may already strike readers as naive in valuing the power of individual intentions over the larger societal functions of one's occupation, little would seem to prevent the constitutively unsettled Gesine from dissociating herself from said bank: the working conditions there clearly differ from her depiction of a democratic socialism's freedoms, which would include individuals' determination of the uses of the means of production

(*AN* 448/*JT* 690). While Gesine ascribes no more importance to her employment than a mere means to other ends, *Jahrestage*'s attention to the force of economics in its mediation of the Prague Spring will weigh far more heavily.

Where Gesine's casual dismissal of the repercussions of her professional activity may already appear tenuous, her seemingly categorical commitment to socialism proves a still more complex and engrossing issue. It is a piece of social conditioning and individual responsibility at once—and part of her own pathogenesis that she seeks to fathom and substantiate in the reconstruction of her biography. The depiction of her commitment comes replete with the recollection of socialism as a child's wish (*JT* 990), feigned attempts to fortify herself, in communication with D. E., against susceptibility to mere wishes (*JT* 866), and a reminder—via the same interlocutor—of its standing as an unshakeable aspect of Gesine's orientation: "You've never yet tired of taking the socialists' promises at their word, you persist in challenging the imperialist democracies with their nobly conceived constitutions. . . . If this were naïveté, I would swallow this never-ending pedagogic task with pleasure; but it is hope" (*AN II*, 31/*JT* 818). Johnson's own explanation—"at school she was taught socialism as the only humanly possible alternative. . . . She kept it in mind also because it concerned her home, because [this idea] was administering Mecklenburg"[116]—speaks not only to the inculcation of an ideology in a person, but also to Gesine's subsequent transformative appropriation of socialism: awakened from illusion by the dehumanizing atrocities perpetrated in its name, Gesine develops a discerning and differentiating comportment required by orientation to a utopian ideal. In flight from the GDR, as Johnson notes in the same interview, Gesine first skirts the contradiction between ideal and practice. By itself the notion of the productivity of the gap—between promises and betrayals, between socialism as it actually existed and its emancipatory projections—is nothing particularly new, having been mobilized repeatedly over the course of the history of socialist dissidence through 1989. And while Johnson's language in the interview appears to downplay the status of the socialist alternative,[117] the actual procedures of *Jahrestage*'s narration do more than feed on the gap between idea and reality.

From the beginning of the narration of Jerichow's "New Era" through *Jahrestage*'s "archaeology of a Stalinistically failed state,"[118] Gesine again and again works up differences between socialism's concrete possibilities from below and the actual realities thereof imposed from above into sharp contrast. As Gary Baker has maintained, Gesine's "experiences with socialism are perceived by her as a brush with concretely possible newness."[119] Her procedure adds new emphases to *Jahrestage*'s strategy of juxtaposition, as the documentation of the Prague Spring in the narrative present is set against the Stalinist repressions Gesine had witnessed in East Germany (e.g., *JT* 1415). The good training (*AN II*, 146/*JT* 1001) she claims to have received through her father's decision to remain there with her postwar certainly endowed her with sensitivity for socialism's inner antagonisms. By referring to the coercive variant implemented in Jerichow by Soviet commander K. A. Pontiy as "Pontiy's socialism," for example (*AN II*, 203/*JT* 1103), Gesine uses the possessive attribution to mark the usurpation of the ideal, a takeover that proves all too real in its debilitating effects on new beginnings in the town, including new mayor Heinrich Cresspahl's own approximation of the ideal from below (*AN II*, 193/*JT* 1079). In his probing article, Baker shows that Gesine's narrative exercises do not simply pit some unsubstantiated illusory ideal against the dismal conditions of socialism's forced postwar implementation; rather, they contrast such domination with the ulterior practical possibilities she experienced in her father's laudable efforts to provide for the town's sustenance (*AN II*, 199–206/*JT* 1098–1106) as well as the agrarian socialism practiced at Johnny Schlegel's farm, at which Gesine worked in the summers (*AN II*, 274–279/*JT* 1269–1275).[120] Marie Abs's responsiveness to need in her reorganization of the Cresspahl household, kitchen, and garden to provide equitably for the many refugees stationed there (*AN II*, 242–245/*JT* 1192–1197) constituted another sign of a socialism from below—until such efforts were aborted on her son Jakob's refusal to support her desire to relocate to a small farm of their own offered in the context of the land reform (*JT* 1197–1199). Repeatedly crushed in the historical time of the postwar's coldness, such utopian impulses were no imaginary illusions, but presented progressive social possibilities from which hope and commitment might have derived sustenance. Highlighting such footholds against their controversion in the Soviet practices undeserving of socialist title,[121] the epic's autodiegetic narrator holds utopian possibility against apocalypse in her double optics.[122] The difference may also be explained in reference to the politically peculiar nature of socialism's inner antagonisms, from above and below, within and without legality, constitutionality, and due process, against which processes of democratization enjoyed little chance.[123]

Drawing on her sense of possibility in and for what is still far (her *Fernsinn*), Gesine willfully inscribes the reform course discernible in the Prague Spring on the side of socialism's unfulfilled yet conceivable possibilities, grounds for which she experienced in real living. Gesine's interpretation is emphasized in the commentary she offers atop her June 28 translation of the entire "Manifesto of Two Thousand Words" written by Ludvík Vaculík in consultation with Czechoslovakian writers, intellectuals, and scholars. The document stands out as a symbol of the Prague Spring's "socialism with a human face." Despite the government's rejection of the publication, Gesine enthuses that "if you want to know what is possible of socialism in our times, learn Czech, people!" (*JT* 1447). Attuned to the objective conditions of possibility, Gesine's identification of Prague as the space in which her commitment to the socialist project could be renewed in action is, as Baker has outlined, by no means without reason: he demonstrates how much the initiatives undertaken by the Prague reformers speak to the historical scars and wounds of actually existing socialism in its Stalinist deformations.[124] And as D. G. Bond has emphasized in his diligent unraveling of the Prague plot,[125] reformers' attempts to deliver a redress of the past—as in the exposure, acknowledgment, and sought-out rectification of injustices (e.g., *AN II*, 104–105/*JT* 941)—resonates so strongly with Gesine that she posits Prague as a space of historical difference where a democratic socialism in Europe could disrupt the pattern of Cold War history hitherto. Perceptions of surrounding Warsaw Pact countries' commitments to intervene (*JT* 913, 1209, 1263), repeated signs and verifications of Soviet military maneuvers (which Gesine at first refuses to believe at *JT* 1110, but see *AN II*, 259, 301, 428, 450/*JT* 1222, 1314, 1335, 1522, 1555, 1595, etc.) notwithstanding, Cresspahl's focus on the ČSSR as a potentially sovereign (*AN II*, 97, 344/*JT* 928, 1374, 1537), constitutionally bound (*AN* 448/*JT* 690), and free space for democratic socialism fulfills the criteria she sets for her own political engagement.

A rationally sound procedure? To be sure, *Jahrestage*, characteristically adhering closely to extraliterary realities, does not make this evaluation easy; its tale cannot escape the force of heterodiegetic history against which it holds Gesine's hopes in the balance. As Prague hovers within the narrative between its status as a new beginning and its subjection to the longer streak of democratically deficient and failed socialisms amid the Soviet Union's postwar domination of Eastern Europe, its localizability in historical time is much at issue in the debates staged between Gesine and her deceased relatives. Whereas Gesine tells D. E. in a discussion in the latter's mother's backyard on June 9 that Marie should see the Russians of today (*AN II*, 314/*JT* 1330), that is, not judge people in sweeping national categories that transcend time, her relatives, copresent in her reading of the news and mindful of the Soviet Union's military mobilization that Gesine herself documents as well as the GDR's attempt to exploit its mythically antifascist stance and bind the ČSSR by invoking victims of the Shoah (*AN II*, 231/*JT* 1165), interpret the trend in question as another lead-up to the disappointment that Gesine appears to anticipate in her note on the "irrational walls" she may be constructing around her Bohemian space of hope (*JT* 913). This poetic line from *Jahrestage*'s reflection on historical repetition and difference resonates equivocally. As with the forest surrounding Johnny Schlegel's agrarian socialism that fails to provide more protection for the illusion of peace (*AN II*, 275/*JT* 1271; *Einbildung*), such boundaries will not be able to guard against possible disappointment. Gesine acknowledges her relatives' insistence that the historical precedence of Nazi Germany's occupation of Czechoslovakia disqualifies any German's presence there moving forward (*JT* 1179; see also *JT* 622), but, in defiance of their extension of postwar logic, this Cresspahl denies the past's hold on the future. Gesine's rationality is of another time.[126]

That Gesine conceives of Prague as a break from the past and an escape to the future lends the space of her hope a revolutionary dimension, but as the discourse and practice of revolution in Eastern Europe was usurped by the governing Marxist-Leninist parties, it necessarily appeared as reform, that is, as a process to be managed by the ruling Communist Party of the ČSSR. Led by Alexander Dubček, the Czechoslovak Communist Party would attempt to navigate through the Scylla of its relationship to the Soviet Union and Warsaw Pact countries and the Charybdis of calls for greater and rasher liberalization, including the kind articulated in the "Two Thousand Words" manifesto, from the larger populace. From afar, Gesine reads, weighs, and rereads the wall-writings of an ever more proximate future in the lead-up to her departure for Prague in the epic's countdown. In so doing, *Jahrestage*'s autodiegetic narrator struggles at the heart of actually existing socialisms' political antagonisms. Her remediation of the news, now from *Pravda* and other Soviet and Czech papers, in addition to the *New York Times*, intensifies over the course of volume 4 even as her narration of Jerichow life lingers over the past in ever-greater detail. "That which is written is taking over" (*JT* 1657). As the weight of political domination from above bears down on the Spring, the future peril of socialism's attempted democratization in which Gesine has placed her last hopes—"If this doesn't work either, I give up, D. E." (*AN* 443/*JT* 683)—becomes more and more ascertainable. Ultimately, the historical chapter in question will have conformed to the larger postwar pattern: the impossibility of the course sketched above would again derive from a politics of fear entailing the reassertion of control over liberalization's uncertain trajectories. The final image of the epic on its terminal date of August 20—Gesine's stopover in Denmark, where she and Marie meet Mr. Kliefoth—figures as a precipice against the imminent invasion of the ČSSR in "Operation Danube" by Soviet and Warsaw Pact (but not East German) troops and the subsequent suppression of Dubček's reform course. This backdrop of heterodiegetic history to which the epic is cued brooks no transcendence. And yet, excluding hindsight by the fiat of its calendrically terminal contract, what *Jahrestage* focuses on in its pages are Gesine's travails of orientation within the historical process. Hence the importance of Gesine's remediation of the Cold War in its own time.

Sabine Fischer's close analyses of this stretch of the work read Gesine's mediations of news from or about Prague against their original sources to demonstrate how Gesine deals with socialism's antagonisms as they play themselves out.[127] Focusing in detail on Cresspahl's rendering of the Czechoslovak Communist Party's response to the "Warsaw Letter" of July 15, which condemned developments in the ČSSR as counterrevolutionary, Fischer demonstrates the subjective factor of remediation at work in its full intensity.[128] In contrast to Gesine's verbatim translation of the "Two Thousand Words" manifesto, neither the letter nor the party's response is included in *Jahrestage*.[129] After referring to parts of the former on July 16 and 18, Gesine paraphrases and reworks the latter in her own language on July 19, while maintaining the pronominal *we*. The procedure serves not only as a vehicle of an acerbic critique of both sides. "What I know has more than two sides," Gesine reminds

Marie in another context, when the latter implores her to take one (*AN II*, 258/*JT* 1221). As Fischer demonstrates, Gesine strips the socialist discourse of its ideology in a rehumanizing presentation of the conflicts at hand: the Czechoslovak Party's presentation of "bureaucratic centralism" is reformulated into the dichotomy of governance from above and wishes from below (*JT* 1579), references to military maneuvers are made explicit, and the elaboration of the new constitution is announced as imminent amid what amounts to little less than Gesine's literary usurpation of the party's voice in almost real-time.[130] Where the ideological discourse of the source document—like the SED's invocation of the victims of the Shoah with which they threaten Prague reformers—constitutes, in its ossification, a dead archive, Gesine's deideologizing reformulations attend to the living conflicts in their proper designations. Amid the numerous other emendations Fischer pinpoints, perhaps most to the core of the matter at hand is Gesine's reformulation of the response's closing: the reference to "democracy and socialism" is changed to the "democracy of socialism" (*JT* 1582), a definitive genitive,[131] and one which can be read as an insistence, by Gesine and against the language and practices of the letters' undersigned, on precisely the kind of course that must be stayed. Cresspahl's intervention—uncertain as the status it enjoys in a work of literature is—holds more than one illusion in a tantalizing balance.

As described by postwar historian Tony Judt, the political illusion at the time concerned the compatibility of the enhancement of civil liberties and the continuation of the socialist project under party dominance.[132] This implied the party's ability to steer the process of reform without losing control—that is, to preside over such a course independently of the USSR. Gesine's remediation extols nothing less than a navigation between Scylla and Charybdis at a critical juncture midsummer. Yet the attention she pays to the developments is both hopeful and bare of illusions at once. As prognoses regarding developments in Prague waver in the narrative present, the truth-content of Gesine's analysis stands out for chipping away at the party's dominant role: reformulating the question of reform askew of its restricted party-bound context, Gesine shifts it into its more revolutionary dimension. Because the question she relates from a *New York Times* report on a survey conducted by the Communist Czechoslovak paper *Rudé Právo*—"Could one speak of a socialist democracy, if the leading role is held only by the Communist Party?" (*JT* 1164)—appears to admit only a negative response, Gesine musters a redress of the gravitational pull on the "abaric point" of the relationship between party and people (figure 8).[133] In so doing, she also prefigures the passage of democratic socialism's prospects from within the Eastern European context so familiar to her to those of socialism in democracy. Whereas this horizon constitutes a political vanishing point for *Jahrestage*'s Gesine—she expresses notably scant interest in such political movements taking shape in Western democracies—it pertains very much to the scope of the hope the epic confers across the terminal deadline of its narrative contract. Legacies of the open critique practiced during

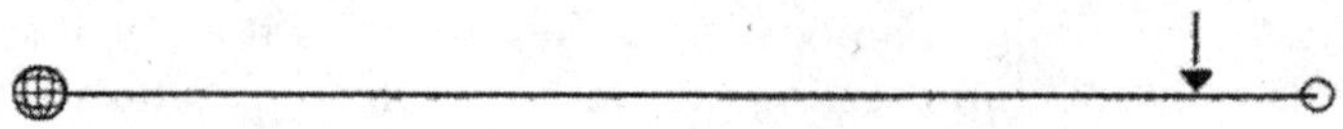

The abaric point between the Earth and the Moon. [Alexander Kluge Archive]

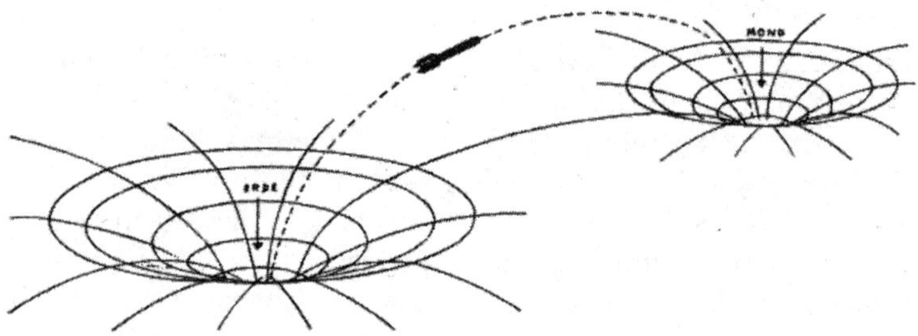

The flight path from the Earth to the Moon—an attempt at rendering the relations between gravitational fields. [Alexander Kluge Archive]

Figure 8. The abaric point. Excerpt from Alexander Kluge and Oskar Negt, *History and Obstinacy*, 377. Copyright © 2014 Zone Books, New York. All rights reserved.

the Prague Spring, Gesine's remediations also work to reset the discourse of socialism beyond its Soviet and Eastern European moorings. Her attempts to inventory and release the democratic and humanizing potentials of spring—"March 24, 1968 is a day in spring, in spring since 1938" (*JT* 914)—resonate not only against the proximate military end of 1968 amid the reassertion of Soviet control, but also in relation to the attention *Jahrestage* pays to the Prague Spring from the side of its economic domination.

Allusions to the military intervention by Warsaw Pact countries led by the Soviet Union and the reassertion of political control over the ČSSR provide ample grounds for the diminishment of Gesine's hopes. Yet *Jahrestage* also speaks to the other side of the Prague Spring's end to insinuate another, perhaps even thornier challenge. Because the political-military suppression stands outside the epic's temporally bound radar, attention shifts to *Jahrestage*'s concern with the ČSSR's relationship to the geopolitical blocs in economic terms. Consistent with the work's sagacious materialism, Johnson's epic captures the emergence of the new age it personifies in the figure of Gesine's boss and vice president of the bank. If Gesine's political orientation wishfully held the Prague Spring as an escape into the future in view, de Rosny's economic machinations—the "maneuvers" (*BU* 421) of his bank's "non-aggressive" policy (*AN* 308/*JT* 466)—suggest that the future has already arrived, albeit in the form of a Western winter. Where Gesine's Prague could constitute nothing short of a whole century's "salvation,"[134] for de Rosny it presents opportunity for capital's gain via economic inroads into socialism carrying geopolitical consequences. In musing over *Jahrestage*'s end today, our attention indelibly reverts to Mr. de Rosny, through whom the end of the Prague Spring and Cold War alike are writ large, not via deference to Soviet suppression, which reinforced the status quo ante until the arrival of Gorbachev at a later historical hour, but rather to finance capital's eastward expansion. While de Rosny's machinations may not appear aggressive, they are no less diabolical in their slyness. Keen to expose the curious pliability of de Rosny's politics of money—"de Rosny understands politics in terms of what is harmful to money" (*JT* 1471)—*Jahrestage* treats its personification of an ascendant neoliberalism as money incarnate (*AN* 307/*JT* 465; see also *AN II*, 88/*JT* 916). An "ideal man for our times" (*AN II*, 87/*JT* 915), de Rosny's free market ideology does not prevent him from viewing the market as something to be manipulated behind the scenes. In preparing a large loan in the hard currency of dollars for the ČSSR, his plans would benefit from secrecy's shrouds, which is why increases in transparency stemming from Czechoslovakians' public pronouncements of their financial affairs and demands (*JT* 933) as well as budgetary practices (*AN II*, 178/*JT* 1057–1058) so unsettle him. More reassuring is the outright Soviet prohibition of any such loan (*AN II*, 332/*JT* 1359), which only spurs de Rosny's clandestine efforts. Gesine's own ideas about her activity appear secondary to signs of the larger new world of finance capital in the making. Noticeably, de Rosny hardly appears in a better light than the epic's fascists and Stalinists—see *AN II*, 539/*JT* 1738 and 1746 for something of a final evaluation on Gesine's part. Toying with his would-be victory in Prague is *Jahrestage*'s way of prefiguring the Cold War's later historical end. By no means is the economic domination on display in the epic unrelated to the reorganization of socialist countries' economies after 1989. Inviting this thread of retrospective associations, *Jahrestage* keeps its nimble fingers on the pulse of a transition stretching from the end of 1968 through the ossifications of actually existing socialism and the dismantling of social welfare in capitalist societies in the wake of the 1973 oil crisis and recession to the rise of a global capitalism that Johnson himself would no longer witness. While the author may and perhaps could not have a full handle on this trajectory—in an interview, Johnson insisted, perhaps to sustain the plausibility of Gesine's fiction, that the currency loan could have been managed effectively, that is, in consistency with the protagonist's political ideals[135]—the curious collusion of political domination from the East and economic domination from the West lends intensive force to the epic's investigation of the conditions of political commitment and the prospects of social transformation beyond Gesine's express grasp thereof.

While this epic strain of *Jahrestage* reveals how little the time of the individual human subject might govern its interpretation, Gesine's own position remains absolutely integral to Johnson's mediation of the Prague Spring and his work's passage through the terminal horizon it pierces. Evocative in its implicit and explicit references, the epic's ending situates Gesine herself as an abaric point, radiating as an interstice of time and space against the backdrop of 1968's historical watershed. As some of the epic's most important scholars have argued,[136] in its formal orchestration of its ending, *Jahrestage* ultimately confirms and preserves Gesine's hopeful orientation in its utopian dimension, even as it simultaneously registers and mourns—in conjunction with (readers' knowledge of) heterodiegetic history—the obsolescence of what Ernst Bloch would have called its tendency, that is, the bridge to utopia's concrete realization.[137] While Prague will not be able to sustain Gesine's predication of what it signifies to her, *Jahrestage* eschews the presentation of the fallout, figuring Cresspahl instead as a "*Homo volans*" in the sense privileged by Alexander Kluge and Oskar Negt: "For more than two thousand years, the FLYING HUMAN has been represented from the point of view of the fall. Icarus fell. At the same time, however, flying is an ideal in all reformation movements of the twentieth century" (*HO* 409, capitals there). That *Jahrestage* resolutely frames Gesine at the metaphorical dawn/dusk (*Dämmerung*) of her flight—the final chapter actually narrates August 20 in the light of day—cannot be reduced to a deceit of the temporally bound narrative contract Johnson cued to the onset of Operation Danube. As Horst Turk has argued in his Kantian interpretation of the June 29 chapter, Gesine's subjective constitution demonstrates an "unfulfilled disposition for the future."[138] On top of Turk's reference to the first of Kant's critiques, *Jahrestage* also develops the question of the philosopher's third. The futural dimension of the epic's closing is inscribed into the frame it grants Gesine's hope, not simply in relation to the specifics of the Prague Spring's history, but also as the very precondition for the perceptibility of human beings' meaningful political engagement. Summarizing Bloch for *Jahrestage*, Baker has written that hope "must exist as a common principle of both subject and object; otherwise, there can be no possibility for concrete utopia."[139] Gesine's interpretation of Prague as the concrete possibility of a new beginning anchors this hope, localizing it in the objective world. Riding the tumultuous waves of its pasts and presents, *Jahrestage*'s storytelling retains its adherence to the quest for an orientation that is aspirational and realistic at once. While it remains uncertain what (dys)function Gesine's "irrational walls" would suffer in the heterodiegetic world of her own subsequent future, at midafternoon on August 20 prior to her departure from Copenhagen to Prague, an anticipatory Gesine hands over to Kliefoth 1,875 pages of the *Jahrestage* manuscript about "how life is treating us" (*AN II*, 644/*JT* 1891). The present tense contrasts with the epic's use of the past participle *gewesen* in its crepuscular opening. "History is a concept or draft," still working itself out. Marie promises Kliefoth that she will take care of his friend Mrs. Cresspahl. Respect, warmth, and commitment come together in Marie's formulation, values that have meaning against the past she and her mother have reconstituted and shared and against their Bohemian horizon. Closing prior to reaching any real Prague, *Jahrestage* frees its own anchor from its mooring, turning "Prague" into a nonidentical metaphor for a future, therewith reopening the question of the future's spatiotemporal location. In closing with a Gesine in transit at the Baltic on the Danish coast, *Jahrestage* contributes to a whole culture of hope,[140] outfitting it with both the subjective dimensions of a studious ideal as well as the objective identification of its real anchors. In this rendition, hope may make for less than a model of the world's course as a long trajectory of emancipation to which *Die Ästhetik des Widerstands* swears. But what *Jahrestage* facilitates in its balanced appraisal of reality's subjective-objective matrix is the pluralization of hope's projections (*Entwürfe*) into the currents of a scrutinously remediated objective reality.

The closing of the epic thereby suggests the general spatiotemporal transferability of Gesine's radar. As seen above, in her attempt to wrest the energy of the Prague Spring from the party's control and into its revolutionary direction, Gesine—perhaps inadvertently—also drew attention to the need for and prospects of socialism in democracy. The role played by de Rosny in *Jahrestage* certainly suggests the lingering urgency thereof. Where the history of the Prague Spring constitutes the epic's heterodiegetic end, the end of *Jahrestage*'s own diegesis is less final. That *Jahrestage* stages the many endings Holger Helbig has teased out in his analysis of August 1968's daily chapters may point to the work's apprehensiveness with regard to having any ending at all.[141] Returning from its implicit figuration of socialism's democratization as an opportunity that will have been missed, Gesine's daily practice of narration—in accordance with the undular epic's hydropoetics of tidal fluctuation addressed above—reverberates back onto everyday life experiences in a center of finance capital itself. "Homesick for New York in the middle of New York" (*AN II*, 637/*JT* 1882) since 1964, Gesine's recollection of the life she is leaving reveals a far more intricate relationship to the city than her more negative descriptions of alienation there suggest. While one might be hesitant to ascribe to the politeness occasionally experienced in the underground world of the subway the status of a utopian latency,[142] the double reference to New York City in the line cited clearly pertains to the critical diagnoses of society that *Jahrestage* spans out over its cityscape. In pitting New York's many realities and possibilities against one another, *Jahrestage*'s continuation of incessant remediation seldom fails to pinpoint the redress of the city's social ills. Although Gesine tends to reserve her political filter for European contexts, the work to which her epic's radar is put in her foreign home invites rereadings of its mediations of New York life in transformative resets of *Jahrestage*'s critical realism.

Combining a careful approach to social life with an investigation of attempted implementations of ideals in historical time, *Jahrestage* crafts a different kind of balancing act than that seen in the culminating dialectics of Weiss's *Ästhetik*. Johnson proffers little overreaching assertion of art's higher reality with *Jahrestage*. In contrast to Weiss's drive toward reality's aesthetic transfiguration that Burkhardt Lindner deemed indicative of an imaginary desire for a transformative appropriation of the world,[143] Gesine's stories hover ambivalently between the rooms they construct for living and the tidal waves they ride through reality. Where Weiss's great tale musters a whole aesthetic education for self-emancipation, *Jahrestage* concedes its constructed character vis-à-vis the history it fathoms. This contrast holds in the very fibers of each work's poetic delivery. Consider a telling line from *Die Ästhetik*'s Heilmann on the aesthetic lodestar of Weiss's epic:

> Heracles, son of a god and a mortal, bore the earthly and timeless within, he was first a human being, then a hero, then became a god, what could this development mean other than that we in our own existence pass through stages, constantly grappling with our own limitations, he always saw Hercules before him, he said, at the outermost edge of the world, with the Hesperides, there where the imagination [*Vorstellungskraft*] reached its end, and yet wanted to extend itself further still. (*ÄdW* 3:169)

By portraying the imagination's relentless reach in this way, Weiss's *Ästhetik* confirms the dimension of human subjectivity as the plane of its contribution, while inspiring human beings to ever new efforts. *Jahrestage* figures the vanishing point of its narrative with greater trepidation: "Friday. Thirty-nine days to go. Not even six weeks. Whatever the employee Cresspahl may do, there will be the twentieth of August" on which she will depart for Prague, as the English translation's compressed rendering of the July 12 chapter reads (*AN II*, 418/*JT* 1537–1538). The limitations she faces are not only those of her own. Where a Heracles absent from the Pergamon frieze circumscribes the subjective position to be occupied in *Die Ästhetik*, *Jahrestage* attends assiduously to the objective spaces in which epic hope might anchor itself at a distance from Prague itself. As aesthetic symbol and signifier of a historico-geographic space, Heracles and Prague constitute horizons of epic sense in *Die Ästhetik des Widerstands* and *Jahrestage*, respectively.[144] Akin to "two halves of an integral" genre "to which however they do not add up,"[145] the two works develop powerful literary expositions of the relationship between projective aspirations and their sociohistorical and political supports. Their expositions transfer resonantly into a century neither author could foresee. Who or what is Heracles? What or where is Prague? These questions can and do not expire, but rather constitute guidelines of the epic quest for subjective and objective orientation vis-à-vis the dynamic and delicate realities of the twenty-first-century world.

As the respective vanishing points of two exponents of the modern epic genre in the Cold War, Heracles and Prague simultaneously constitute literary conditions for the possibility of realistic narration in the programmatic sense spelled out by Thomas Metscher, discussed in chapter 1. With the primacy of praxis in mind, Metscher pinned his conception of an aesthetically plural, experimental, and socially critical realism to the possibility and meaningfulness of social action.[146] Weiss and Johnson's focal points speak to the indispensability of such narrative lodestars even with regard to those historical times in which the possibility and meaningfulness of social action appear questionable and/or unclear. In other words, Prague and Heracles not only lend the two overarching epic narratives their relative wholeness. They also demonstrate more generally how orientation works. Without such lodestars, however fictional, *Die Ästhetik des Widerstands* and *Jahrestage* suggest, horizons of alterative possibility cannot be seen. Tenable, socially meaningful orientation becomes difficult, if not impossible, to achieve. The conclusion of Weiss's epic articulates this explicitly (*ÄdW* 3:265). By wedding its focal point in space to a specific historical moment in time, *Jahrestage* underscores the fragility of the relationship between narratability and the prospects of social action. The perceived passing of an opportunity for socialism's democratization in Europe would appear to mark not only the end of Gesine's story, but also that of the epic undertaking—as conceptualized by Metscher—as such. Hence the importance, as argued above, to the formal orchestration of *Jahrestage*'s actual ending, which both depicts Gesine as an Icarus in ascendance and entices readers back into the many resources to be gleaned from the work's numerous transnational tides.

Modulating subjective hopes and the search for their objective anchors in time and space, *Die Ästhetik* and *Jahrestage*'s symbolic lodestars reflect the critical impulses of both authors, whose works cling to the prospects of human beings' emancipation from entanglements in alienation and guilt, denial and expropriation. Through their reconstitution, expansion, and review of the senses and poles of epic orientation out of the twentieth century's catastrophic history, *Die Ästhetik des Widerstands*, with the self-activation of the aesthetic sensorium as a register for a human world, and *Jahrestage*, with its investigation of the objective conditions and possibilities of a such a world, set courses valid for the next century. As two ways of dealing with the indeterminacy of historical processes and experiences—with different emphases in approach and commitment, in subjective and objective orientation, and in the modulation of projects and history—they indeed belong together and complement one another,[147] even if they cannot possibly achieve, individually or together, a poetic encapsulation of a social totality that has imploded and remains broken. If *Jahrestage*'s literary mediation of the Prague

Spring registers 1968 as a last possibility for steering the process of history into the direction of human emancipation, as some commentators attuned to the work's undeniably melancholic traits have suggested,[148] and if, following Metscher, the link between literature and social emancipation appears severed thereby, then a chapter of the twentieth century's socio-critical literature that derived energy and resources from its liaison with the larger emancipatory project of socialism, either as idea or reality, would appear to have closed. It is not only the standing of such an ideal that would warrant critical review. The semblance of the severance in question—to which the subsequent evolution of the modern epic attends—calls for fuller examination. Amid the implosion of the spatiotemporal conditions on which Weiss and Johnson still based epic form, something resembling the epic would again reemerge, transforming and resetting the vast search for renewed and open-ended orientation. It would fall to Alexander Kluge, who, with the post–Cold War publication of *Chronik der Gefühle* at the turn of the millennium, would persist in telling stories in the ruins of epic form from which possibilities of resistance and emancipation had never entirely evaporated. In his literary monument to the Cold War, Kluge simultaneously trains the epic's gaze on the great plurality of the spatiotemporal sites in which human survival—in the broadest sense—holds out.

Chapter 4

✦

Epic Storytelling and Human Survival

Alexander Kluge's *Chronik der Gefühle*

> The novel is the epic of a world that has been abandoned by God [*gottverlassenen Welt*]. The novel hero's psychology is demonic; the objectivity of the novel is the mature man's [*sic*] knowledge that meaning can never quite penetrate reality, but that, without meaning, reality would disintegrate into the nothingness of inessentiality.
>
> —György Lukács, *The Theory of the Novel*

> With Hegel's gigantic world map, one cannot undertake a tour on foot.
>
> —Ernst Bloch, "On the Ontology of Not-Yet-Being"

> Rescuing oneself fosters curiosity.
>
> —Alexander Kluge, *The Power of Emotion*

Opening Time

The subtitle of the first story of Alexander Kluge's two-volume, two-thousand-page *Chronik der Gefühle*, published in 2000, adumbrates its narrative core in advance: "Two days before his bankruptcy, the building contractor Simon Weigel calculates the seconds of his life" (*CdG* 1:15). Prototypically titled "Der Eigentümer" (The Owner), Kluge's five-page opener concerns a day in this life on which Weigel travels to Berlin to meet with colleagues and visit his company's construction sites. An unnamed narrator's swift contextualization of the background for this visit orients readers to the historical terrain of Kluge's storytelling. We find ourselves in new times, the days of which Weigel will count, the temperatures of which *Chronik* will measure. Amid the political upheavals of the Transition (*Wende*), a process that began with protests in the German Democratic Republic and led to German unification in 1990,

Weigel's miscalculations and mismanagement of real estate property transactions in (East) Berlin have put his company at the brink. He had envisaged ambitious projects that would transform, on the model of "Schumpeter's creative destruction," socialism's architectural "ruins" around Berlin Alexanderplatz into a new commercial center (*CdG* 1:17–18). Like the airplane parts Weigel scavenged out of the "caves of Junkers" as a young boy in 1945, the sites of the soon-to-be-former GDR's capital readily appeared to his firm as booty for the taking in 1989. But absent any forthcoming demand for the kind of transformation that Weigel imagined and in which he overinvested, the excavated lots of his company's construction sites turn into indicators of his own ruin. Sensing his impending social death—Weigel "knew he would soon no longer count among the living in a capitalist sense" (*CdG* 1:18)—yet still ignorant of the disintegrative forces organizing themselves in his biological body, Weigel attempts to take stock of his life hitherto. Looking back, he can, in some contrast to Uwe Johnson's Gesine Cresspahl, "only vaguely orient himself in his own past," which rather appears as a "topography of divested time" (*CdG* 1:18; *der veräußerten Zeit*). The markers of official time—political watersheds or the deaths of prominent politicians, e.g., the news of Kennedy's assassination—too feebly help him sharpen the memory of his own life. In the quiet solace of his Berlin hotel room that evening, he measures the minutes and seconds of life missed, while intending, in the pending final battle against his competitors, to retain composure (*Haltung*) as the last piece of property he owns (*CdG* 1:19).

Weigel's calculation of the temporality of his own life is far from the only kind of measurement Kluge undertakes at *Chronik*'s opening. Deploying a number of literary techniques, Kluge situates the story's narrative core within multiple frames that suggest the epic scope of the work that *Chronik der Gefühle* will unfold. Whereas the story's ostensible site can be read as a reference to the last German bildungsroman,[1] Alfred Döblin's urban epic *Berlin Alexanderplatz*, "Der Eigentümer" begins by elaborating its atmospheric setting in relation to a northwest storm brewing over Berlin in what has been described as an homage to Robert Musil.[2] A vast view of the North Atlantic's meteorological space, stretching from Newfoundland to the Urals, evokes Musil's rapprochement of Vienna from above in 1913 at the opening of *Der Mann ohne Eigenschaften*.[3] What is more, the structure of Kluge's acrobatic encapsulation of the story's two-day temporal horizon, announced in the tale's subtitle and iterated, almost to round the circle, at its closing, constitutes a sinuously proleptic narration of time, a technique at which Musil proved a master: "Two weeks later Bonadea had been his [the protagonist Ulrich's] mistress for fourteen days," reads an early relevant example from his modern epic.[4] Kluge's prolepsis, in the first part of its formulation in the subtitle, conveys Weigel's pending bankruptcy with equal certainty. Yet its second part is deferred until the end of the tale, where it contrasts the business foes who want to destroy Weigel with the more dangerous forces at work inside him (*CdG* 1:19). In other words, Kluge splits the prolepsis in two and with that time's wholeness, recapitulating Weigel's situation between the broken halves of what Musil conveyed in a single sentence. In lieu of sewing these back together again in any explicit follow-through, "Der Eigentümer" projects Weigel's last attempt at perseverance and stubborn protest against the social and biological ends with which he is imminently confronted.

While the evocation of such major purveyors of the modern epic genre as Döblin and Musil indicates the kind of literary net that could be spun from a single short Kluge tale, "Der Eigentümer" ventures a further expansion of its temporal radar, building up its own complexity through the multiplication of its techniques of measurement. In sweeping chronicle fashion, Kluge includes references to Hitler's sighting of the moon on a similarly stormy night in November 1936, Napoleon's view of the like during his short stay in Berlin in 1806, as well as Bismarck's repeatedly recorded observations of such weather over the Prussian capital (*CdG* 1:16). The superstitious link between moon sightings and the significance of this celestial body for events occurring in the human world is undercut in part by the narrator's observation that the temporality of the moon's influence far outstrips any single human course of life. Only across some fourteen generations, the narrator's distant sense (*Fernsinn*) would have us believe, could the moon's impact on any pattern of fate become discernible.[5] Establishing a still greater distance from Weigel's immediate concerns, the first of the story's three footnotes refers to Dante's measurement of the size of giants as recounted in Galileo's lectures "On the Shape, Location and Size of Dante's Inferno." The second recalls Nazi architect Albert Speer's plans for Germania, the Third Reich's capital that was not to be. The third and last footnote describes the disintegration of the primordial animals Leviathan and Behemoth in order to explain Weigel's approach to Berlin's real estate via analogy and contrast: composed of individual living components, the footnote surmises, these creatures met their demise in such a way that their composite parts perished along with them. The contrast drawn relates clearly to the GDR's abrupt end and the living remainders (not simply real estate, but actually existing people, ideas, and emotions) that its sudden passing leaves behind, to Weigel, whose lingering perseverance is projected into an uncertain future, and more broadly to the epic genre itself, which for Kluge consists, after its death, of living parts in lieu of any organic whole.

While no single story could possibly convey the vastness of Kluge's narrative endeavors, just as none could by itself describe globalization, as he remarked during his work on *Tür an Tür mit einem anderen Leben* (*Door to Door with Another Life*),[6] "Der Eigentümer" serves *Chronik* well as its opener due to its suggestive modulation of extensive and intensive times.[7] The exercises of the story's heterodiegetic narrator in the former provide a depersonalizing contextualization for Weigel's measurements of the latter. Of the roughly thirty-six thousand days that might constitute a human life, Weigel is just past the halfway mark (*CdG* 1:18). Whereas the narrator's perspective extends space outward and time backward, Weigel subdivides the time he has lived thus far down into seconds and binds these to the idiosyncratically long blinks of his eyes for which his friends know him. Modernly measured chronos yields to a corporeal marker of time by a man in whose brain self-regulating forces are advancing his biological demise. In view thereof, the narrator folds Weigel's individual existential fate back into the larger cycle of all organic nature that *Chronik* will set in relation to cosmological time.

"Der Eigentümer" evinces recurring features of Kluge's epic approach to *Chronik*'s diverse city- and landscapes in other ways. The incorporation of superstition, giants and other mythical creatures into chronicle-style narration alongside seemingly scientistic appeals to mathematics and weather patterns suggest an unwieldy combination of rational and irrational elements. The admixture echoes, but also differs from that of Musil. Amid the protagonist Ulrich's attempts, in *Der Mann ohne Eigenschaften*, to outfit the soul with greater precision, mythic discourses, including those of the Habsburgs in which Ulrich participates, are palpably subjected to more irony than science is. Kluge's "Der Eigentümer" and *Chronik* generally extend enlightened reason's forays into the scientific and mythical aspects of human orientation evenhandedly. Galileo and numerous other real and fictional scientists at the crossroads of the calculable and the imaginable make frequent appearance in Kluge's tales.[8] What is more, with "no one speaking about giants anymore anyway, at most about a gigantic city" (*CdG* 1:16; where *Riesenstadt* is neither a *Stadt der Riesen* nor of much reason), Kluge's rendering of the relationship between moon, clouds, and storm in the heavens above Berlin includes pointed reference to György Lukács's concept of *Gottverlassenheit* as the terrain of modernity (*CdG* 1:15). The stories constituting *Chronik* all take place in a secularized and disenchanted world abandoned by God and void of spirits and demons, but not at the cost of any narrowing of narration's rational and irrational, profane and spiritual referentiality. "The doctrine of probability in literature is of a different order from the doctrine of physics," Kluge explains to interlocutors Christian Schulte and Rainer Stollmann, who press him on his fascination, for example, for the fountains of the gods, which were, as a story in *Chronik* relates, to be filmed in a collaborative project with Andrej Tarkovsky based on Rudolf Steiner's *Akasha Chronicle* (*CdG* 1:472–478).[9] "I can sense the poetic in physics at any time, but physics cannot intervene in the world of texts and the positions of trust" that they establish with each other and other spirits of the literary imagination.[10] That said, one of the most striking metaphors for the navigation of the timescapes of *Chronik*'s textual world is closer to physics and nature than the divine: Kluge's narrator flies not as an angel, but as a bat practicing echolocation in all directions.[11] "Knocking against the walls of our cage-like world," this flight will find articulate echoes of human life, including both the spiritual and practical dimensions of its feelings, in the chronicle's throws of secular time.[12]

The epic strokes with which Kluge sketches Weigel's plight contain a final resonance worth highlighting in this context relevant to its placement at the beginning of *Chronik*'s first chapter, "Der Eigentümer und seine Zeit" (The Owner and His Time). The protagonist's role as a building contractor during the Transition sets the stage for *Chronik*'s exploration of the collapsing edifices of the construction project of modernity, including the socialist and capitalist, emotional and existential variants thereof: "First, human beings build the tower of Babel. The tower falls. Centuries later, this construction emerges anew inside human beings. That is modernity," Kluge would later write in the foreword to a chapter in *Das fünfte Buch: 402 Neue Geschichten* (*The Fifth Book: 402 New Stories*) called "Passages from Ideological Antiquity: Work/Obstinacy."[13] From the vantage point of the new century's second decade, "Ideological Antiquity" already includes Kluge's own theoretical labors in the renewal of the resources of Marxist theory with Oskar Negt. But time's compressed acceleration, or what Kluge calls its withdrawal (see *CdG* 2:901 and cf. *CdG* 2:457), afflicts modernity's theorists and contractors alike. The *Chronik* chapter steering Kluge's storytelling into the post–Cold War age announces its representative protagonist—not Weigel himself, but rather the social category of The Owner as such—in uncertain terms: as Weigel's story suggests, the days of "Der Eigentümer und seine Zeit" may be numbered. At the very least, Kluge's modulation of disparate times puts modernity's various construction sites into view at a time when the brand-new century's constructions provide unclear residence.

Corporeal time; social, economic, and political time; lunar time: the different registers of storytelling's perhaps oldest function of counting on display in Kluge's opener interrelate the most minute and vastest stretches of temporality. *Chronik der Gefühle* will unfurl time's intensive and extensive modalities across the diverse historical spaces of its large chapters of countless stories. The sprawl of their great plurality appears overwhelming enough to defy any overview. Kluge himself disavows the view of any whole, regarding such a notion as atavistic,[14] for which reason *Geschichte und Eigensinn* reformulates the older concept of totality into that of relationality (*Zusammenhang*).[15] In the narrative terms of Kluge's storytelling, the inaccessibility of any holistic view compels a humility of perspective and procedure. Such comportment corresponds to the view from below in Kluge's stories, especially in those tales in which perspective is, at least to some extent, internally focalized through characters such as Weigel. Part of the curious magic of Kluge's modern epic tales consists in their ability to deploy characters who are sketched swiftly as typical and seemingly impersonal placeholders or vehicles for some aspiration and yet simultaneously remain quirky and endearing as individual human beings. Seldom is there any disparagement: their narrator often manages to cast them in representative roles without forfeiting sympathy, thereby setting a beguiling play of aesthetic identification and distanciation into motion. In this, the aspirations of Kluge's own storytelling occasionally appear to intermingle with the naive or perilous attempts of his characters to dig out of various forms of rubble and ruin and/or surmount numerous inner and outer obstacles. Yet whereas Weigel's measurement of time appears as a countdown to his end, *Chronik* is unquestionably able to count up, additively, and seemingly unto infinity. The sheer volume of Kluge's narrative tomes constituting his main line of literary production from *Chronik* onward would seem to belie any real difficulties here, including questions as to the viability of storytelling in the face of past, present, and future catastrophe. And yet such appearances of literary discourse's self-evidence can also deceive. Kluge's stories are not only generally fraught like few others by the contortions of modernity that impact even the intricacies of their forms. Whereas the aforementioned view from below may seem at odds with the flight of *Chronik*'s bats that narrate over vast stretches of time and space, the metaphor for the work's heterodiegetic narration is consistent with Kluge's apprehension regarding any totalizing views: bats fly blindly; they are no bearers of vision in any straightforward sense, but rather indicate Kluge's investigative and experimental narrative conduct across *Chronik*'s leaps and bounds.

A Monument to the Cold War

As the foregoing analysis of "Der Eigentümer" suggests, Kluge's narrative echolocation of *Chronik*'s time-spaces is too diffuse to be bound to any straightforwardly linear conception of historical time.[16] The work's numerous framing devices nonetheless bring the perspectives embedded in protagonists' various predicaments on the ground and the blind flight of echolocating bats above into greater narrative focus. Whereas the overall scope of *Chronik* is minimally confined, an ascertainably discrete period of political history stands out as its main stage. While the work's anchorage in the history of the twentieth century's second half is hard to overlook, readers may be forgiven for getting lost in *Chronik*'s forests. For this reason, a tentative summary of the work's appearance and constitutive parts must be wagered, along with some notes on navigation therein. Combining such impressions of the *Chronik*'s two volumes substantiates a description of Kluge's work as a monument to the Cold War and modern epic alike.

For starters, *Chronik der Gefühle*'s book carton depicts a couple walking through a post–World War II urban rubble landscape on its left side and an overhead shot of the Berlin Love Parade (first held in 1989) at the Victory Column in Berlin's Tiergarten on its right (figures 2 and 3). In between *Chronik*'s cardboard bookends are housed just about all of the contents of Kluge's literary publications from 1962 through 1984 in addition to scores of new stories published for the first time at the turn of the new millennium. In the first positively formulated foreword of his prose writings ever, Kluge announces and justifies the undertaking of *Chronik* as follows: "What human beings need in their life-courses is ORIENTATION. Like navigating ships" (*CdG* 1:7; capitals there). As with the designation of *Geschichte und Eigensinn* as a handbook (*DuM* 2:5), *Chronik* presents itself with an eye toward its value in use. Finding one's way through the book may already constitute something of a preliminary exercise in orientation. Kluge accommodates the need for some counsel by outlining *Chronik*'s general arrangement. Highlighting his editorial arrangement of the texts in the roughly reverse order of their publication, Kluge likens such an organization to the functioning of memory (*CdG* 1:7), first and foremost, that of the author, but also that of his readers: as Kluge claimed in the foreword to his 1977 *Neue Geschichten: Hefte 1–18: "Unheimlichkeit der Zeit,"* retained within and revalidated by *Chronik* where it opens its second volume of *Lebensläufe* (*Case Histories*), his stories take place, regardless of their historical or contemporary content, in the present (*CdG* 2:11; **Jetztzeit**, boldfaced there). In other words, Kluge has proven and remained a contemporary author in an emphatic sense not only by embracing the narrative treatment of even the most recent events to deliver commentary on the news of the day, but also by implicitly rendering or explicitly marking each story as a view from the contingent present of its writing. For this reason, previously published stories or collections reappearing in *Chronik* generally tend not to assume forms identical to their past editions. They populate new arrangements and may enjoy new forms of connectivity and cross-illumination therein. With the reference to memory, Kluge introduces the principle of reverse chronology that *Chronik* follows in loose semblance of a linear time being traced backward. Thus, the beginning of the first volume, *Basisgeschichten* (*Base Stories*), situates us alongside Simon Weigel and the economies of time unfolded by the first chapter in *Chronik*'s postsocialist and neoliberal present. In the second chapter, "Verfallserscheinungen der Macht" (Symptoms of Declining Power), we enter the anterior present with stories from the Transition and transformative years of 1989–1991. *Basisgeschichten* also provides the title for the shorter and less thematically focused third chapter, components of which appeared in Kluge's earlier publications and can be dated to the 1980s. Introducing tales about "human beings looking for their place in the world," the chapter's foreword conveys this quest with allusions to epic seafaring and related motifs (*CdG* 1:309). The fourth chapter presents a new narrative block featuring, in its titular and leading story "Heidegger auf der Krim," Martin Heidegger's fictional field trip to a front of the war on Crimea in 1941, whither the philosopher was commissioned as part of a team of scholars to research and extract the remains of Ancient Greek and East Gothic settlements and where he witnesses criminal acts of genocide close-hand (*CdG* 1:417–434).[17] The fifth republishes *Schlachtbeschreibung*, Kluge's only ostensible almost-novel, on the Battle of Stalingrad; first issued in 1964, Kluge had since put several different versions of this text into circulation.[18] The first volume's final two chapters present materials mostly new to the public. The sixth, "Verwilderte Selbstbehauptung" (Self-Assertion Running Wild), introduces the play-drive that it will explore in the narration of artistic fantasies and practices as well as of the critical theory evoked in the chapter's title, which varies a formulation of Adorno's *Negative Dialectics* regarding wild self-preservation (*CdG* 1:989; cf. *CdG* 1:297). The seventh, "Wie kann ich mich schützen? Was hält freiwillige Taten zusammen?" (How can I protect myself? What holds voluntary deeds together?), turns to dimensions of human cooperation in the face of grave dangers, at least, in must be said, in terms of what its title, foreword, and cursory readings in the chapter suggest. Entering into the thicket of any single Kluge story or assembly of stories can induce vertigo and consternation, also with regard to their editorial location and relation to Kluge's framing devices.

Chronik's second volume, *Lebensläufe*, continues the loose arrangement of materials in reverse order of their publication and will thus be more familiar to Kluge's readers, since it contains the previously published "*Unheimlichkeit der Zeit*" notebooks (making up nearly half of the second volume here), *Lernprozesse mit tödlichem Ausgang* (*Learning Processes with a Deadly Outcome*), and *Lebensläufe*, albeit differently configured across chapters 8 through 11 of *Chronik*. The twelfth and final chapter, "Der lange Marsch des Urvertrauens" (The Long March of Primordial Trust), offsets the reverse chronology in form as well as content, embracing the longest durations of epic time in its presentation of mostly new stories. The guidance Kluge offers in *Chronik*'s opening foreword is helpful only to an extent in all of this. The danger of vertigo meets one at every turn, to the point that Kluge's potentially well-intended signposts can also become something of a distraction. It may nonetheless be unavoidable to proceed as Kluge himself recommends: "No one," he advises in the general foreword, "will read so many pages at one go. It is sufficient, if he, as with a calendar or, indeed, a CHRONICLE, verifies, what applies to him" (*CdG* 1:7, capitals there). Invited by an author revoking his authority to cut their own paths through aggregate, malleable assemblies of narrative, readers can posit patterns that emerge from their scrutiny of the stories' interrelations. In an epic world abandoned by the gods, these patterns come to stand in for the starry constellations of yore evoked at the beginning of Lukács's *Theory of the Novel* (*TN* 21/29). Mapping the larger constellations in play, one becomes increasingly aware of the centripetal and centrifugal forces exerting themselves over *Chronik*'s differentiated assemblies of its short-circuited narratives. "From a central point of my interest," Kluge noted while discussing the publication, "I tell stories in all directions."[19] This centrifugal tendency is evident from the considerable sprawl of individual chapters, especially those less thematically focused, such as the third, sixth, and seventh. As Wolfgang Reichmann has noted in his analysis of *Chronik*, although linear chronology hardly structures the contents of individual chapters in any exacting way, there is definitely a discernible genealogical approach at work across the work's narrative flights.[20]

For example, given the concern of "Der Eigentümer und seine Zeit" with surveying the onset of the new millennium as an age of neoliberalism, one will find its narrative treatment of contemporary finance capitalism and the effects thereof juxtaposed to earlier pertinent tales from economic history, including returns to Black Friday (i.e., October 24, 1929's Black Thursday, from the perspective of Central European Time), a farewell to the industrial age, stock exchange tales, and so on. Somewhat similarly, as the second chapter, "Verfallserscheinungen der Macht," identifies an interest in the decomposition of political formations, Kluge will proceed—roughly speaking, of course—from Germany's Transition through stories about the implosion of the geopolitical order at the end of the Cold War on a more global scale backward through the end of the Nazi dictatorship, then onto the Napoleonic Wars, reaching as far back as the *Epic of Gilgamesh* (which manages to include Heiner Müller's views on the narrative procedure under way in *Chronik* at *CdG* 1:300), before circling around to a living remainder of the GDR in its final story, thereby anchoring the sudden and surprising Transition into a longer duration of mostly modern turbulence. On the basis of such genealogical procedures, Kluge is clearly rolling his *Chronicle* backward in time, in order to move forward, in wild spirals . . .

If a centripetal force is at work in this, it promises little overall coherence, not to mention any clarity as to where one might be able to arrive. An opposite movement can nonetheless be gleaned, especially from thematically focused chapters such as the science fiction novella *Lernprozesse mit tödlichem Ausgang* (chapter 11) or *Schlachtbeschreibung*: "The book," Kluge wrote in the 1978 edition of the latter, "like every fiction (including that consisting of documentary material) contains a grid, on which the fantasy of the reader can be pegged when it moves in the direction of Stalingrad."[21] With this, Kluge focuses on the movement's directionality in lieu of its stabilization: the Battle of Stalingrad exerts a centripetal force over the narrative without fixing it. While the passage cited is omitted from *Chronik*'s version of *Schlachtbeschreibung*, the newer collection improves on the print mediation of a related point in the "Stalingrad as Report" section of the text (figure 9).[22] "'The closer one looks at a word, the farther it looks back.' *Germany*" also makes an appearance in Kluge's 1979 film *Die Patriotin* (*The Patriotic Woman*). Its core aphorism stems from Karl Kraus, that great Viennese purveyor of literature's shortest genre.[23] Rendering Kraus's line on page 740 of *Chronik* along with a fortuitous addendum of his own, Kluge's remediation in print suggests a vertiginous rapprochement of the cinematic medium, an intermedial reference that mimics the zoom effects intimated in Kraus's sentence.

While the signifier "Germany" repeatedly eludes fixation on reality's open construction sites in Kluge's cinematic and literary work, the point of the foregoing overview of *Chronik* is not only to canvass its epic sprawl and highlight some of its vertiginous effects, but also to identify the cornerstones of its politico-historical stage. The markers of German history of 1945 and

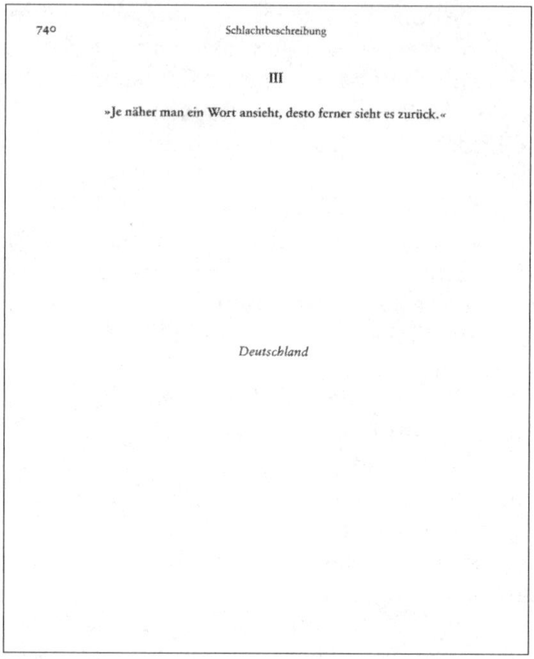

740 Schlachtbeschreibung

III

»Je näher man ein Wort ansieht, desto ferner sieht es zurück.«

Deutschland

Figure 9. "'The closer one looks at a word, the farther it looks back.' *Germany*." Excerpt from Alexander Kluge, *Chronik der Gefühle*, 1:740.

1989 stand out as watersheds of political time in *Chronik*'s narrative focus, qualifying it as a monument to the Cold War. This backward glance is also part of the book's genealogical procedure. Even while numerous stories take place far afield of the "territory . . . called Germany" (*HO* 235/*DuM* 2:500) and freely transcend this time frame in multiple ways, these two incisive dates mark the temporal parameters of the national politics, predilections, and pathologies that Kluge interrogates. His personal close-hand witness of the repercussions of the first date gave rise to what would become his perhaps single most famous story, *Der Luftangriff auf Halberstadt am 8. April 1945*, a montage-oriented approach to the Allies' bombing of his hometown, first published in "*Unheimlichkeit der Zeit*" (see *CdG* 2:27–82). Almost all of *Chronik*'s chapters tell and retell stories from World War II, frequently circling around 1945 as a year in which catastrophe and liberation could not have been more closely entwined.[24] While the focus on World War II radiates clearly from the inclusion of narrative segments such *Schlachtbeschreibung*, *Der Luftangriff*, and the aforementioned story on Heidegger, no fewer than five of *Chronik* chapter forewords—in addition to the very first—refer implicitly or explicitly to 1945. "In the middle of the twentieth century," reads the preface to chapter 4, "the world departs from thought"

(*CdG* 1:415; *kommt die Welt dem Denken abhanden*). The narrative interest that Kluge has afforded this watershed confirms 1945 as a caesura in the life courses of Germans (*CdG* 2:457). It is also one that gave rise, from the beginning of Kluge's literary production, to a highly unusual experimental prose through which he has sought to render experiences of destruction and disorientation, along with the resulting outer and inner debris, narratable.

New with *Chronik* is the explicit demarcation of the posterior perimeter of the period in question. The unification of Germany at the end of the Cold War makes for but one reference in a whole series of dates marked in the book's general foreword from 1945 to the turn of the millennium. And these are not yet categorized according to the distinction between "specious transformations" and "real metamorphoses" that Kluge introduces there (*CdG* 1:7). The foreword to the 2003 *Die Lücke, die der Teufel läßt* more determinately frames 1989 as a watershed year.[25] An interview Kluge gave in *Der Spiegel* on *Chronik*'s publication in 2000, however, is indicative of the effects 1989 and its aftermath had on him. The Transition also appeared to influence his decision to redirect his artistic activity to his preferred medium of literary production.[26] By this time, Kluge had become better known to the German public as a filmmaker and television producer. After contributing to the force of New German Cinema with a number of challenging films, his last narrative film from this period, *Der Angriff der Gegenwart auf die übrige Zeit* (*The Attack of the Present on the Rest of Time*, 1985), featured a blind director, whereas his shift to television was prefigured in the format for his last film for cinema, *Vermischte Nachrichten* (*Diverse News*, 1986).[27] In the 2000 interview "Ich liebe das Lakonische" (I Love the Laconic), *Der Spiegel*'s Mathias Schreiber and Volker Hage thus sought to grasp what compelled Kluge back to the literary print medium after a considerable hiatus:

> DER SPIEGEL: You mean the events of the past decade have tempted you back to the desk?
>
> KLUGE: Yes. During the 1980s I did not really have anything to communicate that pointed to the future [*Zukunftsweisendes*]. That changed with the turn of the times [*Zeitenwende*] ten years ago, when the Russian gigantic empire broke apart. At that time, all of the energies that were being preserved and locked up in the USSR freezer could suddenly emigrate. That changed us also. Thus emerged, at least for fantasy, a whole new world, which attracted my curiosity from the beginning—for example when orchestra musicians from Odessa are suddenly found playing at a health-resort on [the German island of] Sylt and many other, very concrete, seemingly absurd stories suddenly become possible.[28]

While Kluge attests, in the same interview, to never having been anything other than a storyteller and writer, as his comments cited here suggest, the transformations of 1989–1991 had tremendous repercussions on his narrative interests and motivations. Kluge's recalibration thereof would not only attend to the twentieth century's last decade as a time "in which changes more drastic than those of 1945"[29] made themselves felt and gave rise to life courses that overtook those circling brokenly around the previous date, but also to the excavation of future (*Zukunftsweisendes*) from out of the various legacies of the second world.[30] While *Chronik*, in contrast to Peter Weiss's *Die Ästhetik des Widerstands* and Uwe Johnson's *Jahrestage*, has no discrete set of embedded narrators, its key poetological figures include the likes of Xaver Holtzmann and Andrej Bitow. Their backgrounds are not incidental. The former, an East German historian of the Early Middle Ages removed from his academic post amid the GDR's demise, passes time with playwright Heiner Müller in the canteen of the Berliner Ensemble, where the two develop offbeat defense strategies against a narrowing world (*CdG* 1:198–200). While Müller will also reappear throughout *Chronik*'s pages and in its closing story analyzed below, Holtzmann, for his part, crafts a project for an "Imaginary Opera Guide" to capture, in some seven hundred new works, the "experiential content of our time" against muteness (*CdG* 1:840–842). He also calculates the number of animals on earth in comparison to the (fewer) stars of the Milky Way in order to have a case for a class-action lawsuit should the planet be destroyed (*CdG* 2:958–959). The latter figure, with whom Holtzmann is frequently in virtual contact, is no less fanciful: Bitow, an orthodox monk whose isolated montane cloister along the present-day border between the republics of Kyrgyzstan and Tajikistan was never charted cartographically and thus survived divestiture by the Soviet Union, works on chronicling political and cosmological time (*CdG* 2:952–957). Short on wood, Bitow warms his hands in winter on the console of the computer via which this modern-day Hieronymus remains connected to the outside world (*CdG* 1:125).[31] In conjunction with the focus of the "Verfallserscheinungen der Macht" assembly of Transition stories unwinding in the GDR and Soviet Union, these characters testify to Kluge's interest in rescuing and reformulating the legacies of the second world through the end of the Cold War into a new era in which they intermingle with new fantasies and renewed techniques of orientation.

Monumentalizing the Cold War, *Chronik* clearly reexamines the period for the sake of excavating human emotions formerly tied up with or carried by, in one way or another, the second world's socialist project. Conceived and written in the wake of the twentieth's century's last political watershed, in advance of the first historical incision in the next,[32] *Chronik* is a transitional work through and through—and an epic work for transitions. While the motivation for *Chronik*'s unusual character will be explored from a literary-aesthetic angle in the next section of this chapter in greater detail, three outgoing observations leading deeper into the epic architecture of the construction that is Kluge's *Chronik der Gefühle* serve here to confirm its status as a Cold War epic oriented to the future.

First, *Chronik* marks a novel elaboration—in format as well as form—of Kluge's narrative method. Like Kluge's publications that follow it serially, it is no novel. Nor does *Chronik*'s narrative method—amid changing emphases highlighted in Kluge's forewords[33]—represent any clear departure from his storytelling prior to 1989. A straight line leads from his last significant literary publication, under the same title as his 1984 film *Die Macht der Gefühle* (*The Power of Emotion*), to *Chronik*'s preoccupation with feelings as "the real inhabitants of human lives" (*CdG* 1:7). But what *Chronik* inaugurates at the millennial turn is a series of notoriously gigantic tomes that has yet to cease or even abate since. Published—attractively, if mightily—in a roughly DIN-A-5 size format larger and heavier than the more familiar and handier Suhrkamp Verlag's paperbacks, *Chronik*'s two volumes, along with *Die Lücke, die der Teufel läßt: Im Umfeld des neuen Jahrhunderts* (2003), *Tür an Tür mit einem anderen Leben: 350 Neue Geschichten* (2007), constitute an epic ensemble crowned, Pentateuch-like, with the publication of *Das fünfte Buch* in 2012, an ending that would prove preliminary. The next installment—Kluge's most recent volume, *Kongs große Stunde: Chronik des Zusammenhangs* (*Kong's Great Hour: Chronicle of Relationality*)—both offsets any finality the fifth volume in the series might have marked as well as suggests some counterpoint to its opener by pitting relationality against the emotions. Such output has been accompanied by a sizable number of (for the most part shorter) spin-off volumes, including *Das Labyrinth der zärtlichen Kraft: 166 Liebesgeschichten* (2006), *Geschichten vom Kino* (2007), *Das Bohren harter Bretter: 133 politische Geschichten* (2011, with a guest contribution by Reinhird Jirgl), *Dezember* and *Nachricht von ruhigen Momenten* (2010 and 2013, featuring Kluge's collaboration with the visual artist Gerhard Richter), and *30. April 1945: Der Tag, an dem Hitler sich erschoß und die Westbindung der Deutschen begann* (2014), which all feature thematic arrangements of stories from the narrative project's main supply line in addition to new tales. Most closely accompanying *Chronik* is the attractive and poetologically significant collection *Die Kunst, Unterschiede zu machen* (2003), published in Suhrkamp's *Bibliothek der Lebenskunst* series. This inexhaustive overview does not mention Kluge's vast work in visual media, which has likewise continued in DVD, televisual, and internet-based formats.

While the scope of the main line of Kluge's literary production alone may warrant its designation as a maximizing approach to the modern epic genre, Kluge's formatting choices for his publications are not incidental to their designations as works in the tradition in question. Like the "pickled wishes of elephants" (*CdG* 2:160–163; "Eingemachte Elefantenwünsche") in one of *Chronik*'s poetologically significant tales, the question of the containers (as *Behälter* or *Gefäße* for experiential content or *Erfahrungsgehalt*) is important.[34] *Chronik* is driven by Kluge's motivated interest in establishing forms for transferring the experiential content of the twentieth century, especially that from the second world deemed aberrant by the social system of the first that outlived it, into the next century. Such forms are at no point stable. As a self-avowed practitioner of the avant-garde, Kluge approaches the artistic work as an inherently porous container, unfixed and modifiable in its structure. Yet his publishing choices to outfit his storytelling with a main line of large volumes and their demarcation vis-à-vis one another are clearly repercussions of his own orientation vis-à-vis the times he so closely follows as a contemporary commentator of an ever-unfolding present. Amid reality's spatiotemporal complexities as well as those of its "inflation,"[35] Kluge's constructive-mimetic narrative project—in conformity with the hyperdialectics deployed with great elasticity in the theoretical undertaking that is *Geschichte und Eigensinn* (cf. *DuM* 1:240–241, 710ff./*HO* 256ff.)—radicalizes the dialectics of social content and artistic form to keep pace with the reality he wishes to render exactingly and protest against.[36] Part and parcel of the project's constructive dimension, Kluge's arrangement of his many stories into in(ter)dependent works, their divisions and subdivisions into topical clusters, and the parameters of the whole's organization codetermine the meanings of the texts in the play of interpretation.

Kluge's approach to the dialectics of social content and narrative form speaks to the division of *Chronik*—whose individual volumes their author counted as respective installments in the five-part series—into *Basisgeschichten* and *Lebensläufe*. To be sure, any absolute divide between their contents and qualitative distinctiveness is hard to advance beyond the observations outlined above. As Wilfried F. Schoeller has written in his review of *Chronik*'s landscapes of rubble, "I cannot distinguish between *Basisgeschichten* and *Lebensläufe*."[37] Kluge's subtitles for *Chronik* and their accompanying predications are nonetheless suggestive for evoking nothing other than Marx's famous (and also maligned) distinction between productive forces and the institutions and social practices that uphold their relations: that is, the base and its superstructure.[38] If, as Kluge writes in his foreword to the first chapter of *Basisgeschichten*, people reside in their *Lebensläufen*, then these are clearly being conceived in terms of their contingent relationality. *Lebensläufe* are "fragile containers," as *Chronik* elsewhere puts it (*CdG* 2:5; *Gefäße*). *Basisgeschichten* would address their contents, which are akin to productive forces—"the emotions" themselves—as "the true residents of human lives" (*CdG* 1:7).[39] Kluge's metaphoric allusion to Marx's concepts does not entail any reductive or deterministic understanding of the relationship in question: the description of the third chapter, *Basisgeschichten*, in volume 1's table of contents declares the most fundamental thing (*Basis*) to be "interpersonal relations" (*CdG* 1:5), which inscribes relationality onto the side of the productive forces, whereas *Lebensläufe*, to concretize the metaphor, are inconceivable without some productive force doing the walking. Base and superstructure, productive forces and institutional relations, feelings and relationality, social content and narrative form are dialectically interwoven completely throughout. This is why Schoeller, like the rest of us, has trouble distinguishing between the kinds of stories included in *Chronik*'s *Basisgeschichten* and *Lebensläufe* volumes. What is additionally suggestive here with regard to the epic genre is the notion of a backtracking, the gestural élan of a move back to basics, a return to essentials, which includes both the counting of time on display in "Der Eigentümer" as a rudiment of storytelling as well as all of the disparate meandering searches through vast time-spaces to mediate, among other things, the Transition begun in 1989 as well as the passage into the next millennium. In other words, whereas the historical experiences of 1945 and 1968 compelled Weiss and Johnson to strenuous years at the desks from which *Die Ästhetik des Widerstands* and *Jahrestage: Aus dem Leben von Gesine Cresspahl* would emerge, 1989 drove Kluge back to his "main work"[40] and the only literary form that presented itself as viable to Kluge for the elaboration of his project: the modern epic, or rather, the transformative appropriation of that genre's ruins.[41]

The appellation "epic" thus derives not simply from Kluge's admiration of Musil or Döblin (or of practitioners of shorter epic forms, such as Kleist and Büchner), nor from his suspicion of the dramatic structure of tragedy and his fondness for reworking operas,[42] nor alone from the extensive scope of his circumspect pursuit of reality and his indeed encyclopedic review of the artistic means that have been deployed to render it (often highlighted by his renarrations of past literary works and films). A final dimension of epic in play here is Bertolt Brecht's call for the "separation of [any artwork's] elements," a set of techniques that makes an indelible mark on Kluge's narrative method.[43] From the beginning of Kluge's work, the epic procedures associated with Brecht's approach to drama as well as prose served not only as a benchmark for the exactitude and complexity of literary production, but also as a resource for the development and renovation of any art. This can be seen in the 1965 essay "Wort und Film," which Kluge cowrote with Edgar Reitz and Wilfried Reinke and which proved seminal for the pioneering work of New German Cinema.[44] Devoted to advancing the language of film amid the creative energies fostered and focused by the Oberhausen Manifesto, the authors advocate for an autonomous film production that would fully mobilize the constituent components of the cinematic medium. The "epic possibilities"[45] of film touted by the essay go hand in hand with a differentiated combination of "subjective and objective, linguistic, acoustic, and visual elements" that stands to be realized.[46] What is striking about the authors' approach is their strong appeal to the previous development of the literary medium—for example, its "high level of organization" and "historical advance"[47]—as indicative of the kind of artistic language and power that film can and must achieve, not by mimicking literature's plots or genres but by building up the complexity and expressiveness of its own medium. While Kluge's many films and visual media projects aspire to no less, his fiction writing continues to explore and experiment with epic techniques in the literary medium. In stark contrast to Weiss and Johnson's practices of intermediality as forms of strictly literary remediation, however, Kluge's literary work is by no means confined to the print of its words; rather, it incorporates a great number of photographs, sketches, diagrams, maps, and other visuals into his stories and onto his book's pages. In so doing, Kluge develops his literary method, born out of the experience of war too close to home, reshaped and honed during cold times, out of literature's previously accumulated advances in conjunction with a newfound openness to visual media. Facilitating the transfer of his project through the end of the Cold War to the new century, Kluge's literary works, beginning with *Chronik*'s new assembly, constitute epics of the last century also crucial to the narration of a twenty-first in which words have fallen in value. In this, the unprecedented radicalization of the modern epic that Kluge has achieved is much more a consequence of literary tradition than its cancelation.[48] But to understand the nature of that radicalization and the transfer efforts performed by *Chronik* at the end of the Cold War demands a fuller appraisal and analysis of the modern epic structure Kluge has adopted in his challenging narration of modern times.

Implosions of Epic Form

Populating ruins, Kluge's tales inhabit and unfold in the hollows of an epic form eviscerated by catastrophic history. Kluge meets the challenges of modern epic narration at the level of a formal innovation more conspicuous than that of his erstwhile contemporaries Weiss and Johnson. The first aspect of Kluge's radicalization of epic form pertains to the principle of the relative independence of epic's components. As noted in the introduction to the modern epic as "A Genre for Cold Times" above, the claim that the epic afforded a looser relationship of its parts to the whole goes back at least as far as Goethe and Schiller, who themselves based their reflections on Ancient Greek poetry. The radicalization of the independence of the epic's components in Kluge's work, however, is induced by and part of a response to explosions in space and implosions in time characteristic of (the author's experience of) twentieth-century modernity. It is for this reason that poetological significance accrues to the passage of *Geschichte und Eigensinn* cited and discussed in chapter 1 in which Negt and Kluge ascertain the tasks of antagonistic realism in reference to "the analysis of a site of an explosion" (*DuM* 2:348). While one may be prone to associate the "analysis of what has happened" and the "collection of what the explosion has scattered" (*DuM* 2:348) with theoretical and narrative discourse respectively, Kluge's narrative prose and theoretical work both evince tendencies toward analysis and collection, applying the precepts and procedures of antagonistic realism to both venues. While neither can undo the destructive forces that manifest themselves in explosive and implosive events, Kluge's theorizing and storytelling, separately and in tandem with one another, work toward fathoming catastrophic history in order to guard against its repetition.

A key challenge on this front stems from the gigantic network that presumes cohesion and supplies coherence to modern life. This is what Kluge means by the false realisms of society's normative "novel of reality"[49] and what Negt and Kluge, from *Öffentlichkeit und Erfahrung: Zur Organisationsanalyse von bürgerlicher und proletarischer Öffentlichkeit* onward, have theorized as "public spheres of production" (*Produktionsöffentlichkeiten*).[50] No less nefarious than catastrophe itself, society's putative realisms gloss over the disturbances, destructions, and other kinds of deformation that stem from and can perpetuate catastrophe, in addition to forcibly adapting human beings to society's pseudo-rationality by subsuming them under capital.[51] What is more, the "historical fictions"[52] of reality's (contestable) realism overlay such subsumption with highly orchestrated manipulations of human emotions, setting their bearers off-balance and impoverishing their capacities for differentiation, resistance, and self-determination. Tracing emotions back to their origins in human beings' basic sensory and perceptive faculties in the short programmatic text "Unterscheidungsvermögen" (The Capacity for Differentiation), Kluge defines feeling as the cohesion of sensations making a statement in the direction of another human being.[53] "Feeling is not something sentimental," he writes, "but has been subjected to sentimentalization in the nineteenth century as a process of commercialization."[54] Zeroing in on the Frankfurt opera house as a "power plant of the emotions," an evocative segment of Kluge's film *Die Macht der Gefühle* notes that "something went wrong at the very beginning of the project" and proceeds to film the excavation and repair or replacement of its rotted underground cables.[55] The mechanisms underlying manipulations of feelings in the nineteenth century only became more exacerbated in the postwar period. Presuming to suture wounds inflicted by destruction, "reality's novel" not only suppresses or overwrites the narrative of what has occurred. It also continues to provide prefabricated "cables," that is, to predetermine the inner connections between one's feelings and relations to other human beings. Although sensations figure as the most basic sites of differentiation, the fact that the processes via which sensations are formed into feelings are manipulated at micro- as well as macropolitical levels demands critical review. In what can be read as a description of *Chronik*'s task, Kluge calls for an inventory of the feelings in which "this capacity for differentiation that we carry around with us as our actual property" would be tested as to its "usefulness for us and for the commonweal."[56] As these remarks suggest, the bars Kluge sets for human emancipation are at least as high as Weiss's—and more painstakingly elaborated.[57]

Geschichte und Eigensinn's seminal passage on antagonistic realism builds on and is best read in conjunction with Kluge's own succinct historicization of his poetics delivered in the foreword to *Neue Geschichten: Hefte 1–18: "Unheimlichkeit der Zeit."* The narration of *Lebensläufe* effectively begins with a note by Kluge on his own, in which he relates the bombing of his hometown he witnessed at thirteen years of age as a (de)formative experience, not only in personal terms (*CdG* 2:11).[58] The repercussions thereof reverberate in a number of claims that Kluge, preparing readers for what follows, makes with regard to the kind of narrative emerging from such sites of rupture. While the precision of the date—April 8, 1945—and measurement—Kluge's proximity to the impact of a bomb at a distance of ten meters—represent spatiotemporal exactitude in the demarcation of a historical experience, the author guards against any notion that his historical tales are confined to the past, hence his emphasis on a present (*Jetztzeit*) in which the past and its narration converge.[59] By the end of the volume that opens thus—and in conformity with the chronicler Bitow's conception of compressed time (*CdG* 1:124–125)—this present will have been expansively grasped as the propulsive force (*CdG* 2:7; *Schubkraft*) of some 20 billion years. Second, Kluge bids classical artistic forms for the harmonization of form and content a seemingly final farewell: "We human beings are bound [*bestimmt*] by the war that form and content wage on one another" (*CdG* 2:11). The abbreviated and condensed character of the stories (which Kluge calls *Verkürzungen*) is itself an effect of history that no act of the creative will can brook or transcend, but must recognize as epic narrative's ground zero. Destruction and debris, disturbances and deformation thus make for unavoidable aspects of the disharmonious relationship between the content and form (the feelings and their relationality) of Kluge's stories. While destructive experiences frame Kluge's narrative points of departure against which protest energies will go to work, they less frequently mark their endings, which are often framed openly as vanishing points of the long, continuously self-resetting[60] and self-regulating[61] process of aspiration and struggle, (re)orientation and emancipation.

Adhering resolutely to the experience of catastrophe, Kluge's storytelling attends to the far-reaching repercussions thereof on epic form. History's destructive forces have left too little intact for literary production to continue unaffected through the portal of the twentieth century's caesura. The modalities of time and space, once deemed constitutive of human experience's comprehensibility, no longer serve as stable supports for intuiting reality. The conditions of possibility for such knowledge are themselves broken, rendering epic integration untenable. Kluge has often described how such problems impact the continuities and discontinuities of literary narration. Commenting on Theodor Fontane's realism on receiving the prize named after the nineteenth-century novelist, Kluge notes that "what separates us from him is the radicalization of all temporal relations."[62] This claim goes farther than Ernst Bloch's appeal to the noncontemporaneity (*Ungleichzeitigkeit*) of different times in the present insofar as that concept emerged, in modernist contexts, as a challenge to the established codification of linear time as progress.[63] For Kluge, the "radicalization of all temporal relations" also implies the implosion of the binary opposition underlying Bloch's juxtaposition of

Ungleichzeitigkeit to linear temporality.[64] This results in new demands on the development of narrative techniques, which feed on, but cannot rest with modernist solutions. In some conformity, then, with postmodernism's turn to space[65]—yet in great tension with postmodernism's forfeiture of dialectics—Kluge proceeds, in his essay on Fontane, to outline spatially conceived "strategies of above and below" that bear on sites of destruction both with regard to their literary representation as well as their practical aversion. The former strategy coincides with the military domination of space, as in the organized execution of the bombing raids, whereas the latter relates to the ground-up perspectives of Kluge's many characters in need of orientation. The locus classicus of the juxtaposition of the two strategies in Kluge's work is found in *Der Luftangriff*, where the Halberstadt schoolteacher Gerda Baethe desperately attempts to shield her children from the plummeting bombs on the town's fateful day (*AR* 26–32/*CdG* 2:43–47).[66] The strategic perspective, relates a well-nigh omniscient narrator in an addendum, that would have been able to interrupt the long chain of events leading to the bombing of Halberstadt's civilian population in 1945 would have concerned the collaborative work of some seventy thousand teachers from 1918 onward at multiple organizational levels (*AR* 32/*CdG* 2:46). Years later, near the end of World War II, the temporal diremption between willful intent and necessity holds sway only banefully: Gerda's actual strategy from below—ill-equipped with garden tools against the bombs and cursing and praying to spirits she never believed in (*AR* 30–31/*CdG* 2:44–45)—constitutes but one historically belated and perilously isolated perspective. Only a preemptive unification of intention and necessity—an indirect sense for what is far in conjunction with collective action—could have potentially spared her—along with too many others—such ordeals. *Chronik*'s analeptic narration of the episode, in which narrator and protagonist respectively channel indirect and direct senses, sets the remediation of Gerda's plight in relation to numerous stories that stand in retroactively for the many colleagues in education through whose collaborative labor twentieth-century European history might have enjoyed an alternative course. The passage indicates the subjunctive mood preponderating much of Kluge's remediation of history. Whereas Weiss culminated his *Ästhetik* in the subjunctive mood channeling the transfer of aesthetic resistance through the narrator's own anticipated completion of his tale into the future, and whereas *Jahrestage* largely reserved this verb form for Johnson's scrutiny of the possibility, plausibility, and tenability of both Gesine's and his own narration of reality, in Kluge the subjunctive conveys strategies of anticipation circumscribing the practical tasks of what would have to have been done in the unwieldy throws of chronicled time.

Stark differences radiate between Kluge's approach to modern epic form and that of Weiss and Johnson. Like Kluge's previous works, *Chronik* no longer aspires to the kind of integration achieved in Weiss's *Die Ästhetik des Widerstands* by way of the triumph of the subjective factor featured in the autodiegetic narrator becoming the work's author, nor that of *Jahrestage*, which mobilized the fictional narrative contract between Cresspahl and Johnson to recount the history of the twentieth century and probe the objective spaces of political engagement in which that history might have been redressed. While the overarching story lines of both epics had relied on the intactness of heterodiegetic time and space, one can sense strains being placed on the epic's imaginative capacities for integration in both cases. As discussed in chapter 2, Weiss's ambition to render the epic tale of aesthetic resistance through the integrative power of an embedded autodiegetic narrator (cf. *NB* 810) is already stretched to considerable limits. The narrative teamwork between Cresspahl and her author in *Jahrestage*, as addressed in chapter 3, registers strain on the genre through the epic's explicit self-reflexivity: where Gesine's memory at first detects only splinters of the past she seeks to recount (*AN* 47/*JT* 63–64), it falls to her conarrator to help her (re)assemble them into a whole in which Gesine is superseded. In Kluge, no embedded autodiegetic narrator—no Gesine and no angel of history, nor any figure like Musil's Ulrich—emerges who could possibly put storytelling's mimesis of catastrophe back together again. To be sure, *Chronik*'s individual stories frequently feature embedded narration, often by an unnamed I (whose identity can sometimes be ascertained), or, alternatively, highly focalized third-person narration, via which Kluge sets plays of uncertain perspectives into motion. Where a seemingly omniscient, bat-like narrator can be detected, as in "Der Eigentümer" and *Der Luftangriff* discussed above, such instances—amid the playful perspectival experiments undertaken for sensing epically what is very far—also prove difficult or unreliable. The rule of case-by-case analysis, already demanded by Johnson's forfeiture of narrative norms in a quotidian writing shorn of habit, holds equally for Kluge. As master heterodiegetic narrator, he can himself barely hold the strewn sprawl of stories populating *Chronik*'s volumes together: the point is less to lay claim to (or retain a hold on) any whole than to enact a narrative method that would contribute to human survival.

Figured in *Chronik* as the wounds of history themselves, the splinters of past experiences inflect Kluge's truncated stories of fraught feelings and foiled aspirations, the forms of which mimic but cannot suture such wounds. At the same time, Kluge's volumes retain the outer form of the modern epic as their shell. In this, they resemble Johnson's comparatively far more literalized use of the calendar for the day-by-day narration of *Jahrestage*'s clearly demarcated chronicle of a year. *Chronik*'s forewords, as glimpsed in the previous section, even suggest differentiated unities of a whole. While such directives are crucial navigational tools, they do not proscribe confusion and disorientation in Kluge's narrative thickets. This not only makes for part of the reading pleasure of getting lost. It is also integral to the self-activation of readers' own capacities for orientation.[67] We can appreciate the deliberateness of an author who has revoked his authority in this: Kluge's mimetic presentation of epic's catastrophically induced implosion is as much an artful ruse as Weiss and Johnson's respective solutions to the challenges of modern epic form. In other words, Kluge's literary mediation of destruction orchestrates destructive literary forms to prevent the neutralizations or transfigurations of history. In this, *Chronik* is epic construction through and through, holding fast and true to the historical and imaginable experiences of destruction to which Kluge so often refers, in order that readers participate in the mapping and reconstruction of history's basic elements, including their own sensations and feelings. Provisions for any other form of orientation would risk sacrificing emancipation's humanizing promise.

From its title outward, *Chronik* repeatedly sets the respective subjective and objective poles of epic orientation elaborated in Weiss's *Ästhetik* and Johnson's *Jahrestage* in relation to one another. Whereas the combination of the two resists resolution into any definitive matrix, their disunity fuels the investigation of what Kluge and Negt call the "subjective-objective" relations of modern life (*HO* 220). If the link between the viability of storytelling and political emancipation—marked by the fraught prospects of democratic socialism in the small European country for which Gesine disembarks—appears to recede in *Jahrestage*'s ominous closing, Kluge's *Chronik* reinvestigates and reasserts that link, in what will make for a still-rockier journey, after Prague became a memory and the Cold War met its official end: where Gesine parts on her way to the ČSSR via the Copenhagen airport, Kluge reconceives spatiotemporal maps for navigating the waters rising around the archipelago of his narrative sites in search of vessels and rescue (cf. figure 1).

In contrast to *Chronik*'s traverse of its archipelagic story-world, *Die Ästhetik des Widerstands* and *Jahrestage* stand out as the last modern epics of their kind in German literary history to asymptotically encapsulate modern social content in poetically integrated story lines. Kluge's *Chronik* eschews any straightforward arch—linear, dialectical, revolutionary, or otherwise—via which the narration of society could be streamlined. The many diffuse stories of the two volumes appear to abound in anarchy, operating not only beyond the confines of objective space and linear temporality, but also pushing the limits of—and demanding a suspension of disbelief regarding—logocentrism, without jettisoning the search for orientation or a reliance on an enlightened and playful reason, which literature's newfound fantasy and acrobatics rehabilitate. Despite the emphasis on the radicalized character of unstable spatiotemporal, semantic, and social relations, Kluge's constellative storytelling neither quite constitutes a "hysterical philosophy of history"[68]—since Kluge's scenarios of dedramatization undercut the accuracy of such adjectival appellations—nor abandons itself to the inessential nothingness of bad anarchy; rather, it unfurls a sustained investigation of the hidden and offbeat, expansive and elusive grammars of modern experiences. Strewn about, like the particles resulting from the explosion addressed in Negt and Kluge's account of antagonistic realism, Kluge's stories are obstinate (*eigensinnige*) splinters, mere sketches (*Entwürfe*) that cannot return to themselves.[69] The broken prolepsis in the story of Simon Weigel addressed above is a simple example of this. The comportment he commits to maintaining as his last piece of property is an expression of obstinacy (*Eigensinn*). As indicated to readers in the foreword to *Chronik*'s first chapter, this is the only other kind of property human beings own besides the time of their lives (*CdG* 1:11; *Lebenszeit*). *Eigensinn*—"one own's sense" (*HO* 292), a "self-will"[70] and a "will to meaning,"[71] a form of obstinacy paramount to the power of resistance in Negt and Kluge's conception of history—is derivative of and a response to experiences of the expropriation of meaning as well as the senses (*Sinne*).[72] On the order of Lukács's characterization cited above as an epigraph to this chapter, it is the kind of "meaning [that] can never quite penetrate reality," but without which "reality would disintegrate into the nothingness of inessentiality." The battle between the two forces—in Kluge's instantiations, the assertion of (one's own) meaning against its denial—is staged repeatedly across *Chronik*'s stories. The ensuing difficulty of their interpretation is bound up with their author's observations of the temporal acceleration that induces meaning's withdrawal: "*Sinnentzug*," we read at the beginning of its ninth chapter, is "a societal situation in which the collective life-program of human beings falls apart faster than new life-programs can be produced" (*CdG* 2:457). Where the temporal compression in play here appears subjectively as well as objectively determined, a related definition from *Geschichte und Eigensinn* frames the issue in more basic dichotomous terms: "[**The withdrawal of meaning**] The category that something has meaning. Departure and return must be imaginable, for something to have a meaning. There must be something that both in itself and at the same time for me yields a cohesive movement [*zusammenhängende Bewegung*], so that I can say: that makes sense. This 'for me' however is not provided for in the construction of society's machinery" (*DuM* 2:376; boldface in the original). This passage's emphasis on departure and return as a cohesive movement frames meaning as a question of narrative structure, even if the arch of this structure, *pace* Hegel, whom Negt and Kluge's prepositional phrases evoke, is denied. While the splinter-like character of Kluge's stories reflects that very problem, the denial in question results in the need for a narrative network of production that counters that of society's machinery (cf. *DuM* 2:89/*HO* 121). Contesting the relations through which society produces and distributes meaning, this counterproduction assumes forms of theoretical mediation in Negt and Kluge's writings and poetic mediation in Kluge's narrative network. Whereas Negt and Kluge's collaborations analyze the conditions, relations, and possibilities of labor power and *Eigensinn* in relation to history and political economy, Kluge's storytelling addresses the dimensions of the struggle poetically to supply *Eigensinn* with an aesthetic economy in which it might thrive on its own terms. At this level, his mimesis of destruction enjoys a dialectical reversal. Converting the splinters of destruction into the thorns of protest,

Kluge's literary art—as a gigantic modulation of so many broken stories—more than mimics history. Mobilizing the narration of *Eigensinn* and the *Eigensinn* of narration, the networks of Kluge's stories redress catastrophe and reconnect and recuperate elements of experience disaggregated by history to effect a remediation of humanity's emancipatory potentials.

In this, the adherence of Kluge's method to catastrophic realities of the twentieth century gives no issue to default or resignation. While his stories retain, in their formal character, the quality of being torn asunder,[73] Kluge's development of his narrative method out of its historical conditions points to a great reassembly under way: "Either social history narrates its novel of reality [*Real-Roman*] without regard for human beings, or human beings will narrate their counter-history [*Gegengeschichte*]. They can only do this, however, at the levels of reality's complexity. That demands in the most literal sense of the word the 'artistic object' [*Kunstgegenstand*], an aggregate of artistic objects [*Kunstgegenständen*]. Sensuousness [*Sinnlichkeit*] as method is not a natural product of society."[74] In this programmatic passage—the logic of which clearly evokes and develops Brecht's canonical definition of realism discussed in chapter 1 above—Kluge asserts both the viability of counterstories in their singularity as well as highlights the importance of their larger relationality. With regard to the former, Kluge's predilection for great brevity and condensation has been duly noted. As Winfried Menninghaus has put it:

> Kluge's goal is nothing less than to salvage the function of great art in anti-esoteric form for the average citizen. "These would, in light of their day jobs, presumably prefer to read the substance of one thousand pages [Joyce's *Ulysses*] or the highly organized faculty of memory of Proust's work as a short story from at the most one to two DIN-A-4 size pages." As right as this diagnosis of need may be, the ambition with which Kluge thereby burdens his "oeuvre" is downright adventurous.[75]

While critics have appreciated the democratizing impetus of the procedure Kluge describes here,[76] others such as Michael Bray have expressed concern that Kluge's embrace of aesthetic openness can also induce social hermeticism.[77] Weiss contended that readers of his *Ästhetik* would have to go through "the same exertion" as the book's characters and their author to appropriate the depicted experiences as their own; similarly, if the two-page DIN-A-4 story functions in the way Kluge describes it, it alone would demand some gargantuan force of insight to be fully apprehended.[78] The intricate complexities of Kluge's individual texts often appear harrowing enough. But that analyses thereof easily and inadvertently far outstrip their objects in length is not just a feature of scholarly writing. The interpretations unraveling Kluge's tales rather corroborate his distinction, related at the beginning of this study, between experiences that devour our time and those that repay our investment. What is more, it is not clear that the assessment of their sociopolitical and aesthetic functions turn exactly on Bray's criteria. That the fullness of understanding is about as feasible as totality is attainable does not present any absolute obstacles: the enticements of Kluge's storytelling already make themselves felt at the very beginning of the process of readers' apprehension thereof. Any form of unsettlement is a chance for a new direction. Oscillating between simplicity and complexity in the epic constellations Kluge establishes to enhance human beings' orientation, the stories yields flashes of insight and accumulating rewards to anyone lingering along the paths Kluge paves for the practice—not possession—of emancipation.

While the abundance of Kluge's forewords in *Chronik* can be likened to programmatic claims reminiscent of the theoretical work he has pursued with Oskar Negt,[79] the poetological significance of many of the epic's tales stems from their reinstatement of artistic procedures, methods, and goals at the level of narrative. This is without question part of *Chronik*'s own self-reflexivity. Two such stories straddling the work's 1989 watershed can serve to illustrate a perceptible shift in the calibration of Kluge's own procedure across that divide. The first is the aforementioned "Eingemachte Elefantenwünsche" from the sixth notebook of the "*Unheimlichkeit*" chapter, which depicts the work of one A. Weber on what might be the beginnings of a modern epic. Weber, however, is stuck at a rather rudimentary stage of the process: in what reads as a narrativization of the problems of "cohesive movement" addressed above, Weber's extensive work on the manuscript circles obstinately around the impossibilities of its development. As a result, he has some eighteen hundred pages of sketches, only a few of which he is willing to share with interviewer Heiner Boehncke, who has become curious about the project in his capacity as an editor. According to Weber, the pieces, vaguely defined as materials for a tragedy, do not admit of any larger pattern or coherence (i.e., relationality, *CdG* 2:161; *Zusammenhang*) whatsoever. The interlocutors' interview canvasses parallels to Kluge's own storytelling, including Weber's fascination for elephants as bearers of long memory. What is less clear from their conversation, however, is the pickling. Weber claims that his allusive title marks the need to compensate for the nonexistence of elephant memory in nature (*CdG* 2:162). He is clearly interested in appropriating the idea of elephant memory into human beings' cultural realm. The significance of that transferal could well compensate for the unsustainable character of any of his sketches, each of which he professes to be compelled to write from scratch: those included in the story barely reach over four lines each. While temporal development is denied, a spatial arrangement of individual canning jars emerges, preserved for some future out of the story's view, as if wishes were being prepared for hibernation through cold times. It is difficult, in other words, in the context of this study as well as Kluge's *Spiegel* interview referenced above, not to read Weber's procedures as indicative of Kluge's conception of his own writing during the Cold War.

A more recent story from *Chronik*'s first chapter complements this image suggestively. Reading the jars of pickled elephant wishes as the recapitulation of Weber's problems at the higher level of Kluge's biding time in lieu of "having something to say that points to the future,"[80] "The Twilight of the Idols in Vienna" reveals a curiously eager and positive principle of discovery at work (*CdG* 1:66–73). Dedicated to Heiner Müller and citing him on the "brutal beauty of the recording of an opera" for the epigraph ("What was never broken, can never be saved"), Kluge's story traces the emergence and transferal of the most unusual of artworks. Richard Wagner's opera was allegedly to be performed in Vienna in March 1945 as a final cry of resistance and self-affirmation against advancing Allied forces. Numerous historical and technical complications befall this project, the twists and turns of which elude reconstruction in this context. Yet the film recording of what must be veritably cacophonous fragments of an opera—rehearsed across the spatial locations of the performers in bunkers, recorded amid air raids and technical shortcomings of cameras, and so on—is transported to the basement of the City Museum of Sotschi in the Soviet Union and forgotten, then discovered there in 1991 by a young composer, reconstructed in its fragmentary character in Paris, and discussed by two visitors to the Cinétyp film laboratories there. The destructed character of the work is the imprint of history itself, its truth-content a testament to the self-destructiveness of its attempted broadcast, the Reich's murderous ideology, and an indication of the only form in which Wagner's music is accessible after culture passed through the portal of its death: "One should *always*," writes a contributor to the *Cahiers du Cinéma* in an illustration of Müller's claim, "'fragment' Wagner in this way" (*CdG* 1:70, emphasis there). At the end of the story, in commenting on the passage of the undertaking's filmic documentation through time and space, one of the workers at Cinétyp notes that there are likely to be many such finds in the world. "You must assume that for six thousand years, there have always been things hidden somewhere or forgotten" (*CdG* 1:73). With such a finding, Kluge *also* signals his curiosity in the released dispersal of energies from their erstwhile containers during geopolitically colder times. Advancing a new collection of such energies as a positive project, *Chronik* builds on Kluge's previously honed strategies for revealing the negative and destructive forces of society through their remediation, to constitute, through countermediation, an aesthetic economy of human emotions, protests, and visions.

Remediation and Countermediation

With *Chronik* and the series it inaugurates, Kluge has established a new framework for his storytelling. Accompanying it is a shift in emphasis that I account for by describing strategies of remediation and countermediation underlying Kluge's narrative method. My use of these two terms in what follows aims to convey the stakes and techniques of Kluge's narrative project appropriately. Building on the dual sense of mediation—of *Vermittlung* and *Mediatisierung* discussed in chapter 1—the terms "remediation" and "countermediation" speak both to the level at which Kluge's poetic intervention into society's novel of reality operates and prove useful for delineating distinct tendencies at work in his epic prose. Often dialectically intertwined, neither of the two strategies is entirely new to *Chronik*. Yet the spirit of the new departure the epic associates with the end of the Cold War warrants a differentiating investigation of Kluge's literary activity that reveals subtle and firm shifts from strategies of remediation to strategies of countermediation. To make the case, this section of the chapter lays out the purchase of each term before turning to an analysis of *Chronik*'s second chapter, "Verfallserscheinungen der Macht," as a seminal site of the shift in question.

As argued in chapter 1 above, the modern epic in the Cold War is ambitiously predicated on wresting the self-comprehension of modernity away from its confinement to philosophical discourse. Transformatively appropriating the Hegelian impulse to tell of the whole, to grasp society's totality by way of literary narration (or at least, as with Kluge, gain a degree of orientation therein), Weiss, Johnson, and Kluge's epics adventurously develop forms for a task ridden with difficulty. Their efforts turn on questions of mediation. As nondiscursive fictional works of literature, Kluge's stories, like Weiss's and Johnson's epics, do not mediate with theoretical stringency. Yet Kluge, for whom mediation bespeaks both the interrelatedness of all social phenomena in the grip of society's encompassing machinery as well as that of the individual characteristics of humanity's unrealized potential to shake off such a hold, has not shied away from employing the term in its classic socio-theoretical sense. Literature, he claims in an essay on Gotthold Ephraim Lessing included in *Der unterschätzte Mensch*'s republication of *Maßverhältnisse des Politischen*, mediates between "the immediate, the subjective, and the singular" on the one hand and "the general" on the other to restore substance to the public sphere (*DuM* 1:955). Kluge's prolific activity from the Oberhausen Manifesto onward has refunctionalized society's media in order to intervene in the contestable ways these participate in reality's mediation. To the double resonance of mediation in English, which speaks to the conceptual labor of *Vermittlung* and the work of media alike, Kluge thus adds the larger question of the direction of each, foregrounding their relation to emancipation. Indicative thereof is his obstinate use of the concept of medium to insist on human beings as the fundamental reference points of his work in different venues: what we refer to as media are for Kluge mere forms, means to establish relations that would serve human interests. Human beings themselves, he maintains, are the real media.[81] By anchoring mediation in human activity, Kluge's approach lays the foundation for the aesthetic economy his narrative networks construct: these venture mediation beyond, askew, and against the machinations of society's normative mediation under the dictates of political economy.

As these comments suggest, there is great slippage in the concept of mediation, which proves equivocal in its usage in socio-philosophical as well as artistic contexts. The necessity for distinguishing between different kinds of mediation provides the first rationale for affixing prefixes to the term describing the overarching activity of Kluge's theoretical and artistic work. Remediation and countermediation can be wielded as synonyms for antagonistic realism's respective tasks of analysis and collection. Negt and Kluge's call for "analysis of what has happened" speaks to the activity of remediation. Indeed, Kluge's artistic oeuvre abounds in remediations reminiscent of Bolter and Grusin's use of the term, as discussed in chapter 1 above, to address remakes across different media. This includes Kluge's renarrations of past literary works and films as well as the repurposing of his own narratives for his cinematic and literary productions.[82] More substantively, remediation speaks to the unveiling of society's actual mediation obscured by dominant media's productions of pseudo-realisms as well as their destructive effects. *Unglück*, Kluge's work teaches again and again, is not so much "misfortune" as it is orchestrated.[83] The social totality is indeed mediated through and through, yet the character of its mediation is seldom apparent, for which reason critical theory devoted considerable efforts to disclosing the force of its machinations. Remediation in Kluge is the narrative labor of this disclosure: epic prose's imaginative and socio-theoretical revelation of links in the many chains that led to "what has happened," that is, the conditions that made catastrophe possible. Such work does not square with representation in any conventional sense. The explosive force can hardly be presented again, but constitutes, in texts like *Der Luftangriff*, an absent center circumscribed by Kluge's constructive-mimetic narration. To remediate the April 1945 events that took place in his hometown, Kluge's unusual text unleashes the dialectics of concretion and abstraction, without which they could hardly be fathomed. David Roberts has convincingly demonstrated how the different components of Kluge's reconstruction of the bombing of Halberstadt—"pictures, photos of the bombing, town plans, flight paths of the attacking bombs, flight patterns with lateral, rear and frontal views (schematic presentation), diagrams and specifications of bomb types, first-hand and operational reports, situation reports, quotations of the relevant literature, footnotes, inserted texts, expert discussions, interviews, etc."[84] all combine—along with the depiction of many characters like Gerda affected below in addition to those less unaffected above (e.g., the pilots)—not to "represent" the day but analyze the "multidimensionality of reality and [make] it accessible to empathetic experience."[85]

The disharmonious dialectics of artistic form and social and historical content foreshadowed in the foreword to *Chronik*'s eighth chapter are developed to an extreme in Kluge's remediating texts, which meet Adorno's call for modern artworks to "show themselves to be the equal of high industrialism, not simply make it a topic" (*AT* 33/57; *dem Hochindustrialismus sich*

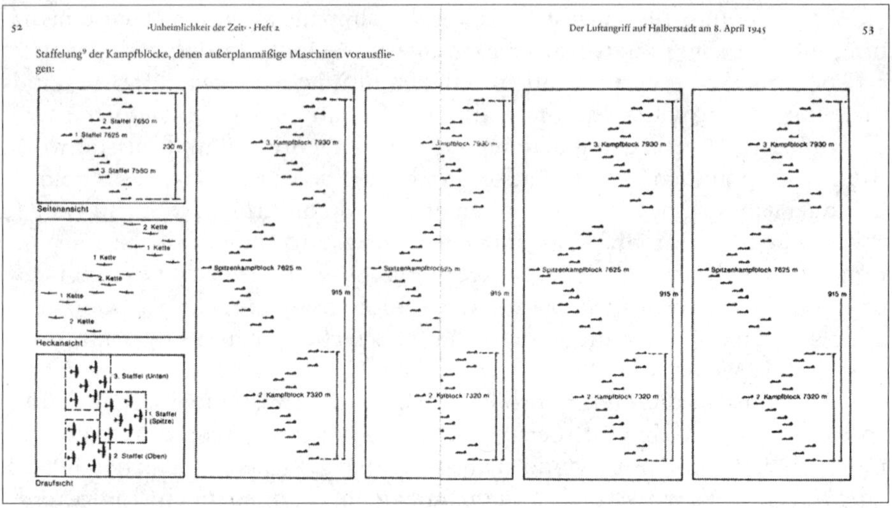

Figure 10. Staggered battle formation with additional aircraft flying ahead. Excerpt from Alexander Kluge, *Chronik der Gefühle*, 2:52–53.

gewachsen zeigen, nicht einfach ihn behandeln). Notably, Kluge's montage assembly of the elements with which he renders the bombing of Halberstadt neither reconstructs any whole, nor coincides with any straightforward approach to its documentation. The abstraction of the diagrams and related schematizations bespeak the kind of imagination necessary to grasp what has transpired and how (see, e.g., figure 10 and *AR* 40–41). They are not readily verifiable as to their authenticity: foreign to conventional fictional narrative, such documentary elements are mounted alongside the equally foreign fictional elements that resemble them, including faked footnotes and interviews that feign documentary authenticity. Such play calls for even greater scrutiny than that demanded by Johnson's *Jahrestage* of Gesine and her readers' reviews of the epic's documentary elements. At a greater distance from Johnson's comparatively ordered narration of the Jerichow past, the New York City present, and the epic's Vietnam and Prague horizons, Kluge's procedure charges readers with the heavy task of grasping the forces of abstraction and concretion in relation to one another as they piece aspects of the narrative remediation together. At the same time, Kluge includes a more forthright address of the subjective factor at work in both the making and the reception of the text. The factor is absent from Adorno's line cited above. Where Adorno appeared to suggest that an equalization of artistic and industrial production in the modernist desecration of art's erstwhile aura might suffice to satisfy the negative-dialectical criteria of art's relation to society and thereby facilitate recipients' responses of insight, Kluge's playful approach to the analogy between industrial and artistic production underscores the constructed character of the latter. It is a form of self-reflexivity within the narrative that both puts the necessarily fictional character of the text's realism on display and guards against its passive reception by activating readers, who can also come to appreciate the necessity of fictional construction.[86]

Remediation thus points to the literary-aesthetic procedure whereby catastrophes such as the Battle of Stalingrad or the bombing of Halberstadt are referred back to the conditions of their possibility in the process of history—back to the whole negative social totality from which they stem. Reckoning with the hubris and gravity of the view from above and its effects on those below, remediation goes hand in hand with the aesthetic negativity that preponderates in Kluge's narration of cold times. The procedure holds not only for stories addressed to war-torn contexts explicitly, but also the many disturbed trajectories spawned by catastrophe in the aftermath of World War II and the Shoah. The stories of Kluge's first publication of *Lebensläufe* cohere, as he repeats again in *Chronik*, in sad history (*CdG* 2:675; *ergeben . . . eine traurige Geschichte*). The title *Lernprozesse mit tödlichem Ausgang* alone compresses a baneful dialectics. Sediments of Kluge's radical mimesis of modern civilization's coldness[87]—"I freeze in summer also," Anita G. tells the court trying her for stealing a fur coat in Kluge's first feature-length film, *Abschied von Gestern* (*Yesterday Girl*, cf. *CdG* 1:734–735)—such tendencies earned him a label as "the heartless writer" Hans Magnus Enzensberger described in his review of Kluge's 1977 publication *Neue Geschichten*.[88] Kluge's practice of remediation, it seemed, indeed extended critical theory's negative-dialectical analyses of postwar capitalism's cold enclosures, but appeared only to signal the necessity of construing exits, ways out, lines of flight, and means of escape.[89] In other words, remediation, in the sense I am giving it here, has the tendency to conform to negative relational patterns dismally confirming the power of the social totality during the perceived standstill of the Cold War's freeze.

The remediation in question, however, by no means rests with the disclosure of total social mediation as a fixed or final mechanism, neither during nor after the Cold War. It is not only that Kluge and Negt refuse the term "totality," replacing it with "relationality." Already in *Der Luftangriff*, as discussed above, can one catch glimpses of an ulterior strategy at work. The desperate defenses of Gerda on display there relate to strategies Negt and Kluge excavate from the landlocked German fairy tales, Heinrich von Kleist's "Michael Kohlhaas," and other sources in *Geschichte und Eigensinn* (cf. *DuM* 2:754–755, 122–125/*HO* 281–282). Features of an obstinate resistance, the many defenses Kluge's characters put up figure as important dispositions to be trained, expanded, and developed: "Those who tell fairy tales," they write in their commentary on "The Story of the Seven Young Kids," "are not in control of the capacity for differentiation. A permanent doubt is at work at the point of contact between inside and outside" (*HO* 287/*DuM*

2:761). Marred by the determining power of the social totality in which they appear, fraught by the expropriation of human senses and meaning, capacities for differentiation and resistance are repeatedly stunted and foiled in the negativity of a historical process of prolonged expropriation, alienation, and disaggregation. Antagonistic realism's second task thus concerns the collection of what has been scattered by society's orchestrated explosions. Effecting a perspectival shift away from the inevitable aesthetic negativity preponderating in Kluge's remediation of catastrophe, countermediation points to the positive reassembly, recollection, and recuperation of humanity's emancipatory potentials. The term's prefix retains the oppositional stance vis-à-vis society's given scenarios of mediation, the negative force of which Kluge's stories can by no means ignore; yet his countermediating strategies narrate from the perspective of emancipation, a standpoint that Kluge's new *Chronik* forewords adopt, against the sad history of yore and prior to the ominous rebalancing of diabolical and human power in *Die Lücke, die der Teufel läßt*.[90] Countermediation connotes the development of an aesthetic economy of *Eigensinn* to match, compete with, and ultimately overturn the political economy to which labor power, as *Geschichte und Eigensinn* lays out, is perennially subjected. The strategy arises as the equivalent, in Kluge's epic storytelling, of the perspectival shift engendering the 1981 *Geschichte und Eigensinn* and 1992 *Maßverhältnisse des Politischen* out of the negative findings of Negt and Kluge's 1972 *Öffentlichkeit und Erfahrung*. A vast reassembly of humanity's otherwise splintered emancipatory potentials, Kluge's countermediating storytelling also speaks to another dimension of mediation: the reconciliation of opposed parties and forces.[91] They thus contribute to the reconstruction and reconfiguration of a faintly existing *Gemeinsinn* (*sensus communis*)—rent asunder in the isolated appearances of *Eigensinn*—that can be recuperated toward the end of reducing and defying catastrophe. As *Der Luftangriff*'s outline of a strategy from below suggests, the full development of the senses would entail both the supplementation of the direct senses (*Nähesinne*) with the otherwise neglected enhancement of indirect senses (*Fernsinne*) as well as a recalibration of *Eigensinn* to *Gemeinsinn*, signified there in the collective dimension of Gerda's work as a schoolteacher in conjunction with thousands of other colleagues. By fostering the interrelation, if not full integration of such capacities, Kluge's artistic counterproductions undertake positive constructions that combat and surpass aesthetic negativity's mimesis of catastrophes.

The two strategies in question also relate to topical and stylistic shifts of emphases in the unfolding of Kluge's narrative cartographies from 2000 on. Rather than indicating strong discontinuities in Kluge's work, these shifts mark different points of focus in *Eigensinn*'s aesthetic economy. One can note not only thematic changes in orientation from German to transnational contexts and from pasts to futures at the Cold War's end, but also emerging shifts in style and tone from coldness to warmth and from antagonism to reciprocity, without entailing any forfeiture of dialectical method on Kluge's part. Kluge's positivity (in countermediation)—the flip side of the alleged negativity (in remediation) of his earlier writings—can be associated with the series of aspirational concepts highlighted in *Chronik*'s forewords: the anti-realism of wishes (*CdG* 1:511), the play-drive (*CdG* 1:797), goodwill (*CdG* 1:895), "primordial trust" and hope (*CdG* 2:923), and so on, to which Kluge is seeking to lend new support. In this respect, countermediation also bespeaks a curious relaxation of the erstwhile fierceness of remediation's radical character impacted by Cold War landscapes of destruction and deformation, division and derealization. The turn to strategies of countermediation perceptible from *Chronik* onward modifies this remediation's impetus. In some contrast to the postulate of innovation operative in and accelerated by Adorno's aesthetic theory, which grasped artistic innovations in lockstep with a philosophico-historically conceived arrow of modernity's corrosive unfurling, Kluge's literary practice (particularly amid the strategies of countermediation I am teasing out here) "no longer stands," as Andreas Sombroek has pointed out, "under a permanent compulsion to innovate."[92] As Sombroek argues, the factors constituting meaning in Kluge's texts can still be gleaned from the relations they establish between the old and the new. And whereas Kluge's aesthetic economy is hardly devoid of corrosion, the breadth of his entertainment of the relation between the old and the new reaches from negativity vis-à-vis aesthetic tradition to variability within a given method. In this way, the countermediating tendencies of Kluge's aesthetic economy contribute to the positive elaboration and development of tenable strategies of orientation in the face of society's disorienting forces. We would do ill to jettison them.

Kluge's brief commentary on Leo Tolstoy's epic novel *Anna Karenina* included in *Chronik*'s first chapter provides an example of the dialectical relationship between remediation and countermediation that I have in mind here. Kluge begins his miniature remake by appealing to an "elementary power" that will appear enigmatic to confused minds and hearts (*CdG* 1:27). In a procedure characteristic of Kluge's search for exits and dedramatization of tragic structures (*CdG* 1:841; *Abrüstung*), the renarration of Karenina's plight drastically transforms Tolstoy's plot. Kluge's one-page intervention into the thousand-page novel zeroes in on Anna and her husband's relation to the child they have brought into the world, whose precarious health compels the otherwise hostile and estranged husband to permit his wife continued residence in the home to take care of their son. The improvised arrangement, devoid of reconciliation, turns permanent. "In [Anna's] confused sense," Kluge writes, "the life of the child that she bore appeared more elementary than [any] story of love. She recalled having read a very similar story from a novel that ended fatally" (*CdG* 1:28). Kluge's fanciful intervention prevents the fatality of Tolstoy's ending. At least the former's footnote relates that in the absence from the home of the French novel that Anna had in mind, she could rely only on her memory thereof, which led her to abstain from any search for forced, violent solutions, on the one hand, and from experiencing the new arrangement as incarceration, on the other. As the footnote champions the avoidance of calamity—Kluge uses "catastrophe" to refer both to Karenin's initial expulsion of his adulterous wife from their home and to a negative turn in the child's health—the magic of the child appears to hold its mother in thrall in a story that seems to mount not only a transformative remediation of Tolstoy's novel, but also a successful countermediation of its catastrophes.

Of course, this would be no Kluge story without the deliverance of cascading uncertainty: thin indeed are "Kommentar zu Anna Karenina"'s feigned resolutions. The first chapter's table of contents grants a clue in the form of a subtitle introducing Kluge's commentary: "One has to narrate this novel from the perspective of the human being to whom Anna is closest" (*CdG* 1:11; *dem an der jungen Frau das meiste liegt*). Kluge's follow-through on this point gives readers to understand that he means Sergei, the child Anna brought into the world with her husband. Driven by a focus on the sickly child, the story's twist—and the moment of its departure from Tolstoy's rendition—arises from the parents' concern for Sergei and saves his mother's life in the process. The peace denied Anna and Karenin thus appears to accrue to the child in this exchange, whose own peace figures as the tale's last word. Yet the story's concluding line prohibits any reassurances. A curious textual *Eigensinn* makes itself felt, here at the level of Kluge's syntactical choices. The peace displayed by the child's closed eyes appears deathly: "His closed eyes showed an expression of peace, the way they would in death" (*CdG* 1:28; *Seine geschlossenen Augen, so sähe es im Tode aus, zeigten einen Ausdruck des Friedens* [my translation fails to capture Kluge's Kleistian syntax]), a line that sends each narrative advance of the story hitherto into a tailspin. In this case, Kluge's use of the subjunctive does not circumscribe any missed actionable possibilities, which the story had detailed by explicitly rescinding Karenina and Karenin's mutual animosity. Rather, the subjunctive raises issues pertaining to multiple perspectives at play here, including that highlighted by the story's subtitle. Not only do readers not learn whether, in Kluge's account of the family's narrative trajectory, the child survives his illness. The entwinement of peace and death also reverberates back onto the improvised domestic arrangement between Anna and her estranged husband. And it stands in tension with the footnote's laconic restraint regarding any possible disharmony between the blood circulating within Anna and her life in the home she never leaves. Neither child nor mother, not to mention the husband, hold any certain position in the text's vortex of meaning.[93] Whose or which elementary power is in play here? Without elaborating any definitive answer to this question, the text demonstrates such a power running through each of its obstinate characters.[94] While Kluge's remediating intervention into Tolstoy's narrative exploits one of its many possible turning points in a few brief strokes, the claim of "Kommentar zu Anna Karenina" as to the presence of an elementary power proves more beguiling. This point of departure grants Kluge's renarration its purchase as it beckons readers to suspend any disbelief in its premise. Holding sway over the story, "elementary power" constitutes a building block of Kluge's strategy of countermediation that *Chronik* is beginning to map and test out.

Kluge's poetic shift from a swiftly delivered and ultimately downplayed remediation of Tolstoy's fictional narrative to the foregrounding of a here still uncertain strategy of countermediation is suggestive. Operating in the folds of a novel, rather than at a site of great historical upheaval, Kluge's story points to the role of poetic construction that goes hand in hand with the positive side of his project. Rainer Stollmann, in the dialogues he crafts around the relationship between theory and poetry in Kluge's work, has maintained that "Critical theory made use of the poetic from the beginning," to which the interviewee responds, in a prolongation, rather than an explanation, of theorizing and storytelling's entwinement: "That is its strength. Reason is a feeling for relationality, just like poetry or music."[95] While Stollmann thus traces the branches of Kluge's various scenarios of theoretical and artistic mediation back to their common denominator, a quasi-originary unity of human faculties, the manifestations thereof in strategies of remediation and countermediation can be, to put it in the formulation of Enzensberger's bon mot for the consistency of Kluge's narrative comportment, "confusingly similar" (*zum Verwechseln ähnlich*).[96] Parsing such confusion, the dialectical unity of Kluge's method can be grasped by associating remediation with the genealogical exposure of modern civilization's negative and destructive potentials, a strategy that will indelibly import healthy doses of socio-theoretical abstraction into Kluge's storytelling, and countermediation with the poetic sets and resets of an aesthetic economy aspiring to grant humanity's emancipatory potentials their own chances to develop, which will thus necessarily rely on equally healthy doses of poetic fantasy. Emphases falling on one or the other side of the method's negative and positive precepts and aesthetic procedures will not turn on any absolute shifts, but rather enact the strategy demanded by the narrative situation at hand, its topic and the conditions of its relatability. Nonetheless: the mostly older *Lebensläufe* of *Chronik*'s second volume tend to remediate, whereas the epic *Basisgeschichten* of the first volume countermediate.

As a keystone of countermediation, the elementary power referred to in "Kommentar zu Anna Karenina" may serve as shorthand for *Chronik*'s large-scale examination of feelings. In setting such a focus, *Chronik* undertakes a rewriting of the twentieth century—in addition to the tales it tells of experiences from other contexts—from the "subterranean" perspectives of the "human instincts and passions repressed and distorted by civilization" in the "known history of Europe."[97] As discussed above, a key site of this rewriting concerns the "Verfallserscheinungen der Macht" chapter's genealogical approach to the Transition. Excavating recent times in which a dynamic withdrawal of meaning accompanies symptoms of declining power, Kluge unleashes utopian potentials—and Marxism's unfulfilled programs (cf. *DuM* 2:144)—associated with the socialist project into uncertain trajectories in *Chronik*'s second chapter.

Like "Der Eigentümer," the chapter's opening story, "Nikolaus 1989," sets its stage and mood in reference to weather patterns. In conformity with those of yore (*CdG* 1:153; *wie zu früheren Zeiten*), the storms of this December 6 stop at the Elbe River, part of which once constituted a short stretch of the German-German border. The story develops a panorama of fourteen different scenes characterized as "Reports from the Front" across its fifteen-page depiction of a single day, four weeks after the Berlin Wall's opening and at the beginning of Advent in the lead-up to Christmas. The first scene juxtaposes the ominously inclement weather conditions confined to points just west of the Elbe within GDR territory (from Magdeburg to Halberstadt) to a sense of urgency in the crisis-ridden politics of the day, the limited "temporal budget" (*CdG* 1:153) of which is running out. No citizen protesters constitute Kluge's list of dramatis personae here, which instead comprises adherents of the "buckling state" of the GDR (*CdG* 1:155). As in Kluge's literary treatments of the Nazi dictatorship in *Schlachtbeschreibung* and elsewhere, adherents of and participants in the systems depicted in crisis or decline make up the vast majority of the protagonists throughout this chapter's stories. The narrative tone appears mostly cool and removed. But in contrast to Kluge's literary reckonings with Nazism, the force of aesthetic negativity in "Nikolaus 1989" remains more relaxed as the investigation of what can be recuperated from the experience of the GDR takes shape. The starkly antagonistic features of Kluge's remediating texts are being reconfigured as the nature of the social antagonism in question swiftly undergoes drastic transformation. Kluge's countermediation of processes in and around 1989—which have little to do with staking out positions for or against unification directly—frame the period as a space of historical possibilities and impossibilities.

The party functionaries depicted in "Nikolaus 1989" are well aware of the subjective volatility of the GDR's citizens in the wake of the border's new porosity. The citizens' protest energies are already giving way to preparations for the Christmas season.[98] In the questionable decorations for a factory party depicted in the second scene, Christian and socialist symbols coexist for a last time. One comrade, Beelitz, ruminates, as he has every other December, over the impossibility of offering something more attractive to the necessarily false consciousness manipulated by the Christian décor (*CdG* 1:154). The strings of lights during Advent pique the expectation of something special—"Never was there as much contemporary history taking place as now"—but to the party functionaries, they remain an "ideological diversion" from which "the West profits" (*CdG* 1:154; capitals of the original omitted). A comrade Friedewald, who cannot fathom the attractiveness of "a Nicholas carved out of birch," admits that "one cannot dip Karl Marx into chocolate" (*CdG*

1:166), but nonetheless proposes miniatures representing episodes from the Paris Commune, climatic moments of the French revolution as well as the Spartacus slave revolt, each of which would look nice in properly lighted window displays. At some distance from these efforts, the guests attending the factory party enjoy their evening; little affected by the various decorations, the most divergent personal and political convictions dissolve into the festive atmosphere.

The third scene outfits the story with an additional and more penetrating layer of historical reflection, analysis, and speculation. Titled "Young Marxists at the Front," the vignette zeroes in on members of a Marx reading group associated with the VEB Plaste (a People's Factory for plastics), who fear the consequences the distracting seasonal festivities may have on their fellow citizens. They are concerned that the impending annexation of their state by the West will transform political hopes into consumerist desires. The concerns of the reading group's members are curious. Although politically ostracized because of their association with a protestant group in Wittenberg prior to 1989, they now constitute a fraction of the SED (*CdG* 1:155). By including this note, Kluge points to the diversity of protest energies as well as the different possibilities of political association at the time. These young Marxists, who rely on the early Marx's "Economic and Philosophical Manuscripts" as well as the *Grundrisse* for their orientation (*CdG* 1:157), are redoubling their efforts to articulate a new agenda. With the ardency of a Martin Luther, they also assume front-line positions: "They wanted a different result in the 'Battle of Systems' than that which would evolve as if naturally, were the state territory of the GDR to subject itself to the West in the form of an annexation" (*CdG* 1:157–158; *Anschluss*). In order to prohibit such suspiciously natural turns of events, they identify a need for "working towards conquest on THE SUBJECTIVE ROUTE" (*CdG* 1:155; capitals in the original). The militaristic overtones of the militants' language stand out. They encounter difficulties in seeking to orient themselves quickly enough to the new situation. It is especially unclear to what extent they can successfully mobilize politically by means of an embattled vocabulary containing terms such as "Front, Conquest, [and] Determination of the Enemy" (*CdG* 1:155–157).

Kluge's narration of their predicament continues to backtrack. In the next scene, "What does 'to the front' mean under these circumstances?" the members of the reading group itemize an agenda that is quickly submitted to some criticism:

> We are concerned with:
> - An analysis of the image of the enemy
> - An analysis of the measure to be taken against the enemy's trickery
> - Our own attack
> - Decision
> - Execution (*CdG* 1:156)

The epistemological aspect of this cautious preliminary work outweighs its practicality. As their vision is overrun by rapidly changing conditions, one of the group's members—if not the narrator himself—asks what "front" could mean if they are dealing with the "effects of an 'invisible hand,' that is, society in the mind of the many millions who constitute the market in its broadest sense?" (*CdG* 1:156). The front line appears to shift its location into the micropolitics of human beings' emotions. While the text attests that what this market offers inside the mind of human beings cannot be bought for money, a reading group member named Pichota, in what reads as a clear example of Kluge's conception of the radicalization of temporal relations, reformulates the "front" concept: "THE FRONT IS DETERMINED BY THE FACTOR OF TIME. The West's TV, of which you just spoke, is only a 'gigantic collection of commodities,' a horde of specters of time [*Zeitgeistern*] that respond to sensibilities that have built themselves up in human beings" (*CdG* 1:157), a claim that appears as a concession to East Germans' susceptibility to the advertisements of the pleasantries of a Western lifestyle. The members quickly realize that they themselves do not have the time to develop adequate counterimages with which to oppose those propagated by Western television's parade of newly accessible commodities. Nor do they have the distributive apparatus to publicize them. The narrator refers them to the media originating at the Deutscher Fernsehfunk, the GDR's erstwhile state-run television. But they miss the opportunity to gain a foothold in the media wars and their own communicative networks—based on withering channels of communication of an apparently ruined party—extend only so far.

The members of the reading group nonetheless gain insight into the problem time poses for them. There is a deep disproportion between the temporal measure of their work on their historical experiences and the urgency of the present: they remain beggars "on the territory of the 'magical attraction of the moment'" (*CdG* 1:157). Kluge's countermediation of such Transition activities clearly foregrounds key aspects of his conception of the radicalization of temporal relations afflicting political modernity. In *Maßverhältnisse des Politischen*, a work devoted to the remediation and reconstitution of a withering public sphere and with that of grassroots politics, Negt and Kluge relate such disproportions (*Missverhältnisse*) to the "incongruity of the subjective and objective" for reasons of which "human beings' responses usually come too soon or too late; they themselves stand in no positive relation to the objective" (*DuM* 1:699). Such temporal discrepancy is part of the reason "why the revolutionary process, in the November Revolution of 1918 as well as the November Revolution 1989, did not outlive the Christmas holiday."[99] One can readily see that the problems of the reading group's members are among other things traceable back to the absence of appropriate *Maßverhältnisse*—especially regarding the question of their political opponent (*gegenständliches Gegenüber*) and the right measure of time (cf. *DuM* 1:700). The absence of a clearly discernible opponent also sends the coordinates of Kluge's own strategies of remediation and countermediation into further spin. Negt and Kluge's timely collaboration in their political-theoretical follow-up to the Transition and the beginning of Germany's own depoliticization into centrist consensus attends to the proportionate conditions that must be fulfilled in order for a commonwealth to be able to both govern and preserve itself in its integrity as well as develop and flourish. These conditions ground the possibility of an emphatic political life to begin with and include, as succinctly captured in the 1992 preface to their book, "time, recognizable spaces, the capacity of subjects for autonomy[,] . . . a fortunate combination of spontaneity and duration, a physically present opponent, the free play between the withdrawal and concentration of efforts. [. . . Such] parameters (forms) combine to constitute politics in an emancipatory direction when they find the right proportion to one another."[100] Although the preoccupation of the young Marxists with the identification of a political opponent must strike one as a problematic aspect of the GDR's legacy, if one can speak of properly political processes only when these conditions are met, then "Nikolaus 1989" reads as the withdrawal of politics from the process of unification itself.

In the face of the situation's complexity, the questions animating the reading group's session become more fundamental—and more epic: "harder than THE QUESTIONS OF A READING WORKER" (*CdG* 1:158). Their movement evokes the vast backtracking undertaken by Weiss's *Ästhetik* in the wake of 1968. In contrast to the thrust of Brecht's poem referred to in the citation, which sought to accompany the proletariat's rise to self-consciousness, no canon of answers for the reading group's questions is readily available. Nothing less constitutes their agenda than a complete revision of the concepts foundational to Marxist revolutionary theory: "What is front? What is Marxist? . . . What is the West? . . . What is to be done?" (*CdG* 1:158). Deconstructing Brecht's canonical appeals to communism's ABCs, that alphabet falls apart at its seams on St. Nicholas Day, without any purchase on the present. In the face of history playing itself out before the comrades' direct senses, the project of such an alphabet's reconstitution is of another time and a longer temporality. (Compare Gesine's challenge to the Warsaw letter's condemnation of the Prague Spring as counterrevolutionary.) On Kluge's watch, the friends' project evinces a comical, almost naive, composure on the one hand and a serious, insistent, critical undertaking on the other. Kluge's footnotes repeat the need to prepare reading lists of original texts for each following week (cf. *CdG* 1:157, 158). Projecting this return to originals as the possibility of a fundamental reset, epic in scope, Kluge's panoramic text, obviously closing before fuller countermediation can be accomplished, figures as a faintly sparkling constellation on a cloudy and stormy day in the offbeat center of a Europe in transformation.

A differentiation between the "original texts" and the experiences of GDR socialism, about which one tends to think that it had precious little to do with the former, is also put forth in the chapter's last story, the two-page "Verweigerter Reisekostenersatz" (Travel Reimbursement Denied). Shortly before the December party convention of the SED, at which the Politbureau resigned, two of the GDR's foreign agents (*Auslandskundschafter*) assigned to London come across seventeen unknown fragments by Karl Marx put up for sale at an auction in Middle England. The two assume that their finding could possess "still decisive value in the crisis of the socialist republic" and procure the fragments (*CdG* 1:304). One of the Central Committee's members, an emigrant now responsible for ideology, recalls the euphoric discovery of Marx's Parisian manuscripts—the aforementioned "Economic and Philosophical Manuscripts" that introduced readers and party members to a "Marx open to criticism" (*CdG* 1:304). The texts found in England reveal a skeptical, rather than radical Marx, who, in commenting on a text by Montaigne, as a footnote to Kluge's fictional anecdote relates, among other things insists that the defending commander of a fortress should by no means give up his position. Since the "worst catastrophes emerge out of attempts at reconciliation," the skepticism of such a Marx must be directed toward the danger of trusting one's enemies. Kluge thus paints this Marx, filtered through the perspective of socialism's adherents, as refusing to give up the fortress's defense. *Eigensinn* in need of countermediation? Regardless of how these strange would-be directives might be interpreted in light of the crisis of the socialist republic, the party secretary does not harbor hope for attracting any interest from the members of the Politbureau. He knows that "we would have had to find these fragments earlier" (*CdG* 1:305). The reader, of course, especially given Kluge's footnote, from which I have cited only one of its meandering qualifications, must wonder: with what consequences? The two agents are not rewarded for their service and they even have to come up with funds to cover their travel costs themselves.

With *Chronik*'s treatment of the German Transition in its second chapter, Kluge stages the undiminished importance of primarily the early Marx's texts. These were not, of course, in any way fulfilled by the historical experience of the GDR, but Kluge locates their projective character and orientational function in this experience—even if this anchor is only depicted as finding soil in the emotions of the protagonists treated ambivalently here. While Kluge's characters appear comical in their naïveté, hopelessly confronted with a world that escapes their influence, their concerns visibly overlap with key features of Negt and Kluge's theoretical works. *Geschichte und Eigensinn* takes great recourse to the raw character of Marx's unsystematic texts, retrieving their analytic resources, reworking the sedimentation of experiences out of their language, as well as rearticulating their proleptic visions in order to expand the direct and indirect senses and establish diachronic and synchronic perspectives[101] on social appearances of "incongruity," such as that of temporal diremption noted above. In this context, the stories from "Verfallserscheinungen der Macht" are particularly illuminating. History produces all kinds of remainders on Kluge's watch: the unfulfilled longings of active human beings—their feelings—linger on as potencies that will fill different containers and assume different directions. Kluge's protagonists neither have time nor opportunity to make their wishes heard before the same are swallowed up or marginalized in the new (old) order of the pseudo-realistic novels of reality or society's *Produktionsöffentlichkeiten*, the sum of which in the central European context yield what is called Germany.[102] The text of "Nikolaus 1989" lingers for a moment on the thoughts of one of the guests at the factory party, Marion Gellert, who holds "the survival of ideas 'after their death' for possible" (*CdG* 1:156). The afterlives of surviving ideas assume spectral forms: the concepts of the young Marxists, the trip to London that never paid off, or the medical service that becomes crucial to one of the GDR's economic functionaries in the last scene of "Nikolaus 1989," who refuses to sell his knowledge to the West Germans and heads for the hospital sensing a malignant growth in his body (*CdG* 1:167)—each such narrative line can be read in a metaphoric sense. They cling obstinately to a forward-looking model of social praxis buried in the GDR itself.

The "Grammatik der Revolution" (Grammar of the Revolution), as another story in the chapter attests, is of a fragmentary character. One of the Leftist German politician Gregor Gysi's associates confirms this in conversation with a woman named Sigrid, whom he meets in the Prater beer garden of Berlin's Prenzlauer Berg. Sigrid is composing a text about revolution:

> SIGRID: Revolutions can develop more grammatical forms than those found in a textbook on grammar?
> REENTS: I am working on that assumption. . . .
> SIGRID: Is there a revolutionary subjunctive? . . . Optative? Wish-form?
> REENTS: That is essential to revolution. . . . If you investigate revolutions . . . you will find 186 different grammatical conditions, some of which are difficult to grasp linguistically. (*CdG* 1:186)

The passage is exemplary for Kluge's attempt to excavate the revolutionary potential buried in the past and present. Such energy, relates this poetologically significant passage, is fragmented into cell-like particles lying asunder, just like the stories of Kluge's epic on the whole. As *Geschichte und Eigensinn* maintains in its departure from traditional schematizations of dialectical processes and as Kluge's intimation—on page 186 of *Chronik*—of the 186 grammatical revolutionary conditions resistant to being captured in language, the grammar of revolutionary processes, like the experiences in which they are housed, prove unwieldy in the extreme. The whole scope of Negt and Kluge's expansion of Brecht's function-oriented conception of realism would be required to sort out the irrational, imaginary, and revolutionary dimensions of reality from one another (*HO* 236ff./*DuM* 2:511ff.). For this, the simple, if insistent revolutionary grammar of Rosa Luxemburg's "I am,

I was, I will be" (*CdG* 1:185) appears limited both in its imagination as well as in its grasp of the splintered multitude of potentially revolutionary energy. At the very least, the "grammatical inflection," as Negt and Kluge write in *Geschichte und Eigensinn*'s consideration of Luxemburg's proleptic formulation, captures little of the "richness of the relations in the real diffracted measures of the non-linguistic grammar of events" (*DuM* 2:712). Kluge's keen short prose text "Grammatik der Revolution" takes stock of the standing of revolutionary energy in the age of its entropy at the end of the Cold War amid the obsolescence of the forms that might have harnessed and guided what remained of its force. The determination of revolutionary energy's fragmented character is only the slightest assurance that it has not suffered a total eclipse. While openly acknowledging the unlikelihood of recollecting the 186 revolutionary conditions into a social movement that would lead to some realm of freedom, Kluge's literary investigations of the same provide for a different perspective on revolutionary processes in history as well as contemporary social reality. Bearing witness to this fragmentation does not signal the denial of theory's programmatic hopes so much as it points again to the necessity of Kluge's countermediation of human energies, feelings, and wishes. Any address of the questions depicted in the work of the reading group in "Nikolaus 1989" with regard to new contexts will prove challenging. Negt and Kluge's theoretical efforts offer guidelines for just such work, and Kluge's stories filter revolutionary potential in epic form in order to uphold and preserve it.

Returning to *Geschichte und Eigensinn* again after the Transition, republishing it in a three-volume revised edition in 1993, Negt and Kluge resisted the notion that socialism's passing is part of some rational historical course. They do not deny that the downfall of the GDR was not in many ways liberating. But they are interested in the effects of a victorious history's demonization of the GDR on its citizens' experience: "That not even the subsidiary flows [*Nebenströme*] of the history of my country retain their meaning, that makes this loss irreplaceable. I lose with that a large portion of my possibilities for the labor of mourning, which is, at the least, dependent on the alternatives or sidelines of the development of my country retaining its meaning."[103] Such forced devaluation is an example of the sensory, semantic, and cultural loss to which Kluge attends in his narrative treatment of the process of German unification. By remediating and countermediating the period in *Chronik*, Kluge incorporates its splinters into the fabric of an epic time's longer march.

Trust-Networks for Plural Futures

If the strategies of remediation and countermediation are set off-balance in the tumultuous and disorienting period of the Cold War's rapid ending, it is in *Chronik*'s final chapter that Kluge's strategy of countermediation is put on exemplary display. "Der lange Marsch des Urvertrauens" embraces the longest durations of epic time already intimated in Weiss and Johnson's practices of chronicle narration in their epics to fathom long-term determinations and, with the help of Andrej Bitow's measure of cosmological time from 20 billion years BCE onward (*CdG* 2:952), expands them to an extreme. "Sketches of time-spaces that last longer than a life-course: the stars, eons, generations," reads the announcement of *Chronik*'s final chapter's theme in the foreword (*CdG* 2:923), where Kluge attributes humanity's survival to primordial trust. It is an elementary power that, likes the others, suffers a mutilation in the process of historical time, such that trust's appearances cannot always be trusted, but demand the same kind of scrupulous review of its constituent components and the processes of their formation or deformation that Kluge's stories set into motion. This does not diminish the networks of trust Kluge continues to weave. While their stakes may appear hopelessly overstrained, because the abounding fantasy of Kluge's poetic constructions turns on experiment rather than integration and on enactment rather than encompassment, the expansion of its entry-points allows for countermediation to take hold at any site at which the capacity for differentiation can be trained and advanced in emancipatory directions.

The poetological principle of such a procedure is captured in the epic's final two-and-half-page tale, another dedicated to Kluge's friend, the (former East) German playwright and poet Heiner Müller. "Heiner Müller und das Projekt Quellwasser" (Heiner Müller and the Project of Spring Water) accompanies the ailing playwright during his stay at a Baden-Baden spa in November 1995 (*CdG* 2:1008–1010). Müller encounters a characteristically obsessive Kluge protagonist there, one Prof. Dr. F. Wilde, a technician, scientist, and businessman from the new German states (i.e., the former GDR). Wilde is pursuing a novel business venture: he wants to capture and market the earth's purest groundwater and solicits Müller as a partner from whom he wishes to gain poetic support for the undertaking. Detailing his study of water's beguiling heterogeneity to the fatigued writer, Wilde focuses on twelve of the earth's groundwater lakes under the Sahara Desert, which are some 66 million years old. His knowledge thereof is framed as a state secret—and curious legacy—of the GDR. The magical quality of the lakes' waters radiates through Wilde's scientifistic discourse. While Müller does not acquiesce to his interlocutor's request for him to join the proposed business enterprise—an undertaking that would relegate poetry to the function of advertisement—he does see in Wilde, "who is examining something as elementary as water as to its rarity" (*CdG* 2:1010; *Seltenheit*), something of a poetic colleague and wishes to contribute some verses. Generalizing this pursuit of the rare and the singular, Kluge elaborates the thesis of the story's subtitle—"Poetry is collection" (*CdG* 2:1008; *Das Poetische heißt Sammeln*)—in the final paragraph of the text. He likens Wilde's activity to the harvest of berries and herbs, a search demanding tenacity, thoroughness, resoluteness and passion. In lieu of providing any closure to such a search, the open-ended character of which will have become evident to any reader rummaging through the many pages of the vast *Chronik*, Kluge ends the story by referring elliptically to Müller's last work as a sketch (hard to decipher) of just such a process of (self-)collection and harvest (*CdG* 2:1010).

Fancifully zeroing in on an environmental feature of the earth as a source of poetic inspiration and imagination, *Chronik*'s positive and hopeful appeal to groundwater at its end also provides—not wholly unlike Johnson's return to the sea at the end of *Jahrestage*—a segue back into the vast heterogeneity of the world and the interactive plurality of its stories. Oscillating, as these have in *Chronik*, between business and poetry, aspiration and defeat, hope and despair, Kluge's "Quellwasser" complements "Der Eigentümer" to set a frame for the work by encapsulating in outer nature the dynamic precariousness of trust stemming from inner nature. The element in which "Quellwasser" takes course, subterranean as well as surface-bound on the blue planet, provides for the diffuse pathways through which *Chronik* connects to the larger networks of trust Kluge ascribes to the writing and reading of literature as collective undertakings. This path leads not only through Heiner Müller's dramatic and postdramatic work, but also into the larger network of the modern epic traversed in this study. Along Weiss's canals, the narrator's imaginative self-location onto Géricault's *Raft of the Medusa*, and Bischoff's journey across the Baltic Sea, through Gesine's multifold traverse of heterogenous water-spaces from Mecklenburg to New York to Copenhagen, to Kluge's broad encapsulation of water's forms in the storm over Berlin with which *Chronik* begins and the elusive spring water under the Sahara with which it ends, the currents of the modern epic flow to invite and permit a world's remediation, and, with Kluge, its countermediation. By encapsulating his narrative constellation in this way, Kluge has not provided any "organological closure"[104] for the whole; rather, he has set storytelling, in its plurality and in the diffusive singularity of its constitutive parts, into relation with the equally diverse fragility of the natural world. It is a relation from which many departures—as numerous and still more numerous than the hundreds of stories Kluge has generated since—can proceed. Craftily situating his *Chronik* at the cusp of two ages, Kluge has offered a countermediation of the Cold War and its ending by mobilizing powers out of the ruins of an unlikely genre, enabling modern epic narration a transfer into the future. The costs borne by a genre seemingly paradoxical in modern times have by no means demolished its viability. Without epic, future presents and future horizons will be increasingly less legible. As Kluge discusses in his text "Fremdling, rede" (Stranger, Tell), storytelling, through whatever forms it may need to take, aspires to set an appropriately moderate temperature for interpersonal encounters between the coldness of indifference (and standstill) and the heat of violence (and destruction).[105] As Kluge's insistence on a moderate temperature for the social body implies, in an age imperiled by the dehumanizing force of both tendencies, the quality of post–Cold War realities will also turn on the fulfillment of this basic human need for warmth. As perhaps best demonstrated by Kluge's narrative project for epic transfer, storytelling's multifold resilience attests to the many possibilities of the present and the future's rehumanization.

Epilogue

✦

Epic for the Twenty-First Century

Most people relate to themselves as storytellers.
—Robert Musil, *Der Mann ohne Eigenschaften*

In one of his some two thousand aphorisms, the Viennese satirist Karl Kraus wrote that "in epic there is something of a frozen superfluousness." Another attributes "the longest breath" to the aphorism.[1] A keen purveyor of literature's shortest genre, Kraus masterfully exploited the aphorism's capacities for paradox, including the versions thereof in play in each of these two examples, between them, and between them and the rest of Kraus's aphoristic network, which assembled larger wholes out of its constituent parts. What Kraus may have dreaded as superfluous at the other end of literature's spectrum appears from a different vantage point as a plentitude—and perhaps also as a way to avoid the paroxysmic literary projectiles of the kind that Kraus hurled into an era of Europe coming to an end on the eve of World War I.

Little has been exhausted in this study's account of Weiss, Johnson, and Kluge's work in a putatively oxymoronic genre. Their groundbreaking approaches to the modern epic raise the freezing temperatures Kraus perceived to a thaw. Empowering the long genre anew to appropriate, renarrate, and countermediate different dimensions of the modern world, *Die Ästhetik des Widerstands*, *Jahrestage*, and *Chronik der Gefühle* transform experiences of defeat and destruction, dereliction and derealization, disaggregation and dehumanization into components of an epic storytelling. In so doing, they set forth narrative worlds in which human beings can learn how to live with history as well as develop their capacities for perception, differentiation, and sense-making on their way to identifying their aspirations and pursuing emancipation.

Attending to the evolution of the modern epic amid its unlikely reemergence postcatastrophe, this study has traced the arch of the genre's development over the course of a relatively short period in time, from around the beginning of the Cold War's second half in 1961 through the chilly standstill of geopolitical opposition in the decades that followed to the final thaw of the Cold War and the dissolution of socialist states in Europe after 1989.

Weiss, Johnson, and Kluge's literary journeys during that time frame yielded works that are as unwieldy as they are rewarding, harboring resources that have only begun to be tapped in the preceding pages. Presenting each epic respectively, chapters 2 through 4 of *The German Epic in the Cold War* have also marked differences between them. The larger arch of the argument has staked out a somewhat paradoxical claim regarding the modern epic's overall advance. From the scintillating drive to the aesthetic appropriation of the world on display in Weiss's *Ästhetik* that reconstitutes resistance from out of the darkest challenges of European history in the twentieth century through Johnson's engrossing investigation of the quest for personal fulfillment in a thorough reappraisal of past, present, and future politics on the waves of a tumultuous year in *Jahrestage* to Kluge's mediations of multiple sites of ex- and implosive destructions and their far-reaching consequences through which he resets the quest for human survival and human futures in *Chronik*, each chapter's analysis of the permutation of modern epic form also suggested a dialectical advance over the previous. There is considerable movement from Weiss's last great aspiration to synthesize and integrate the historical experiences of the twentieth century into a single and exemplary work of literature to the narrative artifice of multiple perspectives Johnson crafts for setting a livable world against the Cold War and again to Kluge's aggregate narration of the Cold War's end and his transferal of second world legacies through epic's democratized ruins to the twenty-first century. Perceived advances here, however, do not point to any supersession, and not only because the series of historical watersheds formative for each epic—1945, 1968, 1989—evince no clear trajectory of progress. These dates suggest a political history that is not readily conceivable in terms of a progressive sublation, not to mention that the democraticizing entropy of Kluge's approach to epic form is unable and unwilling to support such a conception.

The development of modern epic form follows the heterodiegetic history of the period in relation to which each epic is set. What stands out in this relation is the postcatastrophic epic's investment in the project of what, during the Cold War, despite all its dictatorial deformations, was still identified and conceptualized as socialism. As discussed in chapter 2, Weiss already effected a broad extension of this signifier, for which reason this study has tended to opt for the more general—and more epic—concept of social emancipation to discuss the aspirations and hopes the genre channels on Weiss, Johnson, and Kluge's watches. From the perspective of the Cold War epic, the relationship between narration and social emancipation—codified in Weiss's reset of resistance, scrutinized in Johnson's mediation of actually existing and possible socialisms, and reasserted as an object of investigation in Kluge's post-1989 revival of the narrative quest for orientation—has become still less clear since socialism's passing. For this reason alone the stubborn persistence of each writer's approach to emancipatory epic remains attractive. While the chances for the humanization of the present and future still appeared, during the Cold

War, in the guise of socialism's untapped democratic potentials, the modern epic's labor during the period confers at least two charges to the post–Cold War age: a measured incorporation of socialism's history and a reformulation of the prospects and promises of emancipation in and for the twenty-first century. Curiously, from the perspective of the current century's second decade, this has become more urgent outside a unified Germany, which sadly stands out as a country that has incorporated its catastrophic pasts to a greater degree than others and has displayed at least some modicum of political sanity amid the rising temperatures of grave political regressions elsewhere around the globe.

Kluge's sagacious denial of any whole that epic could encapsulate corroborates the genre's asymptotic relation to totality. In lieu, therefore, of presenting any sublation into finality, the interrelations between Weiss, Johnson, and Kluge's projects addressed here confirm the impression of a great literary network being set to work. The August 2 chapter of Johnson's *Jahrestage* includes a note on the character Dieter Lockenvitz's fondness for a Christian Morgenstern poem about a knee traveling through the world (*AN II*, 514–515/*JT* 1706). It is a reference that resurfaces in Kluge's film *Die Patriotin* and that serves as a general metaphor of connectivity.[2] Cross-references, only a few of which have been highlighted in the preceding chapters, abound between the three epics. Many turn on the postcatastrophic focus of the genre on the past's remediation: "The path to emancipation leads through the hells of the past," Kluge warns in the foreword to *Chronik*'s seventh chapter, "Verwilderte Selbstbehauptung" (*CdG* 1:797, cf. *CdG* 1:861), which Weiss's narrator and Johnson's Gesine demonstrate equally, whereas Weiss's Bischoff, who sets on documenting and memorializing the work and fates of fellow resistance fighters against their future obliteration from cultural memory, finds herself so "filled with the dead [that] her own death had to appear as a collective death" (*ÄdW* 3:232), a line that could almost be mistaken for a description of Gesine Cresspahl, who so extensively concerns herself—and converses with—the deceased. Her approach to storytelling is driven less by the aestheticized appropriation of the world—though she and her daughter manage this in their own ways, too—than by the search for self-fulfillment through concrete political engagement. *Jahrestage* thus approximates the practices of Kluge's *Chronik* more than Weiss's *Ästhetik* not least because Kluge, like Johnson, mediates artfully, smuggling aesthetic vertigo and playful destabilizations into the stories themselves with seemingly less struggle and strain than Weiss, while rearticulating directives and commitments at the programmatic levels of his forewords, which are akin to the theorization to which *Die Ästhetik*'s characters submit their own efforts in self-liberation and self-realization. This kind of inventory of cross-references and contrasts between these exemplars of the genre could easily be extended,[3] not least because Weiss, Johnson, and Kluge all take seriously the charge that any reconstitution of narration after catastrophe had to work through the recent past and the travesties wrought by Nazi Germany and fascism as well as Stalinism therein. And yet *The German Epic in the Cold War* has not emphasized the epics' contributions to coming to terms with the past (*Vergangenheitsaufarbeitung*) on the whole. This stems from an interest in conceiving each writer's project and approach to epic narration as an intervention in the present of its writing and publication as well as the possible futures each might enjoy. The political watersheds marked here—1945 and 1968 for both Weiss and Johnson, 1945 and 1989 for Kluge—compelled each writer to undertake epic resets at specific historical junctures. The epic return to basics proceeds in terms of analepsis as well as anamnesis, taking broader stock of experiences in longer durations of time to explain the unexpected. At the same time, each author directs his critical examination of the past to the future to contribute to the prospects and quality of human survival. Moreover, the analyses advanced in chapters 2 through 4 have sought to ascertain the legacies of the techniques of epic narration each author develops for future critical use. While this dimension is on clearest display in Kluge, who alone of these three lived through and wrote about the Cold War's end, setting them beside one another in an epic network archives their tenable, reliable, and trustworthy literary mediations of reality as resources for the living.

As anticipated by Kluge's relaxation of the epic's integrative strategies and his radicalization of the genre's tendency to thrive on the autonomization of its parts, the epic imagination bounded by the generic framework and its characteristic features addressed in this study need not be confined to a single genre in any strict way. Weiss, Johnson, and Kluge all draw on Bertolt Brecht and Walter Benjamin's ecumenical conceptions of modern epic, which were not anchored in preoccupations with genre per se, but directed toward what critical artistic production, across different venues and media, could accomplish.[4] While *Die Ästhetik*, *Jahrestage*, and *Chronik* together constitute a tremendously resourceful network of epic narration on their own, they are equally suited to become part of the broader collective canon of works and writers that Kluge has conceived as necessary for the new millennium to have any human face.[5]

On the other hand, it is both useful and interesting to see how the pluralization and diversification of epic narration is opened up from within the genre itself. This can be pursued by raising the simple question "Whose epic?," already implicitly posed by Weiss's narration of the proletarian appropriation and transformation of culture under the sign of a Herculean labor. The first work considered in this study's second chapter delivers a balancing act between the centripetal force of the narrator integrating the tale of antifascistic as well as broader resistance that will become *Die Ästhetik* and the centrifugal expansion of his epic radar compelled by the critique of the historical Left it develops. In other words, *Die Ästhetik* already opens the epic up to its feminist and postcolonial appropriations, in defiance of notions that the genre is inherently male or Eurocentric. As Edward Said noted in a review of Eric Hobsbawm's *Age of Extremes*, "The surprising renaissance of the novel, which in places like Russia, Latin America, and parts of Asia and Africa is an exception to the general eclipse of the major traditional aesthetic genres."[6] While Said focuses on the novel by name, his point also relates to the second question, "Where is epic?," as does the following passage in Hobsbawm: "If we look for the great novels and the great novelists of the second half of the century, the ones which took an entire society or historical era as their subject, we find them outside the central regions of western culture."[7] These observations by Said and Hobsbawm explain why Franco Moretti's turn to Gabriel García Márquez's *One Hundred Years of Solitude* in the final chapter and epilogue of *Modern Epic* is so salient (*ME* 231ff.). As the transnational positionality of the German epic in the Cold War suggests, the question of where epic is may also relate to any form of transcultural space or experience. Indicative of this is Emine Sevgi Özdamar's 2003 *Seltsame Sterne starren zur Erde: Wedding—Pankow 1976/1977* (*Strange Stars Stare Down to Earth*),[8] which, in narrating the author's journey from Istanbul to West and East Berlin and traverse of the second city's inner divide to learn Brechtian theater at the *Volksbühne*, evinces many, if not all, of the epic characteristics and techniques analyzed in Weiss, Johnson, and Kluge's works.

Finally, the question of "why epic" pertains to epic storytelling's fundamentally human dimension. As argued across the foregoing study's pages, a main recurring agenda of the modern epic in the Cold War is the reconstitution and training of the human senses. Weiss, Johnson, and Kluge all, in different ways and with different concepts as well as intermedial practices, devote considerable energy to the development of human beings' capacities for using direct and indirect, spatial and temporal, realistic and imaginative senses appropriate to modernity's various challenges as well as humanity's many potentials. This, too, is an unfulfilled program that, as Negt and Kluge's work remind us, stems from the early Marx's tremendously prescient focus on the need to establish and elaborate human sensibility (cf. *HO* 98ff., 201/*DuM* 2:45ff.), which has yet to enjoy emancipation, socialization, and humanization.[9] It is precisely Marx's call for the unification of sense and theory in the conception of the senses as "practical theoreticians" that sets an indispensable bar for living humanly in the modern world: "The direct senses are working, no work has been done on the indirect senses. They first and foremost constitute no society. That is a political problem of the present and [responsible for] the distortion of our basic relationship to history" (*DuM* 2:597; original boldface omitted). Kluge knows that sensuousness as a method is not a natural product of society,[10] but must be built up and trained. This too is a lesson the modern epic can teach, and to do so it must remain modern. Epic narration therefore continues into an age that needs it still more desperately than the already catastrophic centuries of the past.

NOTES

Introduction

The epigraph is from Eric Hobsbawm, *Fractured Times: Culture and Society in the Twentieth Century* (New York: New Press, 2013), ix.

1. This study associates the second half of the Cold War with the process of stabilization between the U.S. and the USSR beginning with the construction of the Berlin Wall in 1961 and the resolution of the Cuban Missile crisis in 1962. See Tony Judt's chapter titled "The Politics of Stability" in *Postwar: A History of Europe since 1945* (New York: Penguin, 2005), especially 254–255. Focused on Germany, Mary Fulbrook offers a similar periodization in the second part of her *History of Germany 1918–2000: The Divided Nation*, 2nd ed. (Malden, Mass.: Blackwell, 2002). Stressing global economic, rather than political factors, Eric Hobsbawm identifies the early 1970s, specifically 1973, as the period's watershed moment, after which decades of crisis were to follow in *The Age of Extremes: A History of the World, 1914–1991* (New York: Vintage Books, 1996), 225ff. The diagnostics of the alleged standstill ranged widely across Europe's eastern, western, and nonaligned vantage points in the 1980s.

2. Christa Karpenstein-Eßbach, *Deutsche Literaturgeschichte des 20. Jahrhunderts* (Munich: Wilhelm Fink Verlag, 2013), 123. All translations from German sources unavailable in English are my own.

3. Karpenstein-Eßbach, *Deutsche Literaturgeschichte des 20. Jahrhunderts*, 127.

4. In Kluge's appeals to *Eigenerfahrung*, *Betätigungslust* (the pleasure of activity), and even *Eigensinn* (obstinacy) as originary forms of purposive human activity, the legacy of Karl Marx and Friedrich Engels's anthropological conception of self-activity (*Selbstbetätigung*) lives on. Cf. Kluge in Rainer Stollmann, *Die Entstehung des Schönheitssinns aus dem Eis: Gespräche über Geschichten mit Alexander Kluge* (Berlin: Kulturverlag Kadmos, 2005), 84ff.; Marx and Engels, e.g., *The German Ideology: Part I*, ed. C. J. Arthur (New York: International, 1970), 87ff.; and Marx and Engels, *Die deutsche Ideologie*, in vol. 3 of *Werke* (Berlin: Dietz Verlag, 1958), 72ff.

5. Addressing the Cold War as a Cold Peace amid economic growth and social transformation lasting from around 1950 to the early 1970s, it was not only with irony that Eric Hobsbawm named the second part of his history of the twentieth century "The Golden Age." See Hobsbawm, *The Age of Extremes*, 6, 225–228.

6. See Annette Vowinckel, Marcus M. Payk, and Thomas Lindenberger, eds., *Cold War Cultures: Perspectives on Eastern and Western European Societies* (New York: Berghahn, 2012), 1–2.

7. While humanities scholars have addressed and are well poised to analyze critically the cultural terms in which conflicts are expressed, it is not possible to

rule out a certain collusion whereby humanities discourse has also contributed to obscuring social and political conflicts by focusing on seemingly irreducible forms of cultural difference and antagonism.

8. The American literary and cultural theorist Michael Denning has written in his *Culture in the Age of Three Worlds* (New York: Verso, 2004) that to "speak the word 'globalization' is to say that these worlds [in the geopolitical designation of the Cold War] and their ideals have not only failed, but are gone, over. The task of the various forms of critical globalization studies is to understand why, to find the fault lines that generated the earthquake, to read the history of the age of three worlds against the grain" (27).

9. On human beings as future-makers, see Arjun Appadurai, *The Future as Cultural Fact: Essays on the Global Condition* (New York: Verso, 2013), especially chapter 15.

10. The first volume of Peter Weiss's *Die Ästhetik des Widerstands* has been translated into English as *The Aesthetics of Resistance*. Johnson's *Jahrestage* has appeared in an abridged English translation in two volumes. While segments of Kluge's two-volume *Chronik der Gefühle* have been translated into Russian, French, and Swedish, some of the story-complexes included in it have appeared in comparatively shorter independent English publications.

11. Two omissions from this study's selection of Cold War epics written in German that quickly come to mind are Ingeborg Bachmann's *Todesarten* project (including *Der Fall Franza* and *Requiem für Fanny Goldmann*), the first part of which was published as the novel *Malina* in 1971, and a consideration of the novels of Günter Grass, e.g., the Danzig trilogy beginning with *Die Blechtrommel* (*The Tin Drum*) in 1959, through the lens of epic.

12. Transnational Cold War epics represent a continuation of what Denning outlines as "The Novelists' International" in *Culture in the Age of Three Worlds*, which constituted a "globalization of the novel" in "the early decades of the [twentieth] century" (11–12, 51–72). As discussed in more detail in the following chapter, Hegel's evaluative comparison of the ancient epic with the modern novel in the *Aesthetics* turned in part on the limitation of the former to "the total world of a *nation* and epoch," whereas he set the latter against the wide background of a whole (no longer poetic) *world*. See G. W. F. Hegel, *Aesthetics: Lectures on Fine Art*, trans. T. M. Knox, 2 vols. (Oxford: Oxford University Press, 1974), 2:1044, 2:1092, my emphasis.

13. Katja Leuchtenberger, *Uwe Johnson: Leben, Werk, Wirkung* (Frankfurt am Main: Suhrkamp Verlag, 2010), 26.

14. *Speculations about Jakob* was translated into English by Ursula Molinaro and first published by Grove Press in 1963.

15. The Allies' bombing of Halberstadt is captured in Kluge's *Der Luftangriff auf Halberstadt am 8. April 1945*, the most recent edition of which Martin Chalmers translated as *The Air Raid on Halberstadt on 8 April 1945* for Seagull Books in 2014.

16. Hajo Cornel recounts the beginning of Kluge's literary activity in "Alexander Kluge: Ein Intellektuelles Profil," an introduction to the Russian edition of *Chronik der Gefühle* previously available on Kluge's website, accessed October 4, 2004, http://www.kluge-alexander.de/vorw-chronik-russland.shtml. *Lebensläufe*, translated into English as *Case Histories* by Leila Vennewitz (New York: Holmes

& Meier, 1988), also provides the title for the second volume of *Chronik der Gefühle*, which includes parts of the 1962 publication as chapter 10.

17. Weiss's reminder that he was never German prominently frames Jochen Vogt's presentation of his life in the monograph *Peter Weiss* (Reinbek bei Hamburg: Rowohlt Taschenbuch Verlag, 1987), 7. Analogously, the beginning of Gesine Cresspahl's father Heinrich's section at the end of the second volume of Johnson's *Jahrestage* reads: "He never thought of himself as a 'German.' He kept with those in Mecklenburg who spoke of 'Prussia'; even before his stays in Holland and Great Britain he thought of 'the Germans' [Johnson's text renders the term in Low German: *de Dütschen*] as the others. He had no desire to be responsible for them, neither for their world wars nor for their image in the world"—and yet is pulled into the vortex of German history all the same, even as his regional identity as "Mecklenburger" remains (*JT* i). While the opening of Cresspahl's addendum delivers a powerful focalized account of identity's possible predications from the national through the regional to the individual, the epistolary exchange between Weiss and Johnson reveals another vexed episode of identity's nationalization. In the context of political turbulences in the Suhrkamp Verlag in the fall of 1968, Weiss wrote Johnson on October 25 to criticize the arrogant tone with which Johnson had reprimanded him for his absence from a meeting called by publisher Siegfried Unseld (Uwe Johnson-Archiv Rostock [Depositum der Johannes und Annitta Fries Stiftung], UJA/H/251547, Mappe 15, Bl. 20). Treating this tone as representative of the climate of rampant "irreconcilability in the country," Weiss provoked Johnson's protest at the former's "making him into a German." Highlighting the insinuations accompanying such a term, Johnson reiterated his recommendation that their communication cease in a follow-up letter also copied and sent to Suhrkamp publisher Siegfried Unseld the next year. See *Uwe Johnson—Siegfried Unseld: Der Briefwechsel*, ed. Eberhard Fahlke and Raimund Fellinger (Frankfurt am Main: Suhrkamp Verlag, 1999), 584–585. Some years later, Unseld facilitated exchange between the two again by forwarding Weiss's request for historical maps of Berlin needed for his work on *Die Ästhetik des Widerstands*, which had begun in June 1972, to Johnson (*Uwe Johnson—Siegfried Unseld*, 753–754). In the brief bit of collegial correspondence between the two writers that followed, one can detect a greater reconcilability driven by their simultaneous work on their respective epics (UJA, 251550–251552, Mappe 15, Bl. 23–25). Johnson attended Weiss's funeral in Stockholm in 1982. For more on their relationship, see my "Uwe Johnson, Peter Weiss und die Möglichkeiten des modernen Epos," *Johnson-Jahrbuch* 23 (2016): 183–206, especially 193–194.

18. Edward W. Said, "Reflections on Exile," in *Reflections on Exile and Other Essays* (Cambridge, Mass.: Harvard University Press, 2000), 186. Alexander Honold's short comparison of *Die Ästhetik des Widerstands* and *Jahrestage* is one of the few to stress Weiss and Johnson's respective dislocations and the repercussions thereof on their epics. See Honold, "Working on German Memory: Peter Weiss and Uwe Johnson," in *German Studies in the Post-Holocaust Age: The Politics of Memory, Identity, and Ethnicity*, ed. Adrian del Caro and Janet Ward (Boulder: University Press of Colorado, 2000), 206–213.

19. Whereas Weiss and Johnson completed their works in Sweden and England respectively, the distance of Kluge's epic from West and East Germany is temporal, rather than spatial, with the publication of *Chronik der Gefühle* ten years

into the Berlin Republic. While German self-distanciation from Germanness was a characteristic feature of the period, the positions of Weiss, Johnson, and Kluge at the margins of nation clearly facilitated their epic exercises in inner and outer perspectives on the country and its division.

20. The evolution of Ralf Schnell's work on post-1945 German literature is a case in point. As indicated by its title, *Die Literatur der Bundesrepublik: Autoren, Geschichte, Literaturbetrieb* (Stuttgart: J. B. Metzlersche Verlagsbuchhandlung, 1986) was devoted to West German literature. The publication of the first edition of his more comprehensive *Geschichte der deutschsprachigen Literatur seit 1945* (Stuttgart: J. B. Metzler, 1993) after unification addressed West and East German literature in two large sections. In the second and revised edition of this work, published in 2003, the material yielded to a more interrelated treatment on the model of chronological periodization rather than spatio-political separation.

21. Weiss's perspective on socialism was more global than it was oriented to the GDR. While his 1965 statement of socialist solidarity "10 Working-Points of an Author in the Divided World" appeared in the East German paper *Neues Deutschland*, in addition to its publication in Sweden's *Dagens Nyheter*, Weiss's critical contributions to socialist discourse and culture were not always welcome in the GDR, to which his relationship would remain fraught.

22. Emmerich fled East Germany in 1958. His resourceful study of East German literature, *Kleine Literaturgeschichte der DDR: Erweiterte Neuausgabe* (Berlin: Aufbau Verlag, 1995), was first published in West Germany in 1981 and revised after unification.

23. Negt and Kluge's theoretical collaborations are collected in *Der unterschätzte Mensch*, the second volume of which contains their central work *Geschichte und Eigensinn*, which has been translated into English by Richard Langston et al. as *History and Obstinacy*.

24. In Karpenstein-Eßbach's recent German literary history of the twentieth century, Weiss's book appears more accurately situated in her chapter "Nation, Migration, andere Räume" (Nation, Migration, Other Spaces), 261ff. Right after unification Norbert Mecklenburg published an essay on Johnson as the author of multiple German literatures, ultimately categorizing his oeuvre as a literature of emigration in "Uwe Johnson als Autor einiger deutscher Literaturen," *Literatur für Leser* 1 (1991): 1–7.

25. Enforcing the separation of East and West Germany, the Wall also facilitated the stabilization of their coexistence. The relaxation of tensions in the context of the West German SPD chancellor Willy Brandt's New Eastern Policy led to the Basic Treaty (*Grundlagenvertrag*) of 1972, in which the two countries, downplaying their commitments to unification and normalizing their relations, first recognized one another and respectively pledged allegiance to the principles of the United Nations, which they subsequently joined.

26. Uwe Johnson, "Berliner Stadtbahn (*veraltet*)," in *Berliner Sachen: Aufsätze* (Frankfurt am Main: Suhrkamp Verlag, 1975), 10.

27. Johnson, "Berliner Stadtbahn (*veraltet*)," 10. See also Gary L. Baker, *Understanding Uwe Johnson* (Columbia: University of South Carolina Press, 1999), 15–16.

28. "Eine Kneipe geht verloren" is the only story in the *Berliner Sachen* essay collection (64–94).

29. "A Secret Life: Uwe Johnson in Sheerness," BBC Radio Feature by Patrick Wright, April 19, 2015, accessed July 31, 2015, http://www.bbc.co.uk/programmes/b05qyjsr. Although virtually all his works deal with German-German difference, part of Johnson's criticism of the label had to do with the simple fact that he was not permitted to be read in the GDR (*BU* 336–337). Whereas *Zwei Ansichten* and *Das dritte Buch über Achim* (*The Third Book about Achim*) focus on East-West Germany, his two acclaimed works *Mutmassungen* and *Jahrestage* are cued to the non-German events of the 1956 Hungarian Uprising and the 1968 Prague Spring, respectively.

30. For passages not included in *Jahrestage*'s abridged English translation, only the German pagination can be provided.

31. An incisive imposition onto urban space, the Wall's construction clearly posed challenges to aesthetic orientation at both basic sensory as well as artistic levels for Berlin residents, eliciting a number of site-specific responses. For a survey thereof relevant to this study's focus on epic prose, see my forthcoming article "Divided Berlin and Cold War Aesthetics."

32. In his introduction to *Massenmedien im Kalten Krieg: Akteure, Bilder, Resonanzen* (Cologne: Böhlau Verlag, 2006), 11, editor Thomas Lindenberger calls attention to mass media as political weapons and manufacturers of social and cultural realities. West and East German media, each tied through financial and political institutional structures to the FRG and GDR respectively, competed with one another on this very front. By contrast, cognitive mapping, as theorized by Fredric Jameson in *Postmodernism, or, The Cultural Logic of Late Capitalism* (1991; Durham, N.C.: Duke University Press, 2001), 51ff., designates an aesthetic approach to reality that is attuned to human needs and opposes the market-oriented and political imperatives of dominant media.

33. Walter Benjamin addressed the encroachment of information and new media on forms of epic narration in "The Storyteller: Reflections on the Works of Nikolai Leskov," in *Illuminations: Essays and Reflections*, ed. Hannah Arendt, trans. Harry Zohn (New York: Schocken, 1969), 88–89.

34. Bertolt Brecht, "The Modern Theatre Is the Epic Theatre: Notes to the Opera *Aufstieg und Fall der Stadt Mahagonnny*," in *Brecht on Theatre: The Development of an Aesthetic*, ed. and trans. John Willet (New York: Hill and Wang, 1992), 37; Brecht, "Anmerkungen zur Oper *Aufstieg und Fall der Stadt Mahagonny*," in vol. 24 of *Werke: Große kommentierte Berliner und Frankfurter Ausgabe*, ed. Werner Hecht et al. (Berlin: Aufbau Verlag/Frankfurt am Main: Suhrkamp Verlag, 1988–2000), 79.

35. Throughout this study, I use "literary cartography," "narrative maps," and related terms in conformity with the work of Robert T. Tally Jr., who has stressed that "literary cartography or literary geography [which may not include actual maps, diagrams, or illustrations] operates precisely by virtue of the specifically *literary* nature of the project," in *Spatiality* (New York: Routledge, 2013), 5, emphasis there. Literature's potential for narrative mapping can be grasped in terms of the medium's evolving formal characteristics by which it exercises procedural autonomy. Thus, in the phrase "narrative map," the specific mediating activity of literature can supersede the conventional opposition between maps and narratives as fundamentally different media.

36. On the orientation of Kluge's work toward posterity, see Devin Fore's introduction to the English translation of *Geschichte und Eigensinn* in Kluge and Negt, *History and Obstinacy*, 16. Kluge's modification of the metaphor of bottled messages into glass shards and echoes conveys perspectives particularly germane to his storytelling. See Kluge in Richard Langston, "'Das ist die umgekehrte Flaschenpost': Ein montiertes Interview mit Osker Negt and Alexander Kluge," *Glass Shards: Alexander Kluge-Jahrbuch* 2 (2015): 47–75, here 50.

37. Kluge, *Schlachtbeschreibung: Der organisatorische Aufbau eines Unglücks* (Frankfurt am Main: Suhrkamp Verlag, 1983), 7.

38. On "time-space compression," see part 3 of David Harvey's *The Condition of Postmodernity: An Enquiry into the Origins of Cultural Change* (Malden, Mass.: Blackwell, 1990).

39. Due to overlaps between the narrator's biography and Weiss's own, *Die Ästhetik* has been read as a "wishful autobiography" (*Wunschautobiographie*) of Weiss's life. See Klaus R. Scherpe, "Reading the Aesthetics of Resistance: Ten Working Theses," trans. James Gussen, *New German Critique* 30 (1983): 97–105, here 99–100 and chapter 2 below.

40. To describe the narrative situations of the modern epic, I rely on Gérard Genette's distinctions between story (as the represented plot), narrative, and acts (or the activity) of narrating laid out in *Narrative Discourse: An Essay in Method*, trans. Jane E. Lewin (Ithaca, N.Y.: Cornell University Press, 1980), 27ff.

41. In a key passage near the end of the third volume, the narrator notes that the "meaning of my long waiting . . . would consist in the clarification of what happened by way of future insights" (*ÄdW* 3:261). Resolving the narrator's lingering doubts (cf. e.g., *AoR* 112/*ÄdW* 1:130) as to whether the tale could ever be told, Weiss transforms the narrator's expectation of future fulfillment into a future made present for readers.

42. Baker, *Understanding Uwe Johnson*, 8.

43. *Lebensläufe*'s embeddedness in an FRG that is tied to the Nazi past as well as *Chronik*'s chapter titled "Verfallserscheinungen der Macht" (Symptoms of Declining Power), which lingers on 1989–1991 in (East) Germany and the (former) Soviet Union, may be taken as indicative of the book's (nonexclusive) historical orientation. That Kluge's more recent volumes leave the watershed dates of 1945 and 1989 behind speaks to epic's continual outreach in an age as global as it is digital: Kluge's emphatic appeals to literature as a trustworthy network set against more predominant ways of combining and disseminating information seek to confirm its future. See Alexander Kluge, "Das Innere des Erzählens: Georg Büchner," in *Fontane Kleist Deutschland Büchner: Zur Grammatik der Zeit* (Berlin: Verlag Klaus Wagenbach, 2004), 73–86, especially 75.

44. The principle of the relative independence of epic's parts was highlighted in Friedrich Schiller's exchanges with Goethe (cf. the entry "Lyrisch—episch—dramatisch," in *Ästhetische Grundbegriffe: Ein historisches Wörterbuch in sieben Bänden*, ed. Karlheinz Barck et al. [Stuttgart: Metzler, 2004], 3:717) and revisited by Alfred Döblin, for whom "with an epic work, as opposed to a dramatic, one can as it were take a pair of scissors and cut it into individual pieces, which remain fully capable of life," as Bertolt Brecht cited him in "Theatre for Pleasure or Theatre for Instruction," in Willet, *Brecht on Theatre*, 70.

45. In conversation with Stollmann, Kluge notes that we must "draw maps of experience by telling stories, laying out maps of human behavior" (*Entstehung*, 90). And Kluge refers repeatedly to cross-mapping as an integral part of narrative strategy and human orientation generally. See, e.g., Kluge, *The Devil's Blind Spot*, 316. In his article "Distant(ly) Reading Alexander Kluge's Distant Writing," *Alexander Kluge-Jahrbuch* 1 (2014): 29–41, Günter Martens traces Kluge's use of cross-mapping to Guy Debord (39).

46. For a short introduction in English to the work of Werner Krauss and Victor Klemperer with regard to German's linguistic ruination, see Karlheinz Barck, "Intellectuals under Hitler," in *A New History of German Literature*, ed. David Wellbery (Cambridge, Mass.: Harvard University Press, 2004), 830–835. Karpenstein-Eßbach's literary history delivers a broader overview of the linguistic dimension of the problem in her chapter on the postwar diffusions (*Zerstreuungen*) of German (163ff.).

47. The 1963 premiere of Rolf Hochhuth's play *Der Stellvertreter* (*The Deputy*), which examined the Vatican's relationship to the Shoah; Peter Weiss's internationally acclaimed and much debated play of 1965, *Die Ermittlung* (*The Investigation*), based on the Auschwitz trials in Frankfurt; and Alexander and Margarete Mitscherlich's psychoanalytic study *Die Unfähigkeit zu trauern: Grundlagen kollektiven Verhaltens* (*The Inability to Mourn: Principles of Collective Behavior*), first published in 1967, were each part of this development. With a broader context in mind, Michael Denning has ascribed a delay to historical novels that tend to appear nearly a generation after the era to which they refer in *Culture in the Age of Three Worlds*, 54. This is not always so: Anna Seghers's *Das siebte Kreuz* (*The Seventh Cross*) appeared in 1942 to constitute something of an exception to the rule. While Weiss's historically discrete epic squares superficially with Denning's point, all three of this study's modern epics multiply their spatiotemporal reference points such that they neither conform to the genre of the historical novel nor are confined to the delayed memorialization of the past.

48. Jean-François Lyotard, *The Postmodern Condition: A Report on Knowledge*, trans. Geoff Bennington and Brian Massumi (Minneapolis: University of Minnesota Press, 1984), xxiv (first published in France in 1979); Karl Markus Michel, "Ein Kranz für die Literatur: Fünf Variationen über eine These," *Kursbuch 15* (1968): 169–186; Peter Demetz, *After the Fires: Recent Writing in the Germanies, Austria, and Switzerland* (1986; New York: Harcourt Brace Jovanovich, 1992), 29.

49. For overviews of the issues at stake, see James E. Young, *Writing and Rewriting the Holocaust: Narrative and the Consequences of Interpretation* (Bloomington: Indiana University Press, 1988); Saul Friedlander's introduction to the anthology *Probing the Limits of Representation: Nazism and the "Final Solution,"* ed. Saul Friedlander (Cambridge, Mass.: Harvard University Press, 1992), 1–21; and Berel Lang's *Holocaust Representation: Art within the Limits of History and Ethics* (Baltimore: Johns Hopkins University Press, 2000).

50. Auschwitz is "the caesura of our times. . . . No (re)presentation of it is possible," wrote Philippe Lacoue-Labarthe in *Heidegger, Art, and Politics: The Fiction of the Political*, trans. Chris Turner (London: Basil Blackwell, 1990), 46. See also Günter Grass, *Schreiben nach Auschwitz: Frankfurter Poetik-Vorlesung* (Munich: Luchterhand Literaturverlag, 1990), 10.

51. Burkhardt Lindner, "Hallucinatory Realism: Peter Weiss' *Aesthetics of Resistance*, *Notebooks*, and the Death Zones of Art," trans. Luke Springmann and Amy Kepple, *New German Critique* 30 (1983): 127–156, here 127–128.

52. Weiss, Johnson, and Kluge all self-critically engage the "epic naïveté" that was the focus of Theodor W. Adorno's dialectical reassessment of the possibilities of epic narration in a short essay of the same title in *Notes to Literature*, vol. 1, trans. Shierry Weber Nicholsen (New York: Columbia University Press, 1991), 24–29.

53. While Adorno consistently placed culture under the erasure of its negation, his work also contributed to the emergent culture of principled negativity, nonconformity, and the self-identification of a critical intelligentsia in West Germany, as Klaus Scherpe reminds us in *Stadt, Krieg, Fremde: Literatur und Kultur nach den Katastrophen* (Tübingen: Franck Verlag, 2002), 317.

54. Adorno, "Cultural Criticism and Society," in *Prisms*, trans. Samuel Weber and Shierry Weber Nicholsen (Cambridge, Mass.: MIT Press, 1983), 34, translation modified; Adorno, *Prismen: Kulturkritik und Gesellschaft*, in *Kulturkritik und Gesellschaft I*, vol. 10.1 of *Gesammelte Schriften in 20 Bänden*, ed. Rolf Tiedemann (Frankfurt am Main: Suhrkamp Verlag, 1997), 30.

55. Adorno, "The Position of the Narrator in the Contemporary Novel," in *Notes to Literature*, 1:30, 32, italics there; Adorno, "Standort des Erzählers im zeitgenössischen Roman," in *Noten zur Literatur*, vol. 11 of *Gesammelte Schriften*, 41, 43, italics there.

56. See especially *Aesthetic Theory*'s chapter titled "Society" (*Gesellschaft*) and Peter Uwe Hohendahl, *The Fleeting Promise of Art: Adorno's Aesthetic Theory Revisited* (Ithaca, N.Y.: Cornell University Press, 2013), 166. I return to this point in a discussion of Peter Weiss's labor-theory of culture in chapter 2 below.

57. Adorno, "The Meaning of Working through the Past" and "Education after Auschwitz," in *Critical Models: Interventions and Catchwords*, trans. Henry W. Pickford (New York: Columbia University Press, 2005), 89–104, 191–204.

58. By addressing the prospects and human quality of life and survival on individual and collective levels, the Cold War epics examined in this study clearly relate to recent discussions regarding the need for the humanities disciplines to reclaim the concept of life as fundamental to their scientific inquiries. See Ottmar Ette and Vera M. Kutzinski, "Literature as Knowledge for Living, Literary Studies as Science for Living," *PMLA* 125, no. 4 (2010): 977–993.

59. Günter Holtz, "Vierter Teil: Von den frühen Siebziger Jahr bis in die achtziger Jahre," in Bernd Balzer et al., *Die Deutschsprachige Literatur in der Bundesrepublik Deutschland: Vorgeschichte und Entwicklungstendenzen* (Munich: Iudicium, 1988), 485.

60. With a view to the positive contributions literary art can still make against Adorno's emphasis on the dark and the cold, chapter 1's consideration of the modern epic from the perspective of its artistic production takes more recourse to Bertolt Brecht's aesthetics than Adorno's.

61. Benjamin, "The Storyteller," 86; Benjamin, "Der Erzähler," in *Illuminationen: Ausgewählte Schriften I* (Frankfurt am Main: Suhrkamp Verlag, 1974), 388.

62. Jost Hermand, "Obwohl, Dennoch, Trotzalldem: Die im Konzept der freien Assoziation der Gleichgesinnten aufgehobene Antinomie vom ästhetischem

Modernismus und sozialistischer Parteilichkeit in der *Ästhetik des Widerstands* und den sie begleitenden *Notizbüchern*," in *Die Ästhetik des Widerstands*, ed. Alexander Stephan (Frankfurt am Main: Suhrkamp Verlag, 1983), 94.

63. In "The Position of the Narrator," Adorno had written that the only contemporary novels of note were negative epics (35/47; *negative Epopöen*). Without denying negativity as a social fact and an aesthetic principle, Weiss, Johnson, and Kluge do not confine their work to negative prescriptions. Signals thereof can be identified in Weiss's narration of resistance as positive social content, as described by Michael Hofmann, *Ästhetische Erfahrung in der historischen Krise: Eine Untersuchung zum Kunst- und Literaturverständnis in Peter Weiss' Roman "Die Ästhetik des Widerstands"* (Bonn: Bouvier Verlag, 1990), 317ff.; Johnson's playfully provocative abstention from the adverb "not" so common to German in his poetological *Begleitumstände* (*BU* 453, highlighted by Leuchtenberger, *Uwe Johnson*, 120); and Kluge's entertainment of the dialectic of enlightenment's "lighter side," as described by Cornel in "Alexander Kluge: Ein Intellektuelles Profil."

64. Lifted from Oskar Negt and Alexander Kluge's self-description of their theoretical work *Geschichte und Eigensinn* (*DuM* 2:5), "Gebrauchsbuch" squares both with Weiss's practical approach to the arts in *Die Ästhetik* (e.g., *AoR* 45/*ÄdW* 1:53), Johnson's comparison of the entertainment (*Unterhaltung*) offered by the novel to that of a bridge or household (VPR 403), and Kluge appeals to his *Chronik*'s service to practical orientation in the publication's foreword (*CdG* 1:7).

65. Weiss's attendance of the East German production of his play *Marat/Sade* in Rostock in 1965 reportedly alerted him to the political power of the scenes he had himself written, an experience that would in part compel his ensuing change of political position. See "Die Unmöglichkeit der Neutralität," the German version of an interview Thomas von Vegesacks conducted with Weiss in Swedish, printed in the newspaper *Sonntag* 33, August 15, 1965, and filed amid Johnson's newspaper clippings (UJA/H/253338, Mappe 4, Bl. 18). West German commentary on the claim was caustic. Writing about the end of Weiss's previously assumed neutral "third path," H. D. Sander attributed to the "Baltic Sea city Rostock" the status of Weiss's "Damascus" in "Das Ende des 'dritten Weges': Peter Weiss und seine politischen Metamorphosen," *Die Welt*, no. 217, September 18, 1965 (UJA/H/253344, Mappe 4, Bl. 23).

66. Looking back, Heiner Müller, in his autobiography *Krieg ohne Schlacht: Leben in zwei Diktaturen*, vol. 9 of *Werke*, ed. Frank Hörnigk (Frankfurt am Main: Suhrkamp Verlag, 2005), would dub this turn the "sanctification of misery" (157).

67. See Hofmann, *Ästhetische Erfahrung in der historischen Krise*, 7–22; Martin Rector, "Zur Kritik der einfachen Politisierung: Die 'Ästhetik des Widerstands' als Nach-68-Roman," in *Literatur, Ästhetik, Geschichte: Neue Zugänge zu Peter Weiss*, ed. Michael Hofmann et al. (St. Ingbert: Werner J. Röhrig Verlag, 1992), 99–114; and Klaus Briegleb, "Widerstand als tätige Erinnerung: Uwe Johnson und Peter Weiss," *Das Argument* 192 (1992): 205–218.

68. Adorno, *Minima Moralia: Reflections from Damaged Life*, trans. E. F. N. Jephcott (New York: Verso, 2010), 15; Adorno, *Minima Moralia: Reflexionen aus dem beschädigten Leben*, vol. 4 of *Gesammelte Schriften*, 13.

69. Wolfgang Fritz Haug and Kaspar Masse make this claim in the introduction to their coedited study of the 1970s as the time of a "culture from below." See Haug and Masse, eds., *Materialistische Kulturtheorie und Alltagskultur* (Berlin: Argument Verlag, 1980), 4.

70. In each case, but with Weiss especially, canonization is a devious affair: *Die Ästhetik des Widerstands*, for example, vigorously contests the very relations of cultural production into which it might be integrated and absorbed. For this reason, critics have explained how it demands political, and not simply aesthetic reception. See, e.g., Thomas Metscher, *Der Friedensgedanke in der Europäischen Literatur: Studien zum Verhältnis von Literatur und Humanität mit einem Essay zu Picassos Guernica* (Fischerhude: Atelier im Bauernhaus, 1984), 166. While the context for political decisionism has greatly changed, any academic treatment of *Die Ästhetik des Widerstands* must grant it its *Eigensinn* (obstinacy/own meaning) to forestall the forfeiture of its edge.

71. Schnell, *Die Literatur der Bundesrepublik*, 339–350. Schnell retained this categorization in his more comprehensive history of German literature after unification, the 2003 edition of *Geschichte der deutschsprachigen Literatur seit 1945*, 489–500.

72. For a description of the function of comparative "medium-level" analysis in literary studies, see Jochen Vogt, *Aspekte erzählender Prosa: Eine Einführung in Erzähltechnik und Romantheorie*, 7th ed. (Opladen: Westdeutscher Verlag, 1990), 218ff.

73. E.g. Holtz, "Vierter Teil"; Peter Bürger, "Über die Wirklichkeit der Kunst: Zur Ästhetik in der *Ästhetik des Widerstands*," in Stephan, *Die Ästhetik des Widerstands*, 293–295; and Norbert Mecklenburg, "Großstadtmontage und Provinzchronik: Die epische 'Aufhebung' des regionalen Romans in Uwe Johnsons 'Jahrestage,' " in *Erzählte Provinz: Regionalismus und Moderne im Roman* (Königstein/Ts.: Äthenäum, 1982), 180–224.

74. Registering the conditions of artistic production in a Cold War still overshadowed by catastrophe, the opening sentence of Adorno's *Aesthetic Theory*—"it is self-evident that nothing concerning art is self-evident anymore, not its inner life, its relation to the world, not even its right to exist"—may apply even more to art's historical situation thereafter (*AT* 1/9).

75. See Kluge, "Das Innere des Erzählens," 86.

Chapter 1

The epigraphs are from Karl Schlögel, *Die Mitte liegt ostwärts: Europa im Übergang* (Munich: Fischer Taschenbuch Verlag, 2002), 44; Fredric Jameson, *The Geopolitical Aesthetic: Cinema and Space in the World System* (Bloomington: Indiana University Press, 2002), 4, emphasis there; and *AN* 197/*JT* 298.

1. The doctrine of the dialectics of form and content once drove Hegel's comprehensive treatment of the history of art and the arts in his *Aesthetics*. Its standing today is a matter of debate. The schematism underlying culture's industrial production subjected the relationship between form and content to arbitrary reconfigurations that would be celebrated in postmodernism, and may mark a development that continues in current appeals to artistic pluralism. Cf. Max Horkheimer and Theodor W. Adorno, *Dialectic of Enlightenment: Philosophical Fragments*, ed. Gunzelin Schmid Noerr, trans. Edmund Jephcott (Stanford, Calif.:

Stanford University Press, 2002), 94ff. I revisit the issue in chapter 4's account of Kluge's storytelling.

2. G. W. F. Hegel, *Aesthetics*, 2:1044; G. W. F. Hegel, *Vorlesungen über die Ästhetik III*, vol. 15 of *Werke*, ed. Eva Moldenhauer and Karl Markus Michel (Frankfurt am Main: Suhrkamp Verlag, 1970), 330; cf. Moretti, *ME* 11–12.

3. Hegel, *Aesthetics*, 2:1092, 1059, 1044; Hegel, *Ästhetik III*, 392, 349, 330.

4. Hegel, *Aesthetics*, 2:1092, translation modified, 1109; Hegel, *Ästhetik III*, 392, emphasis there, 414.

5. Hegel, *Aesthetics*, 1:11.

6. On the different dimensions of the concept of totality, see Martin Jay, *Marxism and Totality: The Adventures of a Concept from Lukács to Habermas* (Berkeley: University of California Press, 1984), 59 and passim.

7. To Christa Karpenstein-Eßbach, writing in *Deutsche Literaturgeschichte des 20. Jahrhunderts*, Lukács's aestheticization of humanity's relationship to reality evokes aspects of postmodernism *avant l'heure* (139), but what sets his approach as well as Weiss, Johnson, and Kluge's modern epics apart is their motivated and realist orientation to totality.

8. Moretti confirms Lukács's appeal to time's constitutive role for modern prose, but claims a new diremption thereof in modern epics: whereas the novel "invents a new language," the epic "produces *a new interpretation of the old language*." In the modern epic, there is "no trace of that great novelistic invention which is the [modern] present," but rather "the great modernist polarity of Archaism and Utopia—with nothing for today" (*ME* 88, emphasis there).

9. For an instructive account of Lukács's work in social and literary theory as an integrated project, see Fredric Jameson's "The Case for Georg Lukács," in *Marxism and Form: Twentieth-Century Dialectics Theories of Literature* (Princeton, N.J.: Princeton University Press, 1971), 160–205.

10. Massimo Fusillo, "Epic, Novel," in *The Novel*, vol. 2: *Forms and Themes*, ed. Franco Moretti et al. (Princeton, N.J.: Princeton University Press, 2006), 33.

11. Fusillo, "Epic, Novel," 40.

12. Additional distinctions that Fusillo associates with the critical myth of the novel's derivation from epic include "nature/culture, public/private, orality/writing, tragedy/comedy [and] masculine/feminine" (34). While the modern epic may be implicated in some of these "dualities on which Western identity is constructed," my inventory includes operational distinctions most relevant to Weiss, Johnson, and Kluge.

13. The nerve struck by Lukács's interest in *The Theory of the Novel* confirmed the book's relevance through the disintegration of experience that Walter Benjamin diagnosed in his own perpetuation of Hegel and Lukács's critical myth after World War I. In "The Storyteller" and related writings, Benjamin sharpened the distinction between epic and novel further still. To the former he ascribed the wisdom of an oral storyteller once able to sink wise counsel into the lives of his listeners, whereas the novel reflected experience's falling course and exacerbated its incommensurability. See Benjamin, "The Storyteller," 86–87.

14. Hegel, *Aesthetics*, 1:605; Hegel, *Ästhetik II*, vol. 14 of *Werke*, 235.

15. In his "10 Working-Points," Peter Weiss wrote that in the West, the writer had a long way to go for his freedom to become no longer harmless to society. See Weiss, *Rapporte II* (Frankfurt am Main: Suhrkamp Verlag, 1971), 17.

16. Jameson, *Marxism and Form*, 171.

17. In *Deutsche Literaturgeschichte des 20. Jahrhunderts*, Karpenstein-Eßbach suggests that modern literature is the consequent continuation of philosophy by other means, 134. The great resources of Hegel's fascinating achievement in the *Aesthetics* notwithstanding, by outfitting his observations with a conceptual architecture that prejudged the relationship between historical content and its poetic treatment, Hegel foreclosed the question as to how the concrete reality of history could be addressed and transformed. The modern epic inherits this issue as an open question to be examined, rather than decided in advance with any finality.

18. Jameson, *Marxism and Form*, 200.

19. Jameson, *Marxism and Form*, 204.

20. Fusillo, "Epic, Novel," 38–39; Moretti, *ME* 56–57.

21. Lukács's later theory of realism, which was accompanied by a retraction of *The Theory of the Novel*, mandated the presentation of the social totality in the form of aesthetic closure and identified the nineteenth-century novel as a model worthy of emulation in socialist contexts. As he had already argued in the debate on expressionism, the artist must "discover [the relationships that make up society] intellectually and give them artistic shape. Secondly . . . he must artistically conceal the relationships he has just discovered through the process of abstraction—i.e. he has to transcend the process of abstraction" to create an "artistically mediated" totality that appears concrete in the work of art. See Lukács, "Realism in the Balance," trans. Rodney Livingstone, in Theodor Adorno et al., *Aesthetics and Politics* (New York: Verso, 2007), 35.

22. Although Moretti's concluding treatment of García Márquez's *One Hundred Years of Solitude* suggests the significance narrative would continue to have vis-à-vis the world-system, it comes almost as an afterthought to his overview of the genre, which focuses mostly on Goethe and James Joyce, effectively concluding with the latter's *Ulysses*. More relevant for the German-speaking context than Moretti's *Modern Epic* is thus Hunter Bivens's recent *Epic and Exile: Novels of the German Popular Front, 1933–1945* (Evanston, Ill.: Northwestern University Press, 2015), which expounds the political tasks and imaginative resources of the modern epic genre in the period preceding the Cold War.

23. While modernity, urban life and the (colonial) world-system remain present as general touchstones of an extra-aesthetic reality in Moretti's study, twentieth-century history rather recedes into its background. Cf. e.g., *ME* 191.

24. For differentiated accounts of Weiss's *Ästhetik* in the context of postmodernism, see Andreas Huyssen, "Memory, Myth, and the Dream of Reason: Peter Weiss's *Die Ästhetik des Widerstands*," in *After the Great Divide: Modernism, Mass Culture, Postmodernism* (Bloomington: Indiana University Press, 1986), 115–138; and Michael Hofmann, "Die Ästhetik der Postmoderne und die 'Ästhetik des Widerstands': Vorüberlegungen zu einem Vergleich," in Hofmann et al., *Literatur, Ästhetik, Geschichte*, 147–163. For Johnson, see Carsten Gansel and Nicolai Riedel, eds., *Uwe Johnson zwischen Vormoderne und Postmoderne: Internationales Uwe Johnson—Symposium 22.–24. 9. 1994* (Berlin: Walter de Gruyter, 1995) as well as Norbert Mecklenburg's categorization of *Jahrestage* as a modernist work in *Die Erzählkunst Uwe Johnsons: "Jahrestage" und andere Prosa* (Frankfurt am Main: Suhrkamp Verlag, 1997), 330–335. In an

interview, Kluge once succinctly remarked, "We are not postmodernists. I believe in the avant-garde." See Kluge in Stuart Liebman, "On New German Cinema, Art, Enlightenment and the Public Sphere: An Interview with Alexander Kluge," *October* 46 (Fall 1988): 23–59, here 57.

25. Neither connotation of totality necessarily returns us to the "totalitarian temptations" Moretti diagnosed in reactionary modernist world texts despairing in the face of modern complexity and seeking to reduce it (*ME* 227–228).

26. The larger outcomes of theoretical analyses of mediation—i.e., whether they serve emancipation (e.g., Negt and Kluge), assert its sufficient theoretical fulfillment (e.g., the later Hegel), or lament its alleged temporary preclusion (e.g., Adorno)—rest on the perspectives, methods, and intentions of each approach.

27. The account Hans-Peter Burmeister gave in *Kunst als Protest und Widerstand: Untersuchungen zum Kunstbegriff bei Peter Weiss und Alexander Kluge* (Frankfurt am Main: Peter Lang, 1985) of the passage of Hegel's "universal mediation" through Lukács's *History and Class Consciousness* and Negt and Kluge's *Geschichte und Eigensinn* to the category of *Zusammenhang* (relationality) in Kluge's artistic production illuminates a relevant stretch of intellectual history. See especially 186–195 there.

28. Haug and Masse, *Materialistische Kulturtheorie und Alltagskultur*, 4.

29. Bertolt Brecht, "From the Three Penny Trial: A Sociological Experiment," trans. Lance W. Garmer, in *German Essays on Film*, ed. Richard W. McCormick and Alison Guenther-Pal (New York: Continuum, 2004), 117; Bertolt Brecht, "Der Dreigroschenprozeß," in *Werke: Große kommentierte Berliner und Frankfurter Ausgabe*, ed. Werner Hecht et al. (Berlin: Aufbau Verlag/Frankfurt am Main: Suhrkamp Verlag, 1988–2000), 21:469. Compressing and further developing Brecht's pathbreaking considerations, Adorno adopted the terms "construction" and "mimesis," effectively capturing the poles of reference in Brecht's passage (cf. e.g., Adorno, *AT* 44/72ff. and 257/381). An echo of their interrelation can be detected in Johnson's characterization of his procedure as delving in "*tatsächliche Erfindungen*" (real inventions) in "Lübeck habe ich ständig beobachtet," in *"Ich überlege mir die Geschichte": Uwe Johnson im Gespräch*, ed. Eberhard Fahlke (Frankfurt am Main: Suhrkamp Verlag, 1988), 79. The differences between the two theorists Brecht and Adorno are not always as large as the latter would have us believe. For an insightful reappraisal of Adorno's relation to Brecht, see Steve Giles, "Realism after Modernism: Representation and Modernity in Brecht, Lukács, and Adorno," in *Aesthetics and Modernity from Schiller to the Frankfurt School*, ed. Jerome Carroll, Steve Giles, and Maike Oergel (New York: Peter Lang, 2011), 275–296.

30. Weiss, Johnson, and Kluge's collective embrace of construction, fiction, and experimentation further justifies the designation of their realist projects as modern epics. Some of the competing terms fall outside the nomenclature of literary genre. Kluge's use of "encyclopedia," for example, captures a relevant tendency of epic narration, but is also open to theoretical discourse of the kind that Kluge himself has separated from his prose works. *Chronicle* is a more challenging competitor, not least in light of Benjamin's opposition in "The Storyteller" of the chronicle to historiography: "Any examination of a given epic form is concerned with the relationship of this form to historiography. . . . The chronicler is the history-teller. . . . [Yet] the historian is bound to explain in one way or another the

happenings with which he deals; under no circumstances can he content himself with displaying them as models of the course of the world, [which is] precisely what the chronicler does" (95–96). In arguing thus, Benjamin was clearly ascribing to the chronicler an artful role, one quite attractive to Weiss, Johnson, and Kluge, who all appealed to the chronicler to insist on the proximity of their works of art to extra-aesthetic realities. While Kluge's embrace of the chronicle is evident from his epic's title, Weiss's narrator describes his activity explicitly as that of a "chronicler, who conveyed collective thinking" and Johnson, as related by Ingeborg Gerlach in *Auf der Suche nach der verlorenen Identität: Studien zu Uwe Johnsons "Jahrestage"* (Königstein/Ts.: Scriptor, 1980), 2, referred to *Jahrestage* as a chronicle. As for that other genre: Weiss's designation of his three-volume *Ästhetik* as a novel in the work's subtitle occurs not due to a commitment to generic terminology per se (which Weiss, like Kluge, seldom deployed in a technical way), but rather to emphasize the work's fictionally free treatment of real persons and events, which could not shield *Die Ästhetik* from attacks on its implied historiography. See Peter Weiss, *Notizbücher 1971–1980* (Frankfurt am Main: Suhrkamp Verlag, 1981), 926.

31. Brecht's charge is found in the "Brecht against Lukács: Popularity and Realism" section of Adorno et al., *Aesthetics and Politics*, 86. "Scientific age" recurs throughout Brecht's writings, as in "A Short Organum for the Theatre," in Willet, *Brecht on Theatre*, 179ff.

32. Brecht, "Can the Present-Day World Be Reproduced by Means of Theatre?," in Willet, *Brecht on Theatre*, 274–275.

33. Hofmann repurposes Kantian terminology to conceptualize Weiss's *Ästhetik* as a kind of transcendental literature in *Ästhetische Erfahrung in der historischen Krise*, 67ff. Ralf Schnell's brief comparison of Weiss and Johnson in "Zwischen Geschichtsphilosophie und 'Posthistoire': Geschichte im deutschen Gegenwartsroman," *Weimarer Beiträge* 37, no. 3 (1991): 342–355, see 347–349 there, confirmed this basic similarity of epic self-reflexivity in their works.

34. Thomas Mann, *The Magic Mountain*, trans. John E. Woods (New York: Alfred A. Knopf, 1999), ix; Thomas Mann, *Der Zauberberg*, vol. 5.1 of *Grosse kommentierte Frankfurter Ausgabe: Werke, Briefe, Tagebücher*, ed. Michael Neumann (Frankfurt am Main: S. Fischer Verlag, 2002), 9.

35. Kluge, "Die schärfste Ideologie: Daß die Realität sich auf ihren realistischen Charakter beruft," in *Gelegenheitsarbeit einer Sklavin: Zur realistischen Methode* (Frankfurt am Main: Suhrkamp Verlag, 1975), 222; my paraphrase adds emphasis to render Kluge's point clearly. For David Roberts's abridged translation of the text, see Kluge, "The Sharpest Ideology: That Reality Appeals to Its Realistic Character," in *Alexander Kluge: Raw Materials for the Imagination*, ed. Tara Forrest (Amsterdam: Amsterdam University Press, 2012), 191–196.

36. Kluge, "Die schärfste Ideologie," 222. In "Das Politische als Intensität alltäglicher Gefühle: Theodor Fontane," in *Fontane Kleist Deutschland Büchner*, 9, Kluge provides a succinct description of critical realism's two tendencies, which consist in "realistic conduct" as the "precision of the representation [*Wiedergabe*] of real experiences" and "antirealistic conduct" against the ways in which real relations bring about misfortune. For Andrew Bowie's translation thereof, see Kluge, "The Political as Intensity of Everyday Feelings," in Forrest, *Alexander Kluge*, 283–290.

37. A comparatively seminal passage concerning Gesine's memory project in Johnson's *Jahrestage* registers related skepticism of the past's retrieval. As the "multilayered sieve of earthly time and causality and chronology and logic that we use for thinking is not served by the brain," its "filter allows scraps, splinters, broken glass, shavings, to trickle through and scatter themselves without meaning over the plundered and spaceless image [of the past], obliterating the traces of the sought-for scene, leaving us blind with open eyes" (*AN* 47/*JT* 63–64).

38. Weiss, Johnson, and Kluge's epics all cultivate the indirect sensory faculty in question here. *Fernsinn* is also a transit-oriented concept, and the accompanying exercises in the epics' "plurality of vision" evoke Said's description of exilic optics noted in the introduction.

39. Brecht, "The Modern Theatre Is the Epic Theatre," 37; Brecht, "Anmerkungen zur Oper *Aufstieg und Fall der Stadt Mahagonny*," 79.

40. Walter Benjamin, "The Crisis of the Novel," in *Selected Writings*, vol. 2: *1927–30*, trans. Rodney Livingstone et al. (Cambridge, Mass.: Belknap Press of Harvard University Press, 1999), 301.

41. The relevant scholarship evinces a rich discussion of artistic practices and techniques of separation. Jochen Vogt ascribes several of these to Weiss's *Ästhetik* in his instructive article "'Wie könnte dies alles geschildert werden?': Versuch, die *Ästhetik des Widerstands* mit Hilfe einiger Vorurteile ihrer Kritiker zu verstehen," in "Peter Weiss," ed. Heinz Ludwig Arnold, special issue, *Text + Kritik* 37, no. 2 (1982): 68–94, especially 78–79, and again with Ludger Claßen in "'Kein Roman überhaupt'?? Beobachtungen zur Prosaform der 'Ästhetik des Widerstands,'" in Stephan, *Die Ästhetik des Widerstands*, 134–163. Bernd Neumann assesses the Brechtian underpinnings of narrative procedures in Johnson's *Mutmaßungen über Jakob*, which is also relevant to *Jahrestage*, in "Uwe Johnsons *Mutmaßungen über Jakob*: Die 'nicht-aristotelische' Gestaltung einer konkreten Utopie," in *Der deutsche Roman im 20. Jahrhundert, Band II: Analysen und Materialien zur Theorie und Soziologie des Romans*, ed. Manfred Brauneck (Bamberg: C. C. Buchners Verlag, 1976), 118–144. Norbert Mecklenburg provides a fuller overview thereof in his pathbreaking essay on *Jahrestage*, "Großstadtmontage und Provinzchronik," especially 201, and Lothar van Laak works out Johnson's critical entwinement of epic narration and mediality with an emphasis on deictic practices in the manner of Brecht in "Johnsons Beschäftigung mit den Medien," in *So noch nicht gezeigt: Uwe Johnson zum Gedenken*, ed. Ulrich Fries et al. (Göttingen: Vandenhoeck & Ruprecht, 2006), 309–332. For an overview of Johnson's use of montage in *Jahrestage*, see Baker's discussion in the "Poeticization of History" chapter of his *Understanding Uwe Johnson*. For Kluge, see most recently Kai Lars Fischer, *Geschichtsmontagen: Zum Zusammenhang von Geschichtskonzeption und Text-Modell bei Walter Benjamin und Alexander Kluge* (Hildesheim: Olms, 2013).

42. See, e.g., Kluge, *Die Kunst, Unterschiede zu machen* (Frankfurt am Main: Suhrkamp Verlag, 2003), 11.

43. Kluge's antidramatic approach to opera—the "disarmament of tragic events" (*Abrüstung des tragischen Geschehens*) delivered by Xaver Holtzmann in *Chronik* (*CdG* 1:841)—is further indication of the influence of Brecht's legacy. That Brecht himself saw epic theater as a general artistic practice is seen not only in his own prose works, but also in his note, to which Neumann draws our attention (124–125), about the incongruence between the "Aristotelian novel's"

singular story line (*Fabel*) and modern content (such as the injustice of the juridical system). Cf. Brecht, "Über den Aristotelischen Roman," vol. 21 of Brecht, *Werke*, 538–539. The work of Brecht's interlocutor Walter Benjamin on modern epic took a similarly ecumenical shape.

44. Moretti claims that world texts address themselves to "*an entire society*" (*ME* 222, emphasis there), but his consideration of readers appears to be confined to a contemplative aesthetics of reception.

45. Examples include Weiss's staging of the narrator's interpretative discussions of artworks with other characters, discussions revolving around Gesine's reconstruction of the past in Johnson's *Jahrestage*, and Kluge's incorporation of the interview format into his short narratives.

46. Uwe Johnson, "Berliner Stadtbahn (*veraltet*)," 21.

47. VPR 403. In *Jahrestage*'s remarkable chapter on Theodor Fontane's *Schach von Wuthenow*, Gesine's teacher Matthias Weserich underscores Fontane's wish for independent readers (*AN II*, 514/*JT* 1705).

48. Karl Marx gave such a conception of knowledge's shared production a sharp formulation long ago. One of his "Theses on Feuerbach" reads: "The question whether objective truth can be attributed to human thinking is not a question of theory but is a *practical question*. Man must prove the truth, i.e. the reality and power, the this-sidedness of his thinking in practice. The dispute over reality or non-reality of thinking that is isolated from practice is a purely *scholastic* question" (Marx and Engels, *The German Ideology*, 121, emphasis there). See also Denning, who writes that "transnational cultural studies will need . . . to write the global history of the intersection of novelists, filmmakers, and musicians with social movements" (*Culture in the Age of Three Worlds*, 33). The rejuvenation of the modern epic genre proceeds from and remains in dialogue with social movements, including not only the West German student movement, but also socialism itself. For this reason, 1968 is as an important a date as 1945, 1961, and 1989 for any historical account of Weiss, Johnson, and Kluge's works.

49. Thomas Metscher, "Über die notwendige Pluralität künstlerischer Formen: Anmerkungen zum Problem einer Theorie moderner epischer Dichtung," *Weimarer Beiträge* 32 (1986): 1626–1650, hereafter cited parenthetically.

50. In an interview conducted with *Der Spiegel* in 2000, Kluge recalled the 1980s as a time in which he did not have much that was "forward-looking" (*Zukunftsweisendes*) to communicate. See Kluge, "Ich liebe das Lakonische," *Der Spiegel* 45 (2000), http://www.spiegel.de/spiegel/print/d-17757645.html.

51. Weiss, Johnson, and Kluge's works are informed by Walter Benjamin's diagnosis of the encroachment of reified information on epic forms of narration. In his account of the increasingly powerful opposition between narration and information, Benjamin effectively conveyed a devolution in the social practice of mediation itself. Information, he underscored in "The Storyteller," lives only in the moment, is shot through with prefabricated explanations, and presses a heteronymous account of reality upon us, whereas the story, eschewing no wonders, leaves space to a listener or reader to "interpret things the way he [*sic*] understands them" and "does not expend itself" (88–90). The postwar epic's restaging of this tension between two fundamentally opposed forms of communication is geared towards the restoral of critical narration from its demolition by informational media and its surrounding discourses.

52. Literature is far from alone in critically mediating other media. The theatrical, cinematic, operatic, and visual arts all present examples of intermedial epic work in this vein.

53. As discussed in chapter 4, I grasp constellation, which Kluge appropriates from Benjamin and Adorno, as a category of *Chronik*'s mediating activity. With regard to the other terms, it is worth underscoring both the difference between representation and *Darstellung* (where the latter does not presuppose a correspondence theory of truth) and the association of *Erscheinen* as a procedure not only with what Hegel thinks underlies the "pure appearance of the Idea to sense" (*das sinnliche Scheinen der Idee*) in *Aesthetics* (1:111/*Ästhetik I*, vol. 13 of *Werke*, 151), but also with Adorno's critique of insufficient mediation in Brecht's plays, in e.g., "Commitment," *Notes to Literature*, vol. 2, trans. Shierry Weber Nicholsen (New York: Columbia University Press, 1992), 84–85.

54. John Guillory, "Genesis of the Media Concept," *Critical Inquiry* 36 (2010): 321–366, here 342–344.

55. Guillory, "Genesis of the Media Concept," 360.

56. The distinction also allows for the critique of informational media (in Benjamin's sense), which tend to "mediate" under the regime of representation and its false transparency, which advances reality's ideologically driven distortion.

57. Jay David Bolter and Richard Grusin, *Remediation: Understanding New Media* (Cambridge, Mass.: MIT Press, 1999), 21ff., 61.

58. Bolter and Grusin, *Remediation*, 15.

59. Bolter and Grusin, *Remediation*, 55.

60. Adorno, "Art and the Arts," in *Can One Live after Auschwitz? A Philosophical Reader*, ed. Rolf Tiedemann, trans. Rodney Livingstone et al. (Stanford, Calif.: Stanford University Press, 2003), 375; Adorno, "Kunst und die Künste," in *Kulturkritik und Gesellschaft I*, 440.

61. See Irina I. Rajewsky, "Intermediality, Intertextuality, and Remediation: A Literary Perspective on Intermediality," *Intermédialités* 6 (2005): 43–64. "Transposition," "medial combinations," and "intermedial references" are three of the terms she deploys to distinguish sharply between different intermedial practices.

62. Kluge, "Das Innere des Erzählens," 75, my emphasis.

63. The critical aesthetics developed by Brecht and Adorno and practiced by Weiss, Johnson, and Kluge in the different ways addressed in the following chapters constitute tremendous resources vis-à-vis contemporary developments in communications technologies, which seldom fail to downplay their own status as mediators. As Bolter and Grusin emphasize, innovations in media technology are driven by a perceived human desire for immediacy that cannot be satisfied, but which nonetheless plays a role in the production of media devices that minimize or obscure their mediating characteristics. See their *Remediation*, 23–24. With regard to the technological remediation of the modern epic, the hypertext possibilities of each text may appear suggestive. The online presence of guides to Johnson's *Jahrestage* such as *Der Kommentar*, ed. Holger Helbig et al. (Göttingen: Vandenhoeck & Ruprecht, 1999), http://www.philfak.uni-rostock.de/institut/igerman/johnson/johnkomm/default.html, and the *Kleines Adressbuch für Jerichow und New York*, the print version of which was published by Rolf Michaelis (Frankfurt am Main: Suhrkamp Verlag, 1983) and revised for print as well as reissued digitally by Anke-Marie Lohmeier in 2013,

http://literaturlexikon.uni-saarland.de/index.php?id=191, confirms the utility of digitally available reference works. But such instruments differ from aesthetic media. And the digital remediation of the modern epic would risk destroying the aesthetically significant separation of literature from other artistic or nonartistic media. While Johnson himself never worked in any medium other than literary prose, faced with the choice of book vs. film, website, digital text, and/or radio play, Kluge has insisted on his preference for the former in the medium of print. As discussed in the next chapter on Weiss's *Ästhetik*, the modern epic facilitates the appropriation of an orientational network as one's own.

64. See Bolter and Grusin, *Remediation*, e.g., 41, 58. The socio-theoretical dimensions of *Vermittlung* are largely absent from their important study.

65. Jameson, *Postmodernism*, 54, 6.

66. Jameson, *Postmodernism*, 51, emphasis there.

67. Jameson, *Postmodernism*, 52–53, emphasis there.

68. Jameson, *Postmodernism*, 51.

69. Jameson, *Postmodernism*, 410ff. The three phases are classical or market capitalism, the stage of monopolistic capital and imperialism, and late or multinational capitalism.

70. Jameson, *Postmodernism*, 411–412.

71. Jameson, *Postmodernism*, 413.

72. Jameson, *Postmodernism*, 53, 54, 409. Jameson deploys Jacques Lacan's term to point to the spaces of language and media in which works of cognitive mapping intervene.

73. Jameson, *Postmodernism*, 52. See also Tally, *Spatiality*, 73, on the usefulness of "intentionally figurative or metaphorical maps." By acknowledging its fundamental corrigibility, the aesthetic strategies of cognitive mapping remain constitutively distinct from cartographic practices bent on domination.

74. Jameson, *Postmodernism*, 416.

75. Jameson, *Postmodernism*, 416–417.

76. Jameson, *Postmodernism*, 418.

77. See Tobias Mandel, *Formen und Funktionen von Intertextualität und Intermedialität in der "Ästhetik des Widerstands" von Peter Weiss* (St. Ingbert: Röhrig Universitätsverlag, 2013), 489–494; Gerlach, *Auf der Suche nach der verlorenen Identität*, 82–84; David Roberts, "Alexander Kluge and German History: 'The Air Raid on Halberstadt on 8.4.1945," in Forrest, *Alexander Kluge*, 127–154.

78. See Baker, *Understanding Uwe Johnson*, 17–20.

79. Nancy Armstrong, *How Novels Think: The Limits of Individualism from 1719–1900* (New York: Columbia University Press, 2005), 10.

80. Throughout *How Novels Think*, Armstrong attends to the genre's masculinist gendering regime, e.g., 102–103.

81. Armstrong, *How Novels Think*, 83. For this reason, it is also possible to speak of the bildungsroman as the genre of the educated bourgeoisie (*Bildungsbürgertum*), as discussed in the next chapter.

82. Benjamin, "The Storyteller," 90.

83. Benjamin, "The Crisis of the Novel," 303.

84. Cf. e.g., *AoR* 268/*ÄdW* 1:305; 2:204, 306; Lindner, "Hallucinatory Realism," 140; and Hofmann, *Ästhetische Erfahrung in der historischen Krise*, 344ff.

85. Cf. Scherpe's related characterization of the structure of Kluge's epic volumes in terms of a "democratic diversity of writing experiments" in *Stadt, Krieg, Fremde*, 329.

86. On Johnson's characters as "invented persons," see Christoph Schmid, "Gespräch mit Uwe Johnson," in Fahlke, *"Ich überlege mir die Geschichte,"* 253.

87. Cf. Robert Musil, "Helpless Europe: A Digressive Journey," trans. Philip H. Beard, in *Precision and Soul: Essays and Addresses*, ed. and trans. Burton Pike and David S. Luft (Chicago: University of Chicago Press, 1995), 131.

88. Kluge, "Die Differenz: Heinrich von Kleist," in *Fontane Kleist Deutschland Büchner*, 36–37.

89. "Just as my father had always laid claim to the cultural goods, so too he had insisted that he owned the things surrounding him at work. Art and literature were means of production, just as the tools and machines were" (*AoR* 308/*ÄdW* 1:350). Delivering a labor theory of culture, Weiss's *Ästhetik* contests the social division between mental and manual labor to retract the alienated character of labor in capitalist society.

90. Uwe Johnson, "Neue Bibliothek" of the Norddeutscher Rundfunk, November 14, 1970, viewed at the Uwe Johnson Literaturhaus, Klütz, June 9, 2016.

91. In his review of "Art and Society in the Thought of Marx," Eugene Lunn has written that there "is in art always an element of self-purpose in which the creation of formal attractiveness is an exercise of a human capacity for playful material activity (the lack of which in modern capitalist labor is a prime measure of its alienation)," in *Marxism and Modernism: An Historical Study of Lukács, Brecht, Benjamin, and Adorno* (Berkeley: University of California Press, 1982), 11.

92. See, for example, Kluge, "Authentische Texte sind klüger als ihre Autoren," in *Verdeckte Ermittlung: Ein Gespräch mit Christian Schulte und Rainer Stollmann* (Berlin: Merve Verlag, 2001), 41–42.

93. "I must, so to speak, establish a framework dictatorially, so that freedom can prevail within the framework, within the 'capillaries,' " Kluge explained in an interview with Stuart Liebman, "On New German Cinema, Art, Enlightenment and the Public Sphere," 34.

94. Axel Honneth, *Pathologies of Reason: On the Legacy of Critical Theory*, trans. James Ingram (New York: Columbia University Press, 2009), 39.

95. Horkheimer and Adorno, *Dialectic of Enlightenment*, 115. The original reads "Vergnügtsein heißt Einverstandensein," in *Dialektik der Aufklärung: Philosophische Fragmente*, vol. 4 of Adorno, *Gesammelte Schriften*, 167.

96. Brecht, "Theatre for Pleasure or Theatre for Instruction," in Willet, *Brecht on Theatre*, 72–73.

97. Robert Cohen, *Understanding Peter Weiss* (Columbia: University of South Carolina Press, 1993), 160.

98. In "Die Macht der Bewußtseinsindustrie und das Schicksal unserer Öffentlichkeit," Kluge noted that the richness of classical publicity (*Öffentlichkeit*) had but one flaw, that it was not accessible to all (DMB 59).

Chapter 2

The epigraphs for this chapter's sections are from *ÄdW* 2:84; *ÄdW* 3:239; *AoR* 295; translation modified/*ÄdW* 1:335; Weiss in Burkhardt Lindner, "Between Pergamon and Plötzensee: Another Way of Depicting the Course of Events: An

Interview with Peter Weiss," trans. Christian Rogowski, *New German Critique* 30 (1983): 107–126, here 118; and *ÄdW* 3:67.

1. Staatliche Museen zu Berlin, Preußischer Kulturbesitz, "The Pergamon Altar," Führungsblatt-Nr.: Ant 1 (engl.), text by Volker Kästner, trans. B. Schubert (Berlin: Staatliche Museen zu Berlin, 2007). The large altar exceeded available exhibition space at the beginning of the century and occasioned the construction of a new Pergamon Museum, which was opened in 1930. The museum is currently undergoing extensive renovations, and the altar space is scheduled to reopen in 2019. Weiss's *Ästhetik* includes pointed skepticism regarding the altar's acquisition by and relocation to Wilhelmine Germany (*AoR* 9, 43/*ÄdW* 1:13, 51–52).

2. In the context of the Ancient Greek division of labor, the contributions of the laboring classes to the Ionian state went unacknowledged. The devolution of aesthetic reception and material production onto different social groups—cf. Marx and Engels, *The German Ideology*, 52—is a divide that *Die Ästhetik des Widerstands* challenges through its labor theory of culture.

3. The remarkable discussion of *Die Ästhetik*'s fifth chapter includes the narrator, Coppi, Heilmann, and Coppi's parents' deliberations on the respective accomplishments of realist, socialist realist, and modernist avant-garde artworks. Coppi and the narrator praise those of socialist realism (*AoR* 57/*ÄdW* I, 65) for their grasp of historical accomplishments and the enthusiasm they impart. Heilmann criticizes them for not demanding a transformation of visual habits (*AoR* 54/*ÄdW* 1:64) and for underestimating the worker (*AoR* 57/*ÄdW* 1:68). Ultimately, art's "mind of its own" (*AoR* 58/*ÄdW* 1:68; its inherent *Eigensinn*) proscribes any normative treatment, for which reason the balance Heilmann has in mind at *AoR* 48/*ÄdW* 1:58 can be taken as an initial guideline: "Both [standpoints] are correct . . . the lunge that yanks the ground out from under our feet [associated with the aesthetic negativity of the avant-garde] as well as the [socialist realist] effort to establish a solid basis for investigating simple facts."

4. Reentering the epic at the beginning of the third volume's second part, Coppi and Heilmann continue the debate about Hercules's qualitative function as their "lodestar" (*ÄdW* 3:169; *Leitstern*). The narrator follows through on this at the epic's end by exploiting the visual absence of Hercules on the frieze as a space of self-empowerment (*ÄdW* 3:267–268). The protagonists' diction and discussion both recall the opening of Lukács's *Theory of the Novel*.

5. Martin Rector, "Örtlichkeit und Phantasie: Zur inneren Konstruktion der *Ästhetik des Widerstands*," in Stephan, *Die Ästhetik des Widerstands*, 124. The phrase *Gang zu den Bildern* evokes Weiss's account of the respective existential dimensions, aesthetic functions, and expressive power of words and images in the speech he delivered on receiving the Lessing Prize in 1965, "Laokoon oder Über die Grenzen der Sprache," in *Rapporte* (Frankfurt am Main: Suhrkamp Verlag, 1968), 170–187.

6. As developed in greater detail below and in chapter 3, the phrase "living archive" designates the appropriation and mobilization of an orientational network on which Weiss's protagonists and Uwe Johnson's Gesine Cresspahl labor, albeit with different points of emphasis.

7. For a more detailed account of the first chapter, see Anne-Kathrin Reulecke, *Geschriebene Bilder: Zum Kunst- und Mediendiskurs in der Gegenwartsliteratur*

(Munich: Wilhelm Fink Verlag, 2002), who observes Weiss's approach to myth as an extension of cognition serving the representation of the narrated present (107) and grasps *Die Ästhetik*'s "reading and writing of images" (126) as honoring the differences of signifying media (94) in an activity that I describe as the work's literary remediation of its source media.

8. See, e.g., Schnell, *Die Literatur der Bundesrepublik*, 341–342.

9. While Mandel's recent *Formen und Funktionen von Intertextualität und Intermedialität* includes the term "intermediality" in its title, much of the focus there is on intertextuality.

10. Cf. Harald Olbrich, "*Die Ästhetik des Widerstands* als Herausforderung: Zum Umgang mit bildender Kunst," in *"Ästhetik des Widerstands": Erfahrungen mit dem Roman von Peter Weiss*, ed. Norbert Krenzlin (Berlin: Akademie Verlag, 1987), 122–134, who writes that Weiss facilitates "grasping artworks as experimental fields for independence and the sharpening of the faculties for perception and judgment" (127).

11. There is a great degree of overlap between the aesthetics of *Die Ästhetik des Widerstands* and Oskar Negt and Alexander Kluge's account of *Eigensinn* as a reaction to the expropriation of one's senses. For a recent account of the latter, see my "*Eigensinn* in Transit: Reexamining a Concept for the Twenty-First Century," *Glass Shards: Alexander Kluge-Jahrbuch 2* (2015): 83–102, especially 88–90.

12. The locus classicus is Immanuel Kant's 1784 essay "What Is Enlightenment?," which also lays out the function of a critical public sphere. See Kant, *Philosophical Writings*, ed. Ernst Behler (New York: Continuum, 1993), 263–269.

13. Weiss's broad-minded approach to the social exclusion of the proletariat by the relations of production and the division of labor pertains to any person's externality to language, culture, and art, which will only become real, meaningful, and valuable when they are appropriated in and through the self-activity of individuals and groups. This is how the gap of the ontogenetic process is to be closed, not via the assimilative acculturation of individuals to any given culture. In Weiss's narrative context, this very much pertained to Germans' acceptance of Nazism at the time, whereas today the phrase and function of "cultural capital" might provide an example of such assimilation's directionality. For an explanation of the expansion of the term "proletarian" along these lines, see Richard Langston, "The Work of Art as Theory of Work: Relationality in the Works of Weiss and Negt & Kluge," *Germanic Review* 83, no. 3 (2008): 195–215, which draws on the work of the latter two to explain proletarian as a relational concept denoting experiences of suppression, expropriation, and exclusion that may befall members of any class in advanced global capitalism (202).

14. Accordingly, in "Örtlichkeit und Phantasie," Rector has stressed the importance of fantasy in art and politics alike to argue that Weiss's correction of the Left's political blindness consists in a redress of "universal rationalization and repression of the abysmal" to "imagine what is unthinkable" (123–124).

15. Fredric Jameson has described *Die Ästhetik*'s "depersonalized collective voice" as a "dialogical agon" in his instructive foreword to the English translation of the first volume, "A Monument to Radical Instants" (*AoR* xxvi).

16. Cf. Marx, "Theses on Feuerbach," in Marx and Engels, *The German Ideology*, 121. Münzer is effectively challenging the tendency of socialist dialectics

to surmount paradox by way of temporalizing contradictions, which too often entailed the sacrifice of the present to an only imagined better future.

17. Compare Karl Marx's succinct formulation on the character of capitalist production in the *Grundrisse*: the human being "steps to the side of the production process instead of being its chief actor" in *The Marx-Engels Reader*, ed. Robert C. Tucker (New York: Norton, 1978), 284.

18. Marcauer inaugurates the line of feminist critique that *Die Ästhetik* develops pluralistically through a host of female characters. In grappling with the dimensions of a feminist aesthetics of resistance at work in Weiss's book, the scholarship has debated its standing. While Genia Schulz, in *"Die Ästhetik des Widerstands": Versionen des Indirekten in Peter Weiss's Roman* (Stuttgart: Metzler, 1986), debunks the existence of Weiss's proposed "dialectics without exclusion" (25), of which these voices would be a part, Robert Cohen, in *Versuche über Weiss' "Ästhetik des Widerstands"* (New York: Peter Lang, 1989), 185–190, has argued for the salience of the antipatriarchal aspects of Weiss's political critique. On the other hand, by detecting the abjection of the feminine by the very narrative system in which the narrator presumes to integrate it, Julia Hell has regarded its status in the novel as a far deeper problem in "Rosa oder die Sehnsucht nach einer Geschichte ohne Stalin," *Peter Weiss Jahrbuch* 6 (1997): 138–163, especially 150 and 157. In the section titled "Epic's Polyphonic Futures" below, I grasp the issue as part and parcel of *Die Ästhetik*'s work on unity and difference, which is less resolved than framed as an ongoing challenge.

19. Characteristically, this occurs even in the direst situations where "rescue was so remote that it seemed as if it first had to be invented" (*AoR* 303/*ÄdW* 1:345; *erdacht*).

20. Robert Cohen has compiled an inventory of all significant characters in his *Bio-Bibliographisches Handbuch zu Peter Weiss' "Ästhetik des Widerstands"* (Hamburg: Argument Verlag, 1989), but notes that at the time he could not gain any independent information on Ayschmann, Marcauer, Münzer, Gallego, and Rogeby. See Cohen, "Vorbemerkung" to *Bio-Bibliographisches Handbuch*, 1. In an interview, Weiss, omitting the narrator's anonymous parents, stated that only the narrator was invented. See Arne Ruth, "'Für den arbeitenden Menschen kann nichts zu schwer sein': Interview mit Peter Weiss [30. Januar 1979]," trans. Michael Kanning, in *Peter Weiss im Gespräch*, ed. Rainer Gerlach and Matthias Richter (Frankfurt am Main: Suhrkamp Verlag, 1986), 232.

21. Jameson in *AoR* xxvi.

22. Müller wrote of Weiss's "monk-like relation to utopia" in *Krieg ohne Schlacht*, 175.

23. In "Prolegomena zu einem Forschungsbericht," Martin Rector observes how the disavowal of socialism after the *Wende* purportedly renders not only Weiss's work but also its interpretation historically obsolete. See *Diese bebende, zähe, kühne Hoffnung 25 Jahre Peter Weiss "Die Ästhetik des Widerstands,"* ed. Arnd Beise et al. (St. Ingbert: Röhrig Universitätsverlag, 2008), 33–34.

24. Cf. Rector, "Prolegomena," 34.

25. Cf. Adorno, *AT* 40–41/67.

26. Weiss in Lindner, "Between Pergamon and Plötzensee," 107.

27. The father appeals to Rosa Luxemburg's exemplary conduct and emphasis on free and self-conscious thinking in her interactions with workers that

contrasted greatly with what party functionaries propagated and practiced (*AoR* 94, 108/*ÄdW* 1:109, 125).

28. Cf. Michael Denning's outline in the "From Text to Work: Towards a Labor Theory of Culture" section of his *Culture in the Age of Three Worlds*, 90–96, which explains how a labor theory of culture can supplement other cultural theories, including those that have focused on ideology and/or consumption.

29. While the cultural turn has downplayed the divide between high and low culture, the failure to set either in relation to labor risks perpetuating culture's opposition to material existence.

30. Cf. Hobsbawm, *Fractured Times*, x–xii.

31. Hofmann develops the term "productive reception" in his analysis of *Die Ästhetik*'s first volume in *Ästhetische Erfahrung in der historischen Krise*, 35–99.

32. Championing the avant-garde's ability to process forms of inner and outer reality's instability, by the end of chapter 6, Heilmann summarizes the protagonists' education that "ran not only contrary to the obstacles of the class society" but "also flouted the principle of a socialist view of culture that had sanctioned the masters of the past but excommunicated the pioneers of the twentieth century. We insisted that Joyce and Kafka, Schönberg and Stravinsky, Klee and Picasso were of the same rank as Dante" (*AoR* 67/*ÄdW* 1:79).

33. "Culture," Weiss wrote in one of his previously unpublished notebooks, "that was first when we came together and spoke with one another." These are now available in Peter Weiss, *Die Notizbücher: Kritische Gesamtausgabe*, ed. Jürgen Schutte, CD-ROM (Berlin: Directmedia, 2006), 7023.

34. While *Die Ästhetik* addresses mostly the production and reception of culture, Willi Münzenberg's work, as discussed in the fourteenth chapter of the first volume, exemplifies the labor of culture's circulation (*AoR* 136/*ÄdW* 1:157).

35. Metscher has drawn attention to the proximity between Gramsci, who finds mention only in this passage of Weiss's book, and the protagonists' transformative appropriation of culture in *Der Friedensgedanke in der europäischen Literatur*, 195–196.

36. In so doing, Weiss undertakes no less for culture than what Marx and Engels, in *The German Ideology* (86) anticipated for social production when they wrote of communism's conscious production of the form of intercourse itself.

37. Denning, *Culture in the Age of Three Worlds*, 94.

38. Cf. Lindner, "Hallucinatory Realism," 127.

39. Huyssen, "Memory, Myth, and the Dream of Reason," 136.

40. In view of this opposition between two sets of the relations of cultural production, the narrator's aesthetic competence need not appear as the prolongation of "that of the narrator in the modern bourgeois novel," as Rector has claimed in "Zur Kritik der einfachen Politisierung: Die 'Ästhetik des Widerstands' als Nach-68-Roman," 112. While Weiss and his narrator appropriate techniques from the tradition in question, *Die Ästhetik* wholly repurposes their use in its drive toward social emancipation.

41. While *Die Ästhetik* does not employ Marx's terms of living and dead labor (cf. Tucker, *The Marx-Engels Reader*, 252–253, 362–363), its approach is consistent with them.

42. Cf. Lukács, *TN* 56/47.

43. For an overview of *Die Ästhetik*'s oneiric dimensions, see Jameson in *AoR* xxviii–xxii.

44. A related outpost of Adorno's *Negative Dialectics* reads: "If thought is not measured by the extremity that eludes the concept, it is from the outset in the nature of the musical accompaniment with which the SS liked to drown out the screams of the victims" (*ND* 365/358).

45. Scherpe, "Reading the Aesthetics of Resistance," 102.

46. Huyssen, "Memory, Myth, and the Dream of Reason," 137.

47. Peter Bürger, "Über die Wirklichkeit der Kunst: Zur Ästhetik in der 'Ästhetik des Widerstands,' " 292–293.

48. Negt and Kluge also entertain this image of the introverted medieval scholar at work in *Geschichte und Eigensinn* (*DuM* 2:1006–1007).

49. Burkhardt Lindner, "Déjà-vu im Zeitriss: Die Erinnerungspolitik der *Ästhetik des Widerstands*," in *Diese bebende, zähe, kühne Hoffnung*, 89; Vogt, " 'Wie könnte dies alles geschildert werden?,' " 76–77.

50. In "Ich Konjunktiv Futur I oder die Wiederkehr des Exils," Lindner focuses on Weiss's use of the subjunctive in the final chapter to culminate the narrative. See Lindner in *Die "Ästhetik des Widerstands" lesen: Über Peter Weiss*, ed. Karl Heinz Götze and Klaus R. Scherpe (Berlin: Argument Verlag, 1981), 85–94.

51. Vogt, " 'Wie könnte dies alles geschildert werden?,' " 74–75. In conversation with Wend Kässens and Michael Töteberg, Weiss called *Die Ästhetik* a novel of development. See their "Gespräch mit Peter Weiss über *Die Ästhetik des Widerstands* (Frühjahr 1979)," in *Peter Weiss im Gespräch*, 244.

52. G. W. F. Hegel, *Phenomenology of Spirit*, trans. A. V. Miller (New York: Oxford University Press, 1977), 49; G. W. F. Hegel, *Phänomenologie des Geistes*, vol. 3 of *Werke*, 72. Like Weiss's, Hegel's path most definitely includes instances of despair.

53. Theodor W. Adorno, "Aspects of Hegel's Philosophy," in *Hegel: Three Studies*, trans. Shierry Weber Nicholsen (Cambridge, Mass.: MIT Press, 1993), 18–32; Adorno, "Aspekte," in *Drei Studien zu Hegel*, in vol. 6 of *Gesammelte Schriften*, 265–277.

54. For further explanation of this aspect of the *Phenomenology*'s structure, see Alexandre Kojève's instructive appendix to his *Introduction to the Reading of Hegel*, assembled by Raymond Queneau, ed. Allan Bloom, trans. James H. Nichols Jr. (Ithaca, N.Y.: Cornell University Press, 1980), 261–263.

55. Although such interruptions provide no solutions by themselves, they allow for breathing space. Cf. Bischoff's association of art with physical exhalation (*Aufatmen*) at *ÄdW* 3:86.

56. Hofmann, *Ästhetische Erfahrung in der historischen Krise*, 67–71. *Die Ästhetik* thus also provides a dialectical model for understanding Weiss's development as a writer against his feuilleton critics, who had questioned Weiss's adoption of varying standpoints. See for instance Helmut Salzinger, "Zwei, drei, viele Standpunkte: Der lange Marsch des Peter Weiss," *Die Zeit*, May 30, 1969, http://www.zeit.de/1969/22/zwei-drei-viele-standpunkte/komplettansicht.

57. Cf. Hofmann, *Ästhetische Erfahrung in der historischen Krise*, 30.

58. Hofmann, *Ästhetische Erfahrung in der historischen Krise*, 333–340.

59. Burkhardt Lindner, "Der große (kommunistische) Traum des Schriftstellers Peter Weiss: Zur 'Rekonvaleszenz,' zur Dante-Prosa und zur 'Ästhetik des Widerstands,' " in Hofmann et al., *Literatur, Ästhetik, Geschichte*, 74.

60. Lindner, "Déjà-vu im Zeitriss," 86–89.

61. Carefully reconstructing Weiss's *Ästhetik* in view of the *Notizbücher*, Lindner's insightful article "Hallucinatory Realism" addresses the fictional accomplishment with more skepticism than enthusiasm, not least due to Weiss's erasure of "the fundamental efforts of documentary investigation" and his "rendering . . . indistinguishable . . . the difference between the depicted past and the present day of the author" (133). Lindner's reservations are directed less at Weiss's fictional construction than at the ways it allegedly conceals its constructed character. On this argument, the work's real self-reflexivity lies not in the narrator's express concerns about the story's feasibility, but behind them, in the workshop of Weiss's hallucinatory realism (142).

62. While Lindner does not use this term, it definitely squares with the curiously Hegelian scheme whereby the narrator's tale is being written behind his back. For the locus classicus of the cunning of reason in Hegel, see the *Lectures on the Philosophy of World History*, trans. H. B. Nisbet (Cambridge: Cambridge University Press, 1975), 89; Hegel, *Vorlesungen über die Philosophie der Geschichte*, vol. 12 of *Werke*, 49.

63. Cohen selects Weiss's original line about a "terribly monstrous book" in the *Notizbücher* (227) as an epigraph for his *Bio-Bibliographisches Handbuch*, 7.

64. Weiss's approach to the publication of *Die Ästhetik* mirrors Uwe Johnson's delivery of *Jahrestage* in installments. The delayed delivery of the latter's fourth and final volume raised questions about the project's completability. In contrast to both Weiss and Johnson, Kluge's work is not subject to the same pressure, since its more aggregate form deflates the drama of epic endings altogether.

65. Cohen's *Versuche über Weiss' "Ästhetik des Widerstands,"* 49–65, provides a fuller account of Weiss's writing process in reference to *Notizbücher* entries.

66. Compare the birth date of Uwe Johnson's autodiegetic narrator Gesine Cresspahl in *Jahrestage*, which falls on March 3, 1933, a bit over a year before Johnson's and the day of numerous arrests of communists in the new Nazi dictatorship, including that of Ernst Thälmann (*JT* 202–205). The contrasting symbolisms determine the perspectives and trajectories of each epic, with Weiss and Johnson focused on the international antifascist resistance and Nazism respectively, as highlighted by Martin Rector in "Wahrnehmung und Erinnerung in Peter Weiss' *Ästhetik des Widerstands* und Uwe Johnsons *Jahrestagen*," *Johnson-Jahrbuch* 12 (2005): 91–100, especially 95–96.

67. The narrator's father is also not Jewish and exploits the Iron Cross he earned in World War I to move through Nazi-occupied Eastern Europe (*ÄdW* 3:12).

68. W. G. Sebald, "The Remorse of the Heart: On Memory and Cruelty in the Work of Peter Weiss," in *On the Natural History of Destruction*, trans. Anthea Bell (New York: Modern Library, 2004), 190.

69. For a more comprehensive account of *Die Ästhetik*'s autobiographical elements, see Manfred Haiduk, "Dokument oder Fiktion: Zur autobiographischen Grundlage in Peter Weiss's Romantrilogie 'Die Ästhetik des Widerstands,' "

in Stephan, *Die Ästhetik des Widerstands*, 59–78. More contentious than the biographical details highlighted above is the aspect of Weiss's "proletarian vs. bourgeois" identity. Adopting a broad definition of the previous term, Weiss himself associated exile with proletarianization, as Scherpe relates in "Reading the Aesthetics of Resistance," 100.

70. Ludger Claßen and Jochen Vogt grasp *Die Ästhetik*'s formal innovations within the novelistic tradition of classical modernism to argue against its detractors in their "'Kein Roman überhaupt'??," especially 140–141. My approach contrasts novel and epic to explore the alternative trajectories and distinctive strengths of the latter genre.

71. Rector, "Örtlichkeit und Phantasie," 105.

72. Rector, "Örtlichkeit und Phantasie," 113.

73. Rector, "Örtlichkeit und Phantasie," 113.

74. Pressed by an interviewer's query as to why he did not entertain much psychology in *Die Ästhetik*, Weiss responded by saying that "with a style of the epic layout that wants to grasp a totality, there was no room for psychological nuances." See "'. . . ein ständiges Auseinandersetzen mit den Fehlern und mit den Missgriffen . . .': Heinz-Ludwig Arnold im Gespräch mit Peter Weiss (19. September 1981)," in Stephan, *Die Ästhetik des Widerstands*, 53.

75. Weiss in Lindner, "Between Pergamon and Plötzensee," 111.

76. Weiss in "'Es ist eine Wunschautobiographie': Peter Weiss im Gespräch mit Rolf Michaelis über seinen politischen Gleichnisroman (Ende September/Anfang Oktober 1975)," in *Peter Weiss im Gespräch*, 217.

77. Ingeborg Gerlach, *Die ferne Utopie: Studien zu Peter Weiss's "Ästhetik des Widerstands"* (Aachen: Karin Fischer Verlag, 1991), 39.

78. Metscher, *Der Friedensgedanke in der europäischen Literatur*, 191–192.

79. Lindner, "Hallucinatory Realism," 139.

80. Claßen and Vogt, "'Kein Roman überhaupt'??," 142; Lindner, "Hallucinatory Realism," 140.

81. Peter Weiss in "Manfred Haiduk im Gespräch mit Peter Weiss über *Die Ästhetik des Widerstands* (30. August 1974)," in *Peter Weiss im Gespräch*, 211.

82. "Perhaps," Moretti writes, "we can . . . see in Faust's inertia the only chance for the modern epic totality. If Hegel is actually right, and in the modern world 'the vitality of the individual appears as transcended', then nothing is left but to seek 'the universal individual of mankind' *in passivity*" (*ME* 16, emphasis there). For Moretti's follow-through on this notion in Joyce, see *ME* 143–144.

83. In conversation with Haiduk, Weiss emphasized the expanse of the narrator's consciousness far beyond his own person (211). With Arnold, he described this expansiveness as crucial to a new conception and constitution of political and cultural struggle (52–53).

84. Vogt, "'Wie könnte dies alles geschildert werden?,'" 76–77, 89.

85. Ursula Heukenkamp, "Angelus Novus oder der Erzähler in der *Ästhetik des Widerstands*," in Krenzlin, *"Ästhetik des Widerstands,"* 105, 110.

86. Heukenkamp, "Angelus Novus," 110–112.

87. Benjamin, "Theses on the Philosophy of History," in *Illuminations*, 257–258.

88. Relatedly, the "shaft that art directs at society is itself social; it is counterpressure to the force exerted by the *body social*; like inner-aesthetic progress, which is progress in productive and, above all, technical forces, this counterpressure is

bound up with progress of extra-aesthetic productive forces" (*AT* 33/56, italics there mark Adorno's use of English in the German text).

89. Hohendahl, *The Fleeting Promise of Art*, 164–166.

90. Cf. Adorno, "Commitment," in *Notes to Literature*, 2:83, 94. In view of Adorno's "premise that social criticism is articulated [by art] without any manifest social content," Lindner saw in *Die Ästhetik* "a significant corrective to Adorno's critique of *Engagement*" ("Hallucinatory Realism," 155).

91. Cf. Scherpe's account of the work's aesthetic construction: "The chorus of voices, dialogue, polyphony turn directly or indirectly against the monologue of the *one* narrative voice, the *one* orientating authority," in "*Die Ästhetik des Widerstands*: Peter Weiss's Traum von der Vernunft," in *Peter Weiss: Leben und Werk*, ed. Gunilla Palmstierna-Weiss and Jürgen Schutte (Frankfurt am Main: Suhrkamp, 1991), 254, emphasis there.

92. For an analogous contrast of seafarers to peasants, see Kluge and Negt's comparison of Ancient Greek myth with the German fairy tales in *HO*, 268–295.

93. While Rector bundles together the upward climbs of numerous characters in their attempts to gain clarity in "Örtlichkeit und Phantasie," 110, the multifaceted movements of the narrator and others along the vertical, horizontal as well as functional, irrational, imaginary, and revolutionary axes that Negt and Kluge deem crucial to any critical realism eschews facile metaphorization, lest it be that of some considerably acrobatic materialist angel.

94. Cf. Rector, "Örtlichkeit und Phantasie," 105–107.

95. Cf. Rector, "Örtlichkeit und Phantasie," 109–111; Jameson in *AoR* xxviii–xxxii.

96. In a telling sequence during one Berlin evening, Coppi's father, to whom the cramped kitchen had become unbearable, jumps up from the table, and turns off the light to open the window in a quixotic action that reacts as much to the situation of confinement as to his wife, son, and friends' discussion of Stalin's doctrine of socialism in one country (*AoR* 58–61/*ÄdW* 1:69–72).

97. The presence of canals in the *Notizbücher* (e.g., *NB* 490, 538) relates to a key moment of the narrator's work with Brecht on the Engelbrekt drama. The fifteenth-century Swedish revolutionary's plan for the construction of an alternative canal route between Lake Mäleren and the Baltic Sea—averting the Stockholm held by his antagonists—so captivated Brecht in his work on the drama that he thought it nearly demanded a play of its own (*ÄdW* 2:245–246).

98. Cf. Mandel, who reads the protagonists' reflections on culture's universality and totality at *AoR* 148–149/*ÄdW* 1:171 as *Die Ästhetik*'s guiding thesis and relates both terms to the concept of network in *Formen und Funktionen von Intertextualität und Intermedialität*, 16–17.

99. Comparing Kluge's work to Weiss's *Ästhetik*, Jens Birkmeyer writes that Kluge fosters a "remembrance of those emotions and affects that stand in relation to events in such a way that this emotional memory can generate points of reference to stabilize traditions, pass on experiences and describe identities" across *Chronik der Gefühle*'s disparate universe of stories. See Birkmeyer, "Eigensinn und Anerkennung: Anthropologische Phantasie bei Alexander Kluge und Peter Weiss," in *Diese bebende, zähe, kühne Hoffnung*, 130.

100. Rajewsky, "Intermediality, Intertextuality, and Remediation," 51.

101. Rajewsky, "Intermediality, Intertextuality, and Remediation," 52–53.

102. Herbert Claas, "Ein Freund nicht, doch ein Lehrer: Brecht in der 'Ästhetik des Widerstands,'" in Götze and Scherpe, *"Die Ästhetik des Widerstands" lesen*, 146.

103. In conversation with Weiss, Lindner noted Brecht's tendency during exile to seek out source material from the countries of his stays ("Between Pergamon and Plötzensee," 111). In fact, the narrator's work on the Engelbrekt drama not only leads to his articulating an increased feeling of "belonging" in Sweden (*ÄdW* 2:255); it also prompts the extensive report on the history of Swedish social democracy delivered by Rogeby and Ström, with which the narrator's remediation of Engelbrekt is interspersed. One can readily surmise that Engelbrekt is for World War II what the recapitulation of the debates between the communist Rogeby and the social democrat Ström is for Weiss's orientation in the Cold War.

104. Jost Hermand, "The Super-Father: Brecht in *Die Ästhetik des Widerstands*," *Communications from the International Brecht Society* 13 (1984): 3–12.

105. Gudrun Klatt, "Korrespondenz und Widerspruch—Brecht bei Peter Weiss," in Krenzlin, *"Ästhetik des Widerstands,"* 145.

106. Mandel, *Formen und Funktionen von Intertextualität und Intermedialität*, 451.

107. Metscher highlights this ending as an admirable piece of Marxist historiography in *Der Friedensgedanke in der europäischen Literatur*, 182.

108. Mandel, *Formen und Funktionen von Intertextualität und Intermedialität*, 456; Cohen, *Versuche über Weiss' "Ästhetik des Widerstands,"* 202.

109. Metscher, *Der Friedensgedanke in der europäischen Literatur*, 191.

110. In their article "'Kein Roman überhaupt'??," Claßen and Vogt make a case for the cinematic character of *Die Ästhetik*'s presentational techniques.

111. Claßen and Vogt, "'Kein Roman überhaupt'??," 152. While Weiss's techniques evoke aspects of Brechtian stagecraft as well as film, most important are the effects of montage's literary mobilization. Remediation highlights both intermedial reference to a film technique such as montage as well as the task of mediation in the sense of *Vermittlung*.

112. "Ich montiere," Weiss cites Brecht in the *Notizbücher* (*NB* 506), an activity Gerlach ascribes to the function of *Die Ästhetik*'s narrator as an "Arrangeur," in *Die ferne Utopie*, 125.

113. As noted above, in "Hallucinatory Realism," 133, Lindner focuses on the blurring of the distinction between the narrator's work and that of the author.

114. Another assertion of continuity concerns Brecht's last request for a change in the draft at the end of the chapter: the members of the Swedish noble family *Natt och Dag*—Engelbrekt's adversaries, including the nemesis who kills him, Måns Bengtsson—were to be called *Nacht und Tag*, thereby connecting to the present via the Germanization of the drama (*ÄdW* 2:255). The narrator follows through on this at *ÄdW* 2:308.

115. Brecht's elaboration of the "Näherrücken weitläufiger Zusammenhänge" would make formidable demands on any theater set design, a constraint to which Weiss's remediation of the drama in prose is not subject (cf. *ÄdW* 2:251).

116. On direct and indirect senses (*Nähesinne* and *Fernsinne*), see the preceding chapter. In Weiss, these also come together as a *Spürsinn*, a sense for traces of "reality's monstrous sprawl" (*ÄdW* 1:341; *Wuchern*; see also *ÄdW* 1:128).

117. Lindner, "Déjà-vu im Zeitriss," 84.

118. *Die Ästhetik* recurrently criticizes the Left's insufficient imagination in the political arena, in particular with regard to its appraisal of the enemy, e.g., "in the inability of the human being to imagine his own extermination fascism founds its presupposition" (*ÄdW* 2:118). Münzenberg's emphasis on the antifascist struggle's ideological dimensions (*AoR* 144/*ÄdW* 1:167) costs him rebuke from a party that believes he is overestimating the power of fascist propaganda and demagoguery (*ÄdW* 2:126).

119. Benjamin, "The Storyteller," 94.

120. On the concept of *Raffung* in narrative prose, see Vogt, *Aspekte erzählender Prosa*, 109–117.

121. Benjamin, "The Storyteller," 96.

122. Weiss in Lindner, "Between Pergamon and Plötzensee," 117.

123. For more detail on this scene in relation to *Die Ästhetik*'s gendering scheme, see Hell, "Rosa oder die Sehnsucht nach einer Geschichte ohne Stalin," 148.

124. With the exception of the final two chapters, the narrator is neither present nor marked as a mediator in the third volume's second half, having receded behind the tale entirely. Of course, all that we read is attributable to his implicit role as the author of the whole, as is evident from the retention of third person narration in Bischoff's chapters.

125. On Bischoff's role in *Die Ästhetik*, see also Briegleb, "Widerstand als tätige Erinnerung."

126. Hell's argument, in "Rosa oder die Sehnsucht nach einer Geschichte ohne Stalin," regarding *Die Ästhetik*'s inability to break free of this abjecting logic therefore focuses more on Libertas Schulze-Boysen than on Bischoff.

127. Both the narrator and Bischoff emphasize the importance of naming the many antifascist resistance fighters, bestowing meaning to the names, and thereby giving them voice (*ÄdW* 3:236, 265–266). Between Weiss's *Ästhetik* and Johnson's *Jahrestage* there is an overlap in the literary politics of naming: in neither do perpetrators of crimes against humanity and other political foes earn such a right (cf. *JT* 1874).

128. Bischoff's project merges with Hodann as well as the narrator's insistence on the need to come to terms with the past, as articulated at *ÄdW* 3:259–260. The polyphonic nature of this charge continues the centrifugal tendencies of *Die Ästhetik*'s concluding chapters.

129. A parallel contextualization delivered in *Jahrestage* concerns the compass of Gesine's *New York Times*, which places news from Germany in the "proper relationship to world news: a minor one" (*AN* 55/*JT* 74).

130. The political activist noticeably treats space as neutral, whereas the emigrant suffers its manifold complexities. Later on in Paris, the narrator "refrains from" challenging Hodann's dread of deracination on the eve of his departure for Norway, which indicates a repression of emigration's effects on political activism on the part of both characters (*ÄdW* 2:71).

131. Rector, "Örtlichkeit und Phantasie," 128.

132. Metscher, *Der Friedensgedanke in der europäischen Literatur*, 188.

133. In "Über die notwendige Pluralität künstlerischer Formen," 1639–1640, 1646, Metscher derives "the organic narrative structure (the coherence of narration) as a basic principle of the composition of epic form" from traditional realism and demonstrates its relevance for the modern epic also.

Chapter 3

The epigraphs for this chapter's sections are from Walter Benjamin, "The Crisis of the Novel," 299; *AN* 169/*JT* 256; *AN* 435, translation modified/*JT* 668; *AN* 417, translation modified/*JT* 643; *AN* 342/*JT* 524; *AN II*, 159/*JT* 1029–1030; *AN II*, 95/*JT* 925; *JT* 913; and Johnson in Jürgen Becker, Rolf Michaelis, and Heinrich Vormweg, "Gespräch mit Uwe Johnson," in Fahlke, *"Ich überlege mir die Geschichte,"* 305.

1. Theodor W. Adorno, "On Epic Naiveté," in *Notes to Literature*, 1:24.

2. Adorno, "On Epic Naiveté," 24.

3. Adorno, "On Epic Naiveté," 25–26.

4. Adorno, "On Epic Naiveté," 27–29. For a fuller discussion of Uwe Johnson's modernist realism in this theoretical context, see Christa Bürger, "Uwe Johnson: Der Erzähler," in Peter Bürger, *Prosa der Moderne*, with Christa Bürger (Frankfurt am Main: Suhrkamp Verlag, 1988), 353–382.

5. See Horkheimer and Adorno, *Dialectic of Enlightenment*, 12–34.

6. See Hofmann's reference to first receptions in "*Ästhetik des Widerstands* und *Jahrestage*: Ansatzpunkte für einen Vergleich," in *Uwe Johnson zwischen Vormoderne und Postmoderne*, 190; Gerlach, *Die ferne Utopie*, 163–164; Heinrich Vormweg, "Uwe Johnson: Bestandsaufnahmen vom Lauf der Welt," in *Zeitkritische Romane des 20. Jahrhunderts: Die Gesellschaft in der Kritik der deutschen Literatur*, ed. Hans Wagener (Stuttgart: Philipp Reclam jun., 1975), especially 375–380.

7. Bernd Neumann, *Uwe Johnson* (Hamburg: Europäische Verlagsanstalt, 1994), 835.

8. Neumann, *Uwe Johnson*, 835. While such a claim suggests that Neumann is missing the modernity of the epic and the Shoah alike, in the very same passage he emphasizes *Jahrestage*'s "contemporaneity, dualistically set against its archaic dimension," as resting in its "specific reliance on the media of its time." Gesine's story straddles the divide in question.

9. Jochen Hörisch, "Anniversaries and the Revival of Storytelling," in *A New History of German Literature*, ed. David Wellbery (Cambridge, Mass.: Belknap Press of Harvard University Press, 2004), 934. Hörisch also highlights the uses of temporal artifice in these two modern epics: "Whereas Joyce compresses the entire complex extent of world history into an everyday microcosm of twenty-four hours, Johnson divides the weight of the world, as it were, and spreads it over 366 days."

10. Gerlach's passage reads, "Wenn Jerichow . . . für sie . . . zum Mythos geworden ist, hängt dies mit Gesines Identitätsverlust und ihrer offensichtlich traumatischen Fixierung auf dieses Ereignis zusammen," in *Auf der Suche nach der verlorenen Identität*, 40. My formulation echoes a line from Horkheimer and Adorno's reading of the *Odyssey* in *Dialectic of Enlightenment,* 25.

11. Mecklenburg, "Großstadtmontage und Provinzchronik," 197. See also Ulrich Fries, *Uwe Johnsons "Jahrestage": Erzählstruktur und politische Subjektivität* (Göttingen: Vandenhoeck & Ruprecht, 1990), 151, 167, who confirms Mecklenburg's claim, and D. G. Bond, *German History and German Identity: Uwe Johnson's "Jahrestage"* (Atlanta: Rodopi, 1993), 15–16.

12. Mecklenburg, "Großstadtmontage und Provinzchronik," 197.

13. See Baker, following Neumann, in *Understanding Uwe Johnson*, 121–122.

14. Adorno, "On Epic Naiveté," 24.

15. A hallmark of his poetics, Johnson first delivered his programmatic account of literary exactitude in "Berliner Stadtbahn (*veraltet*)."

16. Baker, *Understanding Uwe Johnson*, 121.

17. Neumann, *Uwe Johnson*, 779.

18. Neumann, *Uwe Johnson*, 837.

19. Schnell, *Die Literatur der Bundesrepublik*, 354.

20. See Severin Strasky's reference to Johnson's distinction between rivers and seas in "So klares Wasser habe ich nie wieder gesehen: Aspekte der Wassersymbolik in Uwe Johnsons *Jahrestage: Aus dem Leben der Gesine Cresspahl*," *Johnson-Jahrbuch* 11 (2004): 117–149, 118.

21. For a more detailed account of water's narrative functions and a fuller substantiation of *Jahrestage*'s hydropoetics in reference to the relevant scholarship, see my article "An Epic's Hydropoetics: On the Waters of Uwe Johnson's *Jahrestage*," forthcoming in *Germanic Review*.

22. See Gerlach, *Auf der Suche nach der verlorenen Identität*, 30–35, and Fries, "Tod und Struktur," in his *Uwe Johnsons "Jahrestage,"* 77–95, for the analysis of relevant examples.

23. Johnson highlights his one-year contract with conarrator Gesine as the foundation of *Jahrestage* at *JT* 1426–1427 and in the fictional interview "Marie H. Cresspahl, 2.–3. Januar 1972," in Fahlke, *"Ich überlege mir die Geschichte,"* 108. In *Uwe Johnsons "Jahrestage,"* Fries codifies this distinction between the chronological and calendrical in terms of the diachronic and synchronic dimensions of the work, 78.

24. See Johnson, "Einführung in die *Jahrestage*," in *Johnsons "Jahrestage,"* ed. Michael Bengel (Frankfurt am Main: Suhrkamp Verlag, 1985), 15, 25; Johnson in "'Ein verkannter Humorist': Gespräch mit A. Leslie Willson," in Fahlke, *"Ich überlege mir die Geschichte,"* 291; and Johnson, "Brief an Siegfried Unseld vom 25. März 1971," in Eberhard Fahlke, *"Die Katze Erinnerung": Uwe Johnson—Eine Chronik in Briefen und Bildern* (Frankfurt am Main: Suhrkamp Verlag, 1994), 235. As Thomas Schmidt has underscored in *Der Kalender und die Folgen: Uwe Johnsons Roman "Jahrestage": Ein Beitrag zum Problem des kollektiven Gedächtnisses* (Göttingen: Vandenhoeck und Ruprecht, 2000), Johnson's procedure eschews any investment in the official management of memory by way of instituted anniversaries, 213. Moreover, in "Naive Lektüre und Kanonformation: Über den wichtigsten Satz in Jahrestage," *Johnson-Jahrbuch* 22 (2015): 215–234, Holger Helbig analyzes the November 12 chapter (*JT* 286–287) to emphasize the principal equality of each of Johnson's days of the year for memory.

25. Cf. Bond, *German History and German Identity*, 87–128. Schmidt's *Der Kalender und die Folgen* delivers the fullest and most meticulous analysis of *Jahrestage*'s calendrical principle, setting it in relation to the Jewish calendar.

26. Johnson, "Einführung in die *Jahrestage*," 25–26.

27. Bond, *German History and German Identity*, 76.

28. See, e.g., Johnson in Dieter E. Zimmer, "Eine Bewußtseinsinventur: Das Gespräch mit dem Autor: Uwe Johnson," in Bengel, *Uwe Johnsons "Jahrestage,"* 101.

29. Cf. Bond, *German History and German Identity*, 98; Mecklenburg, *Die Erzählkunst*, 255–263. In the expanse of the framework into which Gesine's biographical story is set, *Jahrestage* clearly invites readers into the heterodiegetic

depths of history beyond its autodiegetic narrator's purview and judgments. The very necessity for and use of *Jahrestage*'s *Kommentar*, confirms the work's emphatic porosity to reality, especially those references there which lead not back into Gesine's fictional world, the interconnections of which are presented in Michaelis's *Kleines Adressbuch* and Lohmeier's digitalization thereof at http://literaturlexikon.uni-saarland.de/index.php?id=191, accessed July 1, 2016.

30. See Cohen, *Versuche über Weiss' "Ästhetik des Widerstands,"* 87–107; Mecklenburg, *Die Erzählkunst*, 290.

31. Mecklenburg, *Die Erzählkunst*, 281, see also 344.

32. Cf. Mecklenburg, "Großstadtmontage und Provinzchronik," 192–195, and *Die Erzählkunst*, 276–281, as well as Gerlach, *Auf der Suche nach der verlorenen Identität*, 139–150.

33. Johnson in Martin Meyer and Wolfgang Strehlow, "'Das sagt mir auch mein Friseur': Film- und Fersehäußerungen von Uwe Johnson," *Sprache im technischen Zeitalter* 95 (1985): 170–183, here 179.

34. Strasky, "So klares Wasser," 149.

35. Mecklenburg, "Großstadtmontage und Provinzchronik," 189–190.

36. Cf. Bond, *German History and German Identity*, 119.

37. D. G. Bond, "Two Ships: Correspondences between Uwe Johnson and Johann Peter Hebel," *German Quarterly* 64, no. 3 (1991): 313–324, here 315.

38. I lift this phrase from György Lukács, *History and Class Consciousness: Studies in Marxist Dialectics*, trans. Rodney Livingstone (Cambridge, Mass.: MIT Press, 1971), 166.

39. Bond's iconoclastic reading of *Jahrestage* anticipates the conception of linear temporality's implosion—and with it the tenability of epic integration—operative in Kluge's *Chronik der Gefühle*.

40. I apply Gerlach's claim about the narrator of *Die Ästhetik des Widerstands* in *Die ferne Utopie* (39) to allude to the comparison of Weiss and Johnson's epics developed below.

41. Mecklenburg, "Großstadtmontage und Provinzchronik," 186.

42. Mecklenburg, *Die Erzählkunst*, 239. Mecklenburg places the German word, which points to the network-character of Gesine's narration, in quotation marks.

43. Christoph Brecht, "'You could say it was done with mirrors': Erzählen und Erzähltes in Uwe Johnsons *Jahrestage*," *Johnson-Jahrbuch* 1 (1994): 95–126, here 103–104.

44. "Characters" would be subject to the writer's authority over the fiction, hence Johnson's preference for the latter term. See Johnson in Christoph Schmid, "Gespräch mit Uwe Johnson," in Fahlke, *"Ich überlege mir die Geschichte,"* 253.

45. Jacob Grimm und Wilhelm Grimm, *Deutsches Wörterbuch*, http://woerterbuchnetz.de/DWB/?sigle=DWB&mode=Vernetzung&lemid=GP01991, accessed July 30, 2016.

46. At times skeptical of Gesine's possibly "nontransferable" tales (*AN* 323/*JT* 492), Marie asks why her mother could not "understand that her code, while it had been accepted, was only possible in the other language and not translatable into either thought or action?" (*AN II*, 157/*JT* 1025).

47. "Moral Switzerland" is Gesine's dubious moniker for such a realm (*AN* 251/*JT* 382).

48. In its traverse of the human social experiment that is New York City, *Jahrestage* grapples sensitively with race, class, and gender relations amid the myriad social challenges afflicting the metropolis during Johnson's year. Some instances thereof are closely associated with Gesine, as in her reflection of the translational difficulties bearing on her and Marie's interaction with the latter's African American classmate Francine (*JT* 734). Others stand out on their own, such as the January 5 chapter on the late African American poet then known as LeRoi Jones (*JT* 551–554) or the March 9 chapter on Manhattan's slums (*AN II*, 49–53/*JT* 842–847).

49. By March, Marie will know "more precisely who she is, because her background [*Herkunft*]" will have been "made clear to her" (*AN II*, 30, translation modified/*JT* 817).

50. Marie is quite interested in the behaviors and decisions of Gesine's large ensemble of Jerichow characters. The first significant act of resistance is found there during the attempted Kapp-Putsch of 1920, in the context of which a fourteen-year-old Lisbeth Papenbrock reveals, in Low German, the location of weapons and ammunition to workers who have descended on the family estate looking for them (*AN* 42/*JT* 57). As Fries has suggestively put it, *Jahrestage* contains "not the history, but stories of resistance" in great number, which he begins to itemize in *Uwe Johnsons "Jahrestage,"* 141.

51. The arch stretching from Gesine's approach to storytelling and the epic's final appeal to history as a draft is important to keep in mind given critiques of the pessimistic, deterministic or even fatalistic logic of Johnson's epic. As Mecklenburg has underscored in development of Gerlach's observations, the crux of *Jahrestage*'s situational analyses of history consists in the book's tendency to emphasize equally the "'systematic character of social injustice'" and the irreducibility of "individual responsibility." The materialist and existentialist approaches form an aporetic relationship, but more so as part of its investigation, rather than any ahistorical or preestablished determinism. See Mecklenburg, *Die Erzählkunst*, 298–299. For a closer reading of the cited passage on history as *Entwurf* as well as the other resonances of *Entwurf* in *Jahrestage*, see Holger Helbig, "Last and Final: Über das Ende der 'Jahrestage,'" http://www.germanistik.uni-rostock.de/forschung/uwe-johnson/last-and-final/, accessed October 1, 2015.

52. Musil's epic proceeded by having its protagonist Ulrich juxtapose a sense of possibility to the dominant sense of reality. See *The Man without Qualities*, trans. Sophie Wilkins (New York: Alfred A. Knopf, 1995), 10–13.

53. On this score, *Jahrestage* may be regarded as a continuation of Johnson's investigative, truth-seeking literature (*Wahrheitsfindung*) as articulated in his essay "Berliner Stadtbahn (*veraltet*)," 21.

54. A common feature of the modern epic postcatastrophe, the staging of dialogue in Weiss, Johnson, and Kluge's works often models the communication they wish to initiate among their recipients. Marie's role in *Jahrestage*'s frame narrative as the primary addressee of Gesine's stories can be instructive, but does not exactly constitute an act to be followed. Each recipient, like each of *Jahrestage*'s characters, will come to storytelling from historically and subjectively specific points of departure, with different expectations and needs. Cf. Colin Riordan, *The Ethics of Narration: Uwe Johnson's Novels from "Ingrid Babendererde" to "Jahrestage"* (London: Modern Humanities Research Association for the Institute of Germanic Studies, University of London, 1989), 161–214.

55. This is particularly evident in allusions to tape recordings in the January 12 and 14 chapters: on the latter date, readers are given to understand that Marie plays a voice recording of her mother's storytelling back to her to reinitiate the difficult narration of her father's friend Arthur Semig's persecution in Nazi Jerichow (see *AN* 379, 382/*JT* 581, 589).

56. That the latter claim has become uncontroversial does not detract from the importance of Marie in the *Jahrestage* as a whole, as Riordan's *The Ethics of Narration* has made clear.

57. *BU* 425; Johnson in Becker, Michaelis, and Vormweg, "Gespräch mit Uwe Johnson," 307.

58. Johnson in Becker, Michaelis, and Vormweg, "Gespräch mit Uwe Johnson," 305.

59. Johnson described his contract with Gesine as "Gemeinschaftsarbeit" in an interview with the Norddeutscher Rundfunk, November 14, 1970, on display at the Uwe Johnson Literaturhaus, Klütz (viewed June 9, 2016). *Jahrestage* also depicts the subject of the GDR's national anthem in a related way as the "curious resolution of a multiple subject, a we" (*JT* 1629).

60. While *Vertrag* is largely absent from Weiss and Kluge's works, *Vertrauen* provides for the cohesiveness of *Die Ästhetik*'s collective, at least on Bischoff's account (*ÄdW* 3:223), and is raised in Kluge's *Chronik* to well-nigh mythic proportions. In *Jahrestage*, on the other hand, a skeptical Gesine cannot presume trust, but remains in search of whom and what she can trust, as indicated by her careful attention to the presentation of trust's conditions in her translation of "Manifest of 2000 Words" from Prague (*JT* 1446–1447).

61. See, e.g., *JT* 1578, *AN II*, 475/1650. *Sich vertragen* is also more personable than derivatives of the English word "contract." And as with "person," the term's perceptibly bourgeois provenance does not constitute a problem in Johnson's world: the Countess Seydlitz reminds Gesine that she may err in censuring bourgeois traditions that have been abused, but are in fact humanly necessary (*JT* 75). Related to the book's appeals to an alliance between mother and daughter (*AN II*, 157/*JT* 1025; *Bündnis*), contract goes hand in hand with the discourse of rights underlying *Jahrestage*'s critique of social injustices. See, e.g., *AN II*, 156/*JT* 1024.

62. Cresspahl did also not consider himself in any contract with the GDR (*AN II*, 595/*JT* 1829). Such emphasis clearly relates to Gesine's own appeals to binding constitutions in the U.S. and ČSSR (see *AN* 448, *AN II*, 31/*JT* 690, 818).

63. Given the recurring materialist dimensions of social critique in *Jahrestage*, it is likely that, as Gesine herself believed, the concept of a social contract could be better upheld in a different social order. But this is famously another page, and one from beyond those contracted by *Jahrestage*'s arrangement, which ends precipitously on August 20, 1968, with the Soviet suppression of Prague's Spring.

64. The sharpest encounter between the fictional Cresspahl and "Johnson the writer" occurs in the November 3 chapter, which reconstructs Johnson's prior appearance before the "Jewish American Congress" and where he and Cresspahl enter into a struggle for the control of *Jahrestage*'s narrative (*AN* 167–170/*JT* 253–258). Johnson clearly relies there on his fictional counterpart to process his own frustration with his failed conduct at the earlier event.

65. Johnson in Becker, Michaelis, and Vormweg, "Gespräch mit Uwe Johnson," 306.

66. See chapter 2's related discussion of *Die Ästhetik des Widerstands* as a work of "transcendental literature" in the sense described by Hofmann.

67. That Johnson took this obligation to himself and his readers seriously is evident from his public comments regarding *Jahrestage*'s delayed completion. See Johnson in Becker, Michaelis, and Vormweg, "Gespräch mit Uwe Johnson," 312; *BU* 451–453. And in a letter to the Suhrkamp Verlag on April 17, 1983, Johnson declared, "Thank God it's over" (cited in Leuchtenberger, *Uwe Johnson*, 68).

68. Weiss, *NB* 872. Johnson's copy is catalogued as UJA BP 02224-2.

69. Johnson cites this account from the March 19, 1973, edition of *Der Spiegel* in *BU*, 440.

70. For a differentiation of the respective foci that accompany the contrast in this symbolism, see Rector, "Wahrnehmung und Erinnerung," especially 95–96.

71. For more on this trajectory of the epic, see Gerlach, *Auf der Suche nach der verlorenen Identität*, 30–35; Fries, *Uwe Johnsons "Jahrestage,"* 161ff.; and Mecklenburg, *Die Erzählkunst*, 301–317.

72. For a review of issues at stake in Johnson's relationship to Gesine as a woman, see Mecklenburg, *Die Erzählkunst* and the references there, 224–228. For a tough, yet narratively restrained approach to sexual violence on the Upper West Side, see the January 2 chapter from the women's sauna at the Hotel Marseilles Mediterranean Swimming Club (*JT* 541–543).

73. Schnell, *Die Literatur der Bundesrepublik*, 356–357.

74. Gesine's embedded consciousness resembles the "für-sich" quality of Weiss's autodiegetic narrator. In contrast, however, to Weiss's implied heterodiegetic narrator, whose achievement surmounts a greater knowledge in the execution of his tale, *Jahrestage*'s Comrade Writer commands—despite actual authorial omniscience and the complete orchestration of Gesine's storytelling—no transcendence and no final proposition as to the world's course. In this regard, Johnson's emphasis of his protagonist's independence is no alibi for Johnson himself, nor a prolongation of the illusion of his fictional contract with his autodiegetic narrator, but rather a persuasive and sincere concession, on Johnson's part, to the weight of reality that *Jahrestage* cannot defy.

75. Erstwhile SPD member Heinrich Cresspahl entertains loose connections to the underground political opposition and becomes a spy for Great Britain during the war (*AN II*, 24ff./*JT* 809ff.). The political subplot of *Jahrestage*'s sympathetic critique of the Left—and Heinrich Cresspahl's standing for the whole plight of the German working class—carries enough weight and nuance to warrant comparison with the critical renewal of leftist politics undertaken by Weiss's *Ästhetik*.

76. See Mecklenburg, "Großstadtmontage und Provinzchronik," 184–185, for a synopsis of "Sehen" as a key concept of the work. The significance of the problematic in question can be gleaned from the relatively independent chapter on Heinrich Cresspahl's English friend Mr. Smith's hypothetical visit to Jerichow in 1938. Delivered entirely in the subjunctive case, the chapter's narrative wave consists in variations on the question "Would he have noticed . . . ?" (*AN* 422–426/*JT* 652–657).

77. For comparisons of *Jahrestage* to Proust's *À la recherche du temps perdu*, see C. Bürger, "Uwe Johnson: Der Erzähler," 370; Günter Butzer, "'Ja. Nein.' Paradoxes Eingedenken in Uwe Johnsons Roman *Jahrestage*," *Johnson-Jahrbuch* 4 (1997): 130–157.

78. Both *Die Ästhetik des Widerstands* and *Jahrestage* register the cacophony of the Nazi dictatorship as a veritable auditory flood (cf. e.g., *AoR* 11/*ÄdW* 1:15; *AN* 136/*JT* 202), an aspect of the modern epic's synaesthetics warranting further investigation.

79. Cresspahl has only the "people's receiver" and listens to the BBC illegally with his brother-in-law Paepcke. Repeatedly highlighting the Blaupunkt radio's "magic-eye" feature (*AN II*, 44, 60/*JT* 835, 860, see also the "Mit den Augen Cresspahls" appendix, xvii–xviii), Johnson appears to amalgamate the auditory sense to sight. The skepticism directed at the visual—whether in the films Lisbeth Cresspahl travels to Lübeck to view as if "to dull the senses" (*AN* 446/*JT* 687), the newspaper images that demand interpretative redescription from the beginning (*AN* 10/*JT* 15), or Gesine's opposition to owning a television (*JT* 938, 1026)—underscores how much the epic translates perceptual seeing into a more metaphoric and mediated usage of sight (hindsight, insight, foresight). Prompting Marie's resistance to the prohibition of television (*AN II*, 298/*JT* 1302), the assassination of Robert F. Kennedy also provides an occasion for a thorough analysis of the media spectacle of his funeral (*AN II*, 303–311/*JT* 1317–1327).

80. In its cultivation of epic senses, *Jahrestage* clearly works up what Negt and Kluge have conceptualized as direct and indirect senses, as discussed in chapter 1.

81. Schnell, *Die Literatur der Bundesrepublik*, 352.

82. See Bond, *German History and German Identity*, 140; Sara Lennox, "Die *New York Times* in Johnsons *Jahrestagen*," in *Die USA und Deutschland: Wechselseitige Spiegelungen in der Literatur der Gegenwart*, ed. Wolfgang Paulsen (Munich: Francke, 1976), 103–109.

83. See *BU* 413 and Johnson in Zimmer, "Eine Bewußtseinsinventur," 100, where the author describes the paper as providing Gesine with a "mediation with the world," in an unusual formulation.

84. Deborah Horzen, "Fitting the News to the Novel: Uwe Johnson's Use of *The New York Times* in *Jahrestage*," *Johnson-Jahrbuch* 6 (1999): 183–207. As she argues in her close analysis of the August 21 chapter's complex intertextuality, "such summarization and cross-referencing belies the impression of a quick read on the way to work" (201).

85. Horzen, "Fitting the News to the Novel," 191.

86. Horzen, "Fitting the News to the Novel," 207.

87. Horzen highlights the former, but not in connection to the latter, see "Fitting the News to the Novel," 202. *Jahrestage*'s critique of the paper's mediating practices indicates the criterion to which Johnson's own book must be held. As van Laak has framed the matter in an essay on Johnson's epic as a medial relationship to the world, *Jahrestage* is concerned with mediality in the form of a literaricity that narrates its own medial character. See van Laak, "Johnsons Beschäftigung mit den Medien," 317, 329.

88. *DerKommentar*, http://www.philfak.uni-rostock.de/institut/igerman/johnson/johnkomm/6709/670904.html, accessed July 30, 2016.

89. Cf. Horzen, "Fitting the News to the Novel," 206.

90. Gesine and her writer regularly wield and interrelate the distinctions true vs. false and credible vs. incredible as criteria for mediations of the past and present alike to ensure their tenability, e.g., *AN* 37, 163–164, 417; *AN II*, 147, *AN II*,

307, 316–317, 525, 535/*JT* 51, 250, 643, 1003, 1107, 1321, 1333–1334, 1721, 1733. On Groundhog Day, moreover, Gesine reminds Marie that she has not promised the truth, but rather stories oriented to truth (*AN* 436/*JT* 670). Finally, Gesine's skepticism is no reflex, but rather stems from the German school lessons on Theodor Fontane with Matthias Weserich that provided the foundation for careful reading in one of the epic's most remarkable chapters (*AN II*, 504–516/ *JT* 1694–1707). Careful reading can also be observed in *Jahrestage*'s approach to surface phenomena across New York City. Even where they seem a mere play of arbitrary signs divorced from any historical semantics, as argued by Oliver Simons, "Uwe Johnsons 'New York': Die *Jahrestage* als Amerikatext," *Johnson-Jahrbuch* 22 (2015): 195–213, Johnson's genealogical procedure restores to the Riverside apartment building (*JT* 548–551), Manhattan's slums (*AN II*, 49–53/ *JT* 842–847), and Riverside Park's "originary landscape" (*JT* 1189) the history of their becoming.

91. For the original English, see the *Kommentar*'s citation of the *Times* article, http://www.philfak.uni-rostock.de/institut/igerman/johnson/johnkomm/6801 /680127.html, accessed July 30, 2016.

92. The humor of Johnson's chapter is more sardonic and of a different order than the style of the *Times* article.

93. Eva Schauerte, "Uwe Johnson und die *New York Times*: Ansätze einer Archivologie der *Jahrestage*," *Johnson-Jahrbuch* 19 (2012): 140–159.

94. Schauerte, "Uwe Johnson und die *New York Times*," 154: *Haltbarmachung*; 159.

95. Schauerte, "Uwe Johnson und die *New York Times*," 156–159.

96. D. E.'s presence in and around Gesine's stories stands out as odd amid *Jahrestage*'s large dramatis personae. Much mystery lingers about his actual activities as a physicist working for the U.S. "war industry. D. E. says: 'I work in Defense'" (*AN* 29/*JT* 41), about which Gesine demands more information (*JT* 866). Cresspahl's delay in settling down more formally with D. E.—the option never materializes due to his premature death—tends to present the relationship as a piece of the resignation she seeks to avoid. See her privileging of Prague at *AN* 443/*JT* 683 vs. Marie's wishful rendering of D. E. and Gesine's agreement at *JT* 1591.

97. Schauerte, "Uwe Johnson und die *New York Times*," 151. See also Baker, *Understanding Uwe Johnson*, 132–133.

98. Holger Helbig, "Vom Material zum Roman: Zitieren und Erzählen in Uwe Johnsons 'Jahrestage,'" in "Uwe Johnson," special issue, *Text + Kritik* 65/66 (2001): 149–169, 155, 160.

99. Helbig, "Vom Material zum Roman," 164.

100. These spaces contrast with the many props therein, one category of which—the recurring coffins—are containers for death. See Christoph Brecht's note, in "'You could say it was done with mirrors,'" 122, on *Jahrestage*'s coffins, suitcases, and wooden boxes.

101. Where Immanuel Kant had erected a universal architecture for reason in philosophy, *Jahrestage* undertakes in literature a singular architecture for living. See Kant, *Critique of Pure Reason: Unified Edition*, trans. Werner S. Pluhar (Indianapolis: Hackett, 1996), 663–664 (A705/B 733–A 708/B736).

102. See *JT* 1861: "Heimweh. Ich versteh immer Bahnhof." Omitted from the abridged translation, the line turns on the German expression "to understand only 'train station,'" where train station designates the one phrase from Europe's foreign languages one needs to know in order to travel home. The idiom has been codified as an expression of incomprehension. As homesickness has come to mean *Bahnhof* for a life in transit, translator Gesine pursues the materialization of the expression to discuss her memories of train stations.

103. "A. M." is none other than the Frankfurt psychoanalyst Alexander Mitscherlich, author, with wife and colleague Margarete Mitscherlich-Nielsen, of the 1967 study *The Inability to Mourn*.

104. The terms of the future judgment laid out by Gesine here correspond to Heilmann and Bischof's scale for the past's evaluation in Weiss's *Ästhetik* (see *ÄdW* 3:202).

105. See Mecklenburg's account thereof in *Die Erzählkunst*, 263–264.

106. For a fuller account of *Jahrestage*'s reliance on the chronicle form, see Bond, "Two Ships," especially 318. As Mecklenburg has highlighted in *Die Erzählkunst* however, Johnson's "non-archaic" chronicling refrains from predications on the world's course, 250.

107. For a more thorough consideration of montage as a seminal way in which past and present meet in *Jahrestage*, including a more explicit delineation of its Benjaminian underpinnings and its effects on readers, see Baker, *Understanding Uwe Johnson*, 129–134.

108. For related diagnoses, see Gerlach, *Auf der Suche nach der verlorenen Identität*, 112; Fries, *Uwe Johnsons "Jahrestage,"* 134–135; Mecklenburg, *Die Erzählkunst*, 300.

109. For an account of *Jahrestage*'s anchoring of utopia in real possibilities, see Gary L. Baker, "(Anti-)Utopian Elements in Uwe Johnson's *Jahrestage*: Traces of Ernst Bloch," *Germanic Review* 68 (1993): 32–45.

110. Greg Bond, "Veraltet? Die Beschäftigung mit Uwe Johnson heute," in "Uwe Johnson," special issue, *Text + Kritik* 65/66 (2001): 3–19.

111. Bond, "Veraltet? Die Beschäftigung mit Uwe Johnson heute," 17.

112. Horst Turk, "Europäische Konstellationen: Zur Aktualität Uwe Johnsons," in Fries et al., *So noch nicht gezeigt*, 359.

113. Turk, "Europäische Konstellationen," 359–360.

114. *Jahrestage*'s implicit genealogy of the global present contributes to the kind of "critical globalization studies" outlined by Denning in *Culture in the Age of Three Worlds*, 27.

115. In terms of the coordinates with which Negt and Kluge's supplement Brecht's function-oriented conception of reality, Gesine's orientation to Prague is clearly driven by functional and revolutionary forces as well as an element of irrational protest (*HO* 237–240/*DuM* 2:511–515). Whether the unity thereof is merely imaginary on Gesine's part is debatable.

116. Johnson in Becker, Michaelis, and Vormweg, "Gespräch mit Uwe Johnson," 309.

117. Johnson unpretentiously describes the socialist alternative as "bedenkenswert" (worthy of consideration, thought-provoking) in Becker, Michaelis, and Vormweg, "Gespräch mit Uwe Johnson," 309.

118. Norbert Mecklenburg, "Ein Stück Herkunft, kenntlich gemacht: Realismus und Regionalismus in Uwe Johnsons *Jahrestagen*," in Bengel, *Johnsons "Jahrestage,"* 247.

119. Baker, "(Anti-)Utopian Elements," 34.

120. Baker, "(Anti-)Utopian Elements," 33, 34–38.

121. Examples of such controversion include the Soviet administration's apparent preservation of property and failure to transform the relations of production into any democratic socialist arrangement (*AN II*, 325–331/*JT* 1351–1356), the disassembly of entire industries and transport of labor power into the Soviet Union (*AN II*, 364–368/*JT* 1416–1420), and Cresspahl's mysterious incarceration at Fünfeichen, a former internment camp detailed in one of the epic's most harrowing chapters (*AN II*, 281–295/*JT* 1281–1298).

122. Cf. Baker, *Understanding Uwe Johnson*, 143–144.

123. Contrast the political semantics of democratization and humanization embraced by the Prague reformers, e.g., at *JT* 1440–1441, with the skepticism Gesine's relatives' direct at such vocabulary as "thoroughly worn out shoes" at *JT* 620, a tension found in reflections on the discourse of humanity and humanization in Weiss's *Ästhetik* as well.

124. Baker, "(Anti-)Utopian Elements," 42.

125. See Bond, *German History and German Identity*, 58–71.

126. This reconstruction draws on *Jahrestage*'s own language as well as Negt and Kluge's discussion of the irrational, imaginary, and revolutionary dimensions of reality to parse out the different aspects of Gesine's orientation to socialism and its possible futures. As Baker outlines in "(Anti-)Utopian Elements," the imaginary components of Gesine's fantasy consist in those aspects of the work that tend to stand outside or at the margins of its realistic world, e.g., Marie's Cydamonoe, Gesine's daydream excursions through time and space, but also, to an extent, the elusive Jakob (42–43). They are inflected by a loss of reality and objectivity Negt and Kluge ascribe to the imaginary (*HO* 237/*DuM* 2:511). As Negt and Kluge relate, when reality's construction is foreclosed, the revolutionary "acquires the appearance of the imaginary" (*HO* 240/*DuM* 2:515), for which reason Gesine's "Bohemia-on-the-sea" (*AN II*, 95/*JT* 925) reads as an imaginary construct for a Left seeking a home (*JT* 1210; *Heimat*). The reforms proposed in the context of the Prague Spring, however, constitute the potentially revolutionary reopening of reality as a construction site. That they stand to be squashed and that Gesine's comportment therefore appears "irrational" in hindsight by no means disqualifies it; on the contrary, the irrational constitutes the dimension of protest for Negt and Kluge, "the living critique of so-called rationality" (*HO* 239/*DuM* 2:514). In *Jahrestage* such false rationality includes any too-facile rejection of socialism.

127. Sabine Fischer, "Der Prager Frühling als 'Entwurf': Politische Diskurse in Uwe Johnsons 'Jahrestagen,'" in *Internationales Uwe-Johnson-Forum: Beiträge zum Werkverständnis und Materialien zur Rezeptionsgeschichte*, ed. Carsten Gansel et al., vol. 3 (Frankfurt am Main: Peter Lang, 1994), 53–104.

128. See Fischer, "Der Prager Frühling als 'Entwurf,'" 73–77.

129. For the *New York Times*' English version of the party's response to the Warsaw Letter, see *Der Kommentar*, http://www.philfak.uni-rostock.de/institut/igerman/johnson/johnkomm/6807/680719.html#1579_16, accessed August 10, 2016.

130. In contrast to the retrospective critique of the party delivered in Weiss's *Ästhetik*, *Jahrestage* undertakes its critique in the narrative present, where it unfolds with less deferential and more urgent overtones as a would-be last-ditch effort to influence the course of political history.

131. Fischer, "Der Prager Frühling als 'Entwurf,' " 82.

132. For an overview, see the chapter "The End of the Affair" in Judt's *Postwar*, especially 440–445.

133. In *Geschichte und Eigensinn*, Negt and Kluge mobilize the concept of the abaric point from physics to pinpoint interstices in the gravitational pulls of historical processes (*HO* 377–378/*DuM* 2:789–790).

134. Baker, *Understanding Uwe Johnson*, 8. Cf. Bond, *German History and German Identity*, 58–71.

135. Johnson in Becker, Michaelis, and Vormweg, "Gespräch mit Uwe Johnson," 310. De Rosny's loan would offset the ČSSR's economic dependency on the USSR—see the references to wheat at *JT* 1090 and raw materials at *AN II*, 386/ *JT* 1669—and thereby undercut the latter's political domination, but exchange one form of subjection for another.

136. Bond, *German History and German Identity*, 40, 85–86; Mecklenburg, *Die Erzählkunst*, 316; Helbig, "Last and Final."

137. See Fries, *Uwe Johnsons "Jahrestage,"* 174.

138. Turk, "Europäische Konstellationen," 370.

139. Baker, "(Anti-)Utopian Elements," 33.

140. Gesine's orientation relates to what anthropologist Hirokazu Miyazaki has staked out as hope's very method. Drawing on Bloch, Miyazaki's work facilitates a "radical temporal reorientation of knowledge" devoid of its confinement to retrospection and anamnesis, elevates hope to a strategy that builds up and sustains anticipation across experiences of disappointment, and demonstrates how hope proves an exemplary way of dealing with indeterminacy in experiential and historical processes. See Miyazaki, *The Method of Hope: Anthropology, Philosophy, and Fijian Knowledge* (Stanford, Calif.: Stanford University Press, 2004), 5, 9, 27–28.

141. Helbig, "Last and Final."

142. See Baker, "(Anti-)Utopian Elements," 39, however, for an argument in this direction.

143. Burkhardt Lindner, "Spaltungen: Die Kunst und die Künste bei Peter Weiss," *Peter Weiss—Grenzgänger zwischen den Künsten. Bild-Collage-Text-Film*, ed. Jürgen Schutte et al. (Frankfurt am Main: Peter Lang, 2007), 112.

144. See also Michael Hofmann, who relates Prague to Heracles in "Das Gedächtnis des NS-Faschismus in Peter Weiss' *Ästhetik des Widerstands* und Uwe Johnsons *Jahrestagen*," *Peter Weiss Jahrbuch* 4 (1995): 54–77, here 75.

145. I borrow a felicitous formulation of Adorno's on freedom in art and cinema from his "Letters to Walter Benjamin," trans. Harry Zohn, in Adorno et al., *Aesthetics and Politics*, 133.

146. Metscher, "Über die notwendige Pluralität künstlerischer Formen," 1646.

147. Cf. Hofmann, "Das Gedächtnis des NS-Faschismus," 63.

148. "*What do we have to do with the future?*" Gesine's deceased relatives ask her on July 12, it was Marie who asked "*What is . . . lasting*? We," the voice of the dead respond (*AN II*, 421/*JT* 1541; *beständig*).

Chapter 4

The epigraphs are from Ernst Bloch, "Zur Ontologie des Noch-Nicht-Seins," in *Auswahl aus seinen Schriften*, ed. Hans Heinz Holz (Frankfurt am Main: Fischer Bücherei, 1967), 62; György Lukács, *TN* 88/77; and Alexander Kluge, *Die Macht der Gefühle* (Frankfurt am Main: Zweitausendeins, 1984), 592.

1. Cf. Kluge, *Verdeckte Ermittlung*, 15–16.

2. Schulte and Stollmann in Kluge, *Verdeckte Ermittlung*, 10. Compare the opening of the first dated chapter of Uwe Johnson's *Jahrestage*: "Clearing skies in North Vietnam enabled the Air Force to attack targets north of Hanoi. The Navy bombed the coast with aircraft and fired eight-inch shells into the demilitarized zone" (*AN* 6/*JT* 10).

3. Musil, *The Man without Qualities*, 3; Robert Musil, *Der Mann ohne Eigenschaften* (Reinbek bei Hamburg: Rowohlt Verlag, 1978), 9.

4. Musil, *The Man without Qualities*, 26. If the relationship between time and its narration still appears intact in Musil's turn of phrase, the sentence's tautology ironically marks a unity that will fray over the course of his modern epic, as discussed in the third chapter of Stefan Jonsson's *Subject without Nation: Robert Musil and the History of Modern Identity* (Durham, N.C.: Duke University Press, 2000). On prolepsis, see Genette, *Narrative Discourse*, 40, 67ff.

5. On direct and indirect senses (*Nähesinne* and *Fernsinne*), see chapter 1 above.

6. Kluge, "Rede zum Büchnerpreis-2003," http://www.kluge-alexander.de/zur-person/reden/2003-buechner-preis.html, accessed October 15, 2004.

7. Commentators have noted that time, the uncanniness, pressures, and withdrawal of which have proven long-standing themes of Kluge's narrative interest, constitutes *Chronik*'s overarching topic of investigation: "That feelings (wishes, fantasies)," writes Christian Schulte, "which develop in long time-frames, are, as a rule, overtaken and mauled by the tempo of historical time, this diagnosis belongs to the solid inventory of [Kluge's] storytelling," in "Die Lust aufs Unwahrscheinliche: Alexander Kluges 'Chronik der Gefühle,' " *Merkur: Deutsche Zeitschrift für europäisches Denken* 624 (2001), http://www.kluge-alexander.de/aktuelles/details/artikel/die-lust-aufs-unwahrscheinliche.html. In his review of *Chronik*, Wilfried F. Schoeller concurs that the "profound transformation" found in Kluge's stories concerns "the conception of what constitutes time," as he writes in "Besichtigung von Trümmerlandschaften: Zur 'Chronik der Gefühle,' " in *Maßverhältnisse des Politischen: Öffentlichkeit und Erfahrung an der Schwelle zum 21. Jahrhundert*, ed. Hans-Peter Burmeister (Rehburg-Loccum: Evangelische Akademie Loccum, 2003), 75.

8. Galileo is particularly seminal for Kluge's reckoning with enlightenment's light and dark sides in *Die Lücke, die der Teufel läßt* (Frankfurt am Main: Suhrkamp, 2003), see, e.g., 291–292; Kluge, *The Devil's Blind Spot*, 15.

9. For an analysis thereof, see Bernhard Malkmus, "Intermediality and the Topography of Memory in Alexander Kluge," *New German Critique* 107 (2009): 231–252.

10. Kluge, *Verdeckte Ermittlung*, 27. Kluge delivers his clearest programmatic exposition of literary communication as a network of trust in "Das Innere des Erzählens," which differs somewhat from the "Rede zum Büchnerpreis-2003" available on Kluge's website and referred to above.

11. Kluge, *Verdeckte Ermittlung*, 28. See also Kluge in Stollmann, *Entstehung*, 14, and Kluge, *Die Kunst, Unterschiede zu machen*, 66.

12. Kluge, *Verdeckte Ermittlung*, 30.

13. Kluge, *Das fünfte Buch: Neue Lebensläufe: 402 Geschichten* (Frankfurt am Main: Suhrkamp Verlag, 2012), 161. The volume was published during work on the translation of *Geschichte und Eigensinn* into *History and Obstinacy* and stands in dialogue with the global expansion of critical theory under way there.

14. See Kluge in Langston, "'Das ist die umgekehrte Flaschenpost," 50.

15. See Fredric Jameson, "On Negt and Kluge," *October* 46 (1988): 151–177, especially 170–171.

16. For slivers of the complexity of Kluge and Negt's approach to time's narration from a theoretical perspective, see *HO* 84–88/*DuM* 2:32–37.

17. For analysis of the story, see Gunter Martens, "Reclaiming 'geballte linke Energie': War in Alexander Kluge's Docufiction *Heidegger auf der Krim*," *seminar: A Journal of Germanic Studies* 50, no. 1 (2014): 69–82.

18. For an analysis of *Schlachtbeschreibung* and its different editions, see Richard Langston, *Visions of Violence: German Avant-Gardes after Fascism* (Evanston, Ill.: Northwestern University Press, 2008), 212–228.

19. Kluge, *Verdeckte Ermittlung*, 51.

20. Wolfgang Reichmann, *Der Chronist Alexander Kluge* (Bielefeld: Aisthesis Verlag, 2009), 55–56.

21. Kluge, *Schlachtbeschreibung* (1978; Frankfurt am Main: Suhrkamp Verlag, 1983), 368. The suggestive metaphor of the grid (*Gitter*) figures importantly in Jochen Vogt's insightful account of spatially differentiated simultaneous narration in his study *Aspekte erzählender Prosa*, 137–142, as well as Vogt's analysis of Kluge's (pre-*Chronik*) prose in "Der ratlos-rastlose Erzähler Alexander Kluge: Eine romantheoretische Annäherung," in "Alexander Kluge," special issue, *Text + Kritik* 85/86 (1985): 9–21.

22. *CdG* 1:740; cf. Kluge, *Schlachtbeschreibung* (1978), 299.

23. See Karl Kraus, *Aphorismen: Sprüche und Widersprüche, Pro domo et mundo, Nachts*, vol. 8 of *Schriften*, ed. Christian Wagenknecht (Frankfurt am Main: Suhrkamp Verlag, 1986), 291.

24. While fewer of Kluge's stories address the Shoah explicitly, his extensive literary reckoning with Nazism turns on a structural critique of the object of its analysis, exposing its mechanisms, grappling with its effects, measuring its afterlives. It is a trenchant and far-reaching deconstruction that contributes greatly to coming to terms with terror and catastrophe, even if Kluge's storytelling has stood somewhat afield of Holocaust literature and studies.

25. Kluge, *Die Lücke, die der Teufel läßt*, 7. In *The Devil's Blind Spot*, Kluge opts for the more global reference to the "disintegration of the Russian imperium" (vii) in 1991.

26. See Kluge, "Das Innere des Erzählens," 75.

27. Kluge subsequently recoded the concept of cinema—"immortal and older than the art of film"—into a broader category subsuming his work in visual media. Cf. Kluge, *Cinema Stories*, trans. Martin Brady and Helen Hughes (New York: New Directions, 2007), xi.

28. Kluge, "Ich liebe das Lakonische."

29. Kluge, "Ich liebe das Lakonische."

30. Cf. Kluge's foreword in the booklet accompanying his DVD *Nachrichten aus der ideologischen Antike* (Frankfurt am Main: Suhrkamp Verlag, 2008), 4–5.

31. "Console" renders *Gehäuse* in the passage described above. The term proves resonant in Kluge's work as a whole and indicative of a key thread in the larger networked character of his storytelling. All critique of modernity aside, it is seldom iron-clad; rather, it relates to the construction of homes real and metaphorical (cf. *HO* 175/*DuM* 2:427), the residence of feelings in human lives (*CdG* 1:7), and of human beings in their life courses (*CdG* 1:9). In *Geschichte und Eigensinn*, Negt and Kluge entertained the image of "Hieronymus im Gehäuse" as the introverted medieval scholar at work without disturbance (*DuM* 2:1006–1007).

32. Addendums to *Maßverhältnisse des Politischen* (*Politics as a Relation of Measure*) republished in *Der unterschätzte Mensch* in October 2001 (*DuM* 1:996–1003) and *Die Lücke, die der Teufel läßt* addressed September 11, 2001, as the opening event of the twenty-first century. In 2003, the latter text framed the date as a possible sign of civilization's "relapse" from the spirit of hope felt on the eve of the millennium's turn "into the era of the Thirty Years' War" (*The Devil's Blind Spot*, vii).

33. For an account of the politics of Kluge's forewords, see Harro Müller, "Die authentische Methode: Alexander Kluges antirealistisches Realismusprojekt," in *Gegengifte: Essays zu Theorie und Literatur der Moderne* (Bielefeld: Aisthesis Verlag, 2009), 97–121.

34. Negt and Kluge address their renewal of "unfulfilled programs" in Marx by paying careful attention to encrypted forms of experiential content in the linguistic formulations of *Capital* (*DuM* 2:142–144). Moreover, the *Geschichte und Eigensinn* chapter elucidating their conception of realism refers parenthetically in its title to "Pipes, Bones, Vessels, Baskets" (*HO* 235/*DuM* 2:500) as containers mediating our relationship with and work in reality in Marx's sense (*DuM* 2:505–506).

35. Kluge, "Das Innere des Erzählens," 79. The recurring phrase of reality's inflation builds on Kluge's earlier formulations of the ideological character of reality's own appeal to its realistic character from his programmatic essay "Die schärfste Ideologie."

36. Cf. Kluge, "The Political as Intensity of Everyday Feelings," 284; Kluge, "Das Politische als Intensität alltäglicher Gefühle," 9.

37. Schoeller, "Besichtigung von Trümmerlandschaften," 73.

38. The locus classicus in Marx is found in the preface to *A Contribution to the Critique of Political Economy* of 1859, available in English e.g., in Tucker, *The Marx-Engels Reader*, 4–5.

39. See also Florian Hopf, "'Feelings Can Move Mountains . . .': An Interview with Alexander Kluge on the Film *The Power of Feelings*," trans. Robert Savage, in Forrest, *Alexander Kluge*, where Kluge compares feelings to mighty proletarians at 245–246.

40. The phrase "my books are my main work [*Hauptwerk*]" frequently accompanies Kluge's literary publications during this phase, as in Kluge, *Glückliche Umstände, leihweise: Das Lesebuch*, ed. Thomas Combrink (Frankfurt am Main: Suhrkamp Verlag, 2008), 2.

41. The two generic terms competing most directly with this designation of Kluge's work are "chronicle" and "encyclopedia." Kluge deploys both, whereas

his less frequent use of "epic" mostly corresponds to *episch* in German as a general descriptor of any literary prose. As Gunter Martens has pointed out, *Chronik*'s two-part title already underscores how far Kluge would stray from any conventional understanding of the chronicle as a genre devoted dryly to dates and facts. While encyclopedia, discussed and rejected by Franco Moretti in his study of the modern epic (cf. *ME* 4, 38–39, and chapter 1 above), would also not seem to capture the character of Kluge's volumes as works of literary art, Martens directs our attention to the adventurous, transhistorical, transcultural, and intermedial dimensions of encyclopedic writing to make the case in "'Wann wird man soweit sein, Bücher wie Kataloge zu schreiben?': Alexander Kluge und die enzyklopädische Literatur," in "Alexander Kluge," special issue, *Text + Kritik* 85/86 (2nd ed., 2011): 128–136, especially 129–130. Reichmann, *Der Chronist Alexander Kluge*, 53–67, and Christian Schulte, "Enzyklopädie der Erfahrung," in *Die Frage des Zusammenhangs: Alexander Kluge im Kontext*, ed. Christian Schulte (Berlin: Vorwerk 8, 2012), 9–12, also address Kluge's writing in relation to encyclopedic literature.

42. See Kluge's Holtzmann in *CdG* 1:841 as a follow-through on Kluge's comments on his film *The Power of Emotion* in Kluge, *Die Macht der Gefühle*, 176; Reichmann, *Der Chronist Alexander Kluge*, 45–50; and the writings collected for translation by Miriam Hansen, "Kluge on Opera, Film and Feelings," trans. Sara S. Poor and Mariam Hansen, *New German Critique: Special Issue on Alexander Kluge* 49 (1990): 89–138.

43. Brecht, "The Modern Theatre Is the Epic Theatre," 37.

44. Edgar Reitz, Alexander Kluge, and Wilfried Reinke, "Wort und Film," *Sprache im technischen Zeitalter: Sonderheft: Die Rolle des Wortes* 13 (1965): 1015–1030.

45. Reitz, Kluge, and Reinke, "Wort und Film," 1017.

46. Reitz, Kluge, and Reinke, "Wort und Film," 1020.

47. Reitz, Kluge, and Reinke, "Wort und Film," 1018: *Traditionsvorsprung*.

48. Cf. Schulte and Stollmann in Kluge, *Verdeckte Ermittlung*, 10.

49. Kluge, "The Sharpest Ideology," 196; Kluge, "Die schärfste Ideologie," 222.

50. In *Öffentlichkeit und Erfahrung*—available in English as *Public Sphere and Experience: Toward an Analysis of the Bourgeois and Proletarian Public Sphere*, trans. Jamie Owen Daniel, Peter Labanyi, and Assenka Oksiloff (Minneapolis: University of Minnesota Press, 1993)—Negt and Kluge attended to the betrayal of wishes in a public sphere dominated by private interests. They rely on the term *Produktionsöffentlichkeiten* to describe such institutions as the press, media, culture industry, etc., which are found to serve the reproduction of capitalist society by preprocessing that which can appear in the public sphere. In *Geschichte und Eigensinn*, the term is expanded and deployed to address the production of German history: "Deutschland als Produktionsöffentlichkeit."

51. For an insightful dissection of *Geschichte und Eigensinn*'s point of departure on this score, see Christopher Pavsek, "History and Obstinacy: Negt and Kluge's Redemption of Labor," *New German Critique* 68 (1996): 137–163.

52. Kluge, "The Sharpest Ideology," 196; Kluge, "Die schärfste Ideologie," 222.

53. Kluge, *Die Kunst, Unterschiede zu machen*, 11.

54. Kluge, *Die Kunst, Unterschiede zu machen*, 11.

55. Kluge, *Die Macht der Gefühle*, disc 13 of *Sämtliche Kinofilme* (Frankfurt am Main: Zweistausendeins, 2007). The fanciful montage in play there links the excavation site to the opera.

56. Kluge, *Die Kunst, Unterschiede zu machen*, 12: *Gemeinwesen*. See also 79.

57. For suggestive comparisons of (Negt and) Kluge to Weiss, see Langston, "The Work of Art as Theory of Work"; Birkmeyer, "Eigensinn und Anerkennung."

58. To the extent that the bombing of Halberstadt can be considered a seminal point of departure for Kluge's storytelling, his approach to it contrasts greatly with both the mesmerizing allure of *Jahrestage*'s opening at the sea as well as the self-avowedly sentimental demarcation of its embedded narrator's Jerichow tale as proceeding from "how it was when Grandmother met Grandfather" (*AN* 103, translation modified/*JT* 144), a scene of connectivity worlds away from Kluge's focus on devastation.

59. Kluge deploys Walter Benjamin's term for the present, without referencing the messianic dimension of its shards (*Splitter*). See Benjamin, "Theses on the Philosophy of History," 263; Benjamin, "Über den Begriff der Geschichte," in *Illuminationen*, 261.

60. See the discussion of Kluge's A. Weber in "Eingemachte Elefantenwünsche" (*CdG* 2:161; *Ich muß immer neu ansetzen*) below. From the 1962 *Lebensläufe* onward, the application of the literary generic category of the novel to any of Kluge's texts or collections thereof would remain tenuous.

61. As Negt and Kluge explain in *Geschichte und Eigensinn*, self-regulation is the originary form of *Eigensinn*, prior to its mutilation by the expropriative process of history (*DuM* 2:55–56, cf. also *HO* 98ff.).

62. Kluge, "The Political as Intensity of Everyday Feelings," 289–290; Kluge, *Fontane Kleist Deutschland Büchner*, 17–18. See also Vogt, "Der ratlos-rastlose Erzähler Alexander Kluge."

63. See Ernst Bloch, *Heritage of Our Times*, trans. Neville Plaice and Stephen Plaice (Cambridge: Polity, 2009), 97ff.

64. Relatedly, Bloch's conception of hope as a principle that would restore or, rather, be borne out in the linear time of history is an approach to time on which Kluge cannot rely.

65. Cf. Jameson, *Postmodernism*, 16 and the related discussion in chapter 1 above.

66. For a fuller analysis of the text, see Roberts's pathbreaking essay, "Alexander Kluge and German History: 'The Air Raid on Halberstadt on 8.4.1945.'"

67. As discussed in chapter 1 above, Kluge found that he had to "establish a framework dictatorially, so that freedom [could] prevail within the framework, within the 'capillaries,'" as he explained in an interview with Stuart Liebman, "On New German Cinema, Art, Enlightenment and the Public Sphere," 34.

68. Manfred Schneider, "Die Wiederkehr des Immeralten: Wie sich aus dem Erzählen kleiner Episoden eine hysterische Geschichtsphilosophie entwickeln kann," *Literaturen* (December 2000), http://www.kluge-alexander.de/aktuelles/details/artikel/die-wiederkehr-des-immeralten.html.

69. On Kluge's narratively disturbed stories as "bloße Entwürfe," see Winfried Menninghaus, "Geschichte und Eigensinn: Zu Hermeneutik-Kritik und Poetik Alexander Kluges," in *Geschichte als Literatur: Formen und Grenzen der*

Repräsentation von Vergangenheit, ed. Hartmut Eggert (Stuttgart: Metzler Verlag, 1990), 258–272, here 268.

70. Jameson, "On Negt and Kluge," 158.

71. Andrew Bowie, "Alexander Kluge: An Introduction," *Cultural Critique* 4 (1986): 111–118, 112.

72. Cf. *DuM* 2:766/*HO* 292–293. For a fuller analysis of the term, see my "*Eigensinn* in Transit," from which the following points are drawn.

73. "From the vantage point of NONemancipation," Kluge and Negt write in *History and Obstinacy*, "emancipatory characteristics are something cohesive (as a functional relationality). From the vantage point of emancipation, they are something not (yet) cohesive" (*HO* 220, capitals there, cf. *DuM* 2:32–33).

74. Kluge, "The Sharpest Ideology," 196, translation modified; Kluge, "Die schärfste Ideologie," 222.

75. Menninghaus, "Geschichte und Eigensinn," 263. The Kluge citation is from "Die schärfste Ideologie," 221. While Menninghaus's instructive essay attends to the thorny challenges of this ambition, his exposition of the techniques by which Kluge scales obstinacy in his artistic productions also explains how Kluge releases positive energies thereby.

76. Cf. Scherpe, *Stadt, Krieg, Fremde*, 329.

77. Michael Bray, "Openness as a Form of Closure: Public Sphere, Social Class, and Alexander Kluge's Counterproducts," *Telos* 159 (2012): 144–171.

78. See Weiss in Lindner, "Between Pergamon and Plötzensee," 121.

79. The relation of Negt and Kluge's theoretical collaborations to the latter's artistic production has become an important focus in the scholarship, which has put forth assessments ranging from complementarity to contradiction. The dialectical relationship between the two shuns neither. For a suggestive approach along the lines of the former, see Rainer Stollmann, "Vernunft ist ein Gefühl für Zusammenhang," in *Der Maulwurf kennt kein System: Beiträge zur gemeinsamen Philosophie von Oskar Negt and Alexander Kluge*, ed. Christian Schulte and Rainer Stollmann (Bielefeld: transcript Verlag, 2005), 233–267; for the latter, see Stefanie Carp, *Kriegsgeschichten: Zum Werk Alexander Kluges* (Munich: Wilhelm Fink Verlag, 1987), especially 11.

80. Kluge, "Ich liebe das Lakonische."

81. Kluge, *Die Patriotin: Texte/Bilder 1–6* (Frankfurt am Main: Zweitausendeins, 1979), 294.

82. For a case study of the latter, see Andreas Sombroek, *Eine Poetik des Dazwischen: Zur Intermedialität und Intertextualität bei Alexander Kluge* (Bielefeld: transcript Verlag, 2005), which focuses on Kluge's *Die Patriotin* (*The Patriotic Woman*) as an interrelated film and book project.

83. A recurring subtitle of his narration of the Battle of Stalingrad thus reads "Organisatorischer Aufbau eines Unglücks" (The Organizational Construction of Misfortune), as at *CdG* 1:509, 514. For a relevant analysis of that work along these lines, see Harro Müller, "'In solche Not kann nicht die Natur bringen': Alexander Kluge: *Schlachtbeschreibung: Der organisatorische Aufbau eines Unglücks*," in *Geschichte zwischen Kairos und Katastrophe: Historische Romane im 20. Jahrhundert* (Frankfurt am Main: Athenaeum, 1988), 97–127.

84. Roberts, "Alexander Kluge and Germany History," 129.

85. Roberts, "Alexander Kluge and Germany History," 151.

86. Cf. Roberts, "Alexander Kluge and Germany History," 151.

87. See Nora M. Alter, Lutz Koepnick, and Richard Langston, "Landscapes of Ice, Wind, and Snow: Alexander Kluge's Aesthetic of Coldness," *Grey Room* 53 (2013): 60–87.

88. Hans Magnus Enzensberger, "Ein herzloser Schriftsteller," *Der Spiegel* 1 (1978), http://www.spiegel.de/spiegel/print/d-40693842.html.

89. On techniques Kluge deploys to map such exits, see Stefanie Harris, "Kluge's *Auswege*," *Germanic Review* 85 (2010): 294–317.

90. Kluge, *The Devil's Blind Spot*, vii; Kluge, *Die Lücke, die der Teufel läßt*, 7.

91. Cf. Richard Langston, "Permanent Catastrophe and Everyday Life: Remediation of the Political in Kluge's *Vermischte Nachrichten* and Chernobyl Broadcasts," *Vermischte Nachrichten: Alexander Kluge-Jahrbuch 1* (2014): 101–123, especially 121. Langston's use of remediation encompasses both sides of the distinction I am parsing here.

92. Sombroek draws on Renate Lachmann's work on intertextuality to make this point in *Eine Poetik des Dazwischen*, 113.

93. Kluge's predilection for female protagonists on display here as elsewhere in his work has led to important debates in the scholarship on his idealization of femininity, female labor power, and even motherly love. For a discussion of Negt and Kluge's account of Antigone as an archetype of female *Eigensinn* and the implications thereof for Kluge's work, see Thomas Elsaesser, "The Stubborn Persistence of Alexander Kluge," in Forrest, *Alexander Kluge*, 22–29, especially 26–27 there. For more critical views of Kluge's reliance on and work with female characters, see Heide Schlüpmann, "Femininity as Productive Force: Kluge and Critical Theory," *New German Critique* 49 (1990): 69–78, and Helke Sander, "You Can't Always Get What You Want: The Films of Alexander Kluge," *New German Critique* 49 (1990): 59–68. In his review of the debate, Christopher Pavsek has argued for the reconcilability of Kluge's work with critical feminism; see Pavsek, "History and Obstinacy," 141.

94. While husband and wife are clearer bearers of obstinacy, the child's expression thereof is confined to the self-regulating powers of his body vis-à-vis its illness, which elicit the ameliorative effects compelling his mother to remain to care for him.

95. Stollmann, "Vernunft ist ein Gefühl für Zusammenhang," 239.

96. Enzensberger, "Ein herzloser Schriftsteller."

97. Horkheimer and Adorno, *Dialectic of Enlightenment*, 192; Horkheimer and Adorno, *Dialektik der Aufklärung*, 265.

98. A recurring theme in Kluge's prose works is the heteronymous organization of "free time" by holidays, as in the story "Die Ostertage 1971" (cf. *CdG* 2:504–516). The short life span of protest energy stands in no proportion to the objective necessities demanded by revolutionary transformation (*CdG* 1:156).

99. The lag of human responses to what the times demand is a diremption recurring throughout *Chronik* and heightened in "Nikolaus 1989" through its contrasts of leitmotivic meteorological conditions—including their epically rendered far-reaching prehistory—with the minute-by-minute breakdowns of the activities of the reading group and others across its pages.

100. Negt and Kluge, *Maßverhältnisse des Politischen: 15 Vorschläge zum Unterscheidungsvermögen* (Frankfurt am Main: Fischer Verlag, 1992), 10.

101. Characteristically, to provide an example of an "unfulfilled program," *Geschichte und Eigensinn* includes image of an infant's brain cell network one and three months after birth: "With this apparatus practically everything is possible; everything that was done with it so far, and everything that can still be done with it" (*DuM* 2:144).

102. Expanding their conception of *Produktionsöffentlichkeit* in *Geschichte und Eigensinn* and applying it to German history, Negt and Kluge expound the differences between the actually existing public spheres of production and a self-governing commonwealth in *Maßverhältnisse des Politischen.*

103. In this case, I cite from Oskar Negt and Alexander Kluge, *Geschichte und Eigensinn*, 3 vols. (Frankfurt am Main: Suhrkamp Verlag, 1993), 2:539–540. The passage is inserted at the end of the 1993 edition's seventh chapter, the beginning of which is resonantly retitled "On the Sentence: 'We did not intend all that to be that way.'" The authors managed, however, to include an edited version of this passage in the 2001 edition (*DuM* 2:540), the pagination of which otherwise corresponds to *Geschichte und Eigensinn*'s pre-Transition edition of 1981.

104. Cf. Schnell, *Die Literatur der Bundesrepublik*, 354, cited in chapter 3 above.

105. In Kluge's *Die Kunst, Unterschiede zu machen*, this beautiful piece precedes "Heiner Müller und das Projekt Quellwasser," republished in this volume, 107–111.

Epilogue

The epigraph is from Musil, *The Man without Qualities*, 709; Musil, *Der Mann ohne Eigenschaften*, 651.

1. Kraus, *Aphorismen*, 253, 238.

2. Kluge, *Die Patriotin*, disc 10 of *Sämtliche Kinofilme*.

3. While Johnson was likely the most private of the three writers, he alone perhaps proved the true contemporary (*Zeitgenosse*) of the other two by reading their works, as one can glean from his large library and letters. The relations between the three colleagues definitely present an avenue of scholarship worth pursuing.

4. In *Walter Benjamin: The Colour of Experience* (New York: Routledge, 1998), Howard Caygill frames Benjamin's conception of modern epic not in terms of genre, but within "the planetary extension of technology, which is transforming the collective and individual human *physis* and with it the character of human experience"—a rather different and certainly no less challenging plane on which the modern epic might contribute to experience's reorganization (77).

5. See Langston, "The Work of Art as Theory of Work."

6. Edward W. Said, "Contra Mundum," in *Reflections on Exile and Other Essays*, 479.

7. Hobsbawm, *The Age of Extremes*, 511–512.

8. See Emine Sevgi Özdamar, *Seltsame Sterne starren zur Erde: Wedding—Pankow 1976/1977* (2003; Cologne: Verlag Kiepenheuer & Witsch, 2008).

9. See Karl Marx, "Economic and Philosophic Manuscripts of 1844," in Tucker, *The Marx-Engels Reader*, 87–88.

10. Cf. Kluge, "The Sharpest Ideology," 196.

INDEX